THE CAR BODYWORK REPAIR MANUAL

by
Lindsay Porter

Foulis

Haynes
®

I'd like to dedicate this book to my wife, Shan. Most of the jobs covered here were carried out in our workshop, next to our house, and since the book has taken several years to prepare, she has put up with a lot!

She also checked and typed the manuscript and took many of the photographs, and so there's a lot of her in here.

Books on the following specific vehicles are available in the 'Guide to Purchase & DIY Restoration' series by Lindsay Porter from the Haynes Publishing Group.

MGB (F303)
MG Midget & Austin-Healey Sprite (F336)
Mini (F379)
Morris Minor & 1000 (F442)
VW Beetle & Transporter (F474)

Available soon:
Ford Escort/Cortina Mk. I & Mk. II (F494)

ISBN 0 85429 373 6
ISBN 0 85429 486 4 (trade edn.)
ISBN 0 85429 530 5 (US paperback edn.)

A FOULIS Motoring Book

First published 1985
Reprinted 1985, 1986, 1987

Published by:
Haynes Publishing Group
Sparkford, Nr. Yeovil, Somerset
BA22 7JJ, England

Haynes Publications Inc.
861 Lawrence Drive, Newbury Park,
California 91320 USA

Editor: Mansur Darlington
Printed in England by: J.H. Haynes & Co. Ltd

Acknowledgements

If any person could claim to know every scrap of information carried in this book, I'd like to shake him warmly by the hand! There's so much here that I certainly couldn't claim to be an expert in it all and a great deal of help was freely given by those mentioned below and by many others over the years it took to put all the pictures and information together.

Many companies have lent their expertise but none more than SIP (Industrial Products) Ltd whose welding and spraying equipment has given sterling service. Marketing Director Peter Osborne, a man with both engineering and journalism in his blood, has been unfailingly courteous, friendly and an utterly dependable source of technical information, while Paul Toon has busily set up photographic sessions and supplied pictures at the drop of a hat.

International Paints' training school and technical staff set up some highly informative photo sessions, aided by the planning skills of David Edwards of Leedex, International's PR consultant. At De Vilbiss, the company whose founder invented the paint spraying idea, George Mooney and Ian Bonker were as helpful and informative as can be and I am grateful for the opportunity to use some of the excellent graphic materials produced both by International Paints and by De Vilbiss.

At Murex Ltd, Les Ness kindly arranged the opportunity to photograph a 'how-to' welding session, and the Portapack, produced in conjunction with BOC, has proved to be a super piece of equipment. Much information on gas welding from BOC and from Murex is contained within this book and I am grateful to them both. In that department, Sifbronze have also kindly given their advice.

Tools from Apollo, The Welding Centre, Sykes-Pickavant and Black and Decker have all been used in the situations depicted here and all have been found to be excellent, while materials and equipment from Supra, Unipart and Holts have all been found to give excellent results.

CARS of Stourport, Tudor Webasto, Smith & Deakin, Vehicle Window Centre, Celette Churchill, Clearview Windscreens and Berger Paints all set up photographic situations or supplied pictures and technical information and Austin-Rover kindly allowed me access to many of their in-house line drawings, and Paul Sanderson/*Practical Classics* Magazine were similarly helpful. Also most helpful in arranging work for photographic sequences was John Hill's MGB Centre at Redditch.

My gratitude to my wife Shan for all her help and incredible forbearance is reflected, I hope, in the Dedication at the front of this book. Diane Hayton also typed a goodly number of pages, so thanks are due to her too.

Scott Mauck and his team at Haynes Publishing Inc. in California were tremendously helpful in taking pictures at the locations mentioned in the text while my final 'thanks' goes most gladly to Mansur Darlington who has undertaken the enormous task of editing this complex book with commendable stoicism and enviable efficiency and in so doing has done an awful lot to ensure that the whole package looks as good as I like to think it does.

Addresses of the companies mentioned here and others who have contributed to this book are given at the back of the book.

Using this book

Sometime during the life of every car the bodywork is going to suffer damage of one sort or another, whether it be externally as a result of impact, or internally due to corrosion. Car body problems come in all shapes and sizes from the tiniest scratch through to crash damaged repairs, so there's a lot of ground to cover. In addition to being divided into chapters in the normal way, to help you to find the information you need, when you need it, this book has been split loosely into two kinds of sections which are mixed throughout the book. The first kind is all about 'Techniques', in which is given enough background for you to know where you're going, get-you-started picture sequences and then some more advanced information in case you come across awkward problems and for when you want to take your new skills a stage further.

Having the skills is great, but putting them to use could be something else! That's why there are sections of a second sort dealing with 'Projects'. Project sections show you specific skills or techniques being put to use on real cars, in real-life circumstances where actual rust or accident damage has taken place. Each Project section is fully illustrated with step-by-step pictures of how the experts tackle a job, but in way that the home repairer can follow and use. There has been no attempt to gloss over the problems that come up: you can see for yourself they can occur and what to do about them, and where there is more than one way round a problem, this book gives it. Quite often there is a cheap 'n' cheerful way or repairing car bodywork or there is the high quality approach; the aim here is

to show you all the safe ways out and leave you to choose, basing your decision upon your own aptitude, the value of the car, the equipment at your disposal and so on. To differentiate between the two types of Section a coding is used, starting in the Contents list and carried through to the main headings right throughout the book. The 'Project' Sections are indicated by a ■ against their headings; 'Technique' Sections are indicated by a ●.

To find information on a particular topic go first to the Contents list on pages 5-7, where the contents are listed Chapter by Chapter. Because, however, many of the skills and disciplines required in bodywork repair are interlinked, additional useful information on a particular topic will also be found outside the main topic Chapter. Thus, after the main Chapter contents cross-references are given under the heading 'More Hints, Tips and Information'.

Apart from the above, it is worth reading and digesting the following points if you hope to get the maximum use out of the book.

1) Each chapter is sub-divided into sections. Section headings are in italic type between horizontal lines and sub-section headings are similar, but without horizontal lines.

2) Photograph captions and those for sequences of line drawings are an integral part of the text and therefore the captions are arranged to read in exactly the same way as the normal text. In other words they

run down each column from left to right of the page.

Each caption carries an alpha-numerical identity, relating it to a specific section. The letters before the caption number are simply the initial letters of key words in the relevant section heading, whilst the caption number shows the position of the particular photograph or line drawing in the section's picture sequence. Thus photograph/caption 'DR22' is the 22nd photograph in the section headed 'Door Repairs'.

3) Figures — illustrations which are not integral with the text — are numbered in a manner similar to the photographs. Thus, Figure FWR1 will be the first figure relating to the 'Front Wing Repair' section.

4) We know it's a boring subject, especially when you really want to get on with a job — but your Safety, through the use of correct workshop procedures, must ALWAYS be your foremost consideration. It is essential that you read, and UNDERSTAND, Safety Sense on pages 17-19 before undertaking any of the practical tasks detailed in this book.

Whilst great care is taken to ensure that the information in this book is as accurate as possible, the author, editor or publisher cannot accept any liability for loss, damage or injury caused by errors in, or omission from, the information given.

Contents

The Car Bodywork Repair Manual

Contents

Body Language

Cars old and new have some strange names for their body parts. Some of them date back to the days of horse-drawn coaches but other names seem obscure just to make life difficult. To add to the problems, many British terms are not the same as those in the USA so this section will start off with a glossary.

British	American
Aerial	Antenna
Alternator	Generator (AC)
Battery	Energizer
Bodywork	Sheet metal
Bonnet	Hood
Boot	Trunk
Bulkhead	Firewall
Chassis	Conventional frame
Dynamo	Generator (DC)
Earth	Ground
Engine bay	Motor compartment
Hood	Soft top
Indicator	Turn signal
Locks	Latches
Number plate	License plate
Paraffin	Kerosene
Petrol tank	Gas tank
Propeller shaft	Driveshaft
Quarter light	Quarter window
Saloon	Sedan
Seized	Frozen
Self-grip wrench	Locking pliers
Sidelight	Parking light
Sill	Rocker panel
Spanner	Wrench
Stopper	Glazing putty
Tailgate	Liftgate
Unitary/monocoque	Unitized body
Van	Panel wagon/van
Wheel arch	Wheelhouse
White spirit	Stoddard solvent
Windscreen	Windshield

Figure BL1.   Here are most UK terms for car body parts, although there are plenty of others, such as a 'Sill closing plate', which are not shown but which should be self-explanatory after studying the above figures, looking at 'Sill', 'Wing closing plate' and putting 2+2 together! (Courtesy Paul Sanderson and Practical Classics magazine)

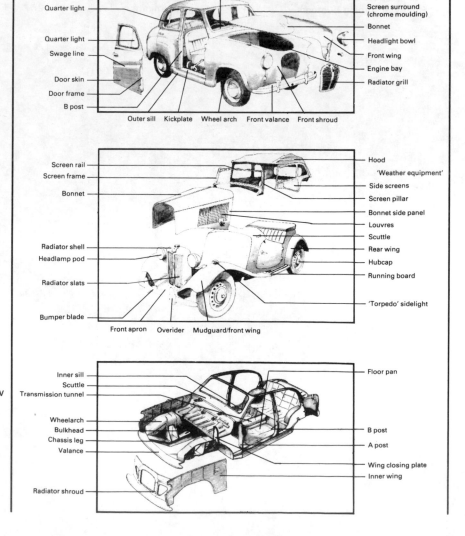

In the old days, a car's bodywork and its frame or chassis were two separate units. The chassis provided the car with its basic strength while the bodywork, which bolted to it, contributed little. Almost all cars are now built along 'unitary' or 'monocoque' lines, where the chassis has become part of the floorpan of the car, the surrounding panels being welded or bolted to the base structure and contributing greatly to its overall strength. Very modern construction techniques take advantage of high-stress steels and the chassis has often disappeared altogether, the shape of the whole car making up its strength.

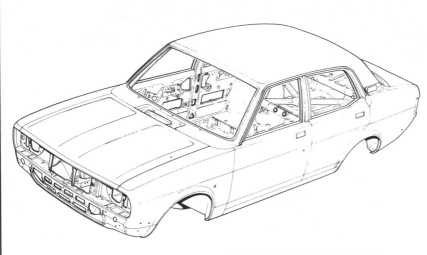

Figure BL2.   This is a very typical completely conventional 'Three Box' saloon, with a central passenger compartment with four doors, an engine bay area at the front and a luggage bay area at the rear.
(Courtesy Austin-Rover)

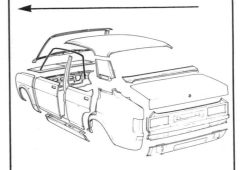

Figure BL3.   Outer panels are bolted or welded on, depending on their position, and add to the strength of the floorpan.
(Courtesy Austin-Rover)

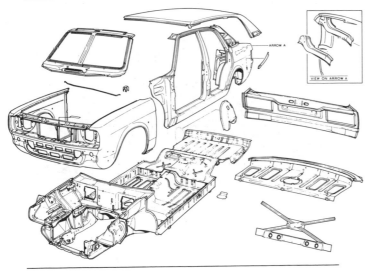

Figure BL4.   The chassis rails on this car have developed out of all recognition. They exist only as box-sections which run front-to-rear at the base of the engine bay and, for example, at the rear shown by 'View on Arrow A'. Note the complex structure of the bulkhead/firewall and the deep ribbing in all panels of any size. These help to make the panels very much stiffer than they otherwise would be.
(Courtesy Austin-Rover)

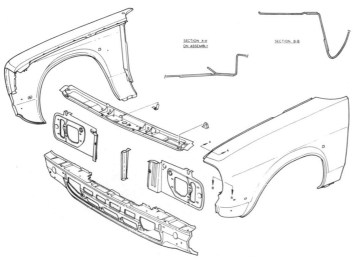

Figure BL5.   These external panels form the front-end outer sub-assembly and are the sorts of panels which the skilled DIY-er could consider replacing. Note from sections A-A and B-B that every panel is joined to another by an overlap. These laps would have been spot-welded together during assembly but it is not always possible for the home repairer to gain access to duplicate these spot welds. Use the alternative welding techniques outlined in this manual. (Courtesy Austin-Rover)

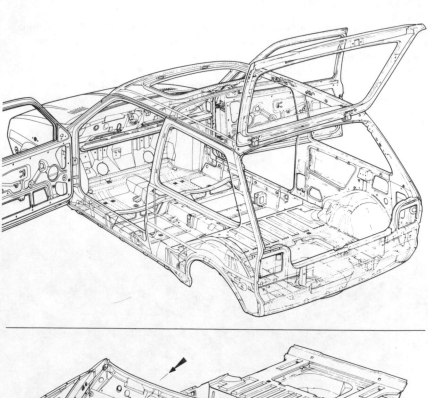

Figure BL6. This is Austin-Rover's Metro bodyshell and represents one of the latest packages around. Gone is the 'Three Box' concept, as the 'hatchback' styling makes maximum use of passenger space. Two door construction adds greatly to the shell's stiffness. (Courtesy Austin-Rover)

Figure BL7. Newer designs of this sort are not just thought up in the old way. Computers work out stresses and twisting forces and other loading factors to the point where design has almost gone beyond the ken of ordinary mortals. The aim here — and the plan succeeded admirably — was to gain maximum strength and rigidity from the minimum number of individual parts. (Courtesy Austin-Rover)

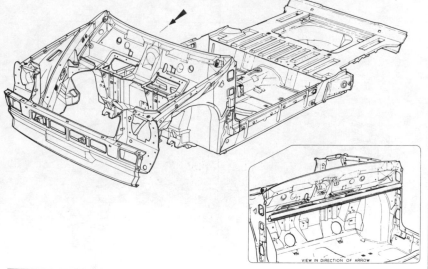

Figure BL8. This time, structures are even more complex than on the previous car and there is now virtually no trace of the old chassis rails. Two important components missing from this drawing are the front subframe, which carries almost all of the Metro's front-end mechanical components and also bridges the inverted 'U' structure of the front-end body assembly, and also the rear subframe. (Courtesy Austin-Rover)

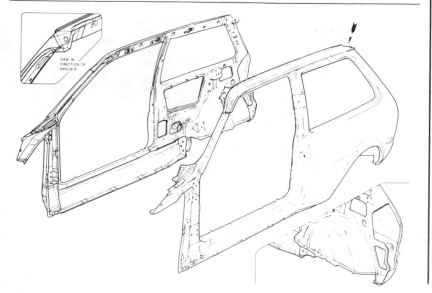

Figure BL9. Even with the addition of subframes, the floor pan in Figure BL8 looks barely rigid enough and indeed it takes the addition of these complete-looking body sides to give the shell much of its strength. Repair panels are available from the manufacturers and from specialist panel makers to repair parts of these assemblies; it is not necessary to go out and buy the whole thing! (Courtesy Austin-Rover)

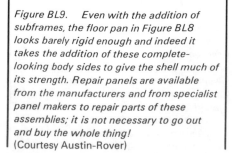

Figure BL10.   These flitch panels (engine bay side panels, not shown in Figure BL1) are the only items where traditional box-sections are used. They take front-end sub-frame stresses back into the bulkhead/firewall. Some say that the lack of box-sections will make these modern cars so much harder to repair when they rot out but they are rust-proofed to a far higher specification than their predecessors. (Courtesy Austin-Rover)

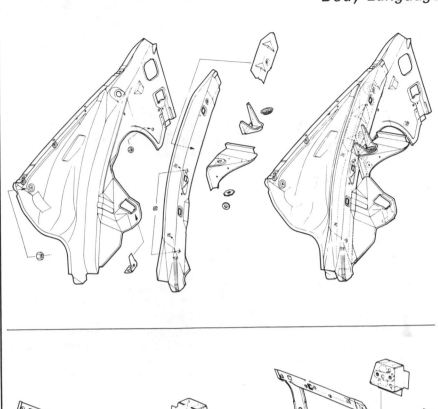

Figure BL11.   This shows how the strength of a whole modern car is crucially dependent upon the bits and pieces it is made from, especially in high-stress areas such as seat-belt mounting points. When repairing panels like this, it is important that all the minor components are re-fitted correctly. MIG welding is preferable to oxyacetylene because many of the panels are of high-grade steel which is weakened by the application of too much heat. (Courtesy Austin-Rover)

A very small number of cars have been built with fibreglass bodywork or GRP – see the Chapter on working with GRP – and others (but a small number) have aluminium bodywork. Aluminium is difficult to work with but is covered briefly in the chapter on 'Welding'. A very small number of cars, mainly pre-1940, were fitted with fabric bodies but work on this type of body is, of course, beyond the scope of this book.

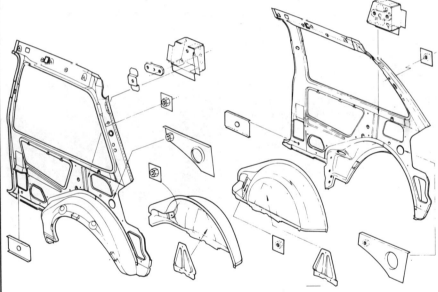

Tools & Equipment

This section shows some of the tools and equipment that the author has used whilst working on this book. If you buy equipment a little at a time, as you need it, you will accumulate a surprising range over a few years. Try to buy good quality equipment if you wish it to last though used continually. It has to be admitted that occasional-use tools, like impact screwdrivers, can be picked up very cheaply. In general, British, German and American hand tools seem to outlast Far-Eastern tools, although most power tools seem to be built there: just look for a reputable maker. Also, when it comes to large and expensive items like a compressor or welder, it pays to stick to a known make rather than to take a chance with an apparently cheap tool whose make you may never have heard of.

Many tools, incidentally, especially the smaller hand-tools, are mentioned within chapters that deal specifically with the job they are used for.

Because this book was written in the UK, with the assistance of British companies, it is inevitable that most references to proprietary manufacturers and materials will be UK orientated. Naturally equivalent equipment and materials are available in the US, in many cases more readily and of a greater choice. Almost all bodywork supplies can be bought from the larger auto parts supplier. More

specialist items can be found at tool suppliers, either locally or through mail order. Businesses that deal specifically with car body and paint supplies can be found through the Yellow Pages. See also the list of leading suppliers in the US, given at the end of the book.

T&E 1. The Welding Centre produce a fully portable gas welding set which looks and feels more like a professional welding set than any other of the DIY sets on offer. When used with a cylinder of Mapp gas (bought from many DIY centres) it gives a flame which is very nearly as hot as an acetylene flame. The only drawback is that the torch controls are a bit sensitive and also running costs are higher than for a full scale set, although the advantages of portability and lower purchase cost can more than balance this out.

T&E 2. MIG welding is, as far as both DIY enthusiast and full professional are concerned, simply the finest type of welding there is. The author uses the SIP Ideal 120N and its bigger brother, the 150, in his workshop, and both are as easy to use as drawing a slow line wth a felt tipped pen — well almost! As well as being the most straightforward form of welding for the beginner to use, it is also far more economical to run than gas welding, and it creates far less distortion. It can also be used for a form of spot welding. Minus points are that it can't be used for heating or bending in the way that gas can and it needs an Argon bottle (Air Products or BOC) or a CO_2 bottle (try the local pub!) to accompany it.

T&E 3. Spot welders work by passing a current through two overlapped pieces of metal, the heat formed actually fusing them together. All that is consumed is electric current. You can reach round obstructions with the spot welder — a particularly useful tool on the Mini with so many external flanges — by using a set of extension arms like these available for the SIP Spotmatic spot welders.

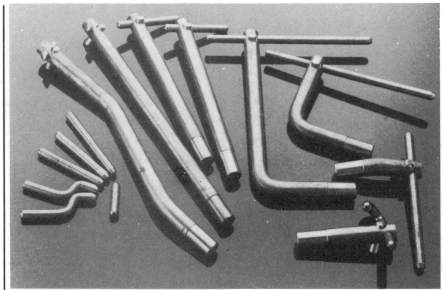

T&E 4. Right down the price scale is the arc welder set which can be bought through national ads and DIY centres at very moderate cost. You have to be a real dab hand to be able to weld thin metals with an arc welder and indeed the conventional wisdom is that you can't do it. Actually, you can sometimes just get away with it if you are extremely careful and just a little accomplished; DC arc welders being easier to handle with thin metals than AC. A carbon arc brazing kit makes working with thinner metals far, far easier, although you are of course restricted to brazing with this part of the kit, and brazing of structural parts is not accepted by British MOT testing stations.

T&E 5. This is the Portapack welding kit comprising small BOC bottles and top-quality Murex portable stand, and Saffire torches and gauges.

T&E 6. Here is one of BOC's many Cylinder Centres where Portapack cylinders can be changed when they have expired. (Find your local centre in Yellow Pages). Packs can be purchased here or at many motor factors.

T&E 7.   This tool, made by Sykes-Pickavant is terrific for cutting out sheet steel. Taking up far less room that a guillotine, it can also cut slow curves. It consists of upper and lower cutting wheels which slice through the sheet while also pulling it through the machine.

T&E 8.   This is another S-P tool, one that is really invaluable for the home restorer. It pulls the edge of the sheet along between two rollers which form a 'set' or a shoulder in the edge of the steel. This allows you to join two flat pieces of metal with all the smoothness of a butt joint but with all the strength and ease of welding of a lap-joint. Wonderful!

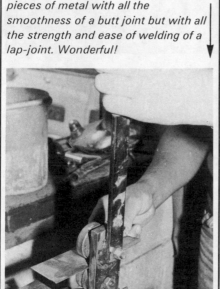

T&E 9.   Although a little more expensive, the Sykes-Pickavant folder is the only way to create perfectly formed folds in sheet steel. It forms very accurate, very crisp folds and even pulls any light wrinkles out of the sheet while it does it.

T&E 10.   This is the size of SIP compressor used by the author in carrying out much of the work featured in this book. It copes with just about every air tool (although an orbital sander is really too much for it and a fully professional spraygun can leave it a little breathless, although it does cope). It is the ideal type of tool for the serious amateur or semi-pro.

T&E 11.   At the smallest end of the scale, the tiny little SIP Jet 30 does remarkably well. It won't power many air tools but it will spray a car, even if a little slowly. It's a real compressor in miniature and a very worthwhile piece of equipment.

T&E 12. One of the things that compressors of all sizes will enable you to do, is blow your own tyres up at home, with the addition of this remarkably inexpensive accessory.

T&E 13. Another useful tool is the gun for blasting solvent onto oily mechanical components. SIP market a set of four or five useful tools including this and the tyre pressure gauge for around the cost of a car tyre.

T&E 14. As your spraying experience develops, you may wish to invest in a better gun. There are many different types available, but for the DIY sprayer the dearest equipment may not be necessary.

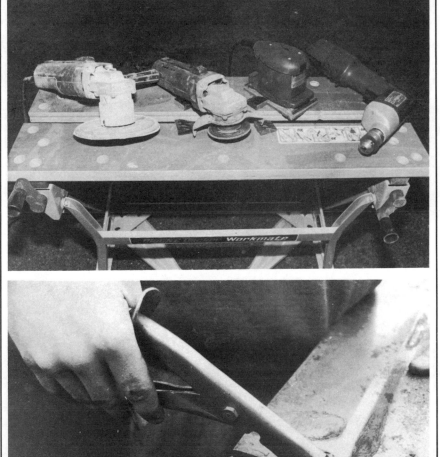

T&E 15. You will certainly find power tools useful and time saving. Black and Decker make the orbital sander shown on the left of this picture, the mini grinder (for grinding and cutting) shown next to it, the palm-grip sander and the tremendously useful electric drill shown on the right, which runs from a rechargeable power pack rather than from the mains, which makes it a really safe and versatile tool for the DIY enthusiast who is likely to be working in, on or under his car in all conditions. Beneath them all is the Workmate, which can be seen throughout this book. (It's so useful, it becomes like a third arm to you!)

T&E 16. This is the Monodex cutter which cuts steel neatly without distortion: It's accurate but hand-achingly slow! You can buy a similar tool to fit your own electric drill, which is of course the most versatile power tool of all!

T&E 17.   Back to welding again, and this is the Welding Centre's top range welding kit. It comes with rechargeable oxygen cylinder, disposable Mapp-gas cylinder (acetylene substitute) and high quality gauges and excellent, lightweight welding and cutting torches. Cheaper models are available.

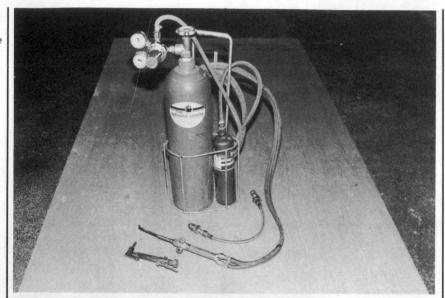

T&E 18.   An arc welder is one of the cheapest ways to start welding and with a carbon-arc attachment can be quite versatile. See 'Welding' chapter for more details.

T&E 19.   The serious DIY-er must consider buying a spot-welder. It welds neatly, cheaply and very rapidly indeed, although its uses are restricted, of course. More expensive models have a self-timer built in which can be a useful though not vital feature, as experience teaches you to gauge duration of a weld quite well.

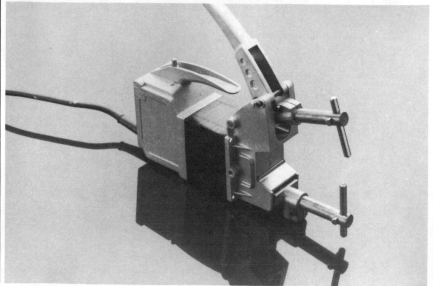

Safety Sense

However enthusiastic you may be about getting on with the job in hand, do take the time to ensure that your safety is not put at risk. A moment's lack of attention can result in an accident, as can failure to observe certain elementary precautions. Long term health hazards, rather than immediate injury, should also be considered a risk if important, yet simple, steps are not taken to protect yourself internally as well as externally from the effects of fumes, dust and harmful chemicals.

There will always be new ways of having accidents, and the following points do not pretend to be a comprehensive list of all dangers; they are intended rather to make you aware of the risks and to encourage a safety-conscious approach to all work you carry out on your vehicle.

Essential DOs and DON'Ts

DON'T rely on a single jack when working underneath the vehicle. Always use reliable additional means of support, such as axle stands, securely placed under a part of the vehicle that you know will not give way.

DON'T attempt to loosen or tighten high-torque nuts (e.g. wheel hub nuts) while the vehicle is on a jack; it may be pulled off.

DON'T allow spilt oil, grease or paint to remain on the floor – wipe it up straightaway, before someone slips on it.

DON'T use ill-fitting spanners of other tools which may slip and cause injury.

DON'T attempt to lift a heavy component which may be beyond your capability – get assistance.

DON'T rush to finish a job, or take unverified short cuts.

DON'T allow children or animals in or around an unattended vehicle.

DO wear eye protection when using power tools such as drill, sander, bench grinder etc, and when working under the vehicle.

DO use a barrier cream on your hands prior to undertaking dirty jobs or those involving solvents and resins – it will protect your skin from infection as well as making the dirt easier to remove afterwards; but make sure your hands aren't left slippery.

DO wear a safety mask, of the correct type, when spraying, sanding or cutting, especially when toxic or fibrous materials are involved.

DO ensure that solvents, cleaners and resins are used or mixed in suitably well-ventilated areas.

DO wear safety goggles when using power tools.

DO keep loose clothing (cuffs, tie etc) and long hair well out of the way of moving mechanical parts.

DO remove rings, wristwatch etc, before working on the vehicle – especially the electrical system.

DO ensure that any lifting tackle used has a safe working load rating adequate for the job.

DO keep your work area tidy – it is only too easy to fall over articles left lying around.

DO get someone to check periodically that all is well, when working alone on the vehicle.

DO carry out work in a logical sequence and check that everything is correctly assembled and tightened afterwards.

DO remember that your vehicle's safety affects that of yourself and others. If in doubt on any point, get specialist advice.

IF, in spite of following these precautions, you are unfortunate enough to injure yourself, seek medical attention as soon as possible.

Fire

Remember at all times that petrol (gasoline) is highly flammable, as is thinner and all like solvents and paint.

Always disconnect the battery before working on any part of the bodywork that involves electrical connections.

It is inevitable that unshielded flames will be around when welding equipment is used, so take intelligent precautions to keep all flammable items well away from the welding area. It goes without saying that special care must be taken when welding close to areas in the body where trim etc. is in place. **Never** weld near a fuel tank.

It is recommended that a fire extinguisher of a type suitable for fuel and electrical fires is kept handy in the garage or workplace at all times. Never try to extinguish a fuel or electrical fire with water.

Fumes and Dust

Certain fumes are highly toxic and can quickly cause unconsciousness and even death if inhaled to any extent. Petrol (gasoline) vapour and certain paints comes into this category, as do the vapours from certain solvents such as trichloroethylene. Any draining or pouring of such volatile fluids should be done in a well ventilated area and a safety mask of the correct type should be used when necessary.

When using cleaning fluids and solvents, read the instructions and follow them carefully. The dust produced when cutting and sanding body fillers, fibreglass and paint can be most harmful if inhaled. The danger is particularly acute when power tools are being employed. So, always wear a safety mask when spraying, cutting and sanding.

Mains Electricity

When using an electric power tool, inspection light etc. which works from the mains, always ensure that the appliance is correctly connected to its plug and that, where necessary, it is properly earthed (grounded). Do not use such appliances in damp conditions and, again, beware of creating a spark or applying excessive heat in the vicinity of the fuel or fuel vapour.

Compressed gas cylinders

There are serious hazards associated with the storage and handling of gas cylinders and fittings, and standard precautions should be strictly observed in dealing with them. Ensure that cylinders are stored in safe conditions, properly maintained and always handled with special care and make constant efforts to eliminate the possibilities of leakage, fire and explosion.

The cylinder gases that are commonly used are oxygen, acetylene and liquid petroleum gas (LPG). Safety requirements for all three gases are:

● Cylinders must be stored in a fire-resistant, dry and well ventilated space, away from any source of heat or ignition and protected from ice, snow or direct sunlight.
● Valves of cylinders in store must always be kept uppermost and closed, even when the cylinder is empty.
● Cylinders should be handled with care and only by personnel who are reliable, adequately informed and fully aware of all associated hazards. Damaged or leaking cylinders should be immediately taken outside into the open air, and the supplier should be notified. No one should approach a gas cylinder store with a naked light or cigarette. Care should be taken to avoid striking or dropping cylinders, or knocking them together.
● Cylinders should never be used as rollers.
● One cylinder should never be filled from another.
● Every care must be taken to avoid accidental damage to cylinder valves.
● Valves must be operated without haste, never fully opened hard back against the back stop (so that the other users know the valve is open) and never wrenched shut but turned just securely enough to stop the gas.
● Before removing or loosening any outlet connections, caps or plugs, a check should be made that the valves are closed.
● When changing cylinders, close all valve and appliance taps, and extinguish naked flames, including pilot jets, before disconnecting them.
● When reconnecting ensure that all connections and washers are clean and in good condition and do not overtighten them.
● Immediately a cylinder becomes empty, close its valve.
Safety requirements for acetylene:
● Cylinders must always be stored and used in the upright position. If a cylinder becomes heated accidentally or becomes hot because of excessive backfiring, immediately shut the valve, detach the regulator, take the cylinder out of doors well away from the building, immerse it in or continuously spray it with water, open the valve and

allow the gas to escape until the cylinder is empty.
Safety requirements for oxygen.
● No oil or grease should be used on valves or fittings.
● Cylinders with convex bases should be used in a stand or held securely to a wall.
Safety requirements for LPG:
● The store must be kept free of combustible material, corrosive material and cylinders of oxygen.

Only cylinders used by known, reputable companies should be used – there have been some horrendous fatal accidents caused by sub-standard imported gas cylinders failing in use.

Work with plastics

Work with plastic materials brings additional hazards into workshops. Many of the materials used (polymers, resins, adhesives and materials acting as catalysts and accelerators) readily produce very dangerous situations in the form of poisonous fumes, skin irritants, risk of fire and explosions.

Jacks and axle stands

Any jack, especially the jack supplied by the maker, is made for lifting the car, not for supporting it. NEVER even consider working under your car using only a jack to support the weight of the car. Jacks are for lifting; axle stands are available from many discount stores and all auto parts stores. These stands are absolutely essential if you plan to work under your car. Simple triangular stands (fixed or adjustable) will suit almost all of your working situations. Drive-on ramps are very limiting because of their design and size.

When jacking the car from the front, leave the gearbox in neutral and the brake off until you have placed the axle stands under the frame. Then put the car in gear and/or engage the handbrake and lower the jack. Obviously, DO NOT put the car in gear if you plan to turn over the engine!

Leaving the brake on or leaving the car in gear while jacking the front of the car will necessarily cause the jack to tip. This is unavoidable when jacking the car on one side and the use of the handbrake in this case is recommended.

Excellent jacking points are; the front cross member (never the engine's sump); the centre of the differential; under either leaf spring; under a closed door at the frame; or with the factory jack, the jack tubes. If the car is older and if it shows signs of weakening at the jack tubes while using the factory jack, it is best to purchase a good scissors jack or pneumatic jack (depending on your budget).

Mini Grinder Safety

The Mini Grinder is a useful but very dangerous tool. Always read the manufacturer's safety instructions before use and, in particular remember to:

i) always wear goggles
ii) wear a particle mask when dust is being created
iii) only ever use the **correct** wheel for the job in hand, fitted with the correct mountings and only use a cutting wheel for cutting and a grinding wheel for grinding. **Never** remove the guard.

Grinding wheels spin very rapidly and can disintegrate if abused with potentially disastrous consequences. Check with the manufacturer for specific and detailed safety instructions.

1 Welding

Large numbers of people are doing their own welding nowadays. From old-car enthusiasts to DIY car-repairers – including those who make useful pocket money out of their hobby – there's a realisation that if you are going to get serious about car bodywork repairs, you really *have* to start welding. We'll take a look at four kinds of welding here, all of them suitable for car bodywork repairs, looking first into the whys and then into a few of the hows. Then, because all kinds of welding are pretty complicated when you start taking them seriously, we will take each of them apart a little bit, and look at the sort of information you will need to know if you're going to take your welding past the beginner's stage.

To understand how welding works, all you have to remember is that any metal will melt if you make it hot enough. Then remember those plastic model kits that most youngsters seem to build. They are held together with a special kind of cement that *melts* the surfaces of the plastic being joined together so that when they are held tight against one another and the plastic re-sets itself, the two surfaces have flowed into one another so that there is a welded joint as opposed to two entirely separate pieces of plastic. Apart from the fact that plastic 'welding' of this sort is carried out with a plastic solvent while metal welding is carried out with heat, the principles involved are much the same. The two bits of metal being welded together are melted around a joint (and more often than not, some extra metal is flowed in to help strengthen the joint) and as soon as the metal cools below its 'freezing' point, you have got a joint

which consists of a more-or-less continuous piece of metal, rather than two separate pieces stuck together with some kind of super-glue. Outside the hi-tech world of lasers and ultrasound there are only two practical ways of getting sufficient heat into the metal: one is by using a high burning temperature bottled gas; the other is electricity.

Brazing

It would really be wrong to go any further without mentioning brazing or 'braze-welding' as it is sometimes called. Brazing has the great advantage that it is one of the easiest ways of holding two pieces of steel together, with beginners usually getting it right within a very short time. Just as in fusion welding, two pieces of steel are held close together and heated up but this time, instead of extra steel being flowed into the joint, a rod of bronze alloy is pushed into the heat of the flame and this adheres to both pieces of metal. It actually 'sticks' extraordinarily well because there is molecular bonding between the braze and the steel, which gives, in effect, something in between a glue and the total fusion you get from a welded joint. Brazing rod is often given the slang name of 'bronze' or 'brass' because it contains the same basic constituents of copper with tin and/or zinc. Strange though it may seem, brazing can be carried out not only with gas welding equipment but also with electric welding gear by using a special adaptor. The disadvantages of brazing are mainly that it is relatively expensive to carry out (the cost of rods is the main reason) and that it is nowhere

near as strong as a full welded joint, so it is not suitable for use with main structural components such as chassis or even sills on most cars. In fact, in the UK, brazing is not accepted at MOT-testing stations on structural components.

Types of Welding ●

Arc welding

Electric arc welding is the easiest to set up and also the cheapest to buy but unfortunately for car bodyworkers, it's just not suitable for welding thin steel, although it can be adapted to carry out brazing. Another snag is that it takes a bit of practice to get it right. The equipment consists of a welding machine, or transformer, which takes the ordinary household current and transforms it into the type of current suitable for safely welding steel. Leading from the machine are two heavy-duty cables; one, the 'earth' cable, has a clamp on the end which must be clipped onto the workpiece, and the other has a special handgrip and welding rod holder on the end of it. A steel welding rod with a special flux coating is gripped by the holder/handgrip and, when the power is on, the end of the rod is touched onto the workpiece at the place where welding is to be carried out. This completes the electrical circuit and the low-voltage-with-high-amperage current pushed out by the transformer causes a bright electric arc to jump between welding rod and workpiece. This melts the steel at the point near the end of the rod and it also melts the end of the rod, too, the molten metal being thrown in liquid droplets into the weld pool. The melting process is pretty well instantaneous so it is a great system for cutting down on heat distortion — in other words the metal is less likely to kink when welded than with some other systems — but it's pretty fierce and it's almost impossible to avoid burning right through thin steel. You can usually arc weld old-fashioned chassis, and even some more modern box-sections when you become more skilful, and bumper brackets and general workshop construction welding is fine with arc welding, but if you want to use the arc welder with thin panels, you have to go over to brazing with a carbon-arc attachment. It is worth pointing out that you can buy a more expensive type of arc welder, one that gives out direct current, which is much less prone to burning through sheet steel.

Carbon-arc brazing

Here a special adaptor is used on the end of the cable which would normally carry the welding rod grip. This consists of two rods of carbon, one of which is fixed and the other is on a slide arrangement. The two rods are held close together and then moved near the workpiece. As the arc is formed, the two rods, in effect, burn against each other which forms a flame. This is used to heat up the workpiece sufficiently for a brazing rod to be fed in and melted. The torch has to be moved, the carbon rods have to be slid close together, and the rod has to be moved and fed in at the same time. Once you have mastered all those simultaneous movements, patting your head and rubbing your stomach at the same time seem child's play although, once mastered, you will wonder why the skills seemed so tricky!

Oxy-acetylene welding

Traditionally, this type of welding has been the staple of every car body repairer and garage, although it has been held back from the DIY market, almost deliberately it seems. With this kind of welding, a special torch is used which mixes oxygen and acetylene in just the right proportions to produce a very hot flame indeed. The gas is fed through tubes from cylinders of the gases being used. The small, hot flame is played onto the steel being welded and when a molten puddle begins to form, a thin rod of steel is fed in. The rod melts and helps build up a good thickness of metal round the joint. Because the torch has to be moved around and the rod has to be fed in and along at the same time, it can take a little while to become proficient at this kind of welding although it is very versatile indeed. In addition, there are many DIY gas welding kits of varying kinds on the market nowadays, a number of which use a substitute gas instead of acetylene. One of the UK's leading gas suppliers, BOC, has started to promote the use of small oxygen and acetylene bottles along with professional-standard hardware by Murex Ltd. Gas welding is very good for brazing, of course, and it can be controlled so that it doesn't burn through car body panels. There is, however, one big snag: transference of heat from the gas flame to the workpiece is inefficient, thus the time taken to raise the weld area to melting point is relatively long. By the time a molten puddle forms, a great deal of the heat energy has gone into the air and much has dissipated through the surrounding steel. The latter aspect causes big problems as a later Section on 'Distortion' shows.

MIG welding

This is the crown prince of car bodywork welding, containing the main advantages of other systems with none of the disadvantages, except that it can't be used for brazing and, compared with gas welding, it is not so versatile and can't be used for cutting metal or freeing stubborn bolts: it just welds, but it does it really well!

MIG welding is based on the idea of arc welding but with very significant modifications. Instead of a fixed length of rod which is clamped to the holder then thrown away when reduced to a stub and replaced by a new rod, the MIG welder has a long coil of welding wire inside the machine casing and a tube which runs out to the welder's handgrip. Also in the machine casing is an electric motor, so when the welder wants to start welding, he presses a button on the handgrip and wire is fed out of the end of the gun on the handgrip. Just as in ordinary arc welding, there is an earth lead clamped to the workpiece and, in the same way, as the wire touches the workpiece the arc is completed and welding takes place. All of this makes the MIG welder very easy to control indeed because all the operator has to do is set the machine controls up correctly, press the button and move the gun at a slow 'n' steady pace. The MIG has another ace up its sleeve, however. The MIG welder does not only push welding wire along the supply pipe to the welding gun (or 'handset' if you want to be absolutely correct), it also feeds an inert gas (i.e. one that does not react in any way with the weld) such as Argon, Argon/CO_2 or even just CO_2 (Carbon Dioxide) along the pipe, through the gun and invisibly around the weld as it takes place. This helps cooling and cuts distortion even further, which means that you are far less likely to end up with rippled panelwork, trim does not have to be stripped out except around the weld area itself, and paintwork only burns back a little way. The only snag with MIG is that, being a little princely, it does insist upon having clean metal to work on, too much rust or paint contamination causing it to cough and splutter in a most un-royal way!

TIG welding

This is a highly specialised arc-welding process but one which is finding its way into some body shops, especially those where a good deal of aluminium is welded, so it will be briefly examined later.

Selecting your Welding Gear ●

These thumbnail sketches of the various types of welding equipment are not intended to be anything like a thorough grounding in the subject, but they should give an idea of what each system is about. So which one is best for the home body repairer? Well, it all depends how much you want to spend and what sort of work you intend to carry out. Here are a few possible 'user profiles': see which one you most closely resemble, then look at the system I think would be best for you.

1.   **You have a few repairs to carry out on your car's body, including structural parts, and you may want to do a little similar welding at some time in the future.** The best choice for you could be one of the really cheap gas welding kits on the market. They can be fiddly to use and are harder to learn with than a more professional kit, but if time is no real problem, so what? They also cost a lot to use because their small gas cylinders need replenishing fairly often and they would work out *very* expensive if you had to use them on a full-time basis. They are widely advertised in the DIY-type journals, but do try to see one before you buy it. Make certain you get one that works from Mapp gas. Anything else is too cool to allow you to weld. Note that none of these kits use acetylene because bottling and handling it is hugely expensive, and risky unless properly controlled.

Recommended supplier: The Welding Centre, Glasgow who sell kits which are slightly more expensive than some but all of which come with a superb welding torch.

2.   **You want a welding system that will allow you to patch rust holes in your car and carry out 101 other welding jobs around the home, such as repairing the gate, making a sledge for winter and so forth. If your car needs major structural welding you'll take it into the garage anyway.** There's no doubt that an arc welder with a carbon-arc brazing attachment will do everything you want! You will be able to braze repair patches to your car's bodywork or on the lawnmower's grass catcher and the arc welder itself will prove invaluable if you're a keen odd-jobber. It's also handy for making lifting brackets, mending tools and constructing one-off special tools in the workshop, although of course any other system could be used for this, but only arc and MIG welding are at all quick where thicker metal is involved.

3.   **You find repairing cars a fascinating hobby. Perhaps you like restoring old cars, or maybe you buy a succession of bangers, tidy them up and sell them on. Maybe you even do the odd job for your friends and neighbours. Or perhaps you just take your hobby very seriously and insist that if you're going to do something at all, you must do it absolutely properly.** You may wish to use more than one welding system, so here are two suggested packages which complement each other well. Neither package comes cheaply but both will do just about every job you could conceivably want in a home workshop.

Package A: A cheap arc welder (for those medium-thickness steel odd jobs) and a good quality gas welding set. The Welding Centre's most expensive offering just about comes into this category but the best DIY gas welding system is the Portapack. Here, a full professional Murex Sapphire welding gun with full kit of accessories including cutting gear and a portable cylinder trolley/stand goes with a pair of Portapack cylinders (oxygen and acetylene) rented out by BOC Ltd from their nationwide distribution system. There is absolutely no difference between the finest welding kits you will find in a professional workshop and this set-up, except that the bottles are smaller and therefore more portable and easier to store, although of course they run out faster and give around 10 or 20 hours of welding burn time per pair, depending upon the type rented. The bad news is that, in the UK, the bottle rental has to be paid all of *seven* years in advance, which can be a rather hefty amount.

Recommended Supplier: SIP (Industrial Products) Ltd for a less expensive arc welder. Murex Ltd for a really top-of-the-range oil-cooled DC arc welder (although this is really more a medium duty industrial piece of equipment). Murex Ltd/BOC Ltd for the complete Portapack hardware/gas or The Welding Centre for something a little less expensive but less professional.

Package B: (This would be my favourite!) A really cheap gas welding set for the few occasions where brazing is necessary. Could also do a little crude cutting, by turning the oxygen up high and would be useful for freeing stubborn nuts and bolts. And a small MIG set, which gives the best quality welds of any system with very little or no distortion. Can also be used on quite thick plate for a few minutes at a time so there are no practical limitations there. In addition, if a lot of welding is anticipated MIG has to be just about cheapest in terms of materials consumption.

Recommended Supplier: SIP (Industrial Products) Ltd for MIG, plus the cheapest supplier you can find offering a useable kit for gas welding (N.B. *not* acetylene).

Welding Concepts and Principles ●

Without becoming at all technical, there are one or two basic concepts involved in all kinds of welding that need to be considered. Briefly, they are as follows:

Compatibility

Obviously, you can't weld just any two materials together; the materials being welded together need to be compatible with each other as does the filler or rod being used. You can't weld aluminium to steel but that apart, as a car bodywork repairer, you don't have to worry about the problem of materials. When buying sheet steel or (in rare cases) sheet aluminium for repairing the panelwork of your car, make sure that your supplier knows what you are going to be using the sheet for and so supplies you with the correct material. Similarly, when buying welding rods or welding wire (for a MIG welder), explain to your supplier what you are welding.

Distortion

As everyone knows, when you heat metal up it expands, and when you let it cool down, it contracts again. In an ideal world, the two would cancel each other out and cooled metal would be exactly the same shape and size as the original. Unfortunately, when you cut and shape pieces of metal, then weld them together, they experience pushes and pulls in all sorts of directions as they are heated up and that's why car body panels are prone to distortion when they are welded. The two main conditions when excessive distortion is likely to occur are when, (i) a great deal of heat is put into the panel, such as with gas welding and (ii) the panel is a large, relatively flat area such as a door skin or bonnet (hood) panel. On a very large flat area, even MIG welding, which is known for being the least distortion-prone of all systems, can cause ripples in the surface of the panel and so can lead-loading a large flat panel or soldering something onto it. The trick when welding is to clamp panels together at close intervals and to tack-weld them together at regular intervals too, before carrying out the welding proper. (Tack welding is explained in later sections, but it is essentially a process of putting little blobs of weld across the joint to hold both pieces together temporarily, the tacks being lost later in the main weld.) Then, avoid welding from one end of the seam to the other in one go. Instead, weld from one end for a little way, stop, cool the panel (but not the area of the weld itself) with a other end a little way and then weld in the centre, cooling the panel after each weld, and then fill in the gaps. This helps to equalise the stresses in the panel and prevents too much heat from building up. When soldering, surround the area with wet rags, so that they draw the excess heat out of the panel rather than allowing it to spread. If distortion does take place and you are left with a 'bump' in the panel, don't despair! Turn to the section on shrinking a panel, which shows how to get rid of the excess metal, this time turning heat and expansion to your advantage. If a panel is left very slightly rippled, you can get rid of it with a thin spread of plastic body filler or even, in very mild cases, with a high-build spray filler.

Impurities

The more impurities there are in a weld, the weaker it will be — that much speaks for itself. It is important to weld with metal that is substantially free of paint, rust, grease or any other contamination because, although much of it is burned off, the residue

gets into the weld, weakens it and makes the weld look lumpy and generally scruffy. Any welding involving an electric arc creates its own impurities unless the air is excluded for the duration of the weld. In MIG and TIG welding a shield is provided by blowing an inert (or 'dead') gas over the weld, while straightforward arc welders use coated welding rods. The coating melts with the rod, floats over the weld and protects it from the air. It then goes hard and has to be chipped away later. Both brazing and soldering require a flux to be applied to the metal, otherwise the oxides formed prevent the solder or braze from combining with the workpiece. Only oxy-acetylene welding requires no shielding of any kind, but it is still important to start off with fairly clean metal.

Protection

All kinds of welding give off a great deal of heat, a lot of bright light and some give off fumes that can be dangerous in certain circumstances.

Take careful note of the 'Safety' section of each welding system described and refer to the 'Safety' section at the beginning of this book for general safety information.

Welded joint types

The illustrations in Figure W1 show some of the most common types of welded joint for sheet steel. Each has its own use according to the job in hand. Before you try a new type of joint, it should be practised on pieces of scrap metal. When butt welding thicker plates together, especially with arc or MIG welding, it is best to use the technique where a first pass is made from one side of the joint and then a second pass is made from the other side, with a slightly higher setting used to encourage the second weld to fuse with the first. Alternatively, use the method shown in Figure W2. Here the plates have been bevelled and are welded together using a series of runs as shown. This method is of course most suitable when access can only be gained from one side of the workpiece.

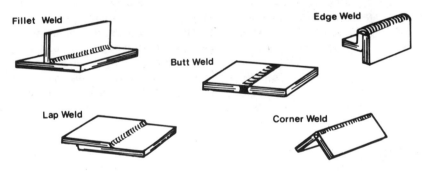

Figure W1.   Basic weld types (Courtesy SIP (Industrial Products) Ltd)

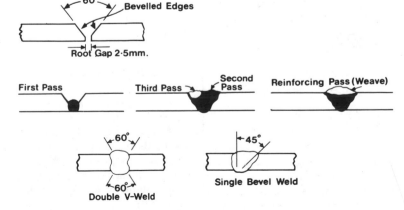

Figure W2.   Multiple-pass welding method (Courtesy SIP (Industrial Products) Ltd)

Welding Techniques ●

There's only one way of becoming really proficient at welding – and that is by getting out there and *doing* it. This section takes each of the main types of welding and shows how to tackle them, right from first principles. Each section shows how to weld on small pieces of metal rather than full panels, because that's the best way to start. Then you can work at a height that is comfortable to you and arrange the pieces in such a way that you can weld them easily. You'll have plenty of opportunity to weld above your head whilst lying on your back later on, when you have mastered the basics!

Arc Welding ●

As already explained, arc welding is the fusing together of two (or more) pieces of metal by means of the heat generated by an electric arc. Figure W3 shows how the process takes place.

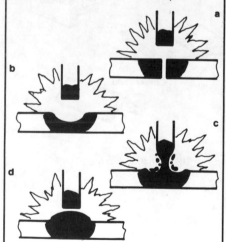

Figure W3.   Arc welding process
(Courtesy SIP (Industrial Products) Ltd)

(a)   Both edges of the metal are heated by the arc until...
(b)   ...they almost immediately melt and flow together forming one piece.
(c)   Simultaneously more molten metal and flux is added from the rod.
(d)   This fills the crater with weld and covers the top of the weld with protective slag.

W1.   *This is one of SIP's basic arc welding kits and, like most kits of its type, includes everything that is necessary to get going.*

Safety

The greatest danger when arc welding comes from the extremely bright light given off during the process. Not only is it so bright that it will damage the eyes if looked at directly, the light also contains a good deal of ultra-violet light which can cause direct and permanent damage to the eyes. *Always* use the full face shield provided when arc-welding and resist the temptation to peek round the edge 'just to start off with'. Since UV light can cause skin damage too, always wear gloves and button-down sleeves. Red hot sparks are thrown off as arc welding takes place, so wear shoes and overalls that prevent a red-hot droplet of metal going down inside your shoe, and for the same reason, keep the overalls buttoned at the neck. When welding overhead, keep the sleeves closed at the wrists. Don't weld in very enclosed spaces without ventilation because the fumes can be harmful. Wear cotton overalls; nylon can quite easily catch fire with disastrous consequences. Take very great care when handling hot metal and keep children and pets right out of the work area so that they can be neither burned, nor affected by the UV rays. Make sure that there is nothing flammable near the area where you are working. When working on car bodywork, strip out all flammable materials from the inside of the car around the area in which you are welding and *never*

weld near the fuel tank, or near plastic fuel or brake lines. Always have a fire extinguisher of the correct type available, for when things get really out of hand, and have a washing-up liquid bottle full of water to douse local outbreaks. *Don't,* whatever you do, allow water to come into contact with mains electricity equipment because of the high risk of electric shocks. When cleaning the weld, clear goggles should be worn because the brittle slag can 'fly' as it is chipped off the weld. If you accidentally look at the weld taking place, you can develop 'flash' or 'arc eye' within twelve hours or so. You will *know* if this happens because the feeling is akin to having a handful of gravel beneath each eyelid. In severe cases hospital treatment may be necessary and it is always advisable to consult a doctor.

If this incredibly long list of safety notes seems daunting; it needn't be. Every one of the points mentioned is of great importance but if you proceed with care and with a sense of involvement, it will all quickly become second nature.

The First Weld

Set up the equipment to the right settings for the thickness of steel being welded. The rod selected should, as a guide, match the thickness of the material being welded. As a starting guide, set the machine in accordance with the following table, but be prepared to modify it according to the results you get.

Electrode diameter	swg	Current required (amps)
1.60mm ($\frac{1}{16}$ in)	16	25 - 50
2.00mm ($\frac{5}{64}$ in)	14	50 - 80
2.50mm ($\frac{3}{32}$ in)	12	80 - 110
3.25mm ($\frac{1}{8}$ in)	10	110 - 150
4.00mm ($\frac{5}{32}$ in)	8	140 - 200
5.00mm ($\frac{3}{16}$ in)	6	200 - 260
6.00mm ($\frac{1}{4}$ in)	4	220 - 340

Make certain that your earth clamp is clamped to the workpiece at a point where a good contact is made and where the metal is clean, otherwise weld quality will suffer.
Find a comfortable position and

support the cable to the electrode holder, perhaps by draping it over the arm supporting the electrode holder.

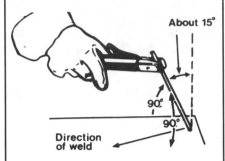

Figure W4. The electrode should be presented to the workpiece at an angle of 15° to the vertical, leaning in the direction of the weld. Practise with the machine switched off until you have the feel of it with your eyes closed – because that's in effect what you will start off by doing! (Courtesy SIP (Industrial Products) Ltd)

W2. When you feel ready to start, switch on, hold the face shield in the other hand to your welding hand, hold the electrode a couple of inches away from the workpiece, pull the shield in front of your face and strike an arc. The main difficulty is in getting the current to flow and the weld buzzing nicely while avoiding the initial momentary tendency for the electrode to stick to the workpiece. There are two ways of preventing sticking: one is to tap the end of the electrode against the place where you want to start welding, allowing it to bounce off again each time until the welding current starts to flow, and the other method is to scratch the electrode across the workpiece, the movement helping to prevent the end of the electrode from sticking. If the end of the electrode should hold fast to the workpiece, try twisting it off, otherwise, simply depressing the lever on the electrode

holder will release it instantly. Even if you are using the screw-up type of electrode holder, a quick twist should do the trick and release the electrode. If you still get tied up in knots, just turn around to the machine and quickly turn it off or take the earth clamp off the workpiece. The electrode **might** be glowing red or almost red hot by now, so pull it off the workpiece when it has cooled down. If a lump of flux has broken away from the end of the electrode, starting up will be even harder. 'Burn' the bare steel back to where the flux is complete by taking a piece of scrap sheet and connecting it up to the earth. Hold the faceshield in place and scrape the electrode rapidly across the scrap steel until enough steel has been thrown off as sparks (watch out for them!) for you to have reached flux covered electrode again.

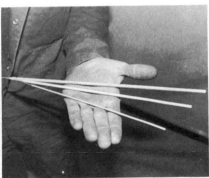

W3. Choose the size of rod (electrode) according to the thickness of metal you are welding. Rod thickness (not including flux coating) should, as near as possible, equal the thickness of the metal being welded. If the flux on the rods has become damp, you will find great difficulty in welding with them. If necessary dry them out before use. Electrodes should be stored in a dry place when not in use. If damp, they can be **gently** dried out in a domestic oven. If they have suffered to the point where flux is cracked and flaky when dry, throw them away.

W4. Some practice may be required before an arc is struck successfully but if you don't seem to be making any progress at all, check that the earth connection is a good one, then try turning the power up, a notch at a time, until you can get started – then if you 'blow' right through the steel, turn it down again. Once you get going, the idea is to move the rod grip down as the rod burns away and also to move it along the workpiece. Try moving the end of the rod right into the weld puddle so that the weld 'splutters' then try to pull away until the arc crackles then snaps out. Somewhere between the two is the ideal distance away from the workpiece.

Figure W4A. Once you have got the hang of moving the rod along, try swirling the end of it by just the smallest amount which helps to give better penetration. (Courtesy SIP (Industrial Products) Ltd.)

W5.   It is important that the correct arc length and correct rate of progress are consistently maintained. If progress is too rapid the weld will be stringy and obviously weak. If too slow, the slag formed will flow in front of the puddle and be trapped within the weld, severely weakening it. This shot shows the weld with the slag in place on top of the weld.

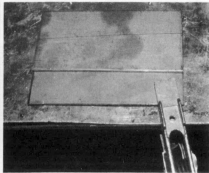

W7.   When you feel confident about running a bead along a flat piece of steel, try welding a lap joint. You will have to angle the rod towards the bottom piece rather than the edge of the piece on top because the weld will tend to burn furthest into the exposed edge. The exception would be steel which is a bit on the thin side when the top sheet would be favoured to reduce the risk of burning through the bottom sheet.

W9.   It is vital that **all** the slag is chipped off and, if necessary, wire brushed from the tack welds before the seam welds are run over the top, otherwise there will be slag inclusion in the weld.

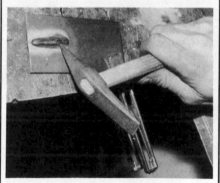

W6.   After the weld has been completed, use the chipping hammer to knock the slag off the top of the weld.

W8.   Start by placing a very short weld at the two outer edges. Known as 'tack' welds, these short welds hold the two pieces together and help to prevent distortion, as the heat of the weld would otherwise cause the two plates to part from one another at the end opposite to that being welded.

W10.   There is very little wrong with a weld where the slag peels off in one piece as the weld cools down leaving a beautifully even, rippled weld beneath it, like this one!

High Bead

CURRENT TOO LOW
Arc is difficult to maintain. Very little penetration.

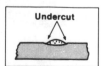

Undercut

CURRENT TOO HIGH
Wide thick bead, undercut. Crater pointed and long. Rod burns away very quickly.

Overlap

TRAVEL TOO SLOW
Metal builds up producing a wide heavy bead which noticeably overlaps at sides.

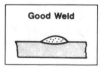

Good Weld

NORMAL CONDITIONS
Uniform ripples on surface of weld. Arc makes steady crackling sound.

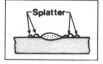

Splatter

ARC TOO LONG
Surface of weld rough. Rod melts off in globules. Arc makes hissing sound.

Undercut

TRAVEL TOO FAST
Small bead undercut in some places. Rough surface and little penetration.

Figure W5.   Arc weld bead faults (Courtesy SIP (Industrial Products) Ltd)

W11. *When welding a fillet weld, the hard bit can often be getting the vertical section to stay upright whilst you tack weld it!*

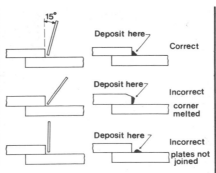

Figure W6. *Lap welding (Courtesy SIP (Industrial Products) Ltd).*

W16. *External corner welds are always easier to carry out if the two pieces of metal are put together as shown, the two edges forming a narrow 'Vee' rather than one edge overlapping the other.*

W12. *After tacking, there is always a certain amount of flexibility in the welds – the trick is in making the tack welds small enough to allow adjustments to be made but large enough for the workpiece to hold together while you tap it into place.*

W14. *Always bear in mind that the more comfortable a welding position can be made, the more successful the weld is likely to be.*

W13. *Then with the rod angled at 45° to each of the two faces – or equidistant from each where they are not 90° apart – a seam weld can be run from one end to another.*

W15. *External corner welds are generally considerably easier than internal welds. Again the same procedure is followed – set-up; tack; clean-up; seam-weld.*

W17. *Many welds have to be carried out in awkward places, so it is necessary to practise welds from different angles. This is a 'vertical-up' weld but 'vertical-down' welds (i.e. starting from the top and working down) are generally easier to carry out. They are best carried out with a smaller rod than normal, with a narrow gap between rod and workpiece (short arc) and by welding straight, without weaving. 'Vertical-up' welding is generally easiest with normal sized rods, a higher current setting than normal (so you have to take care not to burn through) and incorporating a weaving motion.*

Overhead Welding

This can be a slow, tedious operation and should incorporate two or three runs over each joint. Slag and hanging drops of metal are prone to form and they must be chipped and ground away before continuing. The first weld pass should be straight, with no weaving, but subsequent welds can be carried out with a weaving action, covering the first weld. Try turning the power up by around 10% but take care not to burn through. FOR SAFETY'S SAKE: wear a full head screen, leather apron and gauntlet gloves as a protection against red-hot spatter from the weld.
N.B. Always disconnect the vehicle's alternator before arc-welding because the current will damage it.

Carbon-arc Brazing ●

The carbon-arc torch is fitted with two cables: one to each carbon electrode. On welders with screw output terminals, the normal arc welding leads are removed and the leads from the carbon-arc torch are attached to the terminals in their place; one to the electrode terminal and the other to the 'work' or 'earth' terminal. (It is important that the welding cables are removed, because if the earth clamp is left connected to the work, it can have funny 'shorting' effects on the carbon arc in use).

On welders with internally connected output cables, the leads from the carbon arc torch have to be clipped into the electrode holder and earth clamp respectively. The electrode holder and clamp should be placed on a piece of wood or other insulating material.

The carbons are copper-coated, with a chemical core to give a smooth, even arc. (Earlier carbon arc torches were supplied with ordinary copper-coated carbons which were quite difficult to use; people who make the mistake of using non-chemical cored carbons designed for other purposes soon find the difference!) When the carbons are brought together and an arc struck, the resulting 'electric flame' then provides a heat source just as a gas flame does. It is then used with brazing rods, fluxes etc, much like a gas flame.

Of course, the carbon arc torch is not as versatile as a gas flame but is a very good and economic substitute and it allows the owner of an arc welding set to carry out a far wider range of jobs with the set than would otherwise be possible. As well as steel, it is possible to join brass, copper and even aluminium by using the correct filler rods, although the latter material would be somewhat tricky to work with. The set could also be used for heating and bending smallish strips of steel and for freeing rusted nuts and bolts.

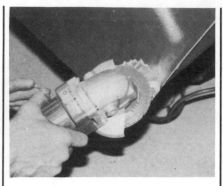

W18.   The first step is to remove any rust, scale or paint from the surface to be brazed, the mini-angle grinder being the ideal tool for the job.

W19.   Then a repair patch can be made up to suit. The patch **must** take the form of a lap joint because there is not enough contact area in a butt joint to allow a sufficiently strong joint to be formed with braze.

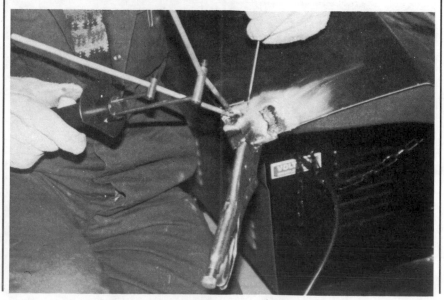

W20.   After clamping the repair patch in place, it should be tack brazed at regular intervals if it is a large patch. Either a pre-fluxed brazing rod should be used, which contains its own flux, or the end of the rod should be heated and dipped in the flux so that a quantity of the powder sticks to it. Then the carbon-arc rods are operated: the thumb slide on the handgrip is moved until the two rods touch, then moved just a little way apart so that an arc flares between the two of them. The operator is **not** brazing without a face shield but simply demonstrating!

*W21. The arc is extremely bright as this picture shows, so **never** attempt to use the equipment without the headshield. (Obviously, unless you have three arms, the usual hand-held shield is useless.) But **never** use just dark goggles as these are designed only to shield the light of a gas flame. The intense light of an arc can cause permanent eye damage even through dark goggles and, in any case, a full face shield must be used to protect the skin from harmful U/V rays. As the rods burn away, they have to be moved progressively together using the thumb slide. The heat from the arc is played onto the workpiece like a flame, the rod is fed in to the joint where first the flux then the rod itself melts and 'flushes' into the joint. Extra braze should be built up over the joint as you go along. The sound produced will be a 'buzz' rather than the crackle of arc welding when the gap between the carbon electrodes is just right.*

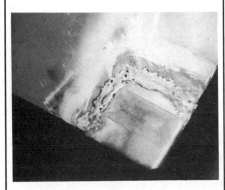

W22. Brazing is very easy to carry out and as long as the simple steps shown here are followed, the result will be a very strong joint, although unfortunately not strong enough for major structural or chassis-frame components on cars.

N.B. Always disconnect the vehicle's alternator before carbon-arc brazing because the current will damage it.

Oxy-acetylene Welding

Oxy-acetylene is the most versatile form of welding equipment to own although, as mentioned earlier, it does have its drawbacks. The most commonly used gases are, naturally enough, oxygen and acetylene although it is possible to gas weld with other gases. Some welding kits offer butane as a heat source, but this is too cool for anything but brazing although another alternative, Mapp gas, is hot enough for welding steels of the thickness of car bodywork.

Full-size welding cylinders can be difficult to get hold of for the home user (the companies involved will generally only hire out to business users) and in any case, the average DIY enthusiast would take ages to get through the gas contained in them. Also, the full size cylinders can be difficult to store and move because of their shape and weight.

Oxygen cylinders contain just oxygen under high pressure (and for that reason the cylinders are heavily reinforced – and expensive to produce). Oxygen is a stable gas and not particularly dangerous to handle, although oil and grease should be kept away from the regulator and other controls because when brought into contact with oxygen spontaneous combustion can occur. On the other hand, if acetylene were to be compressed into a cylinder in the same way as oxygen, it would explode, the critical pressure being as low as 15 lb/sq in. To overcome this, the cylinder is filled with a porous material, such as asbestos, charcoal or balsa wood or some other absorbent material and the material thoroughly saturated with liquid acetone. Acetone absorbs acetylene like a blotter absorbs ink and then the acetylene can reach, say, 250 lb/sq in although it has to be introduced into the cylinder very, very slowly indeed by the filling company.

Acetylene should be handled with care and respect because anything between 2.5% and 80% of acetylene in the air can be ignited with a naked flame. Also, it is possible for an acetylene bottle to explode as a result of a high level impact. Acetylene cylinders should always be kept in an upright position to prevent acetone being blown from the cylinder when the valve is opened.

Safety

Take careful note of all the safety comments contained within this chapter and refer to the additional safety notes in the Appendices.

W23. The Portapack by Murex and BOC is an ideal if somewhat expensive way of equipping the keen amateur or portable professional workshop. Each item is built to top professional standards, but bear in mind that the better the equipment you buy, the easier the welding will be and the better the end product.

W24. Here are the alternative, smaller sized bottles which, although rented for a full seven year stretch, payable in advance, are cheaper to start off with than the larger bottles.

W25. The Welding Centre can supply a top-of-the-range DIY set like this one which is a good compromise between the cheapest DIY sets and the top line Portapack. In general, the cheaper the set, the harder it is to use. The Welding Centre's kit is not as well balanced as the Portapack. The rechargeable oxygen cylinder and Mapp gas cylinders, available through many DIY outlets, mean that there is no rental to pay, although the cannisters of gas would work out expensive if there was a lot of welding to be done. The welding torch supplied with this kit is superb, and an excellent lightweight cutting attachment is also available.

W26. The Murex Saffire FN50 torch is the one supplied with the Portapack. The nozzle and mixer can be changed for a cutting attachment.

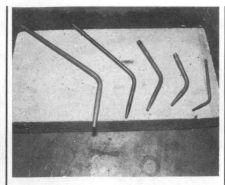

W27. There are several different nozzle sizes appropriate for different applications. Portapack contains three nozzles, nozzles Nos. 1 and 2 being the most commonly used for car bodywork. There is some overlap between the capacities of each nozzle size, but in general, too small a nozzle means that the welder is too close to the heat source while too large a nozzle means that the pressures have to be turned too low for the needs of the nozzle with risk of blowback — see 'Safety' notes at the end of the chapter.

Nozzle sizes – *applications*

Mild steel thickness			Nozzle size
mm	inch	swg	
0.9	–	20	1
1.2	–	18	2
2.0	–	14	3
2.6	–	12	5
3.2	$\frac{1}{8}$	10	7

Note: in all cases shown acetylene and oxygen pressure should be 0.14 bar (2 lb sq in)

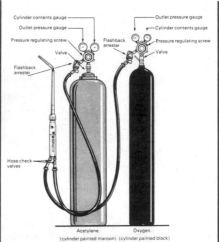

Figure W7. High pressure gas welding outfit (Courtesy BOC/Murex)

In the UK oxygen hoses are blue while acetylene hoses are red. In the USA, oxygen hoses are green and acetylene hoses are red. Before connecting the regulator to a new cylinder, the cylinder should be 'cracked'. This is the 'in' term for blowing out any water or dust that may have accumulated in the valves. All you do is to stand with your face turned away so that no 'UFOs' land in your eyes and briefly open each valve so that the pressure inside blows any unwanted stuff out of the valve.

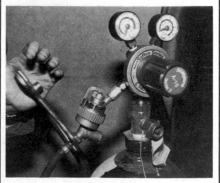

W28. When connecting up, remember that all fuel gas fittings have left-hand threads, while all non-fuel gas fittings (oxygen, carbon dioxide, argon etc) have normal right-hand threads.

Also remember to leave the key on the acetylene valve during use (if that is the type of cylinder you are using; some have a wheeled valve) so that it can be shut down in a hurry if necessary.

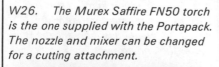

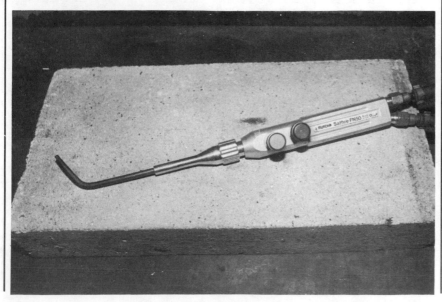

RODS AND WIRES

Mild Steel Applications

		Process	Rod/Wire	Melt-range	Diameters	Remarks
PLAIN	1.	Welding (Oxy-Acetylene)	Sifsteel No. 11 (CCMS)	1450°C	1.2mm, 1.6mm 2.0mm, 2.4mm 3.2mm	No flux is needed. It is copper-coated for long shelf-life.
	2.	Oxy-Acetylene Brazing	Sifbronze No. 1	875°C-895°C	1.6mm, 2.4mm 3.2mm	Flux needed to suit application. This rod has a wide range of uses including joining galvanised steel without damaging the zinc coating.
	3.	Oxy-Acetylene Brazing	Sifbronze No. 2	920°C-980°C	1.6mm, 2.4mm 3.2mm	Contains 9% nickel, providing high strength joints. Excellent for building up worn parts.
	4.	Oxy-Acetylene Brazing	Sifbronze No. 10	870°C-900°C	1.6mm, 2.4mm 3.2mm	Manganese-bronze free flowing rod. Suitable for use with gas fluxer.
FLUX COATED	5.	Oxy-Acetylene Brazing	Sifredicote No. 1	875°C-895°C	1.6mm, 2.4mm 3.2mm	Pre-coated with flux. Ideal for use in high speed continuous welding or for DIY. Suitable for carbon arc brazing.
	6.	Oxy-Acetylene Brazing	Sifredicote No. 2	920°C-980°C	2.4mm, 3.2mm	Pre-coated with flux. Contains 9% nickel for additional strength.
	7.	Oxy-Acetylene Brazing	Sifredicote No. 4	875°C-895°C	2.4mm, 3.2mm	Special aggressive flux for cleaning action. Ideal for brazing where a difficult surface exists, such as rusty metal.
	8.	Oxy-Acetylene Brazing	Sifserrate	875°C-895°C	2.0mm, 3.0mm	Pre-fluxed in pockets to ensure a measured flux-flow with minimum of joint cleaning. Ideal on clean metal.
	9.	Gas shielded arc welding TIG & MIG	Phosphor-Bronze No. 8, MIG 8	—	0.8mm, 1.0mm 1.2mm, 1.6mm 2.4mm, 3.2mm	TIG & MIG brazing on mild steel. Also joining dissimilar metals and building up worn surfaces.
	10.	Gas shielded arc welding MIG	MIG A18	—	0.6mm, 0.8mm 1.0mm, 1.2mm	Often referred to as CO_2 wire.

(Reproduced with permission of Sibronze)

MATERIAL THICKNESS — CONVERSION TABLES

Inches (decimal) to nearest 0.0001'' — Millimetres to nearest 0.001 mm

Inches (Decimal)	Millimetres	British Standard Wire Gauge	American Wire Gauge	Inches (Fractions)	Inches (Decimal)	Millimetres	British Standard Wire Gauge	American Wire Gauge	Inches (Fractions)
0.0201	0.511		24		0.0938	2.381			3/32
0.0220	0.559	24			0.0984	**2.500**			
0.0253	0.643		22		0.1019	2.588		10	
0.0280	0.711	22			0.1040	2.643	12		
0.0313	0.794			1/32	0.1094	2.778			7/64
0.0320	0.813	21	20		0.1181	**3.000**			
0.0360	0.914	20			0.1250	3.175			1/8
0.0394	**1.000**				0.1280	3.250	10		
0.0403	1.024		18		0.1285	3.264		8	
0.0469	1.191			3/64	0.1378	**3.500**			
0.0480	1.219	18			0.1406	3.572			9/64
0.0508	1.290		16		0.1563	3.969			5/32
0.0591	**1.500**			1/16	0.1575	**4.000**			
0.0625	1.588			1/16	0.1600	4.064	8		
0.0640	1.626	16			0.1620	4.115		6	
0.0641	1.628		14		0.1719	4.366			11/64
0.0781	1.984			5/64	0.1772	**4.500**			
0.0787	**2.000**				0.1875	4.763			3/16
0.0800	2.032	14			0.1920	4.877	6		
0.0808	2.052		12		0.1969	**5.000**			

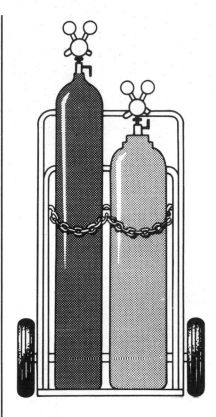

Figure W8. If you are using full-sized cylinders, make sure before use they are contained in a trolley or safety-chained back to a wall. (Courtesy Murex Ltd)

W29. All the valves, however, open and close on the normal anti-clockwise-to-open and clockwise-to-close principles. These cylinders are fitted with re-settable flashback arresters, designed to stop an instantaneous burn-back through the torch and pipe from getting into the cylinder with disastrous results.

The First Weld

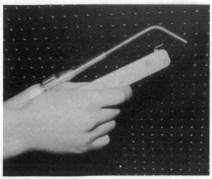

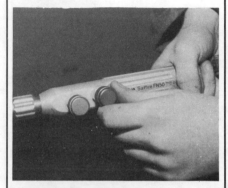

W30. Open the valve on the acetylene bottle and the valve on the oxygen bottle. Now open the oxygen valve (blue) on the torch for a few seconds to purge the system before closing down again. Repeat the process with the acetylene (red) valve on the torch, but leave it open whilst you carry out the step described in the following paragraph.

W31. Next, open the valve on the acetylene cylinder and adjust the regulator to give the correct working pressure.

W32. Use an igniter, held behind the end of the pipe, to light the acetylene at the end of the nozzle. (Oxygen turned off, of course).

W33. In practice, many professional users prefer to over-rule the gauge reading (they can be inaccurate, especially on older, neglected, gauges) and turn the regulator until a bright, bushy flame occurs.

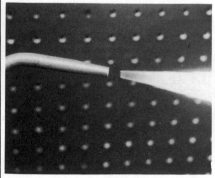

W34. If there is an air gap between nozzle and flame, 'throttle back' until it disappears, then turn the acetylene up again until the bright flame is regained.

W35. Now turn the valve on the torch down until the flame **just** starts to end in a smoky tip. (If you leave it in this state for long, the thick, lazy rolls of smoke will flutter back down as black soot marks all over the workshop!)

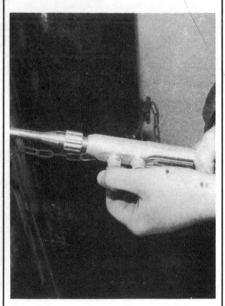

W36. Now turn the oxygen on at the torch ...

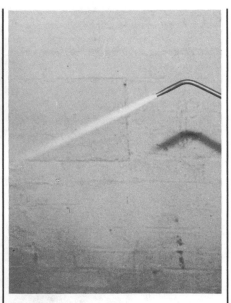

W37.   ... and again, if you wish, adjust the flame at the bottle regulator. Alternatively, and this is the usual approach for both gases, set the recommended pressure at the regulator and tune the flame at the torch.

W39.   Special nozzle cleaning reamers should be used to clean out a dirty nozzle (anything else will only be partly successful and could damage the shape or size of the nozzle).

W41.   Although the full brightness of the flame obscures the cone in this shot, this is how the flame should appear.

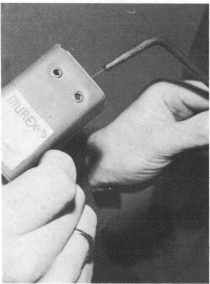

W38.   At this early stage, it could be seen that the flame was coming out of the nozzle at a slight angle, which indicated that there was a small obstruction in the end of the nozzle.

W40.   Simply select the wire reamer of the correct size for the nozzle and slide it in and out, rather like a stiff pipe cleaner. If the nozzle end becomes damaged, it can be restored to 'square' (i.e. 90° to the bore) by rubbing it on a piece of emery paper held flat on a board.

W42.   The first weld has been carried out from (the operator's) right to left, which is normal for steel up to 5.0 mm ($\frac{3}{16}$ in) thick. Note that the plate being welded here does not rest on a surface which could take the heat away from it. Do not, of course, weld on a flammable surface.

*Figure W9.   Start off by holding nozzle
and rod at the angles shown. Play the flame
on the point where welding is to start, until
a small pool of molten material develops –
it will be easily visible through the goggles.
Then begin to swirl or zig-zag the nozzle
slightly, at the same time dipping the rod in
and out of the weld pool at around ½-
second intervals, or as often as necessary. If
the weld pool forms too quickly, you are
likely to blow through when you start
welding, so turn the gas down a little. If it
takes too long to form, turn it up a little. If
more than a little adjustment is needed at
the nozzle, go up or down one size of
nozzle, as required. (Courtesy BOC Ltd).*

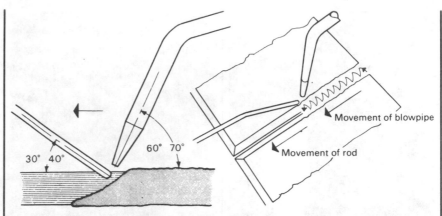

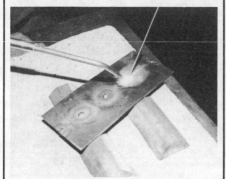

W43.   When joining two pieces of
steel together with a lap joint, start by
tacking them together at regular
intervals. You may find that the pieces
of steel move around between placing
tack welds so that they have to be
tapped back into place with a hammer,
held with a clamp or pushed together
by an assistant with a piece of steel
bar.

W45.   Note also that if you try to
start welding on the end of a piece of
steel, you are likely to burn through
before the weld pool forms.

W47.   The trick is to get sufficient
weld penetration: form the weld pool
then push the nozzle a little way into
the weld pool. If there is sufficient
depth to the weld pool, you will see it
separate.

W44.   Note that the edge of the
overlapping panel heats and burns
through quicker than the piece
beneath. Swirl the flame but
concentrate most of the heat on the
flat steel at the bottom of the overlap.

W46.   When welding a fillet (or inside
corner joint), support the pieces or
clamp them together, then tack weld
them.

W48.   You can weld outside corner
joints without using any rod at all,
although welding rod should be used to
tack the pieces together. This type of
joint is not uncommon in car
bodywork.

Flame conditions for Oxy-acetylene welding

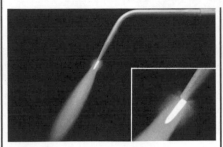

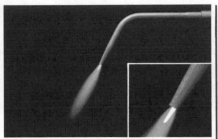

Neutral
Use: Mild steel, stainless steels.
Setting: After lighting the torch as described in the text, adjust the valves until you see a white cone clearly defined with the merest trace of acetylene haze.

Oxidizing *(excess of oxygen)*
Use: Brass and bronze.
Setting: Adjust the valves to give a tighter cone and a pale flame colour. It may cause the nozzle to 'pop'.

(Illustrations courtesy of Murex Ltd)

Carbonizing *(excess of acetylene)*
Use: Cast iron, hard surfacing and stellite.
Setting: Adjust the valves to give a lengthened inner cone. If made too long, insufficient heat may be produced.

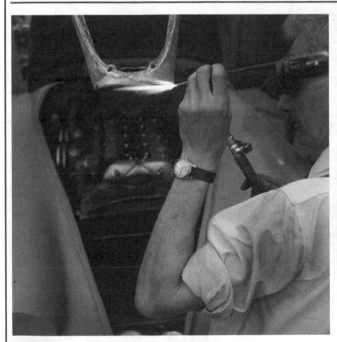

W1.   (Above left) *Gas welding is ideal for repairing thin sheet components and ...*

W2.   (Above right) *... for welding in replacement panels, and patch panels of the type shown being cleaned up here.*

W3.   (Left) *Although more troublesome for use on thin panels the electrical welder is a good DIY alternative for much general work including ...*

W4.   (Right) *.. that of brazing when used with an attachment.*

W49. *Butt joints in thin steel are rather prone to blowing through. Although you should have a gap between the pieces when welding thicker steel, try to close-up thin steel as far as possible. Don't play heat on the joint for too long – after all you are working with* **two** *edges of the type described in W44.*

Figure W10. Unfortunately, much welding on a car's bodywork is carried out in the sort of positions you never find when practising at the bench. These diagrams give an idea of how to approach upright, overhead and horizontal welding. (Courtesy BOC Ltd).

→

Shutting-down procedure

Shut off the acetylene first by closing the blowpipe control valve then follow with closure of the oxygen valve. Close the oxygen and fuel-gas valves on the cylinders, then open and close the blowpipe valves one at a time to relieve pressure in the system – ensuring the gauges register zero – oxygen first then acetylene. Wind back the pressure adjusting screws on both oxygen and acetylene regulators. If the equipment is to be used in the immediate future (i.e. within the next hour or two) it is not necessary to close the cylinder valves or the pipeline valves.

The only exception to the above procedure is when a sustained backfire occurs in the mixing chamber of the blowpipe. In this case the oxygen supply should be shut off first to stop burning internally, followed in rapid succession by closing off the acetylene valve. If this is not done melting of the blowpipe may occur. After quenching the backfire the blowpipe should be allowed to cool down and should be checked over before it is relit.

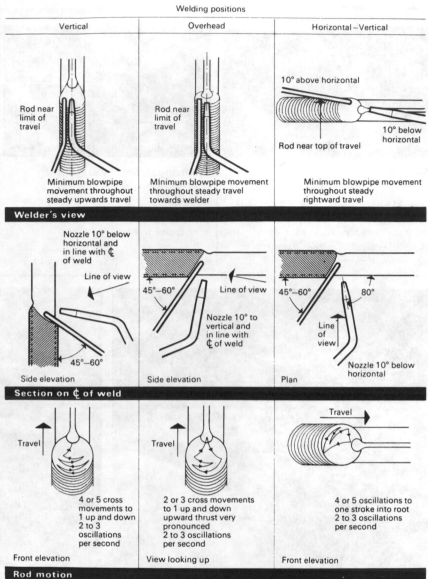

Welding positions

Vertical	Overhead	Horizontal–Vertical
Rod near limit of travel	Rod near limit of travel	10° above horizontal / Rod near top of travel / 10° below horizontal
Minimum blowpipe movement throughout steady upwards travel	Minimum blowpipe movement throughout steady travel towards welder	Minimum blowpipe movement throughout steady rightward travel

Welder's view

Nozzle 10° below horizontal and in line with ℄ of weld / Line of view / 45°–60°	45°–60° / Line of view / Nozzle 10° to vertical and in line with ℄ of weld	45°–60° / 80° / Line of view / Nozzle 10° below horizontal
Side elevation	Side elevation	Plan

Section on ℄ of weld

Travel / 4 or 5 cross movements to 1 up and down 2 to 3 oscillations per second	Travel / 2 or 3 cross movements to 1 up and down upward thrust very pronounced 2 to 3 oscillations per second	Travel / 4 or 5 oscillations to one stroke into root 2 to 3 oscillations per second
Front elevation	View looking up	Front elevation

Rod motion

Cutting ●

As an illustration of the versatility of oxy-acetylene welding, this section shows how to screw a cutting attachment on to the welder's torch and transform it into something that will cut cleanly through steel, which is very useful especially for thicker materials.

W50. *First, you unscrew the torch head by turning the screw in a clockwise direction.*

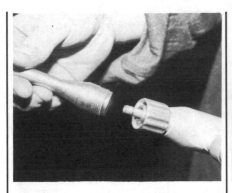

W51.   Then the torch head pulls from the torch body.

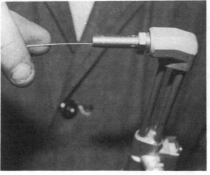

W53.   Check that all nozzles are clear using the reamers already mentioned. Set the oxygen to about 15 lbs sq in.

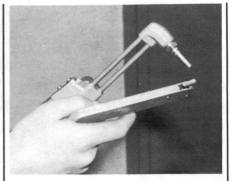

W54.   Turn on the acetylene and light the torch.

W52.   The cutting head pushes on to the torch body before the screw is retightened. The screw will **not** pull the cutter down tightly; it has to be pushed down hard and seated properly by hand first.

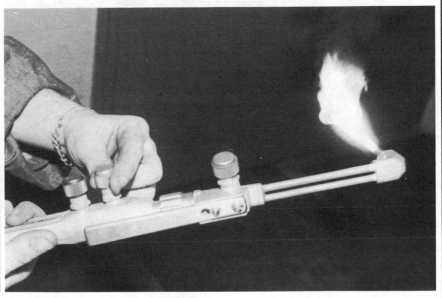

W55.   Turn the acetylene up to give a bushy flame just ceasing to smoke ...

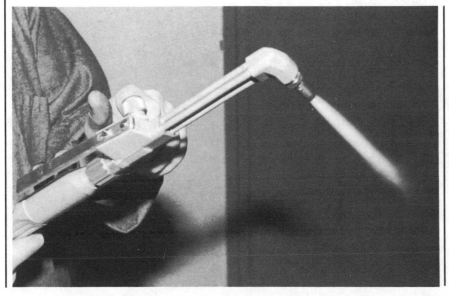

W56.   ... then turn up the oxygen to give a small cone in the middle of the flame, with the cone clearly defined. Next, depress the lever on the cutting attachment and readjust to a neutral flame with the blue oxygen heating valve. If it is found that some of the pre-heat cones are longer than others this can be rectified after shutting down the torch and bottles, then loosen the head nut and turn the nozzle through approximately 30°. Make sure that the head nut is re-tightened with a spanner.

Shutting Down.

Close the red valve on the torch, when the flame will go out. Close the blue oxygen heating valve on the shank. Close the blue valve on the cutter. Turn off both cylinder valves. Open the red valve on the shank and close after releasing the gas in the hoses. Open the blue valve on the shank and the blue valve on the cutting attachment. Close the blue valve on the shank and the cutting attachment once the gas in the hoses has been released.

Note that propane is a perfectly acceptable substitute for acetylene when used with cutting equipment and is certainly a lot safer to carry around than acetylene; a point worth remembering if any work has to be carried out away from home, such as when a scrap car is being cut up for spares.

Hints on Welding Stainless Steel ●

Use a welding rod of similar composition to the parent metal (a cut-off strip is ideal). Coat the underside of the joint with flux and use a neutral flame. Keep the rod in the flame the whole time and at the end of the weld, withdraw the flame slowly to prevent cracking. Do not stop in mid-weld and work as quickly as possible. Carefully remove all oxide and scale when the job is finished.

Hints on Brazing Aluminium Alloys ●

The recommended rod for use here is a 10% silicon, 4% copper aluminium alloy which has a lower melting point than most aluminium alloys. Make sure that the surfaces to be brazed are thoroughly scoured with steel wool, wire brush or file, back to bright non-oxidised metal immediately before use.

Use the correct aluminium brazing flux. The end of the rod is heated and dipped into the flux and the 'tuft' of flux adhering to the end of the rod is then touched down upon the surface of the joint to check the temperature. At the correct temperature the flux will begin to flow smoothly and rapidly forwards along the joint. The aluminium alloy **WILL NOT** change colour before it reaches the correct temperature or even exceeds it and melts and sags. It is most important that the filler rod is not melted into the joint until the flux flows freely. The force of the flame plus capillary action will pull the filler into the joint. Remove all traces of flux deposit as quickly as possible after brazing, or it will attack the aluminium alloy. If possible, buy a weak acid solution from your factor or chemist (drug store) and after using it to wash the joint, wash the joint again with warm water. (Check with your supplier regarding hazards associated with acid usage.)

W57. When cutting, remove rust and scale, if possible, to give a cleaner cut. Heat the edge of the metal with the cutter until it glows bright red. Then press the cutting lever ...

W58. ... and draw the cutter along through the material. Always wear at least one industrial glove (and preferably two) when using cutting gear.

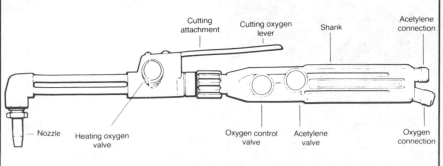

Figure W11. Cutting blowpipe and controls (Courtesy BOC Ltd).

Oxy-Acetylene Brazing

In welding, the workpiece melts as well as the filler rod, but in brazing only the filler melts, forming a strong bond with the workpiece.

Set up the equipment as if you were going to weld, but turn the oxygen on the torch up a little higher than normal to give an oxidising flame.

To minimise distortion, lightly preheat the panel, noting the points at which any initial distortion takes place, then tack it down at this point. On long welds, keep the heat as low as possible by making series of short braze runs at intervals, going back to fill in the spaces later.

Heat the end of the brazing rod in the flame, then dip into the flux. Heat the workpiece and right away, feed the end of the rod into the flame. The flux will melt and then, after a little more heating, the braze will run into the weld. If you use a pre-fluxed brazing rod, it will not require any additional flux added to it. You just push the rod into the flame and the flux inside the rod coats the workpiece before the rod melts.

Brazing is actually a lot easier to carry out then oxy-acetylene welding and there is less distortion because less heat has to be used. Do remember, however, that cleaning the steel to be welded can make all the difference between successful and unsuccessful

brazing. Remember also that a brazed joint is not as strong as a welded joint, and so should not be used where the car's structural safety could be put at risk.

Heat-shrinking a Panel

Every sort of welding depends upon heat to melt the metals being joined together. Unfortunately, it is physically impossible to keep the heat only where you want it (although MIG and TIG come nearest because the gases they blow onto the work help to cool it rapidly) and in the case of gas welding, more heat is transmitted away from the weld area than is used in the weld itself! The result of all this surplus heat is to expand and buckle the metal being worked on, and the flatter it is and the larger the area, the more prospect there is of bad buckling taking place.

Another way of causing metal to buckle is to panel beat it for too long or using the wrong technique. This causes the metal to go thinner, to expand and thus, to buckle – and it can be really difficult for the beginner not to let this happen.

A third and, perhaps the most common, form of buckling occurs when a car is involved in an accident and the metal becomes stretched as it is distorted.

In each of these cases, the metal will form a bulge which can often be 'popped' through from one side to the other without pausing in its correct position, halfway between. The following technique is used to shrink a panel so that the area becomes restressed and reverts back to something much closer to its correct shape. Note, however, that shrinking does have its drawbacks. The metal will not be perfectly flat when it is finished and it will be necessary to use filler or body solder to true it up. The other problem is that metal which has been shrunk can be very prone to rusting. It should be emery-clothed back to shiny metal and painted as soon as the work is finished.

HS1.   There are three ways of judging whether a panel is buckled. The first is simply to look at the panel; all too often any buckling present will be just that obvious! A second way, shown here, is to feel the panel by rubbing the flat of the fingers over it, when any lumps and bumps will be clearly felt. The third way, and the most suitable way for large panels, is to hold the edge of a really true straightedge against the panel and to look for any gaps between panel and straightedge.

HS2.   In shrinking a dent, the centre or highest point of the stretched area must be found because that is where the first shrinking operation should take place. Select a welding nozzle of the size correct for welding the thickness of steel you are working on. Heat a small spot around $\frac{3}{4}$ inch (18mm) to a cherry red heat, holding the flame far enough away so that you don't burn right through the metal. As the metal comes up to cherry red heat, you will see it blister upwards.

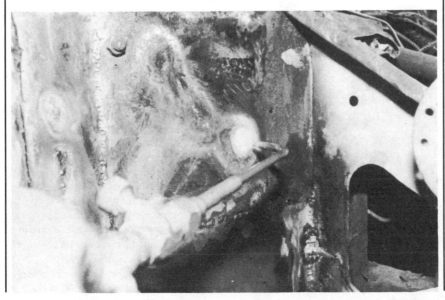

HS3.   *Take away the torch, hold a flat dolly at the back of the panel (or a curved one if dealing with a curved panel) and give several quick, sharp, squarely placed blows with a panel beater's hammer. This pushes the raised metal down but, because the black metal around it is harder than the considerably softened red-heat metal, tends to shift metal into the heated spot, which produces a tightening effect. For this reason, the hammering operation should be carried out before the metal returns to black heat. In practice, it will be found that the metal is far softer than cold metal and hammers down easily. Don't* hammer *too much, or you will just repeat the stretching process.*

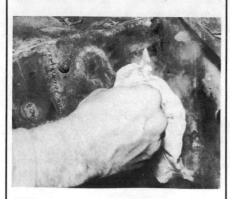

HS4.   *When the metal has cooled to black heat again, quench it with a substantial rag soaked in water. This will pull the metal tauter again in the area close to where you have been heating. Don't quench the metal whilst it is still red hot, or you will cause the metal's grain structure to crystallize which will make the metal brittle and difficult to work. Replace the rag in a bucket of water right away after use and don't touch that part of the rag that has been against the red hot metal – it could scald!*

If one shrink is not sufficient to remove the buckling, it is quite in order to use a number of shrinks but it is best to leave a wide space between them. The heating tends to 'deaden' the areas that have been shrunk, so leave plenty of taut, springy metal around and between each shrink. Make sure that you thoroughly cool the whole panel and those surrounding it after each shrink (you don't want another buckle taking you unawares somewhere else) and remember that a number of small shrinks are better than one large one – as Groucho might have said!

Safety

It is strongly recommended that anyone interested in carrying out oxy-acetylene welding applies to his local institute of education where night classes may be run in the use of oxy-acetylene equipment. In the following paragraphs, a few of the hazards associated with this type of equipment are listed.

● Leaking oxygen can gather in clothing and cause a flash fire or even lead to an explosion. Never drape clothing over bottles and never leave leaks unchecked.

● Acetylene cylinders should always be kept upright.
● Cylinders should always be kept away from sources of heat and should preferably be stored out of doors.
● Cylinders must not be dropped or bumped sharply.
● Chain cylinders to a wall or trolley and keep upright when in use.

● No oil or grease should be used with oxygen equipment, as under pressure it can cause an explosion.

No Oil or Grease

● Check compressed gas connections with a weak solution of washing-up liquid.

● Make sure that the following hose colours are obeyed: In UK: blue for oxygen; red for acetylene; orange for propane; black for argon or argon mix. In the USA: green for oxygen; red for acetylene.
● Never use oxygen as a substitute for compressed air. This is a *highly dangerous* practice!
● Always ensure that hoses are not cracked, split or chafed and that all connections are adequate.
● Never use oversize welding or cutting blow-pipes for the job in hand.
● Don't risk working with damaged regulators.
● NEVER weld without the correct type of goggles. The risk of eye damage is too great.
● Always purge both hoses before connecting them up to a welding torch or after changing cylinders.
● Always make sure that the nozzle is clean because a dirty nozzle can lead to a flashback. It is strongly recommended that a flashback arrester be fitted to each cylinder.

● Always 'purge' (i.e. allow gas to flow from each outlet for a short while) before lighting the torch. This helps to prevent a 'flashback' down the pipe and into the cylinder.

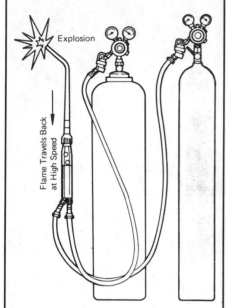

● Use adequate body, hand and foot protection, especially when working beneath a weld.

The list of safety points can make it seem that the process is highly dangerous. If used correctly it is certainly not. BOC Ltd point out that, 'Estimates of one major incident in every 50,000 hours of oxy-fuel gas working (in industry) are an indication of its safety level'.

Just make sure that *your* hours of working don't include that one in 50,000!

Thanks are due to Les Ness of Murex Welding Products Ltd Training School for his assistance with this section.

TIG Welding ●

This is a specialized process but one which is particularly suitable where a lot of aluminium welding has to be carried out. For that reason, it is briefly mentioned here. (TIG stands for 'Tungsten-Inert Gas').

W59.   Here a TIG tack-weld has been made. The 'torch' has a tungsten electrode which makes an arc, but unlike any other form of arc welding, the electrode is not consumed in the process. The shield around it blows argon onto the weld, similarlyy to the MIG welding process shown here.

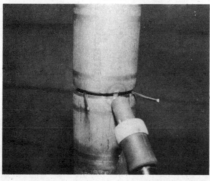

W60.   The pieces of aluminium to be joined are fused together by the addition of a hand-held rod, as in oxy-acetylene welding.

W61.   Good penetration and excellent results such as these can be obtained with aluminium. The process is exceedingly bright and full protective gear must be worn. The argon has to be blown onto the aluminium for a little while after the welding itself is completed.

MIG Welding ●

Allthough the name sounds somewhat similar to that of the preceding section, there is all the difference in the world between them from the user's point of view. MIG welding (the acronym stands for Metal, Inert Gas) is easy to use, gives splendid results with little distortion, and reduced risk of heat damage to surrounding areas. It's just about the quickest way of welding thin steel and in terms of material consumption it must be the cheapest too.

W62.   SIP (Industrial Products) Ltd make a range of MIG welders from the small 120N shown on the right, through machines like its bigger cousin the 220, also illustrated, and on up to those with quite massive capacity for heavy industrial use.

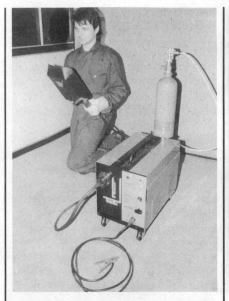

W63.   The 120N is 'small but perfectly formed', as they say. It will do everything that the garage or home workshop user would ask of it, being a fully 'professional' machine. The kit shown here is what you get – apart from the gas bottle – or the welder chap with the faraway look.

W65.   Inside the machine is the spindle (on left) onto which the reel of wire has to be fitted, and the feed mechanism which pushes the wire out and along the supply pipe.

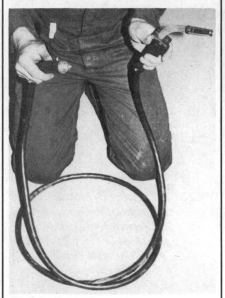

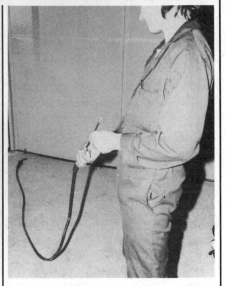

W66.   The supply pipe also has to provide an electric current and this is simply passed into the welding wire at the handset end of the supply pipe. It is this current which melts the weld pool and the wire at the business end.

W68.   Aluminium alloy can also be welded with MIG. It just takes argon gas in preference to argon/CO_2, aluminium-compatible welding wire, and a new supply pipe liner, coated with teflon. This prevents the 'sticky' aluminium wire from binding in the supply pipe.

W64.   MIG is a form of arc welding, except that instead of using an electrode in the form of a stick which has to be changed once it is worn out, the machine contains an almost endless reel of wire which passes down the supply pipe shown here and out of the end of the handset. So, there is no stopping to change rods and no continuous re-adjustment of the distance between torch and workpiece.

W67.   Now this is the interesting bit! Inside the machine, argon or an argon/carbon dioxide mix is fed through an on/off tap into the supply pipe. Then, when the trigger is pressed, the wire is pushed out and the electricity turned on, and the gas (known as shielding gas for reasons that will become clear) is pumped down the supply pipe and out of the end of the handser, to surround the weld.

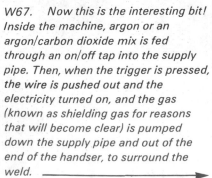

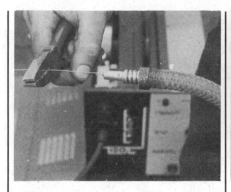

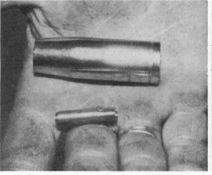

W69.   Once the machine has been set up, the wire is fed through the pipe by holding the trigger 'on' until it emerges, then cutting it off to length ...

W70.   ... before screwing and clipping into place the correct tip for the wire to pass through and the shroud which goes around it and directs the gas.

W71.   BOC Ltd have become aware of the great demand for these small MIG welders and have brought out a range of small Argon-mix and argon bottles, which are absolutely ideal for the DIY user and small garage. They are changeable at any of the many BOC centres.

W72.   It is possible to fit and use a CO_2 bottle of the sort that your local publican uses for making all those things fizzy in the cellar. You have to use a special adaptor and in cool weather the whole thing is liable to freeze up as the high-pressure CO_2 is released. (Industrial users of CO_2 use special and expensive heaters to prevent this from happening.) Argon-mix also gives a better result with a smoother weld, better penetration over a wider spread and less spatter, so it is cetainly preferable to CO_2.

The First Weld

W73.   Simply set the machine to the settings indicated in the handbook for the thickness of plate being welded and clamp the earth lead into place. Then hold the nozzle at 70° or so, with the nozzle opening pointing in the direction that the weld is to take. The end of the nozzle should be held just a little way from the surface of the workpiece.

W74. *When you're ready, pull the mask in front of your face, press the trigger and move the handset at about the speed of drawing a very slow line with a felt-tipped pen. Note how clean the weld is when the machine is set up correctly and there is no paint or rust to inhibit the weld. The gas, blown around the weld, is an inert gas which does not react in any way with the weld, but keeps it clear of the (oxidising) gases in the air until after the weld has 'frozen'. It also helps to cool the weld and so helps to cut down on distortion.*

W75. **Important:** *MIG welding is really very bright, so follow the safety instructions for arc welding. The UV light given off can be very damaging to anyone (even any pet) watching with unshielded eyes. You can tell whether a MIG weld is going well just by the sound. It should give a crisp crackling sound. If the wire speed setting on the machine is too high, the weld will start off burning deep into the metal and then quickly burn through, or the wire may 'bounce' on the workpiece. On the other hand, if the wire speed is too low, the weld will progress with a spluttering sound and may burn back into the wire feed tip.*

W76. *Next try a butt-weld, which is of course much closer to 'real' welding. Select a couple of pieces of scrap of the thickness you intend using, place them close together and hold the handset so that the wire is touching the gap. There is no risk of causing a weld to flash across accidentally because, unlike standard arc welding, no circuit takes place until the trigger is pressed. Hold the mask in front of the face and 'tack' the two pieces together. Run a seam down the joint, zig-zagging very slightly, so that the weld pool feeds equally into both pieces. There is far less risk of burning through with MIG than with any of the other main methods.*

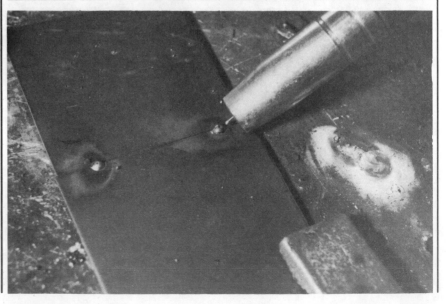

W77.   Before carrying out a fillet weld of this type, place sufficient tack welds to hold the material in place while any necessary adjustment is carried out.

W78.   Bisect the angle between both pieces with the welding nozzle and be prepared to work the nozzle very slightly from side to side, to ensure that there is sufficient penetration into both pieces.

W79.   Here, the more common lap-joint is being tried. Again tack welds have been positioned first.

W80.   Note how the first seam weld was stopped and then re-started with no risk of inclusions as with other weld types. This time, it is important to gain sufficient penetration into the lower piece, so it may be necessary to favour it just slightly at the expense of the edge of the top piece.

W81.   When welding an external angle, try tacking the two pieces together to form a 'vee'. This is much easier to weld and gives a stronger joint than having one piece overlap the other.

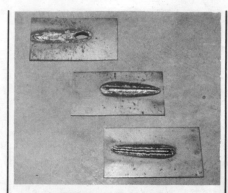

W82.   The top plate here shows a weld where the amperage and/or wire speed settings have been too high; the lower plate shows a thin, stringy weld where either the settings were too low or the handset passed too quickly over the plate; while the centre plate shows a weld that is just about right!

Experienced oxy-acetylene welders should beware that the torch should not be 'swirled' as would be an oxy-acetylene torch. You can weld in either direction but right-to-left for a right-handed person gives better visibility whilst the weld is taking place and improves gas flow over the weld.

MIG-welding in Awkward Places ●

Whenever possible, welds should be carried out flat but sometimes, of course, this is just not possible. Tipping the car over just to run a weld up a split wing is not exactly practical! Vertical welds are best carried out 'downhill', starting from the top, with the smaller sized machines being considered here; butt welds require a straight-on approach while fillets are best tackled with slight zig-zagging. Forehand welding (i.e. in the direction in which the nozzle opening is pointing) is recommended for all vertical or horizontal welds, so that the best gas shielding is obtained.

MIG-welding out of doors is not recommended unless unavoidable because the wind tends to blow the shielding gas off the weld leaving a poor, untidy weld. Try building a localised wind break around the job and turn the gas flow-rate up higher.

W83.   Holes, like these superfluous dashboard holes, can be filled up by welding one side of the hole (say, at the 3 o'clock position) then the other (9 o'clock) then the remaining (12 o'clock and 6 o'clock) positions can be welded, and so on until the hole is filled. The tendency will be for the welder to burn through. Get over this by just pulsing the welder for a couple of seconds at a time.

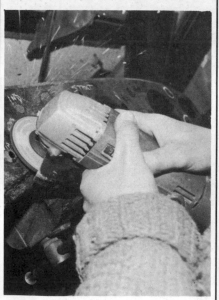

W84.   These short-sharp welds can then be cleaned up to a perfect finish with the linisher, proving that no weakening inclusions are found in a MIG weld.

MIG spot-welding ●

W85.   Here, a repair patch is being MIG welded to the corner of a car tailgate. It is held in place first with a self-tapping screw to ensure a good fit with minimal distortion.

W86.   Small holes are drilled through the top plate only.

W87.   Then, the MIG nozzle is changed for a spot-welding nozzle, which simply holds the wire guide a set distance away from the workpiece. The nozzle is pressed down onto the job rather than held away as in seam welding.

W88.   The right-hand edge was seam welded, but the neat button-spot welds can be seen along the top. There is no point in allowing too much build up. Always practise on scrap metal first and try to lever the finished weld apart with a screwdriver. This proves that settings and timing are correct. All SIP machines larger than the 120N have a timer built in so that pulsed welds and spot welds can be programmed automatically.

W89.   After welding, clean the 'spots' off flush with a mini grinder.

N.B. Always disconnect the vehicle alternator before MIG welding because the current will damage it.

Safety

In general, follow the safety rules for arc-welding (see relevant section and 'Safety' section at the beginning of the book) and remember that newly MIG-welded panels are still hot enough to burn when touched. Care should be taken when flammable materials are near the weld and when a fuel tank is nearby, even though heat spread is less from MIG than any other form of welding except spot welding proper.

Spot-welding ●

W90.   This is an SIP Spotmatic spot-welder. Two pieces of steel are fused together at the point where the two electrodes on the machine are squeezed together using the handle shown. At the point where they come together, an electric current is passed between them, melting the steel at that point and fusing it together.

W91.   All modern cars are put together with thousands of spot-welds; the more modern factories, such as Austin-Rover's Longbridge plant, are dominated by the awe-inspiring efficiency of spot-welding robots dancing and twirling rapidly from one set of welds to another.

W92.   A spot welder gives the cleanest welds of any system and is probably the easiest to use, but it still has to be set-up and used correctly. First, these out-of-alignment electrodes have to be correctly lined up and the electrode tips cut back to the correct profile with the spot welder.

W93.   The arms can be adjusted by slackening them off with an allen key or they can be changed for various shapes and sizes of arm, designed to reach round many of the obstructions found in car bodywork.

W94. The amount of pressure has to be adjusted according to the maker's instructions and on models equipped with a timer, the correct length of weld can be pre-set for the material being used.

W95. Try out the settings on scrap metal before starting to work. Metal **must** be clean and free of rust, paint or any other impurities and it must also be clamped close, without relying on the spot-welder arms to pull the pieces together. The weld on the left looks perfect, but the one on the right looks as though the timer was given too high a setting or, with a 'manual' spot welder, the lever was held down for too long. Always check weld strength on the practice piece by trying to prise it open with a screwdriver. Weak welds are, quite obviously, a great danger.

→

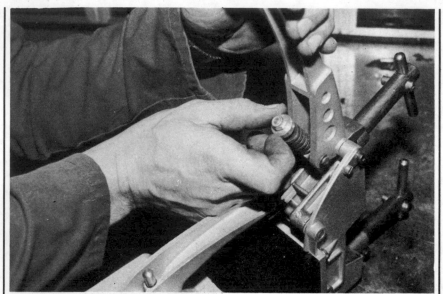

W96. The spot-welder in use. In an ideal situation there will be little or no sparking. If there is too much going on, suspect the weld strength. No special protective clothing or eye shields are needed when spot-welding but take all the usual precautions when working with electrical equipment – see Appendices.

Spot-welding – Notes:

● If you are spot-welding thick metal, line the electrodes up with the metal held between the tips.
● If too much pressure is set, the spot weld will be a deep dimple; if too little, the weld will arc and burn.
● If the tips glow red hot, the welder has been left on for too long, or the tips may need cutting back to the correct profile.
● If you burn right through, the reason will be: metal rusty or contaminated; or, too little pressure set on the arms; or, welder left on too long coupled with too much pressure.

Thanks are due to Murex Ltd, British Oxygen Company Ltd (BOC) and SIP (Industrial Products) Ltd as acknowledged experts in their fields for their kind assistance in the preparation of photographs and specialist information contained within this chapter.

2 Panel Beating

The operation of beating metal is the highest skill in the whole business of vehicle body repair. The ability to control the intensity of the blows delivered, together with the knowledge of how and where to direct the blows, anticipating the result to be expected, is the mark of the expert. Expertise can only be achieved by continued practice, once the basic requirements are understood, so it would be foolish for the complete beginner to start with an ambitious project. If you're interested in panel beating, practise on scrap metal first and take things a stage at a time.

This whole section has been produced with the close assistance of Sykes-Pickavant Ltd, manufacturers of the finest panel beating tools, in a range to suit the beginner and most accomplished expert alike. Fine tools, such as these, cost a little more to buy, but, because they last, cost less in the long run and because they are well balanced and well made, are easier to use than cheap products.

Introduction ●

So, to the first principles ... When a sheet metal panel is bent by accidental force or impact, the force passes through the panel to give an area of direct damage at the point of contact and a wider area of indirect damage. This leaves a series of valleys, 'V' channels, or buckles across the surface, the ridges that appear being hard, rigid areas. In accident repair work it is important to know, or determine, the direction of the force causing the damage, so that exactly the opposite sequence can be applied to correct it. This means that in general, the indirect damage is corrected first and the direct damage last.

Before any repair procedure can be carried out on a panel, the inner and outer surfaces must be thoroughly cleaned, and deadeners and underseal and other foreign matter that might interfere with the application of corrective forces removed. Most of the anti-drumming and other undercoatings used today can be removed by a scraper, or putty knife after softening by the application of heat to the outside of the panel. (Use a large tipped welding torch with a mild reducing flame.) The outside of the panel should be washed down with clean water and any traces of oil, road tar, or asphalt removed with a solvent-soaked rag. The panel preparation will make hand tool straightening more effective, coupled with a reduction in wear and tear on the dollies, etc. The first step in the restoration sequence is to unfold the valleys, 'V' channels and buckles in the indirectly damaged areas as gently as possible, without further stretching or re-forming as they are brought up to something like their original position and contour.

The reshaping should continue with alternative working on the ridges and the low areas as the metal is slowly raised up into line with the surrounding sheet.

Figure PB1 shows a double end hand dolly and suitable beater in such a sequence. The actual force delivered to the metal surface will also depend on the weight of the beater used.

The weight and size of the dolly

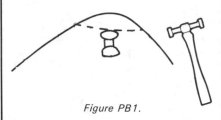

Figure PB1.

or spoon and indeed the area of actual contact with the panel will be factors to take into account. Too great a force between beater and dolly can stretch the metal locally, moving it outwards or inwards, as the metal cannot move sideways to be absorbed within the panel. This action will involve further correction by shrinking (see later paragraphs).

The beater is held loosely, the shaft resting against the base of the thumb and the same distance from the heel of the palm, the fingers hooked over the shaft as shown. Now, by closing the fingers to grasp the shaft, the head of the beater is thrown forward by the strength of the fingers, to a position at 2, passing through an angle of about 80°. This method of beating is most useful when working beneath surfaces, when the beater, or the working area may be out of sight.

When trying this method of beating for the first time, only feeble blows may be possible. Strength in the fingers can only be developed with practice. Throw the head of the beater at the palm of the other hand, without movement of wrist or elbow. Alternatively use a block of soft wood to show if the blows are being received squarely.

Striking with the combined action of the fingers and wrist can be developed by following through from the above description with added wrist action. The movement from 1 to 2 in Figure PB2 is achieved in exactly the same manner as described above. A follow through action of the wrist will cause the beater to make contact with the panel at position 3.

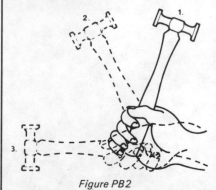

Figure PB2

Some difficulty may be experienced at the initial attempt to strike with this co-ordination of movement so that practice is again essential. Heavier blows, for roughing-out purposes, become more in line with the natural movement of the elbow and shoulder, as in the use of ordinary hammers so that no description is deemed to be necessary here.

In the early attempts at panel beating, some difficulty may be experienced in aiming the beater at the panel so that it strikes squarely onto a dolly below. Place a small dolly below the panel and tap the top surface lightly with the beater. Find the high surface of the dolly by checking for maximum rebound. Once this can be achieved, move the dolly about, following the movement with the beater to develop co-ordination until fairly rapid action is possible.

Metalworking Techniques ●

Beaters should be well balanced i.e. the length of the shaft should give a feel of balance, when the tool is held in the hand, at a point about three-quarters of the shaft length from the head. The handle should not be gripped tightly as this can cause fatigue in the arm muscles when beating over extended periods. When beating on metal the blows should land squarely

on the surface. In all dinging operations the beater should travel in a circular path (Figure PB3) with rhythmic action of some 100 to 120 blows per minute. In this manner the metal receives a sort of sliding or glancing blow resulting in but a small area of contact with the

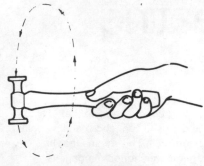

Figure PB3

surface. To level out a panel the beater should be moved about in regular rows, striking the metal at intervals of about 1 cm, with light blows until levelling is completed. Beaters of sufficient size and weight such as those used for roughing-out and bumping are often used alone, or in conjunction with a piece of hardwood to raise the elastic areas of the metal. The non-elastic outer ridges are then re-shaped by 'Spring-beating' or 'On and Off the dolly' techniques. 'On-the-dolly' or 'direct' beating is shown in Figure PB4. The dolly is selected so that its contour, to be held under the ridge, is near to the original shape of the panel at this spot. Beating is then directed at the peak of the ridge, commencing with light blows, increasing in intensity to a level sufficient to push the ridge back. Work along the ridge from end-to-end in a progressive manner, i.e. do not

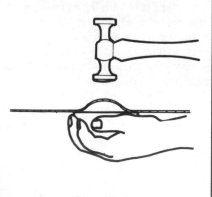

Figure PB4

flatten the ridge completely in a localised area, but take it all down gradually.

In the case of a ridge with an associated depression on one side, 'off-the-dolly' or 'indirect' beating is applied. Again, the dolly is selected to

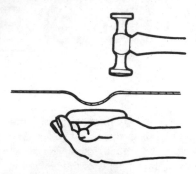

Figure PB5

be close to the original panel shape, and held under the depression (Figure PB5). Beating on the ridge away from the dolly, will cause a reaction to produce an alternating impact on the panel. First impact with the beater and then the impact from the dolly alternatively until the depression is removed. 'On-the-dolly' beating can then be resorted to, bringing the panel up to the final stages of levelling. In panel finishing (Figure PB6) small low areas should be raised by using the side of the round face of the beater, initially. The surface is now checked with the body file to highlight any remaining low spots. Each spot should be raised individually with a blow, or a series of tiny blows, with the pick. Care must be taken not to strike the low spots too hard, otherwise they will become rough and 'pimply' and the metal stretched.

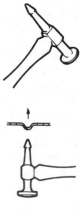

Figure PB6

Mallets ●

Mallet heads are usually made of hardwood fitted to ash handles, to form a complete mallet. Standard round mallets have cylindrical heads. The bossing mallet is sometimes referred to as the 'pear-shaped' mallet. Both patterns are now available in other materials, such as rubber, rawhide and the softer metals, as in copper-faced mallets.

Rubber mallets, with interchangeable screw-on heads, are ideal for use on aluminium and may be used in the repair of panels in sheet steel. Hollowing (Figure PB7) is a process of thinning metal from the centre of a given blank, to produce a double-curvature panel. This can be accomplished by the use of a bossing mallet and a sand-bag. Beating of the metal commences in the centre of the plate, working outwards in increasing circles, until the required curvature is obtained. Uniformity in the intensity of the blows is important to produce a regular shape.

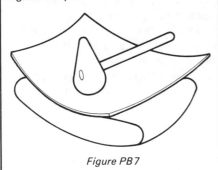

Figure PB7

Applications of Beater and Dolly ●

Reshaping a flange

The utility dolly is placed in the damaged flange (Figure PB8) using the edge most suitable to the shape and size of the original flange. An upward and outward pressure is applied to the dolly. The flange is now reformed by 'on-the-dolly' beating; starting at the inner edge of the flange, gradually working to the outer edge as indicated, until it is back to its original form.

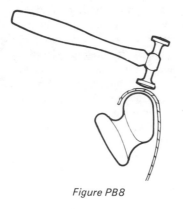

Figure PB8

Spoons and their Applications ●

Spoons are used for bumping and prying (prising), they are also used in place of dollies when direct access to the rear of the panel is obstructed by the internal frame structure. The choice of the spoon for a particular job will depend on the original contour of the metal, the amount of access, the proposed action (roughing or levelling) and the general shape and the length of the spoon.

General Purpose Spoon

The reshaping of the roof panel (Figure PB9) may be possible by the use of a general purpose spoon instead of the curved dolly. Figure PB10 shows the application. The use of a backing piece to prevent local damage to the cant rail and reduce the pressure in this area by distributing the force at the fulcrum will depend on clearances at this point. Prying upwards from a-to-b with a steady force, accompanied with external beating on any ridges that may be present, will restore the shape.

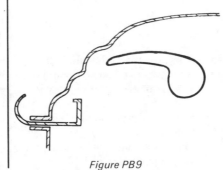

Figure PB9

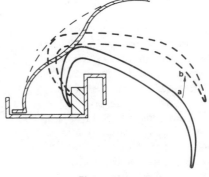

Figure PB10

Provided that a backing piece is employed a certain amount of prying fore and aft may assist the work.

Inside Pry and Surfacing Spoon

Assuming that the outer panel only is damaged, making the repair an economical proposition, the car door provides an example of a double skin structure to illustrate the application of body spoons.

When the door is stripped of interior trim and window glass it should be placed panel down towards the floor or bench, resting on two pieces of wood as Figure PB11. This prevents the panel scraping the floor and gives space for the panel to move, or spring, as force is exerted on the spoon. After roughing out, the spoon can be reversed so that 'on' or 'off' the spoon beating can be used to complete the straightening procedure. Access for this spoon will depend on the pattern of the piercing through the inner structure. If direct access is not possible a Long-Reach Dolly should be employed. Alternatively circular holes may be cut in the inner panel for access and covered by the trim on assembly.

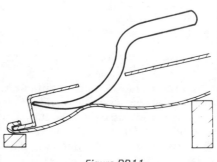

Figure PB11

Heavy Duty Pry Spoon

This spoon can be used for separating outer panels from the inner frame structure, when they have been damaged and squeezed together (Figure PB12). It can be driven between the plates, prying sidewards, or up and down until the desired amount of separation is achieved. The blade can then be used as a dolly, to dress out the outer panel and the inner structure if required. The blade is reduced to a very thin section that can be used for opening door panel flanges, or breaking spot-welded joints that have been previously drilled through the panel or section to be discarded.

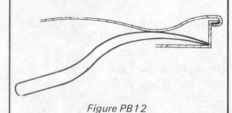

Figure PB12

High Crown Spoon

The high crown, with its broad working surface and high crown is an ideal tool as a dolly, or a spoon for work in confined areas, such as headlamp housings and high crown sections of the body above the waist line (Figure PB13).

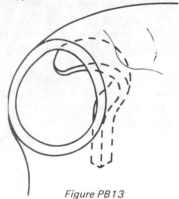

Figure PB13

Spring Beating Spoon

A light pressed-steel spoon is designed specially for spring beating on ridges. The spoon is placed directly on the ridge (Figure PB14) and sharp blows with a beater are delivered to the back of the spoon, spreading the force over

a large area. In this manner marking of the panel is prevented and the damage corrected in many cases without injury to the paint work. The intensity of the blow should be closely controlled so that the area is not forced down below its normal position. This spoon is not made for prying or levering, and its surface, as with other panel tools, should be kept clean and highly polished. Any irregularities on the surface will be reproduced on the panel, in reverse.

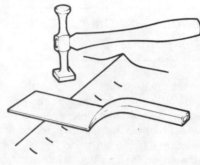

Figure PB14

Bumping Blades

Bumping blades are used for slapping out dents, with or without the backing support of a dolly. For slight dents or a wavy surface, a dolly is not required. The bumping blade should be applied so that glancing blows are received by the panel (Figure PB15). The blade

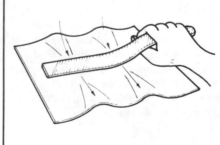

Figure PB15

serrations hold the metal within the area of contact to avoid stretching. Limit the use of blades to slight or moderate damage, as they are not intended to take the role of the body spoon or beater and dolly. Experience will indicate when to use them; try out as a semi-finishing tool.

Panel Finishing ●

Shrinking

In the final stages of panel finishing, some slightly stretched areas of metal may be encountered. The repairer determines the exact location, size and shape of the area by 'hand-feeling' (running the palm of the hand over the surface), by 'eye' or, in the case of a large flat area, such as a door panel, by the use of a straight edge. To increase sensitivity when 'hand-feeling', a lightweight cotton glove could be used to 'feel' the panel. On a paint-finished car body a spray of light oil and a strong light source can be used to show slight irregularities in the surface. Once the stretched area is located the treatment will depend on the amount of stretch involved. (See also 'Heat Shrinking a panel' in the Welding Chapter.)

Shrinking Beaters

For slightly stretched areas shrinking beaters may be used (Figure PB16). The square faced end of the beater is cross-milled. In using this type of beater small amounts of metal are forced into the spaces created by the cross-milling. They can be used on aluminium in a cold condition, but

Figure PB16

working on sheet steel will be speeded if heat is applied to the area. Be careful, however, because excess heat can itself cause more stretching. Whenever possible such beating should be carried out on the inside of the panel to minimise resurfacing work prior to painting.

Grid Dolly

A special dolly is available to facilitate shrinking work. This is the Grid Dolly which has a large crowned grid face on the upper surface. The base is a shallow face for normal finishing work.

SP1   Here, metal is beaten into the groove in the grid dolly, forcing the surplus metal downwards and 'out of the way'! In cases of severe stretching, a second groove can be made, at right-angles to the first, forming a cross.

For information on heat shrinking, see relevant section in this book. In general, Sykes-Pickavant recommend leaving the panel-beating surface marginally lower and under no circumstances should high-spots remain because these are impossible to disguise. The beginner is strongly recommended to leave any small indentations below the surface out of harm's way, rather than to attempt to beat them out, when the result would probably be to stretch and 'belly' the metal. Finish off with a plastic filler: the quantity of filler you have to use will be a good guide to how well your expertise has developed! But once again, go for a successful finish rather than a macho attempt at beating out every last imperfection, because it's the finish that counts, assuming that the job is sound.

Annealing ●

When beating metal, the action of the beater tends to work-harden it. This happens quickly with aluminium; less so with steel. The result is that the metal becomes hard and springy and almost impossible to work. With steel, the solution is to heat it up to red heat then swirl the torch over the heated metal, withdrawing it slowly so that the steel cools slowly. Use this technique only when fabricating a repair panel which needs a lot of working: the risk of distortion is too great with a full body panel. Aluminium should also be heated to anneal it, but remember that it will melt at less than red heat. It will anneal whether allowed to cool in the air or if quenched in water. Quenched steel will not anneal properly.

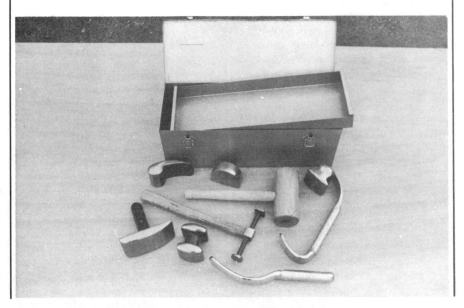

SP2   Sykes-Pickavant make kits ranging from the 'Service Station Kit' for the occasional user and the beginner, through to the 'Master Set' whose name speaks for itself. All are highly commended by the author as fine examples of craftsmanship in themselves!

3 Rust Treatment & Proofing

Rust is your car's greatest enemy. While its engine, gearbox and running gear can be made to go on for hundreds of thousands of miles given remedial treatment when needed, the corrosion of steel is more or less inevitable. You *can* slow it down, and in so doing considerably extend the life of your car, but you can't entirely stop it. Corrosion is part of the nature of things, the process of creation and decay that affects everything around us. Iron ore, a brown rock, is mined from the earth, melted down and alloyed with a small amount of carbon and other elements. This turns it into strong, usable steel. As corrosion sets in, however, the iron content rapidly starts to turn itself back into a brown, crumbly substance, useful only for resmelting and making back into steel again.

To protect steel against corrosion, it is necessary to create a barrier between the surface of the steel and its environment. Car manufacturers have always applied paint to their steel panels, of course, and traditionally, it was considered enough to keep rust at bay for the car's life with the first couple of owners. More recently, pressure from the customer has meant that the manufacturer has had to do much more about keeping rust at bay, and competition has meant that he has had to back up his protection claims with a long-term guarantee. Such procedures make it all the more important to reintroduce corrosion control when repairs to minor bumps and panel replacements are carried out.

The main Section at the end of this Chapter, on rustproofing, shows you how to inject an oily substance into the enclosed box sections of your car, enabling you to dramatically improve the life expectancy of the main structural components. More often than not, however, the dreaded rust has already appeared by the time the owner becomes interested and it is not a preventative procedure that is needed but a remedial one. Rust can never be 'cured', it can only be removed and, where necessary, the underlying metal structure rebuilt before the cosmetic aspects of the body are restored. The basic principles are given below for attention to rust, but greater detail is provided in the various 'project' Sections relating to specific instances of bodywork repair throughout the book. Refer to the 'Contents' for more detailed information.

How corrosion occurs ●

The process of corrosion actually happens as the result of an electric current passing from one section of metal to another. As in the case of a battery, there must be an electrolyte between the two sections (salty water? That'll do nicely!) and oxygen must also be present. As ions flow from the positive 'terminal' (the anode) to the negative 'terminal' (the cathode), the anode breaks down; in the case of steel it rusts. Rusting stops if water, oxygen or the electrolyte are completely excluded, but if any of them get through and the temperature is above freezing point it starts off with a vengeance. Poultices of salt-soaked mud and dust, industrial pollution and soil rich in agricultural chemicals provide corrosion with the perfect opportunity to take a hold on the steel sheets that make up the body of your car.

Fighting back ●

The most effective steps in excluding corrosion are taken during the manufacturing process when a car's internals are most accessible. Obviously, there's not much an owner can do about this except to choose a car made by a manufacturer with a good reputation for rust prevention. In general, cars built by southern European makers, where the climate has provided little experience of corrosion-inducing environments, are more prone to rust than those built in the north of the continent. BL in England (especially since around 1980) and VW in Germany have done notably well at keeping rust at bay while Volvo in Sweden have been consistently second to none.

Once the car is in use, there are two steps that can usefully be taken by the owner to hold back the rust that takes a hold in the enclosed structural sections and those beneath the car. The first is to wash mud and dirt from underneath the vehicle at least twice a year. This can be done in an effective way by many garages at moderate cost using a pressure blast of steam. Steam cleaning removes all the mud from the traps and crevices at which the steam is directed and it also removes any loose paint or underseal which, if left in place, can only accelerate corrosion.

Clearly, it is important to examine those areas that have been cleaned and to touch-up any bare patches. For the keen DIY enthusiast, a fairly effective way of dislodging mud from beneath the car is to make up a lance from $\frac{1}{2}$ in or 15 mm copper tubing and hold it in the end of a piece of hosepipe with a jubilee clip. The business end of the tube can be hammered into a flat slit giving a water jet of increased pressure. But be prepared for a drenching!

The second bit of preventative maintenance worth carrying out on the underside of the car is to spray it annually with engine oil. This is best carried out shortly after the mud has been washed away but after the underbody has thoroughly dried out. The oil will actually stop in place best if there is a covering of dust and light dirt on the underbody and it will do a superb job of stopping rust scabs from spreading and it will not, of course, chip away. Beneath wheel arches, the oil will be fairly rapidly blasted off by the scouring action of debris thrown up by the tyres so use either underseal there, or some 'old sages' recommend a mixture of nine parts underseal to one part oil. The effectiveness of oil spray on the underside of a car has been proven time and time again but two points must be borne in mind. The first is that unless the *insides* of enclosed box sections are similarly treated, they will rot out from the inside; and be certain to treat the

whole of the underside. It is a fact that where any rust preventative is applied, any small areas which are missed by the treatment will be much more prone to electrolytic action than if no treatment had taken place at all.

DBR1.   Many people have reservations about underseal, and prefer paint on the principle that you can easily see when problems in painted steel are starting, whereas rust starting beneath underseal can do its damage without being spotted. In fact, underseal can actually make matters worse by trapping moisture against the metal. Applied over a perfectly sound surface modern 'Body Schutz' type

underseals are much improved over the old-fashioned variety, but they do need to be put on with an inexpensive applicator powered by a compressor rather than a brush. Body Schutz applied to the bottoms of sills and front and rear aprons can cut out stone chips in those areas while on the insides of door panels and on the bottoms of large flat boots and bonnets it can cut down on drumming.

Regular steam cleaning carried out by a garage will show up any defects in older underseal and will remove loose sealant before it has a chance to cause a problem. If you intend inspecting the underside regularly, underseal is probably not a good choice, but if you are the sort of person to leave well alone, then underseal, being preferable to having no worthwhile coating at all on the bottom of your car, is probably for you.

DBR2.   Here rust has started to form from the other side of the panel. There are rust blisters all along the edge of the wheel arch which often means that rust is starting to bubble through after first attacking the inside of the panel. In this case, however, the paint film had broken down letting rust squeeze in beneath the paint. When rust starts from the inside, the rusted-out section of the panel is useless and should really be cut away to stop the rust from spreading. New steel could be welded in or a more temporary repair could be carried out as described in other areas of this book. When you patch a hole with another piece of metal other than steel in order to fill over the top with glass-fibre and filler (see Body Repairs on a Shoestring) be sure to use zinc or aluminium. Both of them will act as an anode to steel's cathode, which means that they will break down first, leaving the steel in one piece. Metals like stainless steel, copper, brass, nickel and lead, although we think of them as being resistant to rust, actually act as cathode to the steel's anode which, in layman's terms, means that in their presence the steel will break down first leaving them intact.

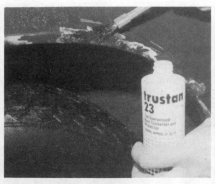

DBR3. The bubbling paint is scraped away with an old wood chisel making certain that all rust and loose paint are removed right back to bright shiny metal.

DBR4. There are several brands of so-called 'rust-killers' on the market but the author has found a brand called Trustan to work quite well. It is brushed onto the rust which is then left to 'neutralize' for 24 hours.

DBR5. This is later followed up by the application of Trustan's own primer. The maker's claim that this is all that is necessary to stop the rust virtually for good was shown to be unfounded when the author left this repair for a few days in rainy weather whereupon the rust started showing through again. In the past, top coat has been applied by the author within hours of applying the primer and that has proved to be far more effective in holding back the rust.

DBR6. One thing that you should never do is to apply paint right over existing rust; this traps the moisture contained within the rust on the surface of the steel and considerably accelerates the corrosion process. Instead, wait until you can properly get rid of as much of the loose and surface rust as possible using a scraper or better still a mini-grinder such as this one made by Black & Decker.

DBR7. Better still is a compressor driven spot sandblaster which gets rid of all the rust, right down to the bottom of rust craters, leaving beautifully clean metal. The main disadvantage of the sandblaster is that it can damage other nearby panels or glass unless they are properly masked off. Also, the dust that it creates is not only untidy but can also be damaging to mechanical components if it gets inside them. You, of course, wear a face mask to prevent the dust getting inside, and damaging, you.

DBR8. Rust prevention is better than cure, and you can go a long way to stop rust reappearing in any repairs you carry out. Here a zinc-rich paint is being brushed into the inside of a door before a new skin is fitted. There is even a weldable paint which comes in aerosol cans and which can be sprayed into all new joints and seams before they are welded (it even allows a spot welder current to flow) without burning off. This means that one of the most vulnerable parts of a car can be given paint protection from rust.

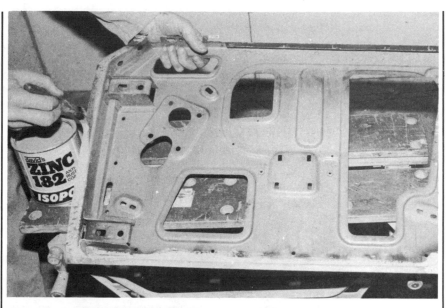

Rustproofing – Wax Injection and Treatment ■

One of the most effective ways in which an owner can guard against rot is to inject all internal and enclosed sections with a wax-based or oil-based rust inhibitor. This can be carried out professionally which has the advantage that the best equipment will be used such as lances for reaching inside hidden members and even, in some cases, a fibre-optics viewing system so that the operator can check that everything has been covered. On the other hand, the motorist can lose out having it treated professionally; after all, the standard of the finished job (regrettably, well hidden) is dependent on the operator's best efforts. With the best will in the world, grovelling around under other people's cars is neither the most glamorous nor fascinating of jobs and who could blame the operator who just got a little bored now and again. Instead the owner could, with the minimum number of tools, carry out the work himself and make sure that it's done properly.

Since *you* are the owner, it is *you* who is going to have to check a few things out. Make sure that the fluid you choose for injection is thin enough to 'creep' into seams and flanges and as far as possible into genuinely hidden areas. If it's thick when you buy it, you can always thin it down, provided that you select the right solvent. Make certain that you can work out how your car is put together; a parts list showing all the body components in exploded detail is best but a good quality cut-

away drawing would be a useful substitute. If nothing of the sort can be found, go round the car and note how it all fits together, especially the hollow box sections running along and across the underside. Ensure that as well as the fluid, you purchase a suitable tool for injecting it, a drill large enough to enable you to get the injection lance through the hole and to manoeuvre it, and a sufficient number of plastic plugs or grommets to fill all the holes you have drilled.

Some rust fluid kits contain all of these items, some do not. The British Automobile Association claim that a car treated in this way will have an extended life of between 3 and 5 years, but they recommend annual inspection and re-treatment with the implication that the car's life could thus be extended even further. The AA, however, make a point that should be noted seriously by any owner of a rusty old car and which seems to challenge strongly what some rust inhibitor makers claim in their literature. Says the AA: "Above all it is important to note that it (rust inhibitor) cannot be successfully applied to retard further corrosion once the flake type of corrosion, rather than a slight red-brown general surface rusting, has set in; at this stage, rust proofer will give preferential protection to the loose or partly lifted off flakes rather than the residual, more or less sound, steel pressing".

The glossy coat of paint which

covers the outside of your car has the dual purpose of giving you an attractive looking vehicle and of keeping surface rust at bay. Rust starting from external sources is rarely as damaging as rust which works from the inside-out but it *can* be if left unchecked. Obvious points to watch are around door, boot and fuel filler edges where the paint can be chipped away and also along a car's leading edge and lower sills where stone chips can cause damage. When you find a paint chip, carefully scrape down to bare metal if any rust is present and touch-up the chip with paint sold for the job. This is especially important where rust seems to have broken through from behind the paint (but not right through the metal). If allowed to continue unabated, this can be the most serious source of external rusting.

Down in the deeps, beneath the car, rust dangers of another sort lurk in the murky half-light. There, salt water, grit and a hundred other damaging objects are blasted against the underside of the car. Most cars are undersealed when new, but underseal hardens with age, lifts slightly and allows salty moisture pockets to form. In other areas, grit blasts the underseal away while on ledges and in crevices, salt-laden mud sits gnawing inexorably at the steel beneath it. If this sounds like a good scenario for a horror tale — it is! Except that it's for real and happening beneath your car. The answer is to 'get out and get under', wash the mud away as already described, scrape at the underseal with a metal scraper (if the underseal stays put, it's OK) and paint any badly protected areas, or if you like underseal, touch-up with some of that.

If all of this sounds like a lot of hassle, just remember the amount of time and money you spend on mechanical maintenance, remember that maintaining your car's bodywork will save you far more money than maintaining just its mechanics, then perhaps you'll question your own maintenance priorities.

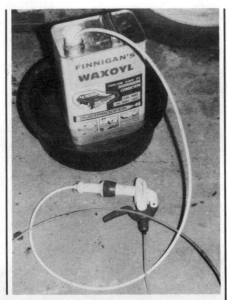

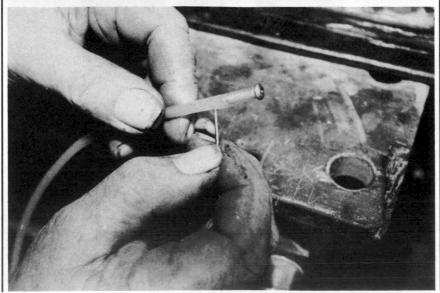

WX1.   This is a shot of one brand of rust inhibitor, Finnigan's Waxoyl shown with one of the injector guns available from Finnigan's as an extra. Here the can of fluid is sitting in a bowl of hot water to give it a thinner consistency. It could be thinned with oridinary white spirit (turps substitute) as an alternative. Make certain that **all** welding has been carried out before using such a fluid; the stuff is flammable and the very devil to put out if it starts burning inside a box section. After it has been in place for some time, its solvents evaporate making it far less flammable. These waxy/oily inhibitors are no use where road dirt can blast them away, such as under wheel arches, in line with the wheels.

WX2.   We found the actual spraying end of the injector to be fairly useless (it just produced one or two concentrated jets) so we cut off the end, which consisted of a nail pushed into the end of the plastic pipe.

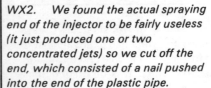

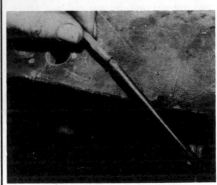

WX3.   A self-tapping screw was selected and fitted into the pipe end, sealing it off.

WX4.   Then holes were pierced radially into the pipe using a pin. By trial and error, sufficient holes were created to give an all-round spray effect.

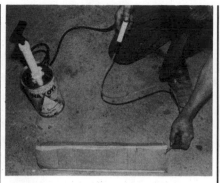

WX5. Here, an improved version of the Waxoyl can is shown. This is a pressure can to which a pump is fitted, rather like that on a garden sprayer. The can is pumped up and then a trigger on the gun simply released when you are ready to spray. The lance is shown being inserted into a test cardboard 'box section', held together with masking tape.

WX7. It will be necessary to drill a certain number of holes to allow injection of the fluid. Mark the spot with a light centre punch mark or place a piece of masking tape over the spot to prevent the drill wandering before it bites. In either case, hold the drill in place without pressing the trigger and rotate chuck and drill by hand in the direction of cut a few times. This provides a safe start for the drill and further discourages wandering.

WX9. In other cases, it may be possible to remove a screw or bolt to gain access such as in the case of this door shut panel.

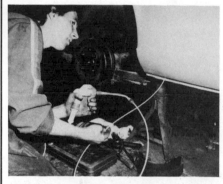

WX10. Here, Terry Bramall has found a sill drain hole through which to inject the fluid.

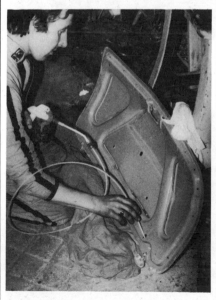

WX6. When the box is opened up, you can see exactly how well the spray has covered and you can also judge your own technique. On the lower part of the box, for instance, it is clear that the lance was moved too rapidly giving insufficient coverage. You can also gauge whether the build up is too high and whether the fluid requires thinning or not.

WX8. There are many places where a lance can be inserted into a box section through pre-existing holes. Here *Practical Classics* magazine's Terry Bramall, rust proofs the boot of one of the magazine's project cars.

WX11. The safest way of ensuring that the entire length of a box section has been covered is to push the lance in as far as it will go or until it meets an obstruction, grip the place where it enters the box section between thumb and forefinger, withdraw the lance and note to where it has reached. Reinsert it, then pump copious quantities of fluid in while withdrawing the lance slowly and rotating it a little if possible.

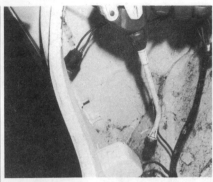

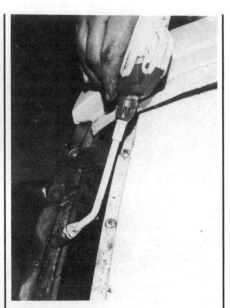

WX12.   Here an older car is being injected through the aperture where the old-style trafficator arm fits into place. Don't forget windscreen surrounds where these comprise enclosed box sections. Approach from behind the trim.

WX13.   This is a different type of gun and gives an effect like any other hand-held sprayer. Use it where some forward motion of the fluid is required such as here inside the boot beneath the rear lamp housing.

WX14.   The inside of the grille is the sort of place crying out for this sort of attention. How else would you get to it?

WX15.   One of the most notorious rot spots of all on any car is around the rear wheel arch where rear wing meets the inner wing. Here the gap between the panels is just close enough to harbour moisture and encourage the sort of electrolytic action already mentioned, resulting in rapid rusting. Spray a good, thin spray of inhibiting fluid well into this area from inside the car (remove trim to give easy access) and hope that it creeps to where you want it.

WX16.   Where a large, open box section has big enough holes in it, the hand sprayer can be used to good effect.

WX17. This bulkhead has been stripped; you may have to search to find the best access holes leading to all the vital, enclosed box sections in this area.

WX20. This floor box section where the handbrake mechanism is mounted is prone to water access and is ideal for the anti-rust fluid treatment. The linkage won't suffer, either!

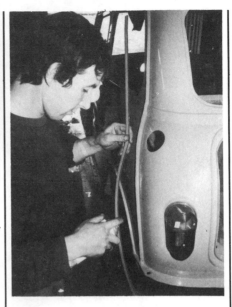

WX22. The same car's seam moulding strips are given the T.B. special treatment.

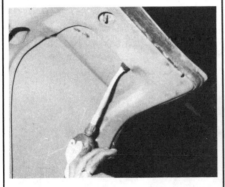

WX18. Stress panels on the boot are often a little way away from the outer skin, leaving plenty of room for access with the gun ...

WX21. There are many places where a really thin rust inhibitor such as those found in aerosal cans come into their own. Here Terry Bramall sprays the number plate mounting brackets on the Practical Classics *project* Mini. The brackets are spotwelded to the front panel, so there is bound to be a tiny gap between them.

WX23. Chrome trim is an especially suitable place to squirt this kind of stuff as it is very 'thin', creeps into all sorts of narrow gaps and helps to keep out moisture and air as well as breaking down the electrical contact between two surfaces. The reaction between two dissimilar metals can be powerful and very corrosive for whichever of the two metals is 'programmed' to be the sacrificial anode.

WX19. ... and the same often applies to the bonnet.

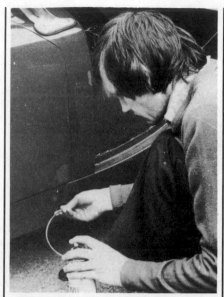

WX24.   Here Paul Skilleter, Practical Classics *Managing Editor injects aerosol fluid into the tricky jacking point mounting at the end of a 'Frogeye' Sprite's cross member.*

WX26.   *If you own a 'woody', stopping rot doesn't stop with the steel-work. Here the drain holes beneath rear window slides are being opened up with a twist drill; they had filled full of silt over the years. Where wood butts up against metal, such as where aluminium or steel panels are pinned or bolted into place, it wouldn't be a bad idea to inject some more of that ubiquitous anti-rust fluid. It seems that in some matters, you can't have too much of a good thing!*

But NB The following areas should not be treated with rust retarding fluid: Engine; gearbox; back axle; prop and axle shafts; wheel hubs; brake drums and discs; brake cables; door mounted speakers.

Mask them off with paper or plastic sheet and masking tape to keep fluid off them. (A plastic bag will be fine for brake drums.) Also, if seat belts of the retractable type are housed within box sections, pull them out and hold them there before spraying. When you have finished, make sure that you have cleared out all bodywork drain holes to allow trapped water to disperse.

WX27.   *The DeVilbiss injection gun does the job in a fully professional way because the fluid is semi-atomised from the end of the nozzle giving very good coverage. The gun set-up costs about a third of the cost of having the work carried out to a high standard, so for anyone with a compressor it represents a good value way of rustproofing a car to a high standard.*

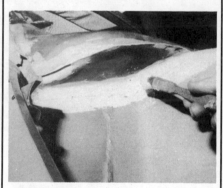

WX25.   *Open seams beneath a car can and should be brushed over with proprietary seam sealer when new panels are let in, simply to stop the ingress of water.*

4 Painting Part 1

Gun lore – types of spray gun ●

The spray gun has a history that pre-dates the motorcar itself. Right at the start of the story, a familiar name pops up. A Dr. DeVilbiss, practising in the United States in the latter half of the last century, was irritated by the problems of getting droplets of nasal medicine into his patients' throat and nose passages. He invented his own solution to the problem and the DeVilbiss atomiser, or nasal spray, soon saw production and began to overshadow the good doctor's medical ministrations. Of course, as we now know, the idea of atomising and spraying went far beyond the world of medicine, and the DeVilbiss company is now a world-wide organisation and acknowledged as one of the foremost manufacturers of spray equipment.

Figure GL1. A simple spray-painting set-up. Nowadays, there are many different types of spray gun in industrial use, some of them involving the use of no air whatsoever. But for the home resprayer the choice is much more simple. (Courtesy of DeVilbiss).

→

Spray guns are precision tools. Any spray gun will blast paint onto a car, but in general, the more you pay for the gun, the better the quality of finish. To the professional, that matters a very great deal because the better the finish 'straight from the gun', the less work has to be done afterwards,

but to the home sprayer, especially to the beginner, the difference may not matter quite so much, until he or she carries out more spraying and becomes more critical.

The way in which the paint is supplied to the nozzle of the spray gun determines whether it is a suction-feed or pressure-feed gun.

Suction Feed

These guns have a flow of air through the top of the gun which pulls the paint up out of the paint pot by a vacuum effect, somewhat similar to the operation of a car engine's carburettor. All suction feed guns have an opening in the lid of the paint pot (to allow air at atmospheric pressure to push down on the paint) and the fluid tip, the centre part of the nozzle, protrudes a little way beyond the front of the air cap. This system is sometimes known as 'syphon feed'. These guns often consume a larger amount of air but are generally used by the 'trade'.

Pressure Feed

This type of gun pushes air down into the pot itself and so pressurises the contents. It is better at lifting heavy materials, such as spray putty, out of a gun with a lower air consumption than the Suction Feed type of gun. Identification: there is no hole in the lid and the fluid tip does not protrude out

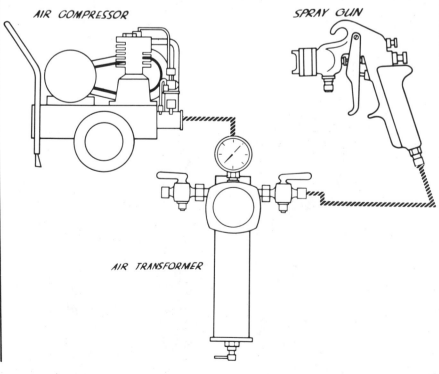

AIR COMPRESSOR

SPRAY GUN

AIR TRANSFORMER

of the front of the air cap (these are generally internal mix air caps).

There is yet another distinction between types of gun!

Bleeder Type

These guns discharge air through the air cap of the gun the whole time the compressor is on, although paint only comes out when the trigger is pressed. They are for simple spray set-ups where there is a small compressor with no air receiver (tank) and so no auto-mechanism for shutting the compressor off when the tank is filled. With this type of compressor, the air created has to go somewhere, so a bleeder type of gun is used.

Non-Bleeder Type

Here the air and the paint are both shut off at the gun when the trigger is released.

There are also two different types of air cap available, which are:

Internal Mix

Here the air and paint are mixed inside the air cap, but if quick-drying materials are used, such as most car finish paints, this type of air cap clogs-up much too quickly. Internal mix air caps are always used with pressure feed guns.

External Mix

These air caps are the ones fitted to most guns and, here, the air and the fluid are actually mixed in the space outside the air cap.

Choose Your Weapon ●

If you buy a complete compressor/spray gun set-up, the choice has already been made for you. But if you're buying your own set

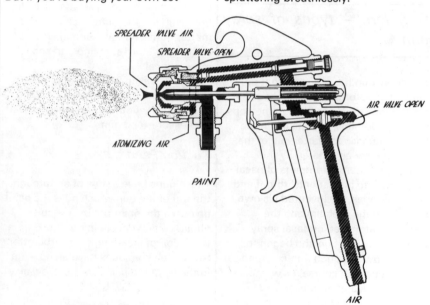

Figure GL2.   Simple air cap types (Courtesy DeVilbiss) ↓

piecemeal, or if you want to uprate the quality of your gun, this is for you.

The primary disadvantage of the suction feed type of gun for the DIY sprayer is that it requires quite a lot of air and therefore rather a large compressor to deliver it. The home sprayer is likely to have a smaller compressor with an inadequate capacity for the operation of a suction fed spray gun. If the compressor is fitted with an air receiver (and all but the smallest are), the reservoir of air would allow the compressor to cope for a short while but it would soon be spluttering breathlessly.

Figure GL3.   The DeVilbiss JGA; the full professional gun. (Courtesy of DeVilbiss)

The major advantage of the pressure-feed system, however, is that it can work perfectly well for the DIY-er on a reduced pressure or volume of air. Its disadvantage is that the spread of the spray will be reduced, giving slower operation than the suction-feed type of gun but that is not generally too important to the home sprayer. Also, the pressure-feed system actually wastes less material in the form of potentially harmful overspray. The external-mix type of cap is a 'must' for the car sprayer, while the owner of a compressor without air receiver must use a bleeder type of gun. If your compressor has got an air receiver, the bleeder type will probably work but a) it will waste air unnecessarily and, b) it will not necessarily be a high

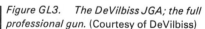

performance gun, being built for lower-priced spray set-ups. The 'Apollo' sprayer, DeVilbiss' 'Tuffy' and 'Beaver' and the SIP 'Jet 30' are all examples of spray set-ups based around the bleeder type of gun and receiverless compressor.

In conclusion, whatever level of attainment you have reached, go for an external-mix nozzle on your gun. Buy a suction feed gun if your compressor will cope with it (ask your supplier for advice) and if you want fast, professional standards of finish; buy pressure feed if you have a medium-small compressor and go for a bleeder type only if your compressor has no air receiver, or tank.

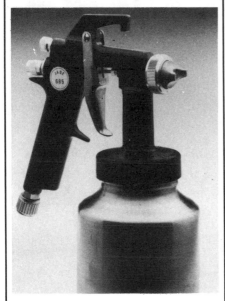

GL1.   The SIP 'Jade' spraygun has such versatility that it can be adapted for suction or pressure feed, bleeder or non-bleeder use or with a special setting for low-pressure use. The Anglo-Italian instructions are a trial, however!

Cleanliness Comes Last! ●

So much for selecting the appropriate gun! There is also a wide range of fluid tips, needles, and air caps available. Their choice and selection is a complex matter, however, and as far as the DIY user is concerned, it's best to stick to standard offerings and to take advice from the factor or manufacturer's

Customer Relations Department if specific problems are encountered. What the individual *can* do to improve standards of workmanship is to learn how to spray properly (see appropriate section for guidance) and to make special efforts to maintain the gun because standards of gun cleanliness and efficiency are absolutely critical in terms of spray quality. It may sounds a little bit Lewis Carroll, but in spraying the end comes first. In other words, the quality of respray depends to a considerable degree on the cleaning carried out after the previous job was complete. It's important to leave time to clean the gun out well after spraying. The following sequence shows how DeVilbiss, at their Bournemouth, England headquarters, recommend that it be done.

DeV1.   This special cut-away spray gun shows just how many passageways and chambers there are in a modern spray gun — and, therefore, just how much there is to keep clean.

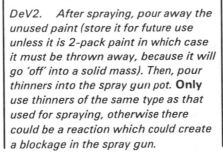

DeV2.   After spraying, pour away the unused paint (store it for future use unless it is 2-pack paint in which case it must be thrown away, because it will go 'off' into a solid mass). Then, pour thinners into the spray gun pot. **Only use thinners of the same type as that used for spraying**, otherwise there could be a reaction which could create a blockage in the spray gun.

DeV3.   Screw the paint pot back onto the gun and shake thoroughly. Empty out the pot, to remove the worst of the paint residue and put more thinners into the pot. Don't leave paint to go hard on and in the gun and NEVER immerse the whole gun in thinners; this will destroy the effectiveness of the gun's sealing glands and allow dirt to get into the airways.

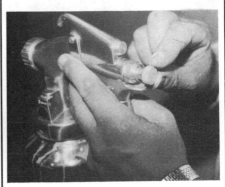

DeV4.   Now unscrew the air valve in an anti-clockwise direction, so increasing the rate at which the gun will deliver fluid when it is triggered.

DeV5. Blast the thinners through the gun so that it cleans all the passageways through which the paint has passed. Carry out this operation two or three times to ensure a thorough clean-out. Be careful where you spray the old thinners; remember that it still contains paint pigment and that it can carry over any nearby vehicles or household fittings.

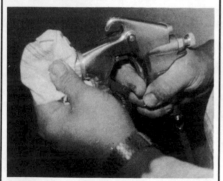

DeV6. Take the paint pot off, cover the air cap with a rag and trigger the gun. This will push the thinners back into the container and dry out the suction tube.

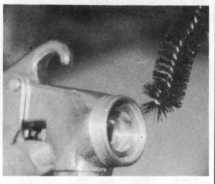

DeV8. Don't just wipe this area with a rag; you need to use a brush to stand a chance of getting inside all the nooks and crannies and the depths of the thread.

DeV10. Clean the fluid tip remembering that it, too, is a critical component in determining the quality of the spray pattern.

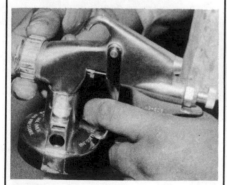

DeV7. Next, unscrew the air cap locking ring, remove the air cap and clean the fluid tip that sits beneath it.

DeV9. Pay particular attention to cleaning the air cap (a build-up of paint can easily form inside it) but resist the temptation to poke through the jet with anything metallic. The jet sizes are finely determined and they can easily be mis-shaped which would ruin the shape of the spray pattern.

DeV11. Inside the neck of the spray gun cup you will find a sealing washer of some sort. (It is best to have a spare standing by; a split or broken sealing washer, or one that has bedded down and which fails to seal, will allow drips through the top of the pot.) Remove the seal, clean it ...

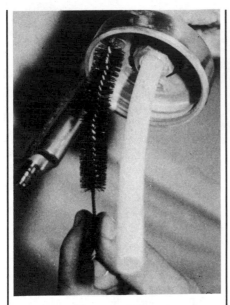

DeV12. ... and also clean underneath it and inside the threads and the air chambers found there. Remember to push the 'flue brush' up the feed pipe, too. Then (for this area at least) put more thinners into the pot and give it a last blasting through ...

DeV13. ... before taking off the pot and wiping it down externally.

DeV14. It shouldn't be necessary to strip out the fluid needle every time you use the gun, but it is a good idea to do so every few spray sessions. When you need to do so, take out the air valve all the way but be careful that the fluid needle spring doesn't jump out and launch itself into oblivion. The needle itself simply draws out backwards. Be careful not to bend the needle end or to abrade or damage the pointed 'business' end in any way.

DeV15. To adjust the fluid needle gland nut, tighten it until the trigger starts to feel stiff, then slacken it off slowly and gradually until the trigger becomes completely free again. Keep the gland lightly oiled.

DeV16. It is important that the trigger should be as free as possible. Although it might seem easy to pull at first, after a lot of spraying has been carried out, the spraying hand can become very tired – and fatigue leads to mistakes.

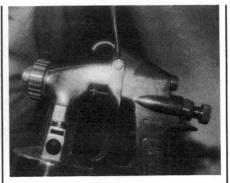

DeV17. Also, oil the trigger pivot, where it hinges on the gun body.

Principal Parts of the Spray Gun ●

The most important features of a spray gun are the following three parts.
The Fluid Tip, which meters out the paint.
The Fluid Needle, which starts and stops the flow of paint.
The Air Cap, which atomises the paint and forms the spray pattern.

It is important to remember that just any combination of these parts will not do; they must be teamed together correctly for the type of paint to be sprayed, the surface to be covered, the amount of compressed air available

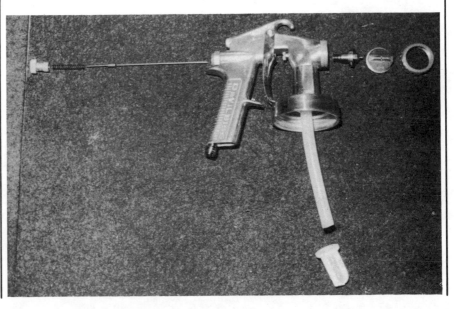

and the speed permissible on the job, although, for general purpose work, the right combination will automatically be supplied with the gun.

The rest of the spray gun consists of the body and handle, the trigger which actuates the fluid needle and the air valve, the spreader adjustment valve and the fluid adjustment screw.

The air valve, controlled by the trigger, starts and stops the flow of compressed air through the gun. The spreader adjustment valve (where fitted) controls the width of the spray pattern, and the fluid adjustment screw sets a pre-determined maximum flow of paint by restricting the travel of the fluid needle.

Putting on the Paint ●

In the motor trade, body repair shops depend for their existence largely upon their ability to turn out cars with a high shine. Naturally, the owner demands a perfect finish, whether the car has been totally resprayed or just spot repaired and so the trade has developed a wide range of techniques for ensuring that the depth of shine achieved is far greater than with paints used years ago. At the same time modern paint is both more durable and cheaper to apply. However, some modern paint systems demand a high level of investment on the part of the bodyshop owner and there are some health and safety snags that need to be considered.

The home car sprayer can most certainly achieve the best standards attainable in the best of the professional bodyshops. The methods for achieving this, however, are likely to be different, particularly in the following areas.

Equipment

For the home sprayer to attempt to achieve a set-up like that of the best equipped professionals would be foolish. A full professional spray booth

and ancillaries could easily cost as much as, say, a top line Jaguar – hardly a cost effective exercise for someone who just wants to spray an old VW 'Beetle'!

There is, however, a great deal of small-scale spray equipment around which will give a first-class spray job, if used in conjunction with the guidelines which follow.

Time

This is where the amateur scores over the professional every time. Whereas the body shop *has* to carry out work in a certain amount of time to ensure that profit does not slip into loss, the home sprayer has no such problem. Say, for instance, that through inexperience, you spray a really heavy coat of paint which then fails to smooth itself out and stays with an 'orange peel' finish. All you have to do is buckle down to several hours of hard polishing to leave a paint finish that is not only smooth but is fantastically shiny! Meanwhile, the pro who did the same thing would have cursed himself for losing a couple of hours and would have finished his machine polishing well before you, the amateur. But then, you wouldn't have been paying his wages. The third main difference comes down to ...

Experience

The professional who has received years of training or practice will have a very wide range of skills that the amateur can't hope to gain. The answer is for the home sprayer to concentrate just on the skills needed for the job in hand, to read up every scrap of information in this book and in manufacturers' own data sheets (such as those available from the factors who sell you the paint) and to spend some time trying out the new skills on a scrap panel or board before attempting the car itself. Again, you can be one up on the pro here: he often becomes stuck in his ways and fails to keep up with the latest developments whereas your information will be topical right from the word 'go'.

Paint – the Constituents ●

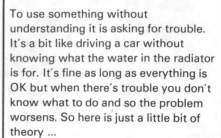

To use something without understanding it is asking for trouble. It's a bit like driving a car without knowing what the water in the radiator is for. It's fine as long as everything is OK but when there's trouble you don't know what to do and so the problem worsens. So here is just a little bit of theory ...

Paints have come a very long way from the days when cavemen exorcized their fears of sabre-toothed tigers by drawing likenesses on the walls of their caves, and indeed, modern paints can be extremely complex chemical brews. All automotive paints, however, are made up of three basic parts which determine their use – pigment, binder (or 'vehicle', as it is sometimes called) and solvent (or thinner or reducer).

Pigment

The pigment in paint is a finely ground powder which gives it its colour and also can carry out other functions. For instance, the pigment in 'red-lead' primer helps to protect against corrosion while the pigment in spray putty gives a good depth of a material that, when dry, can be flatted. The function of pigments in metallic paints are especially important and these will be dealt with later.

Binder

This carries the pigment (hence 'vehicle'), binds the pigment together and makes it adhere to the surface beneath. It also forms a protective, glossy film over the pigment when the paint has dried.

Solvent

This makes the paint runny so that it

can be applied. Although it is obviously an essential ingredient, it has no other use and so it is made of a highly volatile substance (i.e. one that evaporates quickly.) The solvent evaporates both during application and after application leaving the pigment and its binder to form the coat of paint found on the car. Different types of solvents are matched to different types of paint and, when paint is being 'thinned' to the correct degree of 'runniness' for its use, it is essential that the correct solvent is used.

Vehicle Manufacturers' Paint Types ●

Just a few years ago it would have been hard to get confused over common paint types; there were just two. One has the grand sounding name of nitrocellulose lacquer (generally known as cellulose paint, for short) while the other, synthetic enamel, is a cousin of old-style coach paint and of ordinary household gloss paint. However, these paints are now used by a minority of professional finishers while the car manufacturers use paints better suited to mass production systems.

Enamels

Two types of enamel paint are used by manufacturers, both of which form a solid coat of colour by hardening rather than by simply drying. A close analogy is in the difference between 2-pack glue and ordinary wallpaper paste. The paste works by the process of the water (the 'solvent') in the paste evaporating. The 2-pack glue, however, sets by chemical reaction. It is not at all affected by the amount of moisture surrounding it, but like all chemical reactions its setting is affected by heat; the warmer it is, the faster it sets.

The two types of enamel paint used by car producers act in the same way. However, they also contain some 'reducer' to thin the paint down to the correct thickness for spraying. This is allowed to 'flash off' before the hardening process takes place.

If you own one of the many cars made by a small-volume producer such as Jensen, Morgan or TVR note that virtually any type of paint may have been used, though it is more likely to be one of the 'refinisher' paints than one of those used by the large scale manufacturers. Fibreglass-bodied cars may well have their colouring impregnated in the outer coat of the fibreglass. See Section on 'Repairing Fibreglass' for more information on spraying GRP.

Acrylic Lacquer

This is the type of paint usually found in aerosol cans but it can also be used through a standard spray gun. Acrylic Lacquers have excellent gloss colour retention qualities and they dry very rapidly indeed. However, after surface drying full hardness drying can take up to sixteen hours. It is usual to have to compound the paint after spraying in order to bring it up to the highest gloss. It is best if ordinary 'cellulose' undercoats are not used under acrylic lacquers but instead that thinners and undercoats specifically recommended for this type of paint are used. Furthermore, because different manufacturers use different formulations in the production of this type of paint, it is important not to mix different makers' versions of acrylic lacquer otherwise the paint may craze or crack. Because acrylic lacquers forms a thin paint film it is necessary to use a number of coats to build up sufficient depth of paint.

Lacquer paints dry and harden when the solvent evaporates. However, 'Thermoplastic Acrylics' (TPA) as used by the manufacturers, also contain an element of plastic content which can be softened by heat. Consequently, TPA-sprayed cars are baked on the production line to a high temperature. This dries the paint, then softens and smooths the plastic content. TPA can be repaired at home with other lacquer paints where it is allowed simply to air dry.

Refinish Paint Types ●

Manufacturers' paints are not often suitable for refinishing. For instance, if a whole car was baked at a sufficiently high temperature to soften TPA paint, it would also melt the car's plastic trim, seats and wiring! So special paints have been formulated by the paint companies, designed especially to be used for refinishing.

They are available from paint factors under manufacturers' brand names, but their *type* names are: lacquer paints; oil and synthetic resin based paints; low bake enamels; and two-pack paints.

Lacquer paints ('Cellulose')

This dries very quickly which makes it most suitable for use as a DIY refinishing paint, for the problem for most home sprayers is the settling of dust into the paint as it dries. Obviously, the quicker the paint dries, the less chance there is for dust to settle into it. In order to obtain a high gloss finish, 'cellulose' or lacquer paints usually have to be compounded (polished) after the painting has been completed. This type of paint is less expensive than the more exotic, newer, concoctions, carries fewer health hazards (although some still remain) and is fairly durable. The main disadvantage, however, is that it may not be compatible with the paint already on the car, although it is possible to spray a coat of isolator to form a barrier between the two quarrelling paint types. Overall, 'cellulose' or lacquer paints must be considered as the most highly favoured paint type for the amateur. 'Cellulose' paint films are thin, therefore a number of coats have to be sprayed in order to build up the necessary depth of paint.

Enamel (oil-based paints)

Enamel paint is the close cousin of old-style coach paint and today is generally favoured by refinishers of commercial vehicles. It is, like lacquer, a fairly durable paint and it is probably the least expensive type of paint available. It has the advantage that it causes no reaction with any other type of paint that lies beneath it but it also has a number of huge disadvantages. The first is that it takes rather a long time to dry and can pick up every scrap of neighbourhood dust (and twice as many flies as you would have believed possible,) while it does so. Secondly, and this can be a real headache for the beginner, it can take days (if not weeks) to harden off sufficiently to be flatted again – so what do you do if you get runs? (Incidentally, enamels *dry* first in the conventional way, then *harden* by oxidation i.e., the effects of oxygen upon the chemical structure of the paint.) The third problem is that almost every other type of paint reacts by crazing and wrinkling if sprayed on top of enamel, especially if the enamel has fairly recently been applied. And the fourth problem is that it can't be compounded (polished) if you fail to get a shine straight from the gun, although, to be fair, enamel is one of the best paints for instant shine. If a car is to receive a last respray before being run into the ground, or if the car or small commercial has previously been sprayed in enamel then use it. Otherwise, forget it!

Two-Pack Paints

These are the 'magic mixture' paints, the witches' brews of chemicals and compounds that give a fantastic (if rather 'plasticky') gloss from the gun and an extremely hard durable finish together with pigments that seem to fade less than any others, especially in the fade-prone red and yellow ranges.

The big disadvantage with these paints has nothing to do with the paints themselves (although, in being designed for use with low-bake ovens they can be slow to dry and harden unless used with specially activated reducers to give speedier hardening), having more to do with the user's prospects for a long and peaceful life. In short, they can kill if misused. If breathed in whilst in the form of airborne spray, 2-pack isocyanate paints can be lethal. On rare occasions, they have caused fatal spasms after first contact; on other occasions, long-term users of the paint who have not used prescribed breathing apparatus, have been suddenly struck down in the same way. If the correct breathing apparatus is used religiously, there should, according to the manufacturers, be no inherent risk and DeVilbiss, for example, make an excellent filtration/breathing set for around the price of four ordinary tyres. Most ordinary users will conclude, however, that the risks are simply not worth the improved finish, even though, in the motor trade, well over half of all refinishing work carried out is undertaken with this type of paint. Non-isocyanate air-drying 2-pack paint systems are currently under development, but it is understood that there is a problem in getting paint to go hard in a sensible sort of time. Do watch out for this paint, though. When, and if, a safe non-isocyanate 2-pack paint becomes available, it will be the DIY-ers dream!

Low Bake Paints

Low bake enamels are baked at a minimum temperature of 80°C (175°F) and give super results for those bodyshops in the refinishing trade who can afford the large investment of low bake spray booth/ovens.

Metallic Paints

It is important to understand how the increasingly popular metallic paints 'work' in order to understand how to use them. They achieve their metallic effect by the inclusion of tiny flakes of aluminium in the paint. These aluminium chips act as reflectors giving the familiar metallic effect and also the characteristic changes of light and shade in the apparent colour of the paint. The reason for this is quite simple: if the surface of the paint is viewed from above, reflections from the chips of aluminium will be direct, making the surface of the paint seem lighter. If the paint is viewed from one side, the aluminium chips won't be reflecting much light back at you so the surface will seem darker.

Unfortunately, the same car can have areas which vary by how much this is true. In places where the paint has been put on thinly, the flakes of aluminium will have arranged themselves flat against the panel, so the differences between the appearance of the paint from above and from the side will be great. In other places, however, the paint may have been put on too heavily. Where this has occurred, the aluminium flakes will have floated around in the relatively deep paint and will have come to rest at all sorts of angles as the paint dried. In this case, the differences in shading will be small. Next time you see a car painted in metallic paint, try to judge which areas are which. Then, when it comes to spot painting a panel which has been painted in this type of paint, try to ape the style of the person who originally sprayed it so the metallic shadings blend in with the surrounding paint. Metallic paints can be made up of any of the types already shown, the metallic content simply forming a part of the pigment.

Clear-over-Base

This is a painting technique that is becoming popular with some manufacturers. Using this system the colour coat is not applied as a topcoat, but as a matt 'undercoat' which is then covered by one or more coats of clear lacquer. An example of dealing with this type of finish as a refinish task is given in Chapter 5 in the 'Front Wing Repair' section.

Undercoats

It is often said that a successful paint job depends upon successful preparation. That is perfectly true, and it is in the selection of undercoats that the difference between amateurs and professionals is most marked; picking the right undercoat for the job can cut preparation time dramatically and make it so much easier to avoid blemishes which show through the paint and which might even cause outright failure.

Primers are designed to make sure that the paint adheres well to the surface of the panel and to resist corrosion when used over bare metal. Many are required to perform at least one other function. Like everything else a primer should be chosen with a specific purpose in mind. The various types are as follows.

Etch Primers

These contain an acid which eats microscopically into the surface of the bare metal being primed and increases the hold of the paint onto the metal. An etch primer will also help to prevent the spread of corrosion beneath the paint should the paint film become scratched right through, because it holds on tight and makes it more difficult for corrosion to get at the metal.

Primer Filler and Primer Surfacer

These are probably the most versatile primers and can be used directly onto bare metal provided two coats are applied to ensure full coverage even after flatting. Primer surfacers and fillers achieve a compromise between giving good adhesion and also a reasonable level of 'build' – in other words, they leave quite a deep film which hides very minor scratches and blemishes and can then be flatted down.

Surfacers and Fillers

Surfacers and fillers do not attempt to do the job of primer alone and as such are not suitable for use on bare metal but they are superb at filling scratches and blemishes. They give a considerably higher 'build' but they flat out easily to give a fine finish. It is most important that you don't try to overcook the goose when using spray fillers. If too many coats are sprayed on in one session, the coats beneath will

not have had time to dry out and the paint coats could take a long time to dry.

Polyester spray fillers, on the other hand, go hard after the addition of a hardener to the paint before spraying. Since they don't need to dry out, polyester spray fillers can be built up as deeply as you like. Unfortunately the same dangerous health considerations apply to this paint as to the 2-pack paint already mentioned.

Spray Putties

These have a very similar effect to that of the spray fillers already mentioned, although they give an even deeper build. They are 'cellulose' based and so much safer than the 2-packs. They should be left to dry thoroughly *before* flatting, or they may shrink back further after flatting and expose the scratches and chips they were meant to conceal. Spray putties have to be sprayed on without the addition of extra thinners and so they need the services of quite a powerful compressor to pull the thick paint out of the pot.

If your compressor is powerful enough, using a spray filler or spray putty, will help cut down enormously on preparation time. After all, it's the way the pros do it!

Isolator

This relatively expensive but very useful primer is used as a barrier between two incompatible paint types. It can be water-based, wood alcohol-based, or based on anything else that will act as a non-reactive solvent with the common paint types. Just to be sure that it has done the job, try out the first non-compatible coat on a small panel first. *Always* spray a primer-filler over the top within the time specified by the makers and *never* flat the isolator itself.

Sealers

These are rarely used nowadays and were used as a groundcoat to help the final colour match. Modern paint colour pigments don't need such help but

note that a 'sealer' was meant to 'seal' in the colour of the primer and that it won't do the job of an isolator.

Chip Resistant Primer

Chip resistant primers are made to cut down the risk of paint chipping in vulnerable areas such as on sills and aprons and they are worth using when spraying the underside of large flat panels such as bonnets because they also help to cut down drumming noise as well as giving improved resistance to corrosion.

The paints market is an especially competitive one and international manufacturers are coming up with new ideas all the time. It is well worth going into paint factors with an open mind; if you ask to buy something specific you'll get it without comment but if you ask the factors' advice they will be able to advise on the best product to suit your particular purpose.

Pre-Spray Garage Preparations ●

PS1. *The biggest problem in DIY spraying is usually the presence of dust. You don't really notice it under normal circumstances but the blast of air from your spray gun and the movement of your feet around the car will stir up enough dust to make the surface of your newly shiny paintwork look almost like sandpaper if you don't take the right precautions. Start by vacuuming the roof, especially around any beams and also do the walls and any other nooks and crannies where dust can lurk.*

PS2.   *It almost goes without saying that you should sweep the floor out and you should also be prepared to move any dust-gathering lawn mowers, push bikes and any other garage paraphernalia because not only will they have trapped dust but they could also be damaged by overspray and paint dust from the air settling on them when you spray.*

PS3.   *While you're cleaning out the garage, you may be tempted to do something a bit more permanent about the state of your floor. Here Supra Garage Floor Paint is being brushed onto the floor to give a shiny but non-slip, easy to clean floor surface. Before spreading on the floor paint, you must scrub the floor with a broom using lots of detergent, to shift any soaked-in grease, then paint the whole floor with old emulsion paint to seal it.*

PS4.   *Although it's not strictly part of the garage itself, the paint tins you will be using could well have been stored in there during the great 'spring clean' so be sure to blow any dust from around the tin lid before opening up. An air line does the job best of course, but make sure you don't blast any specks into your eyes.*

Preparing to Spray ●

The first 'must' is to find out what type of paint you are spraying onto. As you will have noticed, some paints cannot be sprayed on top of other paints, otherwise a reaction will take place in the new paint leading to cracks and crazing. So it is really important to make sure you are not working with incompatible paint types.

If you are sure that your car has never been resprayed, find the colour code tag (sometimes on the maker's identity plate, sometimes by itself but – sadly – sometimes not there at all, especially on older cars).

If the car has been resprayed, try using the paint-type identification chart shown here or take the car along to the paint factors and ask them to take a look at it. An experienced eye can sometimes tell you which paint type has been used with a high level of probability of being right. If, as most home sprayers do, you opt to spray in 'cellulose' paint, try wiping some thinners onto an area that is not important such as the inside of a wheel arch or the bottom of a door. 'Cellulose' thinners is strong and so, if any reaction is going to take place, it will probably happen fairly quickly. If in doubt, you can always use an isolating primer, but if the surface of the paint shows signs of reaction to earlier

applications of refinishing paint, you would be wisest to strip the paint down to bare metal, at the very least in those areas where reaction is apparent. Stripping the paint is also highly desirable if too many coats of paint have been applied. One more can be just too much and cause bad crazing all over the car and especially on the horizontal surfaces.

Check Back

If you are not sure of the quality of the paintwork that has gone before *now* is the time to sort it out. Follow the plan of work shown here:

a)   Clean the paintwork really thoroughly.

b)   Catch the light on the paintwork and look really carefully for signs of paint film problems. The biggest problems usually occur on horizontal surfaces, so check for: cracking (checking); crazing; micro blistering (hundreds of tiny eruptions in the paint caused by dampness gettiing into the air lines or primer); cratering.

c)   Look out for variations in the paint gloss. Where the paint is dull check for B) again but this time with a magnifying glass.

d)   Make sure that the paint adheres well to that beneath it. Cheap resprays often don't include sufficient flatting of the old paint. See if the paint film has broken away from any edges leaving glossy paint beneath. Any such loose paint will have to be flatted through to the paint beneath.

e)   All of the problems mentioned in B) are best dealt with by stripping to bare metal all those areas affected. Cratering is caused by silicones (from polish) forming no-go inverted islands into which paint cannot run but instead stands off around the silicone spot making a crater. Clean the panel with silicone polish remover *before* and after working on the panel and be sure that you don't transfer the silicone onto any of your tools or equipment. Indeed, it is highly recommended that the whole of the paintwork be cleaned down with a spirit wipe made specially for the job before work commences. It will also remove all traces of dirt, wax oil and petrol on and embedded in the paint.

If you're not sure what type of paint has been used on your car, try the following tests:

Test	Outcome	Paint Type
1. Rub the paint with a rag soaked in 'cellulose' thinner.	A) The colour of the paint comes off on the rag, or the paint dissolves or softens, then –	'Cellulose' paint, or Acrylic lacquer
	B) The paint reacts quite badly, then –	Old oil based enamel paint. Air dry synthetic (not fully cured)
	C) The paintwork is unaffected by solvent, then –	High bake synthetic or acrylic enamel. Air dry synthetic enamel (fully cured)

If the outcome is as B), then perform Test 2.

Test	Outcome	Paint Type
2. Flat with medium grit abrasive paper	The paint clogs flatting paper, goes into balls, feels rubbery, then –	'Young' enamel paint.

To determine the finish type:

Test	Outcome	Finish
3. Rub paint with cloth dipped in polishing compound.	A) The paint colour shows on cloth, then –	Orthodox paint finish.
	B) The polishing cloth doesn't mark, then –	Basecoat and clear topcoat

Flatting (or Sanding) ●

Many home sprayers relegate the job of flatting with abrasive paper to the level of washing the dishes; it's a necessary chore but one to be got out of the way as rapidly as possible. In fact, flatting is crucially important to the finished appearance of the job and should be carried out in the right sequence

The first stage is the shaping of the filler to produce exactly the right contour and shape, especially over repaired areas. The second stage is to make all surfaces true and to remove the deep marks left in stage one. The third and fourth stages involve working through medium grade to fine grade abrasive paper ensuring that each grade takes out all the scratch marks of the one that went before.

Professional body shops use a lot of machine flatting equipment which is very time saving, but if you do have access to these tools make sure that you don't press too hard and cause deep scratching or undulations in the surface.

Flatting can be carried out using either wet-or-dry paper which, in spite of its name is always used with plenty of water, or by using dry flatting paper.

A useful tip when using wet-or-dry is to put a spot of washing up liquid into the bucket of water used for the supply of lubricant. This helps the water to stay on the panel rather than run straight off and it helps to slow down the clogging of the flatting paper. Plenty of water should be used when flatting but the water should be clean to start off with. Be careful not to pick up any grit out of the bucket and if you drop the paper on the floor, wash it thoroughly under the tap to avoid scratching the surface with grit. Each time you change to a finer grade of paper, you should also change the water to avoid picking up particles of the heavier grit used before.

Dry flatting is carried out with 'open coat' abrasive papers, some of them incorporating a dry powder lubricant within them. Grade for grade, open coat papers produce a finer surface than wet-and-dry paper.

On the face of it, open coat flatting is greatly preferable to wet-or-dry. After all, why introduce unnecessary water onto the job when it can cause humidity blisters if not thoroughly dried, it can lodge behind masked off areas only to slither out under the force of compressed air when spraying, it takes time to dry out and it can cause light rusting on bare metal.

Whichever system is used, be sure to clean all traces off after use. Wet-or-dry leaves a paint residue which, if allowed to dry on the panel forms a hard-to-move alkaline residue (so sponge each panel off with clean water as it is finished) and the stearate lubricating powder used in some open coat papers can lead to poor adhesion of the colour coats.

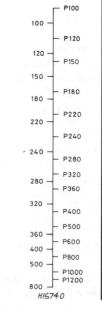

Figure P1. Abrasive paper grades. As a rough rule of thumb, Coarse, Medium and Fine grades of abrasive paper involve the following grade numbers:

	Open Coat Papers	Wet-or-Dry Papers
Very Coarse	up to P80	
Coarse	P100-P180	P100-P220
Medium	P180-P400	P220-P400
Fine	P400-P500	P500-P1200

The grit sizes shown above with the prefix 'P' conform to a relatively recently introduced European standard. The grit numbers are compressed compared with the older grading and the two types can be compared as shown opposite.

How to Flat ●

Start with a coarse grade of paper over areas of new filler where there may still be some marks from the use of the coarser abrasive used in shaping the filler. When all the deeper marks have been removed transfer to a medium grade paper. It is important now that all the marks from the grade you have used previously are removed with the grade you are working with. Don't imagine that the finest grade of paper will remove the coarsest papers scratches – it won't.

If you are simply flatting sound but dull paintwork it should be enough to start with a medium grit paper and then, in all cases, finish off with a fine grit. And again, if you are flatting between coats use the finest grade of paper.

When flatting small areas or concave curves, flatting should be carried out with the flats of the fingers rather than with the finger tips, so that the load is spread evenly over a greater area. At the same time, the fingers should be at right angles to the direction of rubbing. This can seem an unnatural way to move at first but it is important because it prevents 'grooving' caused by the pressure of the individual fingers. When flatting always rub in straight lines. If you flat in circles, the scratches will always show through the paint but if you rub in straight lines, the scratches will not be visible.

Use a rubbing block for more level results on flat or slightly convex surfaces. Remember that the object of flatting is to produce a level surface which is keyed with fine scratches to assist in the adhesion of paint, but is also to eliminate deeper scratches which will show through the paint. It is *not* to remove road tar, polish or other contamination and indeed, flatting will simply push the contamination deeper into the surface. So make sure that you spirit-wipe the surface to be flatted very thoroughly before commencing work.

Feather Edges

Where rust bubbles have formed, where new paint has been applied after a repair or even just where paint is thin, the edges of the paint have to be flatted in such a way that there is no ridge of paint marking where it begins. Flat the paint edges gently to prevent the edge crumbling and flat over a wide area to blend in the edge gently so that it will not be visible under the paint. This process is known as feather edging. As a general rule, attempt to feather edge, to taper the paint back, by two inches for each coat of paint.

Guide Coats

Filler, primer and flatted paint are all matt surfaces and are notorious for hiding faults. These faults will show through, however, once the glossy paint is applied, so find out where they are first. Either use an aerosol can or spray a very heavily thinned coat of cellulose lacquer onto the panel with the spray gun. This gives an almost transparent gloss coat of paint which shows up such faults as are there; they can then be cured with the use of thin stopper. If there are large high and low spots, the guide coat will help to pick them out too, because as the panel is re-flatted, the guide coat will go from the high spots first, leaving the low spots crying out to be filled or stoppered flat.

Try to avoid the use of reds or yellows when applying the guide coat because these colours are more likely than most to 'bleed' through subsequent layers of paint. Do choose a colour that contrasts with the panel, however.

Masking Off ●

The one major disadvantage with spraying compared with painting is that the spray goes everywhere! This makes it essential to mask off areas not to be sprayed.

The well trained pro would often dismiss the use of newspaper as a material for masking off but for amateur use, newspaper is fine; it's plentiful and free. If you are masking off a newly painted surface, however, it would be best to use some other plain paper to avoid the risk of the ink bleeding into and staining the paint.

Choose your masking tape carefully. Some tapes are almost flat and these are frustratingly hard to 'bend' round corners. Others have lots of corrugations built into them and these are the ones to use since they will 'bend' nicely. If your tape won't stick to rubber, don't necessarily blame the tape – old rubber simply won't always take masking tape. If the worst comes to the worst, try painting clear lacquer onto the rubber and letting it dry before attaching the tape. When masking off along a duo-tone line where there is no body moulding bead, be sure to press the tape down carefully all along its sealing edge otherwise paint will seep beneath it.

The worse thing you can do when masking off (next to letting paint through) is to leave crinkles and ridges in the paper. Flatten all folds right down and seal them right off with masking tape.

Avoid wrapping masking tape round and round like the bandages round The Invisible Man. This makes the tape really hard to get off afterwards. Apply tape alone to the edges of all surfaces to be masked off, then add tape and paper to the tape already down – it's the most accurate way of doing the job.

Preparing to Paint – Summary ●

1) Wash the car.
2) Spirit-wipe the area to be painted to remove contaminants.
3) Wash off again with detergent and dry thoroughly.
4) Flat the entire area to be painted, using the following as a guide:
   Where primer is to be applied, use P280 to P400 grade.
   Where colour is to be applied, use P500 to P1000 grade.
5) Feather edge all bare metal areas.
6) Spirit wipe panels once again.
7) Mask off.

Spraying the Primer ●

Earlier in this section, mention was made of the wide number of types of primer available. Greatest mention was made of primer fillers, but perhaps it is worth pointing out that where the highest standards are sought such as when preparing a Classic car for concours respray, or when spraying a panel on a new car, it is worth applying a primer pure and simple. Bare steel should be treated with phosphoric acid cleaner which is washed over the bare steel, following the manufacturer's instructions (including those on safety) most carefully. The phosphoric acid must then be washed off thoroughly before it has a chance to dry.

An etching primer can be sprayed onto bare steel but aluminium panels could, and galvanised metal should, be given a coat of zinc chromate primer as a first coat. N.B. Primer designed for steel will cause paint flaking if used direct on aluminium or zinc plating.

If the work to be carried out is simply a repair to an older car, the quality of the finish may matter less than simple uniformity of colour! In this case the use of a straightforward primer/filler would be fine.

If an older car is to be given a complete respray with a 'glossy from the gun' finish with the minimum of preparation, go for a 'non-sand' undercoat and just use it on the repaired or 'dodgy' areas; where the paint is sound, flat that and use it as your undercoat.

Primer should be sprayed using an approximate pressure of 45 lb sq in and with the gun held about 6 inches away from the workpiece. Spraying primer is excellent experience for someone who has never sprayed before but remember that colour coat flows (and therefore runs) much more easily.

After you have sprayed with undercoat, don't make the mistake of leaving the car out in the rain because primer absorbs moisture and trapped moisture can destroy the finish months after you have painted the car. Isolator is actually hygroscopic – in other words, it seeks out moisture from the air, so never leave it for more than a few hours without a coat of undercoat on top.

Spraying the Colour Coat ●

Once again, base a decision on what type of paint to use upon the type of car being worked upon but also bear in mind the facilities you have. If you are lucky enough to have the correct, safe and necessary breathing apparatus and a fairly dust-free environment in which to spray, the use of two-pack ought really to be the first choice. If you can get hold of a non-isocyanate two-pack (i.e. non-poisonous), then use it by all means, but the problems regarding dust settling into the paint must be taken into account. Do bear in mind that there are special thinners available for speedier air drying.

Otherwise stick to 'cellulose' lacquer for most jobs (and especially for older 'classic' cars where the too-good-to-be-true shine of two-pack paints may look out of place) and benefit from the speedier drying times. Some special customising colours are only available in acrylic paint so be prepared for some hard polishing if you want to go for metalflake shocking pink coachwork!

If your car is an oldster with paint of dubious parentage and you don't want to go to the trouble of stripping off the paint, spray safe and use a synthetic, oil based paint whose thinners are highly unlikely to react with the paintwork already on the car.

When using two-pack or synthetic paint, there is a lot to be said for introducing some heat into the spray area (but beware of fire hazards – use only non-flame heaters such as the electric convector type) unless you are working in high summer. This will encourage the paint to surface dry or go off much more quickly and reduce the risk of dusting. On the other hand, the extra heat could cause dust to circulate ...

Start Spraying! ●

The following picture sequence shows how the DeVilbiss company, makers of what is widely recognised as being the best spray equipment in the world, set about preparing and spraying a door panel at their British HQ in Bournemouth, England. For the purposes of the demonstation, the DeVilbiss personnel used a special extraction booth, so that explains the peculiar looking waterfall present in the background of some of the later shots!

SS1. DeVilbiss chose this perfectly standard door panel to demonstrate the correct techniques. First of all, they ran all the tests to determine paint type and fetched a half litre of colour coat from the stores.

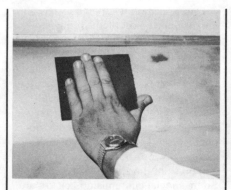

SS2.   Before commencing work, the door was washed, dried, then wiped down with a spirit wipe. Then the panel was flatted all over using a fine grit wet-or-dry. Here the panel is being flatted in straight lines, left to right. Note how the fingers are held flat, the wrist close to the panel and – especially important – the fingers are at right angles to the direction of flatting.

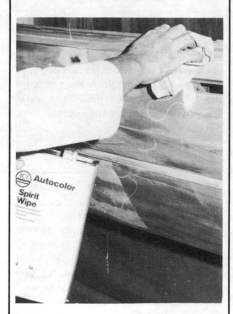

SS3.   Out comes that old spirit wipe again! If you haven't been able to get hold of the correct stuff, it may be OK to use thinners although there is a small risk that thinners will cause problems with cellulose stopper or fairly new paint.

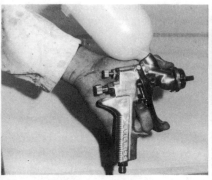

SS4.   On the Continent of Europe, gravity feed spray guns similar to this one are the norm rather than the exception but they are mainly used in the UK for spot work only. There are no real advantages or problems either way – it's simply a matter of what your hand gets used to spraying with!

SS5.   The quality of the air coming into the gun is all too often neglected. Compressors large and small are all prone to introducing water vapour into the air line and thus into the paint. If you haven't got a water trap in your air line or fitted to the compressor, a gun mounted moisture separator is an essential for successful work. This DeVilbiss separator is fitted with a small cock for regular draining. It simply fits on the handle of the gun and the air line fits to it.

SS6.   If water is the enemy in the air line, dirt in the paint is another major foe. A last line of defence in every gun should be a simple, cheap little filter fitted to the end of the tube.

SS7.   Use your air line to blow dust out of the top of the tin **before** opening it. There is nothing more infuriating than to open the lid and see evil little flakes of dirt snuggling down into the shine on the top of the paint.

SS8.   *Pour as much paint as you need into a thoroughly cleaned disposable tin. If you have a graduated measuring stick, place it in the tin first (a steel rule would do, provided that you remember to clean it afterwards) or use the following tip for a 50/50 mix. Hold a clean stick upright in the paint, lift the stick until the bottom of the stick just touches the top of the paint you have just poured in and top-up with thinners until the level reaches the high paint mark on your dipstick. Good idea?*

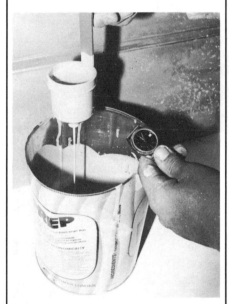

SS9.   *Now you need to know whether the paint is at the right viscosity, i.e. whether it is runny enough or too much so. This is a cheap, plastic viscosity cup — invest in one because it's a 'must'. Stir the paint and thinners very thoroughly together. Now dip the viscosity cup right into the thinned paint so that the cup is brim full. Watch the paint until it reaches the shoulder set in the cup. Start watching the seconds counter on your watch just at that point.*

SS10.   *Here the camera has caught the very split second when you must* **stop** *counting; it's at the instant that the steady flow of paint stops and first begins to break into globules.* **Don't** *wait until all the drips stop too! You may need to try this out a few times to get the hang of it. The paint manufacturer's literature will give you the correct viscosity timing (pick the literature up when you collect the paint — it's free). Make sure that the paint is at the same temperature as the place where you are going to spray. If the paint is too cold it will be 'thick' and if warm it will be 'thin'. Then, when you take it into the spray area, it will take on the wrong viscosity altogether.*

SS11.   *When buying the paint, buy a few disposable filters, too. Filter the paint into a pouring jug or into the spray pot itself. If the pot opening is too small for the filter make it a tighter cone shape by folding one side of it.*

SS12.   *Really, it's best to have all your clean, filtered paint in a pouring jug. Then, when you run out of paint during the respray you can top-up without all the hassle, spills and so on of having to filter the paint just when you want to be getting on.*

SS13.   *Shoulders are much in evidence! Here is the point above which you have overfilled the pot!*

SS14.   *Next job is to regulate the spray fan size and the flow rate. Use the regulator screw(s) (depending upon the type of gun) at the rear of the gun head.*

77

SS15.   The gun should be held 6 – 8 inches away from the surface being sprayed. Conventionally, this is around a hand span with the middle fingers opened. Even the experts try out the gun, the pattern, etc. before commencing work. Don't tilt the gun (Fig. 1, L.H.-side). Holding the gun close causes runs while holding it too far away causes orange peeling (Fig. 1, R.H.-side).

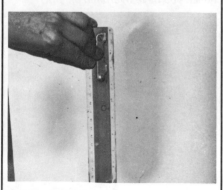

SS16.   A strip of paper was sprayed with the gun held the right distance away. Various fan settings were tried and the one that gave the correct, vertical pattern 8 to 9 inches in length was chosen.

SS17.   Before spraying anything, whether it be a whole car or just a panel, decide upon a plan of action. Our DeVilbiss expert sprayed the rear upright first, starting at the bottom and working up. Note how he has rocked the gun – but **slightly** – so as not to have the full, concentrated vertical spray pattern causing runs.

SS18.   Then he worked forwards and down the front of the window frame, maintaining the right distance away from the work the whole time.

SS19.   His first pass was along the top of the door skin, front to back. After every 'strip' was painted, he shut off the gun momentarily, then restarted it again just before he hit the panel with the paint. In other words, the end and the start of every stroke are aimed at thin air.

SS20.   He worked down the panel, the top of every new 'pass' aimed at the middle of every previous one, so that in effect the whole panel gets covered twice. Note how he has bent his whole body and his arm so that the gun remains at right angles to the workpiece the whole time. The finished door looked terrific!

Bits in the Gloss Coat? – don't panic! ●

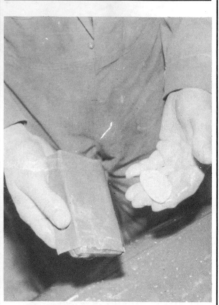

BGC1.   If you find lots of bits in the surface of the paint, either as a result of poor filtering, or airborne contamination, don't despair; at least, not if the paint is thoroughly cured 2-pack or cellulose. Get hold of some P1200 grade wet-or-dry paper and rub soap onto it to soften the effect of the abrasive still further. Rub the paintwork down in the normal way.

BGC2. Use a rubber squeegee to scrape the paint residue from the surface of the panel and examine it minutely for the presence of blemishes. Obviously, you can only do this where you have a good thickness of paint, and in any case, you don't want to take off more paint than is necessary. (The edge of the rubbing block – if you use the rubber sort – makes an excellent squeegee with the flatting paper removed.)

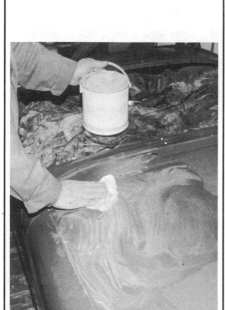

BGC3. When you have removed all the blemishes, set about putting back the shine. Cover an area of about a couple of feet or so square with polishing compound. (Note that 2-pack paints demand a special ammonia-free compound otherwise the surface of the paint will retain a slight haze.)

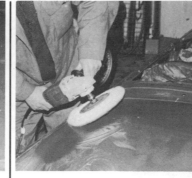

BGC4. This is the Black & Decker polisher which is ideal for the professional and conscientious amateur alike. The depth of shine brought up by this machine had to be seen to be believed, and being electrically powered, it neatly sidesteps the problems of capacity created by air operated polishing mops and the need for a large compressor. The mop operates best, as Black & Decker recommend, used under its own weight, with no downward pressure to burn the paint, and it is especially important not to use the polisher excessively near to edges or on sharp convex curves or it can polish right through the paint. The highest shine is obtained by completing the polishing process with compound and then washing the mop and giving the panel a final polish all over with a fine abrasive such as T-cut.

Painting Pointers ●

● Try wetting the workshop floor with a watering can before spraying commences. This stills the dust, especially on a concrete floor, but don't put so much down that the water lies in puddles; you might splash the car and ruin the wet paint finish.

● If the workshop ceiling is very dusty, try vacuuming it clean. You could even pin up a sheet of clear plastic onto the roof's rafters.

● If you're spot spraying just part of a panel with 'cellulose' lacquer and the paint colour match is not perfect, try fading the edges of the panel. Mask off a much wider area than would normally apply and at the end of each stroke, turn the gun at an angle. The colour of the new paint will then fade into the old and the unavoidable dry spray at the end of each stroke can be polished to a high gloss.

● When spraying an outside corner such as the edge of a door frame, or an inside corner, such as the bottom of a boot or footwell, use Figures GL4 and GL5 as guidelines.

● Always mask off the engine bay. The blast of air around the area can blow dirt onto the panel surfaces and spray can easily creep onto the components inside.

● Never immerse the gun in cleaning fluid; it destroys the lubricant in the fluid needle and air valve packings. Get into the habit of cleaning the gun whilst the paint is soft, right after using it.

● If the paint runs out and there are just a few square inches left, try holding the gun upside down. It may just drain it of the last few drops and save the day!

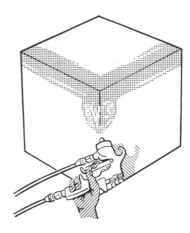

Figure GL4. Method of spraying an outside corner. (Courtesy DeVilbiss)

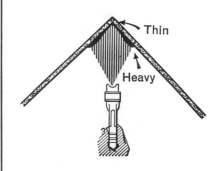

Figure GL5. Method of spraying an inside corner. (Courtesy DeVilbiss)

Spray Gun Trouble-Shooting ●

No matter how excellent spraying equipment is, sooner or later some small trouble shows itself which, if it were allowed to develop, would mar the work done. But this trouble can usually be very quickly rectified if the operator knows where to look for the source of it.

The following list contains the causes and remedies of all the trouble most commonly encountered in spraying.

1. Sometimes the gun will give a fluttering or jerky spray, and this is caused by: (see Figure GL6).
a)   Insufficient paint in the cup or pressure feed tank so that the end of the fluid tube is uncovered.
b)   When a suction feed gun is used, the cup is tilted at an excessive angle so that the fluid tube does not dip below the surface of the paint.
c)   Some obstruction in the fluid passage-way which must be removed.
d)   Fluid tube loose or cracked or resting on the bottom of the paint container.
e)   A loose fluid tip on the spray gun.
f)   Too heavy a material for suction feed.
g)   A clogged air vent in the cup lid.
h)   Loose nut coupling the suction feed cup or fluid hose to the spray gun or pressure feed tank.
i)   Loose fluid needle packing nut or dry packing.

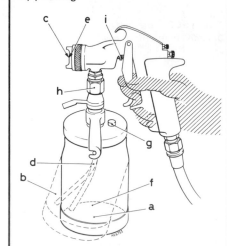

Figure GL6.   Spray gun components.

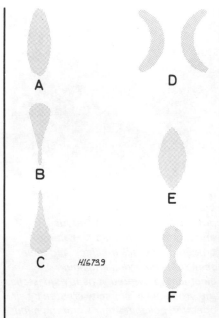

Figure GL7.   Spray pattern defects.

A	Normal	D	Heavy right/left
B	Top heavy	E	Heavy centre
C	Bottom heavy	F	Split spray

2. The normal spray pattern produced by a correctly adjusted spray gun is shown in Figure GL7, as are defective spray patterns which can develop from the following causes:
a)   Top or bottom heavy pattern caused by:
   (i)   Horn holes in air cap partially blocked.
   (ii)   Obstruction on top or bottom of fluid tip.
   (iii)   Dirt on air cap seat or fluid tip seat.
(b)   Heavy right or left side pattern caused by:
   (i)   Right or left side horn hole in air cap partially clogged.
   (ii)   Dirt on right or left side of fluid tip.
c)   Heavy centre pattern caused by:
   (i)   Too low a setting of the spreader adjustment valve on the gun.
   (ii)   Atomizing air pressure is too low or the paint is too thick.
   (iii)   With pressure feed, the fluid pressure is too high, or the flow of paint exceeds the normal capacity of the air cap.
   (iv)   The wrong size fluid tip for the paint being sprayed.
d)   Split spray pattern is caused by the atomizing air and fluid flow not being properly balanced.

Remedies for defective spray patterns

For defects (a) and (b) (top or bottom heavy pattern, or heavy right or left pattern) determine whether the obstruction is in the air cap by spraying a test pattern; then rotate the air cap half a turn and spray another test. If the defect is inverted the obstruction is obviously in the air cap which should be cleaned as previously instructed.

If the defect has not changed its position the obstruction is on the fluid tip. When cleaning the fluid tip, check for fine burr on the tip, which can be removed with 600 wet or dry sandpaper.

To rectify defects (c) and (d) (heavy centre pattern, or split spray pattern), if the adjustments are unbalanced readjust the atomizing air pressure, fluid pressure, and spray width control setting until the correct pattern is obtained.

3. If there is an excessive mist or spray fog it is caused by:
a)   Too thin a paint.
b)   Over-atomization, due to using too high an atomizing air pressure for the volume of paint flowing.
c)   Improper use of the gun, such as making incorrect strokes or holding the gun too far from the surface.

4. Runs or sags on a sprayed surface.
a)   Sags are the result of applying too much paint to the surface, possibly by moving the gun too slowly. Runs are caused by using too thin a paint.
b)   If the gun is tilted at an angle to the surface, excessive paint is applied where the pattern is closest to the surface, causing the paint to pile up and sag.

5. An 'orange-peel' defect such as that sometimes obtained with cellulose and synthetic materials is caused by:
a)   Using unsuitable thinners.
b)   Either too high or too low an atomizing air pressure.
c)   Holding the gun either too far off or too close to the surface.
d)   The paint is not thoroughly mixed or agitated.
e)   Draught blowing on to the surface.
f)   Improperly prepared surface.

6. Paint leakage from the front of the spray gun is caused by the fluid needle not seating properly, due to:
a) Worn or damaged fluid tip or needle.
b) Lumps of dried paint or dirt lodged in the fluid tip.
c) Fluid needle packing nut screwed up too tightly.
d) Broken fluid needle spring.

7. Paint leakage from the fluid needle packing nut is caused by a loose packing nut or a worn dry fluid needle packing. The packing can be lubricated with a drop or two of light oil, but fitting new packing is strongly advised.
   Tighten the packing nut with the fingers only to prevent leakage, but not so tight as to bind the needle.

8. Compressed air leakage from the front of a non-bleeder type of gun is caused by (see Figure GL8):
a) Dirt on air valve or air valve seating.
b) Worn or damaged air valve or air valve seating.
c) Broken air valve spring.
d) Sticking valve stem due to lack of lubrication.
e) Bent valve stem.
f) Lack of lubrication on air valve packing.
g) Air valve gasket damaged.

9. If the air compressor pumps oil into the air line, it is for the following reasons:
a) Strainer on air intake clogged with dirt.
b) Clogged intake valve.
c) Too much oil in crankcase.
d) Worn piston rings.

10. An overheated air compressor is caused by:
a) No oil in crankcase.

b) Oil too heavy.
c) Valves sticking, or dirty and covered with carbon.
d) Insufficient air circulating round an air-cooled compressor due to its being placed too close to a wall or in a confined space.
e) Cylinder block and head being coated with a thick deposit of paint or dirt.
f) Air inlet strainer clogged.

Paint Faults ●

If you have carried out your first respray and you find a few minor faults, you'll probably be so pleased with the general improvement in the appearance of the car that you will hardly notice. However, those who go on from there generally become more critical of what they are doing. The following chart of paint faults and what to do about them has been compiled by the experts at International Paint, so even the most pernickety of operators should be able to see why any fault, large or small, may have occurred and what to do about curing it.

1) Adhesion Loss

Description
In severe cases, the topcoat is easily detached from the primer surface/filler or the old finish, or the complete system detaches from the metal. Generally, thos loss of adhesion is limited to areas which are susceptible to abrasion or impact, e.g. stone chippings, etc. Loss of adhesion will usually be noticed in the paint shop when the masking tape is removed.

Cause
Poor adhesion is the result of improper bonding or wetting of the paint film to the surface being finished. This can occur initially because of poor surface cleaning and preparation, or adhesion can be destroyed later by moisture or other film deterioration.
a) Inadequate surface cleaning and preparation – failure to remove surface contaminants in or on the surface before painting, e.g. wax, oil, water, rust, flatting dust etc. Thus preventing the subsequent paint films from obtaining a good key to the surface.
b) Insufficient flatting of the primer surfacer/filler coat before overcoating will also increase the risk of poor adhesion.
c) Improperly mixed materials. The make-up of paint is such that maximum surface wetting and contact with all components is most important.
d) Use of the incorrect undercoat for either the metal or the topcoat, and poor application, e.g. dry spraying.
e) Failure to use the proper surfacers; use of a surfacer minimises the risk of poor adhesion.
f) Use of incorrect or cheap thinner, or underthinning.
g) Masking too soon on a new colour in a two-tone system. Careless masking may cause bridging which is removal of the paint from the surface when the tape is peeled off.
h) Excessive oven bake time or temperature.

*PF1. When working with aluminium, such as this Land-Rover panel, you **must** use self-etch primer on bare metal (even if you only break through during flatting). If you don't the new paint will flake off for certain.*

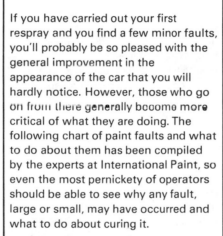

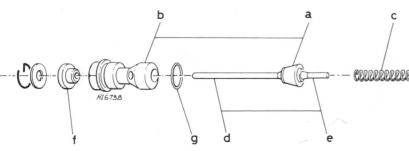

Figure GL8. Air valve components.

Cure

a)   Remove the finish by sanding, over an area considerably larger than the affected area, so as to obtain a good sound base (to metal if necessary).

b)   If loss of adhesion is due to faulty masking technique, flat and feather edge the affected area, and then respray.

2)   Mottling

Description
Spotty, non-uniform, blotchy appearance of metallic paint. Small, irregular areas darker in colour, or spots in solid colour paint.

Cause
a)   Spray viscosity is too high, causing too wet a film.
b)   Solvent is too slow to evaporate. This is a fairly rare occurrence.
c)   Atomizing pressure too low.
d)   Fan on gun too narrow.
e)   Fluid delivery too high.
f)   Applying too much of total film on final coat.
g)   Gun too close to panel.

In all these cases the paint surface must be reflatted, and a new topcoat applied.

Cure
In all these cases the paint surface must be reflatted and a new topcoat applied.

3)   Bleeding

Description
Bleeding occurs when pigment from

the original finish dissolves in the solvents of the refinishing material and discolours it. This usually only occurs with red or maroon coloured finishes.

Cause
a)   Failure to test the original finish before proceeding, by applying a full coat of the colour to be used to a small flatted area.
b)   Failure to use a bleeding inhibitor sealer or isolator as directed.
c)   Failure to remove overspray of a bleeding finish from the surface before painting.

Cure
a)   Bleeding sometimes does not occur until several coats of undercoat and finish have been applied. In this case, the complete removal of the affected paint, and refinishing from bare metal is necessary.
b)   When bleeding occurs after an initial coat of undercoat or finish, the faults can be sealed off with a bleeding inhibitor sealer or isolator.

4)   Blistering

Description
Blistering appears as pimples or bubbles, which can vary considerably both in size and density, in the paint film. It can affect newly applied and aged films, commonly occurring during periods of high humidity followed by sharp frost spells.

Cause
Trapped moisture or air under a paint film causes blistering. Even the best paint films are permeable to water vapour, and when the paint film is subjected to abrupt changes in temperature, the entrapped moisture expands and builds up pressure. This weakens the adhesion between the various coats, and so leads to the formation of blisters.
a)   Inadequate surface cleaning and preparation – the most common cause of blistering is the presence of contaminants, either between the primer filler and metal, or between the topcoat and primer filler. Typical contaminants are oil from airlines, grease from finger marks, flatting dust, dirt and salt. Therefore, ensure that the

surface is clean and dry before spraying.
b)   Wrong thinning – use of non-recommended thinner.
c)   Excessive film thickness and insufficient drying time between coats may trap solvents which, when they later escape, cause blistering of the paint film. Therefore, allow each coat to flash off naturally, do not fan as this merely dries the surface.
d)   Insufficient undercoat/topcoat – adequate film thickness or primer undercoat and topcoat is essential.
e)   Exposure to wet weather or high humidity before the finish is really hard, and also continuous exposure to such conditions will often promote blistering.

Cure
a)   In cases of severe blistering, the finish must be stripped off down to the bare metal. Then reapply the complete refinish system.
b)   In less severe cases, sand out the blisters, and resurface or re-topcoat as necessary.

5)   Sand scratches

Description
A film that appears low in gloss and shows primer and metal imperfections in the topcoat. Normally the film has flowed smoothly with no evidence of orange peel or mottling.

Cause
a)   Film thickness too low.
b)   Poor surface preparation or use of too coarse a grade of paper when flatting.
c)   Poor curing of undercoat or primer.
d)   Poor primer hold-out.

Cure
a)   Where the film thickness is too low the solvent content of the finish coat should be reduced so that a heavier weight of solids is applied.
b)   In most other cases, re-flatting should take place followed by careful re-preparation of the surface using further foundation coats (where necessary) and a topcoat of the correct viscosity.

6)   Solvent Pop

Description
Small bumps in the paint film which, under close examination, can be seen to have small holes in the top. The condition is most likely to occur on edges or areas where film build is the heaviest.

Cause
Solvent pop is caused by too great a film depth being applied in one coat as a result of:
a)   Too high a fluid delivery.
b)   Too high an air pressure.
c)   Too high a paint viscosity.
d)   Moving the gun too slowly, or treating a narrow area to the full spray pattern will over-paint the surface.
e)   Too much overlapping in the spray sequence will over-paint the surface.

Cure
Allow the surface to harden well (bearing in mind the paint depth will affect drying times of oil-based paints) before re-flatting and applying a further finish coat.

7)   Blooming/Blushing

Description
Blooming or Blushing appears as a milky white haze or mist on enamel films. When blooming is seen on a colour coat, the undercoats may also have suffered from this condition. Note that this may not be visible as undercoat surfaces are usually matt – but blistering or loss of intercoat adhesion may occur later.

Cause
Blooming can occur when paint films are applied during cold, humid conditions and is caused by moisture being trapped in the wet film. During the spraying operation air currents are generated which, combined with the rapid evaporation of the solvents, result in the sprayed surface being at a lower temperature than the paint shop. This causes moisture in the surrounding air to condense on to the wet paint film, resulting in a milky white haze.
a)   Use of cheap thinner.
b)   Use of fast thinner in cold or humid conditions. Under such conditions, a non-bloom thinner should be used to prevent blooming. However, use the minimum amount required, otherwise the drying rate will be slowed down considerably.
c)   Wrong gun set-up and technique or excessive air pressure.
d)   Lack of adequate air movement and heating in the paint shop.
e)   Fanning the sprayed surface with the spray gun to speed up solvent release.
f)   Draughty paint shop.

Cure
a)   Slight blooming/blushing – allow the paint film to harden and remove the defect by polishing with polishing compound.
b)   Respray the affected areas using paint thinned with non-bloom thinners.
c)   Respray the whole of the affected area with neat non-bloom thinners. Under some conditions this will remove the milky haze.
d)   If none of the above remedies work, then the temperature of the paint shop must be raised by at least five degrees and all direct draughts avoided.

8)   Cracking and Checking

Description
Checking appears as a large number of unattached very small cracks, which normally require a magnifying glass to be seen clearly. The paint film appears dull and lacking in gloss when checking occurs. Cracking appears as a number of random cracks, often in the form of three-legged stars, which resemble mud cracks present in a dry pond or river bed. The cracks are generally quite deep, penetrating through the top coat and sometimes through the primer/filler coat as well. Cracking is usually the result of a weakness in the paint film such as checking or blistering being exaggerated by normal exterior conditions.

Cause
Cracking occurs mainly as a result of paint film weaknesses that are exaggerated by extended periods of outdoor exposure and so occurs rarely with good quality modern paint finishes that have been properly applied.
a)   Excessive film thickness. Application of excessive topcoat or primer/filler coats will magnify the stresses and strains normally present in paint films and can result in early cracking, even under normal conditions.
b)   Insufficient flash time. The risk of cracking increases when heavy coats are applied without adequate flash off time between successive coats.
c)   Inefficient stirring of the paint before use – this can lead to paint components being improperly mixed. This is particularly important where surfacers are concerned, as failure to stir thoroughly may affect film strength, flexibility and adhesion. The resulting paint films may therefore be weakened and more susceptible to cracking.
d)   Inefficient cleaning and preparation of the surface before cleaning.

Cure
The affected areas must be sanded down to a smooth, sound finish, although in the majority of cases it will be necessary to strip down to bare metal and reapply the complete refinish system.

9) Cratering (Fish Eyes or Cissing)

Description
Cratering is the appearance of small, crater-like openings (small rounded indentations) in the paint film, and can occur either during the spraying operation or immediately after completion.

Cause
The main cause of cratering is silicone particles. These particles (and also other contaminants) repel the paint film so that it fails to form a smooth continuous film, i.e. containing craters or holes in the film. Many modern waxes and car polishes contain silicones which are the most common cause of cratering in freshly painted surfaces. Silicones adhere strongly to the paint film and require extra effort to remove them using a proprietary brand of silicone-removing spirit wipe.
a) Inadequate surface cleaning and preparation. Failure to remove contaminants will invariably cause problems, such contaminants being dried soap, detergent or metal pre-treatment residues. Precautions should be taken to remove all traces of silicone and other likely contaminants, by thoroughly cleaning the surface with wax and grease remover.
b) Airborne contamination of the surface prepared for painting. Minute quantities of silicone in sanding dust, contaminated rags or even from car polish being applied at some distance from the prepared surface can cause contamination and result in cratering.
c) Oil in the airline to the spray gun.
Note. The use of silicone containing additives to prevent cratering is not recommended. These additives can contaminate the paint shop and other work around and also lead to future adhesion failure.

Cure
Re-flat the affected areas and apply a further finishing coat.

10) Dry Spray

Description
A rough, irregular paint surface.

Cause
a) Too fast an evaporation of the solvent either because of incorrect solvent type or low humidity and high ambient temperature.
b) Paint viscosity too low.
c) Air pressure too high.
d) Film build is too low.
e) The gun is being held too far from the surface.
f) Poorly prepared primer coat.

11) Feather Edge Cracking or Splitting

Description
This appears as fine cracks or splits at the feather edge of a spot repair. It occurs during or shortly after the topcoat is applied over the primer-surfacer.

Cause
a) Excessive film thicknesses – heavy applications of primer surfacer/filler without adequate flash off times between successive coats will encourage solvent entrapment and so cause feather edge cracking.
b) Inadequate stirring and the application of improperly mixed, thinned primer-surfacer, will result in a film containing loosely held pigment particles, with voids and crevices throughout – similar to a sponge. When the topcoat is applied, this structure may be broken, causing shrinkage and splitting resulting in feather edge cracking.
c) Too fast a thinner for the primer-surfacer, thus preventing the primer particles from flowing together.
d) Improper surface cleaning and preparation. When feather edges of spot repairs are not properly cleaned, primer-surfacer coats may crawl or draw away from this edge due to poor wetting and adhesion.
e) Fanning the primer-surfacer after application with the spray gun will dry the surface before the air or solvent from within the film can escape so resulting in shrinking and splitting on later drying.

Cure
Remove finish from the affected areas and refinish.

12) Low Gloss

Description
Poor light reflection in relation to expected standard of the paint finish being applied. Note that some paints, such as 2-pack paints, have a much greater from-the-gun gloss than others.

Cause
a) Film thickness is too low.
b) Sand scratches. See item 5.
c) Mottling. See item 2.
d) Poor paint batch.

Cure
Re-flat the surface and apply a further finishing coat.

13) Orange Peel

Description
Orange peel appears as an uneven formation on the film surface, similar to that of an orange skin.

Cause
Orange peel is caused by the failure of atomized paint droplets to flow into each other when they reach the surface and is known technically as poor coalescence. When this occurs the droplets remain as they are formed by the gun nozzle, thus causing a rough surface. Ideally, the droplets should be wet enough when they reach the surface to blend completely or flow into each other, and so form a smooth film.
a) Wrong gun adjustment or technique. Too high or too low an air pressure, excessive gun distance, too little paint flow or too wide spray fan width.
b) Too high shop temperature, in which case use a slower thinner to overcome this.

c) Non-uniformly mixed materials. Many finishes contain components which aid coalescence or flow. If these are improperly mixed, then orange peel can occur.

d) Excessively thick or thin film application.

e) Wrong viscosity or thinning.

f) Incorrect flash time between successive coats, and gun fanning to increase drying rate, will promote the risk of orange peel.

Cure

a) After the colour coat has thoroughly hardened, rub out the orange peel with rubbing compound or Grade P1200 paper, depending on the severity of the condition. Restore the gloss with polish.

b) In severe cases, flat with Grade P1000/P1200 paper and respray.

14) Intercoat Adhesion Failure

Description

One coat of finish peels off or can easily be stripped off with masking tape from another layer of finish underneath. This problem can occur with re-finish or original paint applications.

Cause

a) Contamination between coats by oil, sanding dust, water etc.

b) Excessive bake time or temperature of basecoat or topcoat.

c) Very low film basecoat or topcoat.

d) Poor inter-coat flatting, thus providing poor paint keying.

e) Incompatibility of primer coats and finish coat.

Cure

Flatting of the surface down to the problem base coat and thorough decontamination or keying as a result will normally solve the situation. In rare cases, where successive earlier refinishing has taken place it may be necessary to go back to bare metal.

15) Sags or Runs

Description

Tears or curtains of paint on vertical or inclined areas of bodywork.

Cause

a) Too much slow speed solvent in paint.

b) Too heavy a film build.

c) Film applied too rapidly with no flash-time between coats.

d) Gun too close to surface being sprayed.

e) Air pressure too low.

f) Fluid delivery too high.

Cure

The affected area should be allowed to harden off before reflatting takes place. Bear in mind that oil-based paints 'dry' rather slowly and the depth in a run may be significant. In many cases addition of a further finishing coat will not be necessary.

16) Overspray

Description

Overspray appears as dry or semi-dry atomized paint from the spray gun and so causes unabsorbed paint particles on the painted surface.

Cause

a) Failure to ensure continuity of painting sequence resulting in dry overlaps, e.g. due to the use of a paint with too fast a drying rate.

b) Use of cheap or incorrect thinner, e.g. too fast a thinner in hot, dry conditions.

c) Poor spray gun technique, e.g. careless overspray of adjacent (painted or unpainted) areas.

d) Excessive rebound, due to incorrect air pressure, viscosity or spray gun set-up.

Cure

a) Lacquer overspray is normally dry and non-adhesive and can, therefore, be rectified by polishing the partly dried film.

b) Synthetic enamel overspray is normally wet and strongly adhering to the surface beneath when sprayed. Many of these materials are not easily polished when young and so to remove overspray requires wet flatting and recoating.

17) Pinholing

Description

Pinholing appears as tiny holes – often grouped – in the finish.

Cause

Pinholing can occur for a variety of reasons and is caused by trapped solvents, moisture or air being released from the film while drying. This is often due to poor preparation or application techniques and can occur in the primer-surfacer, putty and body filler or topcoat.

a) Wrong gun adjustment or technique. Gun held too close to the surface, too wet an application or insufficient atomization of the primer filler or topcoat. Pinholes will occur when the air or excessive solvent is released during drying.

b) Fanning a freshly applied finish can drive air into its surface, or cause a skin dry.

c) Application of colour coats over an undercoat or colour coat that has been dry sprayed.

d) Contamination. Moisture or oil in the airline will enter the paint while being applied.

e) Application of heavy coats with an insufficient flash off period between successive coats.

f) Poor knifing technique when applying stopper or body filler. Using the knife at an acute angle causes the material to roll under the blade, forcing air bubbles in.

g) Failure to spot-in areas of body filler or stopper with primer-surfacer before painting.

Cure

a) Where the pinholing is only slight and confined to the colour coat, remove the defect by compounding, or by flatting with Grade P1200 paper and then compounding.

b)   In other cases, wet flat the affected paint to a depth ensuring complete elimination of the holes and then refinish, or remove the affected paint and refinish from bare metal.

On no account attempt to bridge pinholes with successive dry applications or primer-surfacer.

c)   Pinholes exposed after flatting body filler or stopper should be sealed off with a thin spread stopper, applied with the knife held at 90° to the surface. This technique ensures that the stopper is forced well into the holes and also that it is not dragged out again as the knife moves on.

Note: When pinholing is a problem in the paint shop, check and adjust all the conditions that cause rapid surface drying, i.e. paint viscosity, thinner, shop temperature etc.

18)   Dirt

Description
Almost always, except in a case of seed condition (see below), dirt will show up as a rough finish characterized by an irregular pattern with an irregular particle size.

Cause
Dirt can find its way into the finish surface either through the paint in application or after the paint has been applied. In either case, the root cause is likely to be sloppy housekeeping or the use of paints which are unsuited to poor working conditions.

a)   Contaminated paint or solvent. It is unlikely that a new batch of paint or solvent will be contaminated prior to opening the container, though

subsequent contamination can occur easily if dusty lids are removed, or if the paint is stored carelessly after part-use.

b)   Dust from primer sanding not removed.

c)   Airborne contamination either from the area immediately surrounding the work, or from more remote sources. Slow drying paints such as enamels demand a clean, closed application area on two counts. First, the extended drying time allows ample opportunity for dust to settle and embed itself in the finish. Secondly, unlike 'cellulose'-based paints the surface cannot be compounded back and repolished to restore the gloss.

d)   Poor cleaning of equipment and filters will lead to a dirty finish. Quite often a recent colour change, requiring a higher solvent content, will dislodge residue from inside the gun, upstream of the final (pick-up tube) filter.

Cure
To ensure that there is no subsequent breakthrough of the dirt particles, which themselves may be contaminated by oil, solvent etc., the dirty layer must be removed. This can be done by careful sanding down to an unaffected level. Such action is not required when the problem is localized and has been caused by hardened paint deposits being flushed from the gun. In this case merely re-flat and then refinish.

19)   Seed Condition

Description
This appears as a uniform distribution in the film or particles of a regular size and pattern.

Cause
a)   Very low paint film.
b)   Contamination of the paint and poor filtration.

Cure
Re-flat the affected areas and apply a new finish coat.

20)   Poor Opacity

Description
Poor opacity will be found when the original finish or undercoat, etc. can be seen through the topcoat.

Cause
a)   Inefficient mixing, i.e. failure to stir the paint sufficiently to incorporate all the pigment throughout.
b)   Overthinning.
c)   Use of excessively slow thinner, causing the paint to sag before a sufficiently thick coat is obtained.
d)   Use of cheap or incorrect thinner.
e)   Failure to apply an adequate number of coats.

Cure
Allow the paint to flash off and then recoat, or allow the paint to harden completely, wet flat and then recoat.

21)   Sinkage

Description
As drying proceeds, the finish loses gloss and eventually shows all the underlying imperfections, such as the contours of stopper patches and metal scratches, etc.

Cause
a)   Excessively heavy application of any one, or all the materials used in the painting or preparation stages.
b)   Insufficient drying time between coats.
c)   Dry spraying of undercoats, resulting in porosity.
d)   Failure to spot-prime body filler, stopper and sealer patches, etc.
e)   Failure to stir highly pigmented undercoats before use, or poor curing of undercoats.
f)   Use of too coarse a grade of sandpaper.
g)   Poor drying conditions: confined, cold, humid, unventilated.
h)   Underthinned paint.

i) Use of incorrect thinner, particularly in primer-fillers.
Note: Insufficient weight of colour coat will give the appearance of sinkage.

Cure
a) Allow the paint to harden thoroughly. Depending on the degree of sinkage, use either rubbing compound, or Grade 1200 paper to level the surface, and then polish.
h) In severe cases, wet flat with Grade P500-P1000 paper and respray.

22) Slow Drying

Description
The paint film takes an excessively long time to dry and harden.

Causes
a) Excessively heavy coat application, leading to surface skin drying and trapping of solvents in the paint film.
b) Poor surface cleaning and preparation – painting over wax, oil paint stripper or grease contaminants.
c) Poor drying conditions: confined, cold, humid and unventilated.
d) Poor application conditions – lack of air movement or warmth.
e) Insufficient drying time between coats.
f) Excessive use of retarder.
g) Use of cheap or incorrect thinner, e.g. too slow.

Cure
a) Generally, slow drying can be overcome by moving the vehicle to an area of improved ventilation and temperature, or by the application of low heat. If slow drying is due to extra heavy coats, wrinkling may develop, unless great caution is observed so as not to apply the heat too rapidly or directly to the panels of the vehicle.
b) If the slow drying is due to contamination (from paint stripper not properly washed off, for example), neither improved drying conditions nor heat will dry the paint film. In this case, strip to bare metal, thoroughly clean and refinish.

23) Off Colour

Description
The paint does not match the colour standard.

Cause
a) Poor mixing of paint either in main tanks prior to distribution or in small-scale storage.
b) Low film causing transparency and 'see-through' to primer coats. This may be caused by poor application, or as a result of imperfections in the paint.
c) Poor application techniques when applying metallic paint.
d) Variations in the application processes between the original finish and repair finish.

Cure
Flat the existing topcoat and refinish.

24) Water Marking and Spotting

Description
Water marking cannot be removed by rubbing with a cloth, and occurs when a drop of water evaporates from a painted surface, leaving an outline of the drop behind. If a white spot is left behind, this is known as water spotting.

Cause
a) Exposure of the paint film to rain, before it is fully hardened.
b) Abnormal weather conditions, when showers are followed by very strong sun.
c) Excessive wax application.

Cure
a) If repeated heavy applications of wax polish are suspected of being the cause, thoroughly clean off the old wax using plenty of rag, and wax and grease remover. Polish with a liquid polish initially, followed with a coarser polishing or rubbing compound afterwards, depending on the depth of the mark or spot.
b) If repeated polishings are not effective, wet flat the affected area and respray.
Note: In severe cases, the water marks or spots may reappear a few days after the polishing. This may be rectified by repeating the polishing operation once or twice more.

25) Wrinkling

Description
Wrinkling is confined to synthetic enamels i.e. those which dry by a process of oxidation or a thermosetting process in an oven. It appears as a surface distortion or shrivelling, generally during the drying process, although it can occur while the topcoat is being applied.

Cause
Wrinkling is caused by non-uniform drying within the paint film. Synthetic enamels generally dry from the surface downwards i.e. the surface tends to set to a skin due to its contact with the oxygen in the air. When these coats have been applied, the lower coats are not able to release the solvents and set at the same rate as the surface layer, thus resulting in a distortion and wrinkling of the paint film.
a) Non-uniform drying.
b) Excessive film thickness.
c) Use of incorrect or cheap thinner i.e. too slow a thinner.
d) Non-uniform shop temperature; this will cause localized skinning in uneven patterns.
e) Improper drying. When a freshly applied topcoat is baked or force dried too soon, softening of the undercoats may occur, which will cause swelling and wrinkling.
f) Insufficient flash-off time between successive coats.

Cure
a) When wrinkling is slight, allow the film to harden thoroughly. Then flat to remove all traces of the defect and respray.
b) When the condition is severe, strip to bare metal, clean thoroughly and then refinish.

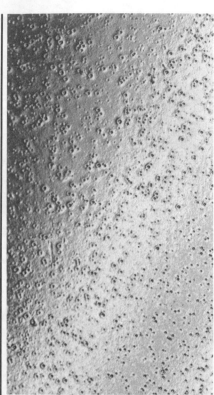

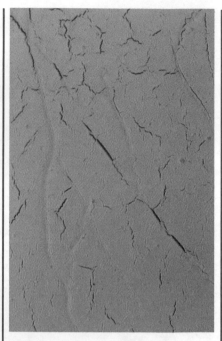

PF1.   Blistering.
(Courtesy Austin-Rover).

PF2.   Sand Scratches. This is an example of scratch marks left by a disc sander. (Courtesy Austin-Rover).

PF3.   Solvent Pop.
(Courtesy Austin-Rover).

PF4.   Cracking. This is a case of cracking, probably caused by a far too heavy application of paint.
(Courtesy Austin-Rover).

PF5.   Cracking. This instance of cracking could have been caused by the application of paint which is incompatible with the paint already on the surface of the panel.
Solutions: strip back to bare metal or sand right through the cracks to a smooth surface and apply an isolator.
(Courtesy Austin-Rover).

PF6.   Crazing. Sometimes, the paint takes on a crazed rather than cracked appearance when the problems mentioned under 'Cracking' are encountered.
(Courtesy Austin-Rover)

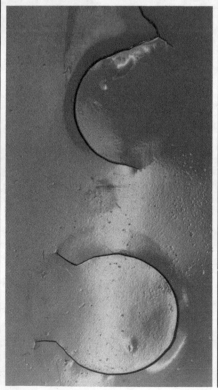

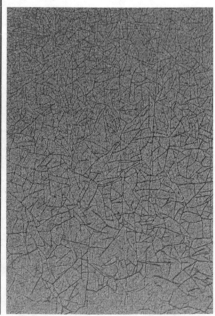

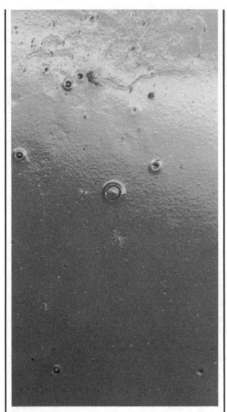

PF9.   Orange peel.
(Courtesy Austin-Rover).

PF7.   Cratering.
(Courtesy Austin-Rover).

PF8.   Low gloss.
(Courtesy Austin-Rover).

PF10.   Intercoat Adhesion Failure.
Paint flaking can occur over large or
small areas and can go right through to
the metal, although it is usually
confined to flaking down to a poorly
flatted gloss coat from a previous paint
job. (Courtesy Austin-Rover).

PF11.   Pin-holing.
(Courtesy Austin-Rover).

PF12.   Dirt. This is the result of a
severe case of dirt inclusion.
(Courtesy Austin-Rover).

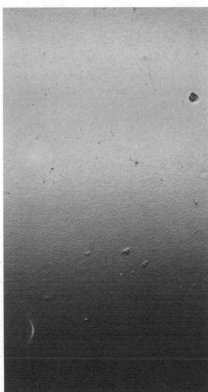

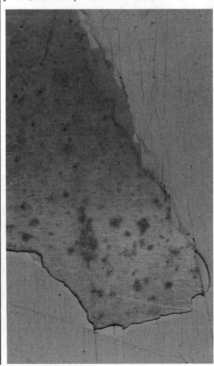

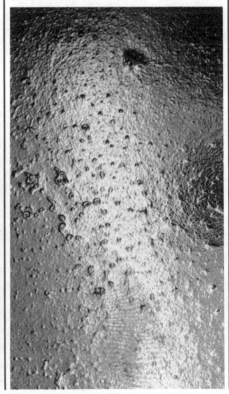

26)   Soft Paint

Description
The paint surface can be marked easily even after full drying has been allowed.

Cause
a)   Too great a film thickness.
b)   Incorrect quantity of catalyst in 2-pack paint.

Cure
The paint surface must be removed by sanding, although almost all paints, but particularly enamels, will respond to some extent to increased drying time. (The information contained in this Section was provided by courtesy of International Paint, Birmingham, England. Cartoons and captions courtesy of International Paint and Paint & Vinyl Operations Ford Motor Co. USA)

Paint stripping ●

Paint stripper is highly caustic and should be handled with great care. Always wear rubber gloves, cover up bare arms and wear goggles when using it. Also, read the manufacturer's instructions on what to do if you spill some onto your skin or into your eyes.

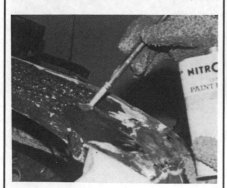

PS1.   Begin by brushing a heavy coat of stripper on the area to be stripped. Try to restrict your activities to no more than, say, a couple of feet square (around half a metre). Be sure to protect any surrounding paintwork with **several** layers of masking paper.

PS2.   Let the stripper attack the paint for a little while before starting work with the scraper. The outer layer of paint, being the newest, will still contain a relatively great amount of solvent and so it should bubble and wrinkle quite considerably.

PS3.   Brush all of the old loosened paint off the surface so that you can see what you are doing. Don't forget that the paint is still coated in caustic paint stripper. Bundle the waste up and dispose of it before it has a chance to do any harm. It could burn your pets (and your children!) quite badly.

PS4.   Coat the next layer with more stripper. It is important to note that each successive layer will become progressively slower to wrinkle and that the lower coats may only soften.

PS5.   Extra weight can be put behind a glazier's three-sided scraper, the sort you pull towards yourself. Remember that scrapers will benefit from being sharpened as much as any cutting tool (although it's necessary only to restore a crisp edge, not to make the scraper razor sharp), but be careful not to dig deeply into the metal.

PS6.   Corrosion of this sort is best tackled after stripping the surrounding area. If only a small area is to be tackled, try stripping it by softening the paint with a blowtorch, but be careful not to cause heat-distortion in the panel. Be prepared for the stripped paint to reveal even more damage, especially since paint stripper works well on polyester resin (the plastic in fibreglass). For that reason, a special type of stripper has to be used on a fibreglass car (if you have difficulty obtaining it, try someone who specialises in Corvettes in the 'States', Lotus or Reliant in the UK or try a boat chandler. Stripper for fibreglass panels is much slower acting than that used on steel panels).

Painting Plastics ●

More and more non-stressed panels on modern cars are being made of plastic and they can present problems when it comes to painting. Some paint types react with some plastics to quite a dramatic degree, making it essential that the correct approach is followed. The trouble is, you can't identify a plastic (and there are many different types around) just by looking at it. And if you can't identify it, you don't know what steps to take to prevent problems arising. The international paint company, Berger, produce an identifier kit called The Stando-Test System which forestalls any risk when painting plastic.

PP3.   ... and rub it onto the plastic panel. If there's no reaction, go on to the next bottle until ...

PP6.   All the rest is routine refinishing; you can proceed safe in the knowledge that there cannot possibly be a reaction because of faulty plastic identification.

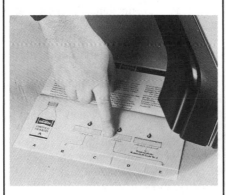

PP1.   The simple flow-diagram that comes with the kit shows how to use the bottles.

PP4.   ... you find one that takes some of the colour off the plastic and onto the cloth.

Mending plastics is no more difficult than mending any other sheet material. You can use fibreglass and filler, although because most plastics are more flexible than GRP, they are prone to cracking out later. Another Berger product, Standox Autoplastic is a stopper made to have built-in flexibility when it has hardened, which makes it ideal for light plastic damage repairs. They also make a plasticiser for adding to Standox finish paint which takes away its brittleness and allows it to flex with its plastic base without cracking.

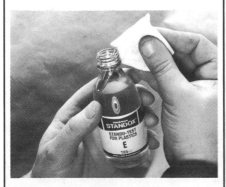

PP2.   The Stando-Test System comes with a kit of bottles of various fluids. You simply pour a drop from one of them onto a cloth ...

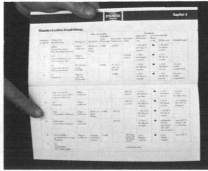

PP5.   You have then identified the key to the whole puzzle. Look along the column for the type of plastic you have just identified and you will be able to repair or paint the panel right through to topcoat.

Compressors – choice and use ●

There is more bull in advertisements for compressors than anything since the hi-fi was invented! No wonder most people buy these extremely useful tools on price and looks above all. A compressor is an indispensable tool for anyone who takes spraying half-seriously and it is also useful for jobs such as blowing up tyres, blasting grease remover onto engines and other mechanical parts, powering a small sand-blaster and also for powering any air tools you may wish to use such as an air chisel, for rapidly cutting away rusty or damaged metal, or a grinder, polisher or random-orbit sander. In fact, when you start taking body repairs seriously, a compressor is the first major item to buy.

A compressor consists of an electric motor (or occasionally petrol or diesel engine) driving a piston in a cylinder, rather like that in a car engine. In this case, however, the piston provides energy in the form of compressed air which is fed to the equipment it powers via air lines.

Whether you are buying new or second hand, perhaps from a garage which is closing down, there are certain points to watch out for. After deciding how much you can afford to spend the first check to make is on the capacity of the machine and it's here that the makers' 'lack of clarity' – shall we call it – sets in.

Larger machines really must be equipped with an air receiver to take out the fluctuations caused by the pumping action of the piston. There are some very small models on the market with no air receiver but, with this type of compressor, progress is very slow in any case so that the pulses in the spray of paint coming from the gun hardly matter. SIP have brought out a tiny compressor which incorporates its own tiny air receiver, which manages to smooth out the flow of air. Compressors which have a larger air receiver have an added advantage in that they can power for short bursts equipment which requires a high flow rate and which the motor itself is not capable of keeping up with. One example would be an air chisel, which uses a great deal of air to keep going flat out. In practice, an air chisel is rarely used for more than a few seconds at a time, the pauses in between giving the compressor time to catch up on the capacity of the air receiver. In general, through, it is false economy to buy a compressor that is going to have to work its heart out to keep up with equipment which you are likely to put to a lot of use. You have to decide how often you will want to use the machine and how much it will bother or inconvenience you if you have to wait for the machine to pick up pressure. At the very least, the compressor must keep up with the

type of spray equipment you intend to use and if you use a top-line gun like the DeVilbiss JGA, you will need a machine which delivers, say, 9 cubic feet per minute (CPU) minimum (250 litres per minute) although there are many less 'greedy' spray guns.

Watch manufacturer's delivery figures like a hawk! Often the figure quoted is the machine's theoretical output which bears little relation to the practical output and is related to the *displacement* figure, which is the volume of the cylinder stroked by the piston. Because of losses and inefficiencies, however, the usable amount of air given out is generally a little over half of this figure. The truly usable capacity of the machine is its *Free Air Delivery* (FAD) and it is the FAD figure which must be related to the tool or tools you intend to use. Air-driven polishing mops, for instance, can consume a hearty 18 cfm (500 lpm) and need that level of output for minutes on end, so you would have to buy a very expensive compressor just to keep up. But most equipment is used only intermittently, so you can make allowances for the time when you are not using the tool and the compressor is rebuilding its tank pressure.

The other figure to look at is the speed at which the machine is running. Smaller DeVilbiss compressors run, typically, at around 650 rpm, SIP run at around 900 rpm, both of which are sensible speeds which ensure reasonable compressor life, but some units which claim a fantastically high output from low purchase cost, run at anything up to a staggering 3,000 rpm, with around 1,400 rpm being the average. Obviously the faster a machine runs, the faster it will wear out.

Other 'quality' pointers to look out for are: safety guards to British Standards Institute, or equivalent, levels of safety; a good quality motor built by a firm with a known reputation; a large air receiver which, as well as the benefits already mentioned, cuts down on condensation because, as the air expands and cools, any moisture in it will condense into droplets and the tank will act as a trap to collect the water, rather than letting it get out onto the job; a tank pressure gauge

which gives a visual indication of unusual tank pressure if the cut-off valve goes wrong, room for top-mounting an air regulator, because there is not always sufficient depth for the regulator body with side mountings; the presence of an inlet filter. Remember also that pressure is far less important than air delivery (FAD *not* displacement). Also, belt-drive compressors are generally quieter running than direct drive.

In Use

Leakage in the air line or connections can cause quite a dramatic drop in the potential of the machine. For instance, a hole measuring only 3 mm across will lose 11 litres of air per second, which is just about the flat-out capacity of the very smallest compressors, so check all connections for tightness. Also, do not choose air lines of too narrow a diameter, especially for longer runs of pipe, because the frictional loss inside the pipe can reduce the air flow volume a great deal. In general, select a pipe size that matches the size of the outlet on the compressor.

You should try to keep the lubricating oil *in* the compressor and water *out*. Accomplish the former by keeping the oil topped up to its recommended level, but no higher, and by renewing the piston rings, when they become worn out. The latter is achieved by draining the tank and/or regulator after every use and by allowing the compressor to run somewhere relatively cool and where it will not draw in particularly damp air. Compressors are best sited outside workshops, if they are to receive very regular use, or inside with a cover and an air inlet to the fresh air, so that abrasive and dirty particles are not drawn into the machine from the air in the workshop. In any case, change the inlet filter or filters at regular intervals. It is all too easy to forget them until they become choked and the machine really has to struggle to keep up.

C1. The SIP 'Workshop' series of compressors are in the same mid-range capacity and are pitched at a more competitive market — being more of an ideal price/quality compromise.

C2. DeVilbiss really is the Rolls-Royce of spray equipment. This unit is well capable of supporting one medium duty spray gun and is well suited to the semi-professional.

C3. For the genuine DIY-ers, the SIP Jet 30 mini-compressor can give amazingly effective results and the cost is less than the cost of having a respray carried out for you. This type of set-up saves money first time out!

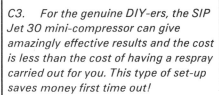

4 Painting Part 2

Respraying a Rear Wing ■

No, there is no reason why a 'Beetle' wing spray should be any different from that of any other car! It's simply that when the author visited the headquarters of International Paints in Ladywood, Birmingham, it was a Beetle that was selected by their man-on-the-spot Ian MacAlister as a suitable car for the demonstration he was about to give. Actually, Ian is very used to being 'on the spot' because as International's Technical Sales Representative he is the man who visits dozens of commercial premises each year as a troubleshooter: finding the cause of difficult problems and demonstrating ways round them.

Identifying the correct refinishing paint

Ian pointed out that the first step, before carrying out any work whatsoever, is to determine the type of paint that has already been used on the car. Knowing the original paint system used is no help at all unless the car's history from new is known. Newish cars may have been accident damaged and older cars are almost certain to have been given a 'blow-over' at some stage by a dealer operating in the knowledge that the seductiveness of a shiny car is a real forecourt asset. There are four principal paint types in use and certain combinations are so incompatible that putting the wrong combination together, such as applying a car with cellulose paint on top of an oil-based paint, will cause a reaction almost as extreme and unsightly as if paint stripper has been sprayed onto the car.

The paint type test in Part 1 of this Chapter will allow you to deduce what the existing paint type is; the accompanying chart shows which combinations of paint can or cannot be used on top of one another.

Original Paint	Cellulose	1-pack Acrylic	2-pack Acrylic	1-pack Synthetic
Refinish Paint				
Cellulose	O	X	O	X
1-pack Acrylic (e.g aerosol cans)	O	O	O	X
2-pack Acrylic (Isocyanate cured hydroxy acrylics)	O	O	O	O (if aged)
1-pack Synthetic (oil-based paint)	O	O	O	O

Note: O denotes acceptable case.

Cellulose paint was once overwhelmingly the most popular paint for original equipment and refinishing use. It does not require sophisticated equipment in its use, it is very quick drying so minimising dust problems and it is relatively inexpensive. It has the ability to be polished back to a high shine (albeit after many hours of elbow grease in many cases) and so if the amateur's initial finish is not perfect, the problem can be remedied. Coupled with its low toxicity (you don't tend to drop dead upon coming into contact with it!) cellulose must remain favourite with the home sprayer.

Where touching-in is concerned, however, 1-pack Acrylic, which is frequently used in aerosol spray cans, is an excellent product and, of course, use of paint in this way involves absolutely minimal outlay. See the section on 'Bodywork in a Can' for further information.

2-pack Acrylic paint is relatively new to the UK although it has been used for some time in Continental Europe. Its qualities are stunning: it completely hides small scratches and so requires less flatting, it can be used over any other paint, it gives a very tough, hard finish and it retains its deep lustrous shine for years and years, requiring only a wash to bring it up like new. But, life being what it is, the enormous advantages are matched by a potentially bigger disadvantage – **Inhaling the spray can be lethal!** The match between the words Iso*cyanate* and *cyanide* is no idle coincidence – they are both killers! Isocyanate 2-packs *must* be used in a sealed booth where the operator is wearing an air-fed face visor so that he breathes only good air from outside the booth. At the time of writing, there are rumours of a *non* isocyanate, air-drying 2-pack being on the verge of being launched, and if that is as good as it promises to be, it could virtually kill off the use of cellulose paint. For the moment, however, 2-packs are simply too dangerous for anyone to even consider them for home use.

The fourth major paint system is 1-pack Synthetic, or oil-based paint, a very close cousin to the coach paint found on very old Vintage cars. Synthetics are used by the commercial respray trade simply because the areas to be sprayed are usually so vast and synthetic is the cheapest paint around. The same virtue makes it attractive to the lowest end of the car respray market but it is possessed of some serious disadvantages: it is very slow to dry and so the risk of its being affected by dust inclusion is commensurately higher; but worst of all is the fact that if there are problems such as runs in the paintwork, it can take weeks before the paint is hard enough to be flatted down again. In addition, apart from another Synthetic, only 2-pack Acrylic can later be used over the top of Synthetic without provoking a reaction and then only if the paint beneath is years old and thus is 'well-cured'.

Actually, it is not quite true to say that nothing can be sprayed over Synthetic paint. It is possible to buy a special barrier paint called an isolator paint which can be sprayed onto an area suspected of being prone to

reaction and which seals it off. Isolators are known to be hygroscopic if used incorrectly (they absorb water from the atmosphere) which means that if a car is left covered in isolator, its paint will act like a sponge. Later, when the finish coat is sprayed on, nothing untoward will occur, until the next good hard frosty spell. Then the tiny droplets of water beneath the surface will freeze and expand, and the surface will erupt with a covering of tiny pimples known as micro-blistering. The answer is to spray a coat of primer over the isolator within the hour and so effectively seal it off from the atmosphere. (It must be said, however, that even primer will absorb moisture if left for a length of time without any top coat – and for that reason, it should *never* be left outside in the rain.)

BWS1.   Ian MacAlister turned up at International Paint's Refinishing School in a fairly well preserved 'Beetle', complete with a few bashes in its rear wing where the owner had argued briefly with a gate post – and lost. Ian knew that the car had previously been sprayed in 2-pack because it had been sprayed previously at the same place. Had he been unsure of the compatibility of the paints being used he would have tried wiping some paint or its solvent onto an unobtrusive area such as a wheel arch flange, or some other out of the way part of the car to be sprayed, then waited to see if any reaction took place.

BWS2.   The next job is to establish the exact colour of the paint. It is possible to identify the colour by its name such as 'Silver Fox', or 'Connaught Green' or whatever. However, it is not always obvious what the colour is called: a visit to the paint factor will bring the assistance of someone with a book of colours called paint chips but the best way is to find the manufacturer's paint code number. Check, of course, that the car is in its original livery. Look inside the engine bay and under the carpets to find the original colour. If the paint is original, the code number will be invaluable because there are often production line variations even with one particular colour name and these 'variants' should be indicated in the code number. Code numbers are usually on a plate in one of a variety of possible hiding places. Look along the front panel, where there is usually a range of information to be found. Alternatively, the plate may be found underneath the spare wheel in the spare wheel well.

BWS3.   Another favourite spot is at the front edge of the bulkhead.

BSW4.   Further 'hiding places' are the door hinge pillar, ...

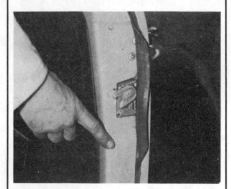

BWS5.   ... the outside edge of the door itself, ...

BWS6.   ... and even the inside of the fuel filler flap, ...

BWS7.   ... as well as the engine bay flitch plates (but, remember, this is a 'Beetle' with its engine at the 'wrong' end.)

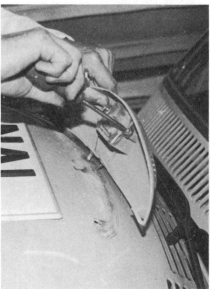

BWS8.   If you can't manage to take the whole of the car to the factor, you can usually find a small part of the bodywork to remove and take along. Here, Ian removes the number plate lamp for the purpose of taking it along to International's own range of paint chips, just to be sure.

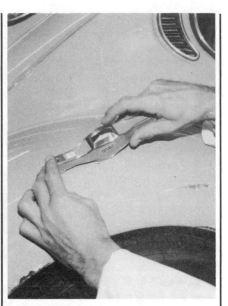

BWS9.   This fiendish little device measures the thickness of the paint already on the panel; the paint factor will probably have one and could do the job for you. Older cars often have layer upon layer of paint on their bodywork and this can eventually cause problems; you can reach the stage where one coat too many can cause a reaction with the paint beneath, necessitating the stripping of the entire panel.

BWS10.   Ian next looked at the blemishes on the panel which, of course, had to be remedied before any painting took place. Here the paint was flaking around a light area of damage. Surface rust had formed and possibly spread a little way beneath the paint film.

BWS11.   Fortunately, the wing was basically quite sound, apart from a shallow dent towards the front of the wing.

BWS14.   Before trying to get rid of the dent, Ian sanded the whole area down to bare metal; it's the only way of being certain of what's under the paint.

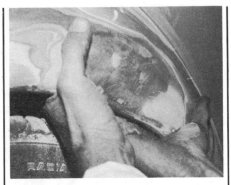

BWS15.   He then 'popped' the worst of the dent by pressing very hard on the back of the panel. Of course, the finish was not perfect but it was good enough for the job in hand. Some enthusiasts might prefer to aim for a perfect finish to the surface of the steel. See the section on Panel Beating.

BWS12.   Ian began by reassembling the equipment he would need for the first stage in the process of repairing the wing: at the front is a random orbit sander (easily replaceable by a free commodity called 'hard work',) and from left to right is a tin of wax and grease remover, a box of sanding papers and a packet of face masks of the type designed to stop the wearer from inhaling dust.

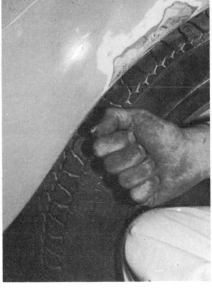

← ——————————————— →

BWS16.   The dent at the rear of the wing couldn't be pushed out so Ian thumped it once with his clenched fist and out it came! An alternative is to use a soft-faced hammer, but it is generally a mistake for the less experienced repairers to use a steel hammer because it can cause more trouble than it prevents, by causing the steel to stand out from the panel.

——————————————— →

BWS13.   The use of wax and grease remover is most important before any abrading work is carried out. Polish, especially silicone polish, can play havoc with paintwork, causing it to form 'fish eyes' where the paint surrounds spots of silicone but doesn't cover them. If silicone is sanded, it is simply pushed further into the remaining paint or steel where it is virtually impossible to remove.

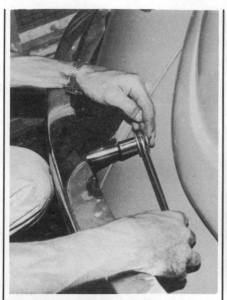

BWS17.   Before proceeding any further, the rear bumper was removed because it would get in the way of the flatting and painting processes. Be prepared for bumper retaining bolts to be difficult to undo. If they are tough going, try: pushing the spanner with your foot; applying releasing fluid to the nut well in advance; heating the part with a welding torch or even a small butane torch, provided that nothing flammable is in the area.

BWS18.   With all the offending areas thoroughly sanded down, Ian provided himself with a tin of polyester filler which requires a hardener to make it set and – a product widely used by the trade but rarely by the home repairer – a tin of cellulose stopper which air dries rather than hardens.

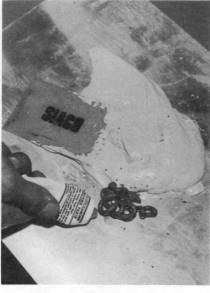

BWS19.   Ian judged the amount of filler to be used and scooped it out onto a clean board using the spreader supplied. The hardener was squeezed out next to it. The proportions of hardener to filler paste are not critical but should be 'about right'. Manufacturers usually supply enough hardener in the pack to satisfy the quantity of filler paste it accompanies, so try to use the proportion of the quantities used as a guide. Remember, though, that if you are working in hot weather, filler 'goes off' (sets) much more quickly while in winter it can take much longer. Be prepared to use a little trial and error and to vary the ratio accordingly.

BWS20.   It is important to mix hardener with filler evenly and thoroughly. The contrasting colours help.

BWS21.   Notice how Ian held the spreader as flat as possible and also shaped it to the contour of the wing. Filler should be left slightly proud, but the closer to the correct shape, the less wastage will occur and the better the final profile is likely to be.

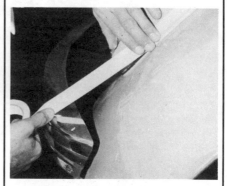

BWS22.   Masking off is best carried out using two layers of masking tape. The first is carefully and accurately placed over the edge to be masked off ...

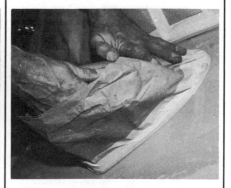

BWS23.   ... while the next is placed over the edge of the masking paper before the paper is stuck down to the tape already in place. Ian carefully folded the paper in on itself as neatly as a Christmas parcel.

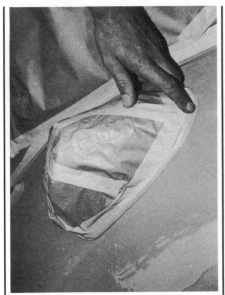

BWS24.   All the edges were then sealed down with more masking tape so that no dust could get trapped in there. Dust blown about by the pressure from the spraygun is the resprayer's Public Enemy No. 1 and great lengths have to be gone to in order to prevent it from causing blemishes on the paint finish.

BWS25.   Ian used the power sander to flatten the filler. An ordinary disc held in a drill is not nearly as good; the random orbit device in this special sander prevents scratching in the surface of the filler. See the section on 'Bodywork in a Can', and also 'Tools and Equipment', for more tips on hand sanding.

BWS26.   The professional way of feeling a panel to check for ripples and bumps is to run the flat of the hand lightly over the panel. At this stage a panel can appear to be perfectly flat to the eye, but once it is painted every ripple will be cruelly exposed.

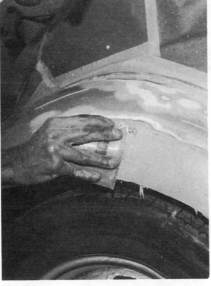

BWS27.   As usually happens, it was necessary to apply a second layer of filler. This time, a really thin skin was all that was necessary.

BWS28.   Belatedly, Ian remembered that he should really have masked off the wheel **before** sanding the filler down to avoid an accumulation of dust there. He used the airline for the task.

BWS29.   More brown paper was used to mask off the wheel. Paper is better than cloth because the latter harbours dust.

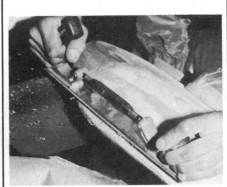

BWS30.   Ian demonstrated a rapid method of removing filler by using a Sykes-Pickavant body file. It has single cut teeth which resist clogging and can be adjusted to give a flat or a concave or convex blade shape.

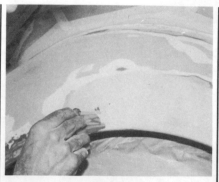

BWS31.   After a further bout of flatting, the surface of the filler was found to still contain small pin holes and other very minor blemishes. Ian used cellulose stopper and a small spreader to deal with them. Cellulose stopper is a very fine filler paste which air dries quite quickly. It should only be used very thinly to avoid the risk of noticeable shrinkage and to keep drying times down. It is also possible to use a 2-pack stopper which is preferable because it is less prone to shrinkage than cellulose stopper.

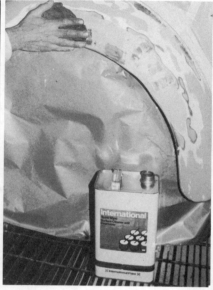

BWS33.   A clean rag was then used with some of International's own Spirit Wipe/Degreaser. It is important to remove all traces of grease at this stage but most people use some of the paint solvent with which the paint is thinned down, although International don't recommend this because they say it could cause 'swelling' or completely remove the cellulose stopper already used.

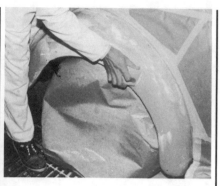

BWS35.   ... and then sanded again with fine grade of paper on a sanding block. This had the effect of highlighting any blemishes that may have escaped attention earlier. A little more stopping was used on the small blemishes discovered. If necessary, more filler would have been used at this stage and, while the professional might rarely need to go back to filler after flatting the primer, the less experienced home resprayer may have to be prepared to do so in order to achieve a first class finish.

BW32.   Stopper sands very easily and the small areas treated were easily hand flatted using the flat of the hand, fingers facing **across** the direction of sanding to minimise the risk of creating grooving.

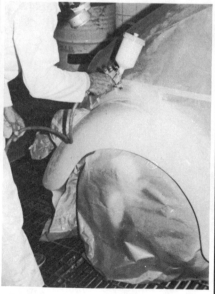

BWS34.   A couple of coats of primer/filler were next blown on ...

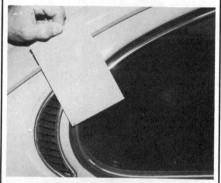

BWS36.   Ian next took a piece of card and sprayed it with just a little of the paint that he was about to use. He then compared it with the shade of the paint on the car's bodywork. If there is a difference between shades, it is better to take the paint back to the factors at this stage where they can often blend the colour to the required shade; after all, paint can fade over a period of time and when that happens, no amount of colour code identification will give you the right shade. Reds and yellows are generally thought of as the most fade-prone colours.

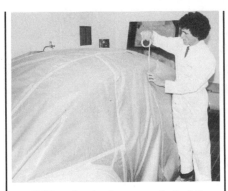

BWS37. Ian had removed all of the masking paper, put there to prevent any damage to the surrounding panel as well as to stop overspray from the primer. His justifiable obsession with dust told him that the old paper was likely to have trapped pockets of the stuff. When masking off a second time, Ian really went to town with the masking paper to make absolutely certain that no overspray whatever could reach the surrounding panels.

BWS38. Before starting to spray, wipe the air lines and the surface of the gun itself to ensure that there were no particles there. This is an important and often overlooked step, important because the forward flow of air which jets out of the front of the gun tends to pull in air — and thus particles if they are present — from behind the nozzle of the gun.

BWS39. The 'man from Mars' outfit that Ian is wearing while spraying the top coat is not just for effect. It's a necessary safety precaution when spraying with 2-pack paint. Fresh, filtered air is fed into the sealed face mask and this keeps out the toxic spray of paint. Needless to say, once the paint has landed and hardened, there is no danger whatsoever. DeVilbiss market an excellent air fed visor kit complete with all the necessary plumbing at reasonable cost — an **essential** investment if spraying 2-pack!

BWS40. 2-pack paints can be baked (i.e. the spray booth doubles as an oven to heat up the car) so that the paint goes off more quickly. If the paint is to be allowed to dry and go 'off' in the air, it is necessary to use a special air-drying 2-pack thinner to allow the process to take place within a reasonable time. An important difference between cellulose and 2-pack is that cellulose hardens mainly by a drying process and is thus liable to shrinkage while 2-pack hardens mainly by a chemical reaction, rather like that in filler and so suffers very little shrinkage. With the paint dry, the masking paper and tape can come off. Tape should not be left in place for more than a few days or it can be the devil of a job to remove. ➡

BWS41.   The newly painted wing looked absolutely splendid! But it was interesting that the surrounding panels, painted a couple of years previously in the same International 2-pack paint, looked virtually as good.

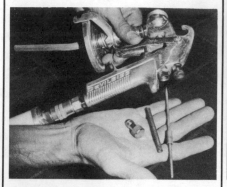

BWS42.   Ian went to great lengths to strip and clean the DeVilbiss gun he has been using, but see the section on 'Spray Gun Care', produced with the assistance of DeVilbiss themselves, for more detail.

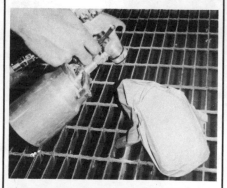

BWS43.   At around the time that Ian MacAlister was respraying the 'Beetle' wing, someone else was carrying out some experimental work on spraying plastics which are finding increasing use in today's cars. (This is a Ford Sierra wing mirror back, receiving attention.) See the relevant section, 'Spraying Plastics', for more information.

Brush-Painted Bodywork – how to deal with it ■

PY1.   This Mazda truck looks OK here and in fact it was a sound old bus, apart from one or two small areas of corrosion. The biggest problem was that it had received the 'kiss of death' – it had been brush painted! Here's how to overcome the problem.

PY2.   The problems with brush painting are usually two-fold: the brush marks are always visible and will show through any additional paint to a horrible degree; and the paint is incompatible with most refinishing paints except oil-based paints. (See 'Putting On the Paint' for more details.)
     The screen was taken out in order to deal with corrosion around the screen surround. ⟶

PY3.   Corrosion around the rear inner wing flange was cut out with the Black and Decker Mini-grinder and a cutting disc.

PY8.   The Black and Decker orbital sander was used to sand the filler down and feather-edge the repair into the surrounding panel. See how the disc looks blurred in this picture? That's because the disc rotates and oscillates at the same time, so that, as if by magic, no scores are left in the panel and the sanding remains flat. Sanding discs used are self-adhesive and just peel off when it's time to replace them.

⟵

PY4.   A Sykes-Pickavant tool was used to put a shoulder on the repair panel so that the patch would lie flush with the surrounding panel ...

PY6.   On this occasion I had run out of filler, so after grinding the welds down flat, inert filler powder was mixed with Cataloy resin to make a filler paste.

PY9.   In fact it was the Black and Decker orbital sander that made the whole job possible because it could be used to remove 90 per cent of the brush marks (some hand-sanding being necessary in the awkward little places), a task that would have taken weeks, or the paint would have had to be laboriously stripped. There are many air operated orbital sanders, made for use in professional shops, but they use a huge quantity of air — more than any DIY compressor delivers. This orbital sander is electrically operated.

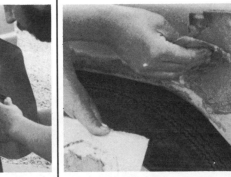

PY5.   ... then the plate was MIG-welded into place.

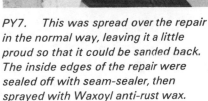

PY7.   This was spread over the repair in the normal way, leaving it a little proud so that it could be sanded back. The inside edges of the repair were sealed off with seam-sealer, then sprayed with Waxoyl anti-rust wax.

PY10.   The bed of the truck was scraped, wire brushed, then treated with rust killer like Supra De-rust, Rust Eater or something similar.

PY11.   The Rust Eater was then washed off and the whole area scrubbed with a hand brush.

PY12.   A small hole in the bed, right over the fuel tanks was repaired with the glass fibre which came in a Holts kit rather than risking welding in that area or going to the bother of removing the tank.

———————————▶

PY13.   Before any spraying was carried out, the whole truck was wiped over with International spirit wipe.

PY14.   The brush marks having been dealt with by using the orbital sander, the paint incompatibility problem was dealt with by using International isolator, followed by International 2-pack primer (used with a safe spray mask — see 'Putting On The Paint'). The isolator does not react with any conventional paint but it does have its own problems: it must not be sanded through (because it obviously can't do its job if it isn't there!) and it must be covered with a conventional primer within a few hours of use to stop it absorbing moisture from the air. The gun used here was a much-used SIP 'Jade' gun with a small SIP Workshop Series compressor, which coped easily with the thick 2-pack primer.

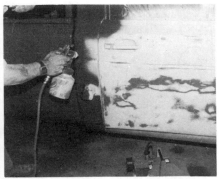

PY15.   The top coat was put on with a tiny SIP Airmate Jet 30 set-up which coped remarkably well, though progress was slow! The inside of the 'load bay' was painted first to quell the dust that remained in that area.

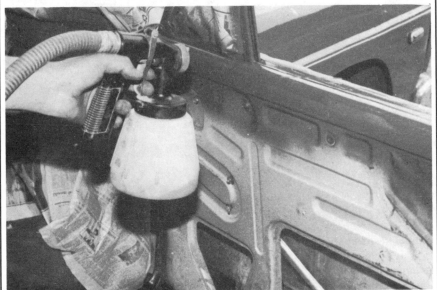

PY16.   Then the outside of the pick-up was painted. 1 litre of International 2-pack paint was just sufficient to paint the whole vehicle. It's expensive and the health problems are acute if the correct breathing apparatus is not used, but it covers extremely well, wears especially well and gives a very deep gloss from the gun, although it can be 'cut and polished' if necessry.

← ─────────────────

PY17.   I experimented with the Apollo sprayer to paint the dash and door interiors. This operates from a blower unit not unlike a vacuum cleaner motor! The air is high volume – low pressure, and there is very little overspray and paint consumption is low. It's easy to gain a fabulous shine with this equipment but progress is slow and the unit has to be switched off to cool down if it overheats, which it would in less time that it takes to spray a whole vehicle.

PY18.   The finished product! Fitted with a new tilt cover for the rear end, a side stripe (see relevant section for how to do it) and with all the chrome and glass polished and the wheels painted with International tyre-black, the old truck looked great!

5 Bodywork Repair

Is it Worth Repairing? – assessing accident damage ●

CARS Ltd are a Stourport, Worcestershire based company specialising in carrying out repairs to crash damaged cars. Their 'parking lot' contains cars in all stages of crash damage, many of which are actually awaiting repair. In the old days, when cars were built around the dimensional rigidity of a chassis, a crashed car could conceivably be reconstructed around a new or a straightened chassis. Nowadays, there are two major differences from the old style of construction. The first is that cars are of unitary construction, as explained in the first chapter. The second difference, made possible because of the first, is that cars are designed with 'crumple zones' which are actually intended to collapse upon impact. Crumple zones are a proven and effective way of shielding the passenger compartment from the worst of the damage in a crash, as the front or tail of the car gradually collapses first and thus acts as shock absorbers.

RI1.   This badly damaged car had skidded at high speed and gone sideways into a tree. No car as badly damaged as this can be saved, not even with the most sophisticated equipment, but it is surprising what can. Read on!

RI2.   This is how a distorted modern car is restored to exactly correct alignment. The bodyshell is placed upon a body jig, of which there are a number on the professional market. This will have been fitted with a set of brackets specially designed for the particular model of car being repaired. Then, using hydraulic rams for pushing or pulling, the car's bodyshell is forced back into correct alignment. Once the major structural components are back in line, straightforward body repair techniques can be used. If any major strcture sub-assemblies have to be let-in, the body jig is the ideal place to do it as it guarantees correct alignment. It would be quite in order for the highly proficient amateur, determined to rebuild a badly damaged car, to have this vital work carried out at a fully equipped garage such as at CARS Ltd. (Courtesy Cellette-Churchill Ltd)

RI3.   This Volvo Estate is typical of the cars that CARS Ltd rebuild. Note how the rear end has begun to collapse down and inwards leaving the rear of the cab pretty well intact.

RI4.   The rear pillar has been distorted and there is obviously severe structural damage here. Can it be repaired? After all, even the doors don't fit any more.

RI5.   The front isn't quite as bad, but even so ... 'Repairing this is everyday work to us', they say at CARS Ltd. At the time of writing, this car's value was around £12,000. Its scrap value was a quarter of that while repair cost would be around the same again, making a total of about £6,000. Even if a new Volvo is out of your range, it makes you realise how economic a rebuild could be, even if the bulk of the panel and body work was left to the experts.

←

RI6.   Perhaps this example would be a bit more like it, for the really skilful amateur. Most of it seems to be a straightforward panel swap. But wait – what about that front wheel? It's obviously had a heavy clout and been forced backwards quite a way. Well, that's the sort of vital, structural job best left to the experts with the right equipment, but quite a saving could be made by the person able to carry out the rest of the work.

RI7.   Now let's take a closer look at one particular crash damaged car. This vehicle was written-off by the insurance company and sold for around a quarter of its true value. It had obviously received a good front end 'smack', but were things worse than they at first seemed?

RI8. With bonnet raised, it was obvious that the front panel had been pushed back a long way and the radiator was bearing against the engine. If you are doing a rebuild for yourself, perfectly good parts such as a bonnet, grille, bumper and lights can be obtained from a breaker's yard. For ease of fitting, however, it is always best to go for some new components such as front panel, valence and inner wings. Not only are they so much easier to fit, but you know that they are dimensionally correct, especially if you stick to the maker's own equipment.

RI10. Looking down one of the rear corners of the engine bay, the gusset plates, inner wings and 'chassis rail' side members seemed to be fine.

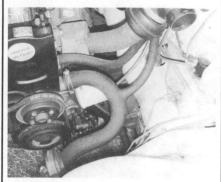

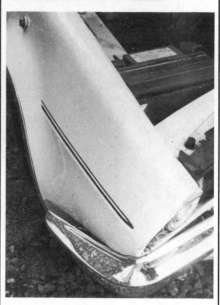

RI9. At the rear of the engine (and remember that the Austin Princess had a transverse engine) there were absolutely no signs of bulkhead damage. The engine mountings were all sound and only under the slightest stress from the impacted front panel. In fact, everything in this area looked pretty good!

RI11. When the other wheel arch was examined, two areas of important damage were found. Arrow 1 shows a kink in the inner wing, just behind the battery carrier, while Arrow 2 shows the first signs of deformation starting to take place in one of the holes let into the sidemember rail. These areas are part of the car's 'crumple zone' system and should always be examined in these circumstances. On closer examination the other side could be seen to be similarly afflicted.

RI12. The car's front wings were undoubtedly saveable and would pull to fit the shape of the new panels beneath them. The inner wings and chassis rails would all have to be cut out and replaced.

Verdict: This car was certainly saveable and would be a piece of cake for the professional bodyshop. The highly proficient amateur could try tacking the new panels into place then trailering the car to a bodyshop to check them for alignment and final, sound welding whilst on a body jig. Alternatively, the home repairer could be content with stripping all the old parts off, having all the structural work carried out for him then fitting back up with new or second-hand parts.

RI13. This is how Austin-Rover engineers go about designing crash crumple-zones into their cars, using computer graphics to indicate how and where bodywork will 'give' first in the event of a crash.
(Courtesy Austin-Rover)

RI14. This lightly damaged Buick, photographed at All Valley Auto Body in Simi Valley, California, is a perfect example of a DIY-able repair, involving, apparently, only bolt-on outer panels.

RI15. The wheel alignment on this Simi Valley police car is being checked prior to repairing crash damage — a precaution that a DIY-repairer should have carried out for him by a specialist. It is also essential that the basic structure is checked over on a jig as shown in the next section.

RI16. This is the welded-on door hinge arrangement on a Chevrolet Citation. To remove the door, you have to knock out the hinge pin, a task which can sometimes be carried out with a drift but sometimes requires the use of a special tool, available from accessory dealers.

RI17. Another welded-on hinge here, this type being fitted to late-model Chrysler products such as this 1981 Dodge Aries. If welded-on hinges are bent inwards in a crash, they can usually be bent back out by heating the bent portions with a welding torch and bending the hinge with a one-off tool you can make yourself out of stout steel. If a hinge is not bent inwards but is bent backwards (or forwards), the repair will be very much more difficult and will probably mean that the door pillar itself is distorted, which will be a job for the professional, equipped with a body puller.

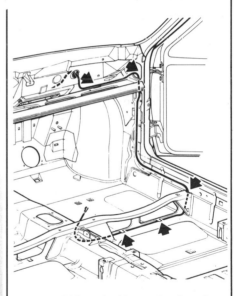

RI18. Although this section is only primarily concerned with assessment, do remember when welding near structural members that there could well be part of a wiring loom or rear screen wash tubes inside the member. They must be removed first.
(Courtesy Austin-Rover)

The Use of Body Repair Jigs

The DIY-repairer could not expect to own or even to have personal access to such specialised equipment, but many crash-repairers equipped with the sort of jigs shown here would be prepared to check you accident-damaged car for accurate alignment on their own 'universal' jig and may be prepared to pull a distorted body frame back into shape and dimensional accuracy, leaving you to fit up the outer panels.

A car is 'jigged' in order to determine whether the underpan has been distorted during the impact of an accident, and if so, to what extent. It is essential for the correct and safe handling of the repaired vehicle to restore the location points of vital components (such as suspension location points, engine mountings, gearbox mountings and steering component fixings) to their correct position, while the rest of the underbody must also be correctly realigned to allow replacement parts and panels to fit exactly.

Jigs and their brackets basically follow the methods of monocoque construction, in which the various components are clamped in position by specially constructed metal support brackets while the whole is welded up. Because each vehicle model is different, each usually requires an individually designed set of jig repair brackets.

Another system of jigging a car is on the 'measurement system'. With the aid of a datasheet which gives the correct height, width and length dimensions, it can be seen whether the underbody has been distorted and if so, to what degree. Generally, bracket-based systems will be the more time- and cost-effective repair method where damage is extensive, because of the progressive anchorage that brackets provide. Damaged metal is pulled back into its correct position and then clamped in place on the bracket, thus ensuring that it is not disturbed by subsequent pulls. The brackets also act as a welding support, clamping new parts in precisely the correct position during welding.

Clearly a measurement system cannot itself provide this progressive anchorage and support. The result is that with major damage, generally more material has to be cut away rather than straightened, and alternative measures must be taken to provide anchorage, usually meaning that the repair will take considerably longer.

On the other hand, a measurement system is very often the

fastest repair method where damage is relatively minor, and it is the ideal method for checking a vehicle for distortion of the underbody. A comprehensive check can be carried out without the removal of any mechanical units (engine, suspension, etc.), whereas this is not normally possible with jig brackets, which require more extensive stripping in order to perform a full check. A measurement system can be immediately available on the premises, whereas jig brackets are normally hired by the repairer since the immense range of vehicle marques and models on the road today make it impossible financially to offer a comprehensive vehicle body repair service using brackets which are the garage's own property.

RI19. Using Celette jig brackets on the MUF7 Mobile Bench. The brackets clamp new parts in precisely the correct position during welding. (Courtesy Celette-Churchill)

Using Body Filler ●

Plastic body filler is one of the most useful materials around when it comes to repairing car bodywork. Unfortunately, it's gained itself a lousy reputation, mostly because the stuff is so good, so effective and so easy to use that a number of folk have been known to misuse it. Filler can be applied over any surface that will support it until it goes hard – and that *includes* rusty metal, or even a hole shored up with newspaper! Used

properly, though, it's an absolute godsend.

First of all, it's worth mentioning that there are one or two places where it is best not to use plastic filler, because of the relatively brittle nature of the stuff. It is best kept away from the edges of door and door pillars, and any other part of the car with an exposed edge that might get chipped. Also it's no use expecting it to bridge a hole structurally unsupported. Finally, it *won't* hold back rust for more than a few winter weeks because it is porous.

On the other hand, it is stronger than most people realise and it clings very tenaciously to the surface, right up to the point where the surface may receive collision damage. There is no reason to believe that filler will ever lift or flake from a well-prepared surface, provided that the following rules are followed.

There are basically two kinds of filler in common use. One is a simple, smooth paste; the other contains chopped strands of fibreglass which gives it a great deal of strength. You should always wear an efficient particle mask when sanding filler, especially when machine sanding, but a mask is ESSENTIAL when sanding filler with chopped 'glass strands in it.

Preparation

The first job is to wipe the damaged area with a spirit wipe, or a rag dampened with paint thinners. This removes all traces of contamination which is *not* completely removed by sanding, but which is often just stirred around by it, so that it pops up later and ruins the paint finish. Then, using a sanding disc in a drill or a mini-grinder, the paint should be sanded from the area being filled. (If you intend filling a rusted-out area, be aware of the fact that the repair will only be temporary, and take a look at 'Repair On A Shoestring' and 'Bodywork In A Can' for project ideas.

Use

Open the can of filler and if there are pools of liquid on the top mix it well.

Use a clean plastic spreader with a dead-smooth edge and take a dollop of filler from the can. Place it on a smooth, clean surface and next to it, squeeze the right amount of hardener from the tube supplied. (Read the maker's instructions for advice on quantities.) The quality of the filler will be reduced if you use too much hardener and one maker's hardener may not work with another's filler — which can leave you with a very sticky problem on your hands, and on your car, too!

Mix the filler and hardener very thoroughly and spread the paste over the repair. If you're not sure whether you are too high or too low, use a throw-away straight edge (e.g. the back of an old hacksaw blade) to gauge the correct amount. You will almost never get it right first time, so don't even try: make the first coat a foundation, with its high points as high as you want to go.

The important thing about filler is that it hardens by chemical action rather than drying by evaporation so there is little shrinkage and everything happens much more quickly. The filler should go off (hard) in around 20 minutes, to the point where you can't scratch it with your nail. When it's hard, take off the highest peaks and test the surface with a straight edge. Judge where the low-spots are and apply more filler.

BUT: Don't use the same scraper without thoroughly cleaning it; don't use the same mixing surface even if it looks clean because it will pick up hard bits which scour across the surface; and don't scoop out more filler with a dirty spreader. Filler that hasn't gone off can get into the tin and set off all the material in a couple of days, or bits can get into the filler.

Sanding at this stage can be with a single-cut file or 40 grit paper. Go through the sanding/rubbing routine until you have the level where you want it, bearing in mind the advice on sanding flat in the two project Chapters mentioned. Finally, use a cellulose or 2-pack stopper to get rid of the finest blemishes. Spread it on like ordinary filler but much thinner. Give cellulose stopper plenty of time to dry, because it dries by evaporation but 2-pack stopper is really a 'thinner' version of body filler. Both are about the consistency of face cream or margarine.

Two points that the first timer often gets wrong: don't use filler to try to get rid of high spots in metal by building up all around them. The result will look absolutely awful, so have the courage to tap the high spot down first. And when you're sanding filler, try to sand right across it. It's easy to make the outsides of the filler look level with the surrounding area but to leave a mound in the middle, which will stand out like a Dutch mountain when the car has been painted.

BF1.   Filler must be mixed throroughly with its hardener before use. Only experience can tell you exactly how much hardener to use at a given temperature so, if you are a beginner, mix a relatively small amount at a time. Care taken when spreading the filler can save a lot of material, a lot of nuisance from dust, and a great deal of time and effort.

BF2.   A single cut file is an excellent tool for removing filler quickly, and without the health hazards associated with the use of power tools. Also ,it clogs a great deal less readily than the standard metalworker's bench file.

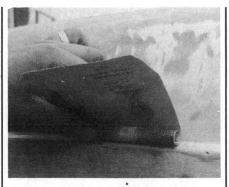

BF3.   Where filler has been used in the area of a body moulding, a rolled-up piece of abrasive paper is often perfect for retaining the shape when rubbing down.

BF4.   This is filler with chopped 'glass strands in it, to give additional strength. Any old, clean lids, can sides or pieces of stiff card can be used as a mixing board.

Using Body Solder ●

Have you ever wondered what the professional body repairer did before the days of plastic filler? In fact he did use a 'filler' of sorts for smoothing out ripples and shallow dents, and that filler was a far stronger substance than today's more common substitute. Old-style filler, known as body solder, consists of an alloy of lead and tin and has the effect of strengthening repairs, unlike plastic filler which simply sits on top of them.

Most people have seen molten electrical solder and will know that it runs as freely as water. How then can body solder be persuaded to stay on vertical surfaces without simply running in an expensive stream onto the floor? The answer lies in the properties which tin and lead develop once they are alloyed together. Tin has a melting point of 450°F (232°C) and lead melts at 620°F (377°C). Whenever tin and lead are mixed together, however, the melting point of the resulting alloy is considerably lower than that of lead. Also, body solder, having a combination of 30% tin and 70% lead (and thus commonly known as 30/70 solder) has the remarkable property of going into a plastic almost putty-like, state at around 360°F (180°C) and staying like that right up to a temperature of around 500°F (260°C) at which temperature it turns to a liquid.

This means that body solder can be apread around like butter if it is kept within this temperature range, but of course, there is rather more to it than that ...

Where to Body Solder

There's no doubt that body solder is greatly superior to plastic filler in many respects though its advantages are often exaggerated. Plastic filler has earned some of its bad reputation for the paradoxical reason that it is so good! It can be used over any surface and so it's frequently used to patch rusty holes which, of course, break right through again. Body solder can't be used in this way. When plastic filler is used over totally sound metal however, it has excellent qualities. So, unless you are an out and out traditionalist, you will probably want to use body solder only in those places where it will do most good. The joint between two panels is one ideal place because the solder will run into the joint and both strengthen it and – more importantly – help to seal it against further corrosion. Another perfect place is where steel has become pitted on one side through corrosion, without

having broken through. Here, the corrosion is sandblasted clear then the pitted area built up with body solder. A third area which is perfect for the use of the material is where a corner of a bonnet, or some other small projection, is completely missing. Again the area has to be completely cleared of any corrosion and this time a great deal of solder has to be used in one spot in order to build up sufficient material.

It has been emphasised several times already that the surface of the steel has to be thoroughly cleaned before soldering. This is because the solder will just not stick to steel that is not both chemically and physically clean. One of the strengths of solder is that it combines *chemically* with the surface of the steel, while plastic filler just sticks on top. If any contamination is left, it forms a barrier which prevents the process taking place.

How to Body Solder

BS1. On the left are shown a few sticks of 30/70 solder, next is a pot of solder paint and a brush. On the right is a stainless steel spatula used for spreading the solder while in between is the booklet supplied by the small UK firm, Radlen Body Products, which supplied all of the items shown here as a complete kit. Each of the materials shown can be purchased individually from paint factors and a spatula could be made from a piece of smooth wood. Since tin became one of the world's semi-precious metals, body solder has become expensive.

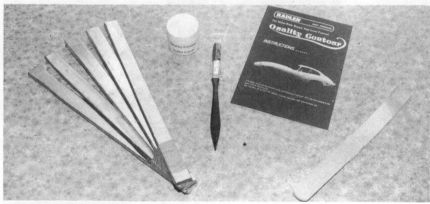

BS2. This is an ideal place for the use of body solder. Here a classic car's wing has been repaired using three separate repair sections. One is a replacement wheel arch panel while the others complete the front and rear of the wing. Each panel was joined to the others via a 'step' in the adjoining panel so that there was a small overlap but the panels lay flush with one another. This left panels which lay beautifully flat and true but with joints that would be susceptible to corrosion in several years time, unless something was done about it.

BS3.   That something, at least as far as the outsides of the panel were concerned, was to lead load it. Before that could be done, the joint was thoroughly cleared of any of its protective paint with a spot sandblaster run from a standard compressor. This scoured out all of the paint right from inside the joint and also removed any traces of rust that might have developed. If no sandblaster is available, it is important to spend some time scraping and sanding every bit of corrosion out of the joint, otherwise the solder just won't take.

BS4.   The paint also was cleared off, about an inch or so back from the joint, using a medium grit sanding disc, sanding until all traces of paint were removed. Paint can also be removed by heating it until it curls and then scraping off while it is still soft. Either the welding torch can be used with a soft flame to remove the paint or a butane torch, the sort that is mounted on top of a disposable cartridge, could be used.

Quite often, when metal has been dented or rippled it is extremely difficult to sand all of the paint or corrosion off the surface. A useful tip is to take a sanding disc and cut it into a square or an octagon shape. Then the 'points' of the shape will reach down into the concave parts of the panel.

BS5.   Old-timers would 'tin' the surfaces of the steel before starting to load the solder. This has the effect of putting a thin coat of solder all over the surface onto which the solder can be built up. Steel does not have the same ideal affinity for solder as copper, for example, so the tinning process must be carried out thoroughly. The old-style way of doing it was to coat the surface of the steel in flux first of all. Flux is necessary to stop the surface of the steel going black as it oxidizes (reacts with the air); it melts at a lower temperature than solder, runs over the surface and keeps the air out long enough for the solder to flow over the steel and combine with it. Here, in the picture, you can see an alternative to flux and stick solder being used. Solder paint is being brushed onto the surface of the joint. This is simply flux in which powdered solder is held in suspension. Naturally it has to be stirred well before use because the solder grains tend to sink to the bottom, then it should be painted onto the surface fairly heavily.

BS6.   The next step is to play a flame over the solder paint until the solder 'flushes'. In other words, the solder has to be melted at which point it flows across the surface of the steel. The point at which this takes place should be fairly obvious because the dull matt grey of the solder paint will be replaced by the silvery gleam of fresh solder. A common mistake when carrying out this job for the first time, especially for those who are used to welding, is to apply too much heat too rapidly. The biggest risk comes when a welding torch is being used, simply because there is so much heat 'on tap'. If the metal is overheated, the flame will burn the flux away and oxidize (blacken) the surface of the steel before the solder has had a chance to melt. If you intend using a welding torch, choose a medium nozzle, have a 'soft' flame (oxygen turned down a little) and play the heat lightly over the job from a respectful distance, not up close such as when you are welding.

BS7. No matter how hard you try to clean the metal, there will almost certainly be some impurities left – so it's a good job that flux has a slight cleaning action to go with its ability to keep oxygen out. As a result, the flux throws up a small quantity of black waste onto the surface. This must be removed thoroughly before attempting to add any more body solder. The flux itself is water soluble and so it can be removed along with the waste by scrubbing it with a wet rag.

BS8. The next stage is just a little bit tricky to master and involves one of those sets of actions where you have to do and think about two different things at once. (After a while, of course, it becomes automatic – do you remember the first time you drove a car and how you seemed to have to do so much all at the same time?) The blowtorch has to be used to heat the panel over an area which covers no more than, say, the size of a playing card. At the same time, the solder has to be held on the edge of the flame so that it is being pre-heated, but not by enough to melt it. When, after a minute or two, you judge that the panel is hot enough, try pressing the end of the solder stick onto the joint. If everything is ready, the solder will become droopy and waxy and at the same time stick to the tinned surface of the steel. You should now try to deposit 'dollops' of solder at close, regular intervals along the joint or across the surface of the panel. Don't even begin to think about making a smooth surface; all you are doing at this stage is heating the solder to its plastic stage (between 360 – 500° F; 180 – 260°C) and depositing the material onto the panel.

BS9. The next stage is the one where you smooth the solder out. Throughout this, and indeed throughout the previous stage, it is best to have a piece of steel on the floor beneath the area being soldered. You can waste an awful lot of the stuff, especially if you are inexperienced; as has been pointed out before, it's very expensive. When you have finished, collect together all the splash shaped scraps and store it. When you have enough, make up a mould from a piece of right-angled steel and blank the ends off with lumps of ordinary household glazing putty. Put the solder scraps into a discarded can and grip the edge with a self-grip wrench. Now heat the bottom of the can with the butane torch or with a **very** soft oxy-acetylene flame (keep it moving so as not to burn through the can) then, when the solder is melted pour into your mould. Hey presto, you've got a 'free' solder stick! And you'll be amazed at how much you can save!

The spreader (or paddle) used for spreading the solder can be stainless steel, although old-timers used hardwood paddles made of beech or boxwood which they kept smooth and burnished with oil. The beginner tends to get the paddle into the flame, so perhaps stainless is best – it doesn't burn. If you look at the range of temperatures between which solder is soft, it looks pretty wide, but in practice, the range seems narrow when you're actually holding the torch. Heat a blob of solder and hold the paddle close by. Periodically, remove the flame and press down on the solder with the paddle. At first the solder will start to move but in a rather crumbly way; heat it for a little longer and it will spread like butter on a summer's day. Heat it too far, however, and it will slip in a silvery stream onto the floor – a demoralising sight! Again, don't worry too much about having a smooth finish at this stage. Try for a consistent, even thickness which is slightly proud of the surface you want to finish up with.

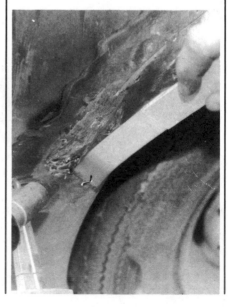

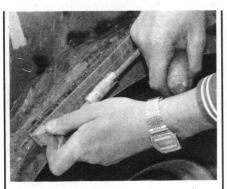

BS10. *The solder can be filed down using a body file, which is a single-cut file and thus one which resists clogging. It is easy to take off too much of the solder, especially if the file is new, because of the softness of the solder relative to the hardness of the surrounding steel. Professional body repairers often keep a semi-blunt file solely for filing body solder, just to prevent digging-in. An important safety point here is that body solder should never be removed with a power sander. The lead would become air-borne dust which could then be inhaled with HIGHLY INJURIOUS CONSEQUENCES! Filing should be done from all angles, working from the outside edges of the soldered patch if it is a large one, and working inwards. Long, smooth strokes should be used wherever there is room and just enough pressure should be used to prevent the file from skidding over the surface without touching. Final sanding of the solder should be carried out with 80 or 100 grit paper.*

Where the solder is found to be a little low, you have three options open. You can follow a risky, perfectionist's path and attempt to build up more solder; you can console yourself with the thought that the joint is sound and strong and finish off with a skin of plastic body filler or, if the depression is really shallow, you could follow the path of the old timers and use a skin of cellulose putty although really this is inferior to plastic filler with no real advantages.

Finally, a tip worth remembering in connection with the heat input involved. When applying body solder to a large, flattish panel such as a door skin for example, it is easy to cause heat buckling, especially if a wide area has to be covered. Buckling can easily be prevented by having a pail of water and a rag to hand and by soldering a small area at a time then quenching it with the rag afterwards. This restricts the flow of heat through the panel and shrinks the localised area back down to its original size, provided that it has not been expanded too far.

Soldering Aluminium

Aluminium can be soldered using ordinary 30/70 solder but it has to be prepared in a rather different way. It is possible to buy a special bar of solder which has to be used for tinning the aluminium first. The surface of the aluminium has to be thoroughly cleaned up first in the usual way and then the special tinning bar is melted onto the surface of the metal. Next, a slightly strange process has to be carried out. Whilst the tinned surface is kept molten, a sharp tool such as a scriber has to be scratched vigorously all over the area which has been tinned, reaching through the molten solder and scratching through the surface of the aluminium beneath. This has the effect of scratching away the outer layer of the aluminium while giving oxides no chance whatever to form and allowing the special tinning aluminium to combine with and key into the metal. From then on, the process is exactly the same as in using body solder on steel and exactly the same materials are used.

Body Fittings ●

Not unnaturally, car makers fit their trim and body fittings in such a way that often you can't readily see how they're fitted from the outside. But since it is really only possible to glue, clip, screw or bolt fittings in place, a little creative thinking usually shows how it's done. The following section shows some of the usual ways of holding body fittings in place.

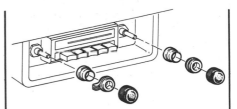

BF1. *Inside the car, most radios and radio/cassettes are removed after first easing off the knobs, bezels and other controls, then undoing the nut behind each control. (Courtesy Austin-Rover)*

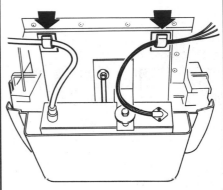

BF2. *Behind the dash there is almost always another mounting bracket. The aerial/antenna wire plugs into the set but the feed and speaker wires will have to be disconnected either at source or at their first junction. (Courtesy Austin-Rover)*

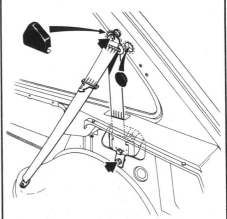

BF3. *Where inertia reel seat belts are fitted, they are bolted to a sturdy mounting, often behind a trim panel. High-up brackets are usually covered in a clip-on cover. When unbolting, be certain to keep track of the sequence of all spacer washers otherwise any swivelling movement in the bracket will be lost. (Courtesy Austin-Rover)*

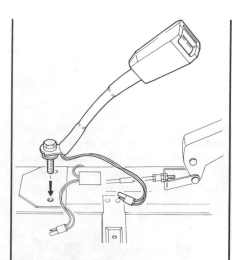

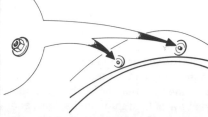

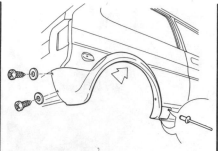

BF4.   Floor mountings are straightforward but, this time, the wiring for the seat belt warning light also has to be uncoupled. (Courtesy Austin-Rover)

BF7.   Sometimes, threaded screws are built into parts which are then held into place with plastic nuts. They have built-in washers which cannot be separated from the nut. (Courtesy Austin-Rover)

BF9.   Here self-tapping screws hold the rear of this wheelarch flare while the front is pop-riveted into place. To remove them, it is necessary to drill the head off (taking care not to allow the drill to bite into the plastic) and fit new pop-rivets when refitting. (Courtesy Austin-Rover)

BF5.   External fittings can be held on by a variety of means. The extensive grille components from this model of Chevrolet are held on with a mixture of hex-head and screwdriver head coarse-thread screws. ➡

BF8.   This VW Golf/Rabbit wheelarch shield is held on in this way. The nuts are simply spannered off in the normal way.

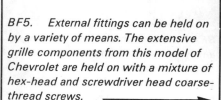

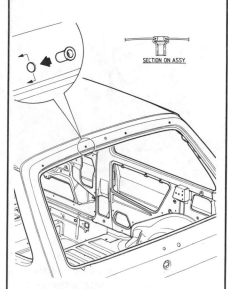

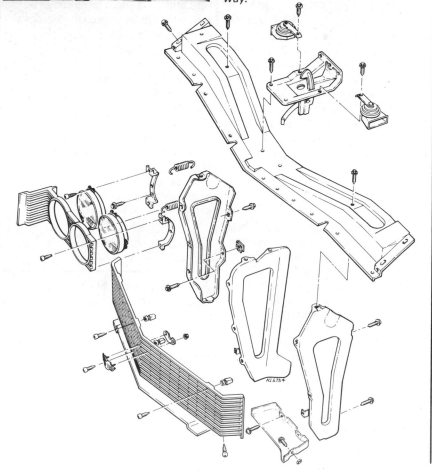

BF6.   A Metro tailgate spoiler is held on with screws which screw into plastic anchor nuts which are pushed into pre-stamped holes. (Courtesy Austin-Rover)

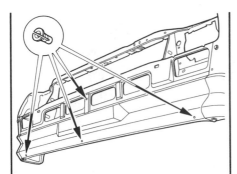

BF10. Where self-tapping screws are used, Locut nuts are pressed into ready-cut holes, or, on some applications, special spring clips are fitted into which the screw is fed. (Courtesy Austin-Rover)

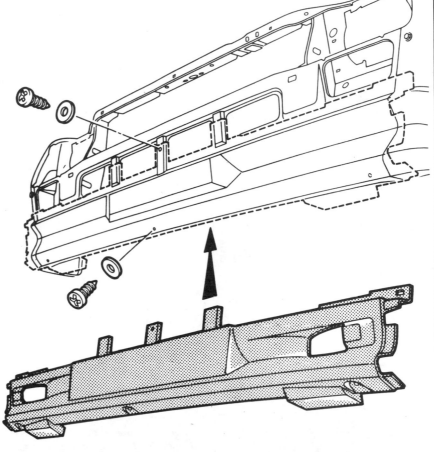

BF11. In this case, the Locut nuts enable a front spoiler to be fitted without the risk of the self-tapping screws cutting into the body and causing corrosion. →

BF12. Almost all trim strips clip down onto special clips. Remove them by carefully prising up from beneath. The clips themselves usually fix in place with special pop-rivets, built into the clips. Buy them from the relevant main dealer.

BF13. Increasingly, badges are stuck on. Remove by pushing a thin-bladed scraper under and along the badge; don't try to prise the badge off.

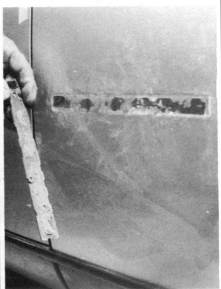

BF14. The sticking medium is usually a double-sided tape. Obtain some from your local friendly body shop rather than having to buy a complete roll.

BF15.   The old tape can then be scraped off the body ...

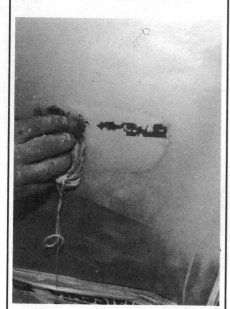

BF16.   ... before the sticky residue is removed with a spirit wipe or white spirit.

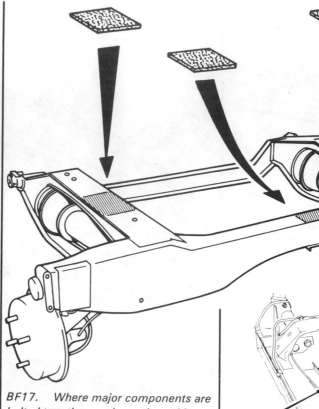

BF17.   Where major components are bolted together, such as where this Metro rear subframe fits against the body, or where some fuel tanks bolt tight against bodywork, be sure to use self-adhesive rubbing pads to prevent squeaks and groans from rubbing bodywork. (Courtesy Austin-Rover)

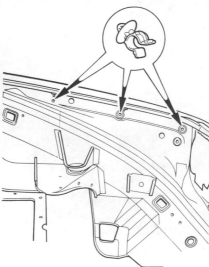

BF18.   Using the correct clips for wiring, fuel and brake pipes is essential for both neatness and safety. These plastic clips push straight into pre-drilled holes ...

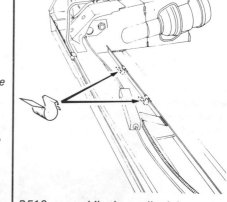

BF19.   ... while these clip tight over the edge of a panel. (Courtesy Austin-Rover)

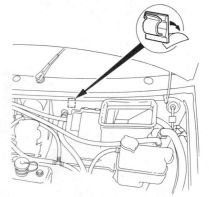

BF20.   Other clips are self-adhesive and these can be really useful when wiring in new components or where old clips are missing. Be sure to thoroughly degrease the mounting area with some kind of spirit wipe to ensure good adhesion. (Courtesy Austin-Rover)

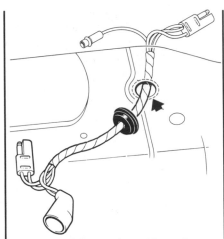

BF21. Whilst on the subject of wiring, always use and re-fit the correct grommets, especially to the bulkhead/firewall area. It is surprising how much in the way of fumes and noise they can keep out. (Courtesy Austin-Rover)

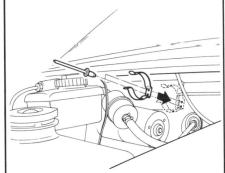

BF22. This fuel filter clip is held on with a couple of pop-rivets, direct to the bodywork. (Courtesy Austin-Rover)

Removing Stubborn Fixings ●

One of the most basic rules in carrying out any sort of dismantling work is to make a plan of action before the work actually commences. The reason for this is two-fold. First, it enables you to ensure that no unnecessary work is carried out – and just about every mechanic can tell of the time spent in dismantling a stubborn part only to find that it didn't need to come off at all! Secondly, it enables you to get plenty of releasing fluid on all the parts that are likely to be seized-up with rust, and heaven knows, on older cars there are

certainly enough of those! The most heavily rusted parts will come off a lot more willingly if they are soaked in releasing fluid on each of three days before the work is carried out.

One of the most versatile methods for the freeing of rust-seized nuts and bolts is to get some heat on the seized parts. This is one of those occasions where every enthusiast wishes he had an oxy-acetylene outfit but in fact the heat from the increasingly popular carbon-arc torch fitted to an arc-welder or even that available from a simple butane torch can make quite an amazing amount of difference. What happens is quite simple. The two parts which have been sitting in cosy proximity for so long that they have virtually welded themselves together with rust are made to move against each other by the action of the expansion of metal, thus helping to break down the bond between them. Also a nut will tend to expand making it a looser fit on the bolt so it is obviously sensible to remove said nut while it is still hot.

Of course, where a lot of heat is being applied safety precautions are of the greatest importance. Under no circumstances should parts situated near to a fuel tank be heated; that much is common sense. What is sometimes not realised, however, is that on more modern cars the fuel line itself is made from plastic which will easily melt and cause a nasty fire if heat should be accidentally played on it. Rubber bushes can also catch fire and·if one of those should burn you could end up with the awful situation where you find yourself in more trouble than you started with. Remember also to clear everything flammable from inside the car in the area to be heated and it is best to have a helper keeping an eye on things armed with a washing-up liquid bottle full of cold water ready to use as a fire extinguisher, just in case something you hadn't thought of, such as undershield or mastic, goes up in flames. Don't assume that a proper fire extinguisher can be dispensed with; always have one to hand when using any heat source.

Sometimes a really unfriendly nut is encountered; one which refuses to budge no matter how much

encouragement is applied. It is then best to cut your losses, admit defeat and remove the thing by less delicate means. Wherever possible the nut should be sawn off rather than chiselled off to avoid risk of damage caused by the action of chiselling. In picture RSF1 you can see the technique of sawing a nut by making a cut in its thinnest part which is parallel to the hole in the nut. By this means it is often possible to preserve the bolt intact and it can often mean less sawing than trying to go through the whole bolt. In any case, in trying to saw underneath the nut the saw usually encounters the spring washer which, being hardened steel, can't be sawn through with a hacksaw blade. However, where there is room to get under the nut, a hacksaw blade held in a pad-saw handle can often be used where there is insufficient room for an orthodox type of hacksaw. In practice, there is sometimes no room to wield a hacksaw of any sort and then a nut just has to be chiselled off. Where this is the case a hold should first be drilled down the nut (again parallel to its hole) before chiselling down (not across) the much weakened nut. Incidentally, chisels should always be ground sharp before use in this way, and it is better to use a relatively heavy hammer (say a 2 pounder) and wield it lightly than to try using a light hammer heavily – the user loses a lot of control that way.

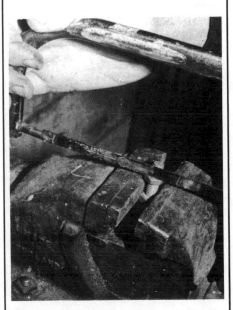

RSF1. Removing a nut by hacksawing across the thinnest part.

On occasions the nuts themselves cannot be reached or, as in the case of bumper bolts, it is virtually certain that the nut and bolt will be impossible to remove. (Bumper bolts are held in place by a squared portion of the shank of the bolt, just under the dome. This sits in a square hole punched into the bumper blade, which allows sufficient purchase for the bolt to be held firmly in place for the first couple of years of the car's life but thereafter there are nearly always problems in removing the nuts). After centre-punching the centre of the bolt head (do it well to break through the chrome plating) the head can be drilled off the bolt allowing simple removal of the bumper.

Coach bolts, which are used in bolting bodywork to woodwork, are virtually the same shape as bumper bolts. The process is older than cars themselves (hence the name) but was still being used in volume production as late as 1971 on the Morris 1000 Traveller. Unfortunately, coach bolts can be just as awkward as bumper bolts, usually simply turning in the wood when they are being untightened instead of being held in place by the square on the shank. If they stand proud of the surface of the wood it is sometimes possible to saw a screwdriver slot on to the dome but if, as usually happens, the dome has sunk below the surface of the wood it will be necessary to remove the nut or the bolt head in one of the ways already described.

A more modern but no less problematic method of fixing bolt-on bodywork is by bolting into captive or caged nuts. In their struggle for freedom these nuts often bend their cage outwards as an attempt is made to undo the bolt, particularly if the threads are tight. When this happens the best solution is to chisel off the cage completely using a slim but sharp cold chisel. Then a spanner can be placed across the flats of the square nut to be found underneath and when the bolt is replaced it can be held with an orthodox type of nut held tight by a spanner.

There are occasions when all the 'trad' methods have been tried and there seems to be no way out. It is then that one of the various gadgets on the market can come in useful. One device which most people wonder how they ever managed without once they have got one, is the impact screwdriver. The impact screwdriver consists of a fat screwdriver body, like that shown in picture RSF2 inside which is a ratchet. The ratchet is operated by striking the end of the screwdriver with a hammer and can be adjusted to work in either direction, enabling it to work with either left or right hand threads and for either screwing or unscrewing. Before using an impact screwdriver it is essential to clean any rubbish out of the screw head, otherwise the point of the screwdriver will not seat properly and rounded screw heads could easily be the only result. With most models, it is also possible to substitute a $\frac{1}{2}''$ socket drive for the screwdriver tip, giving another weapon in the armoury against seized nuts.

A poor man's impact screwdriver can be made up for emergency use by selecting a screwdriver with an impact resistant handle, fixing a self-grip wrench to the upper end of the blade and while putting a slight rotational pressure on the wrench, tapping the end of the screwdriver firmly with a hammer.

RSF2. The indispensable impact driver set. (Courtesy Sykes-Pickavant)

Frequently nuts are rounded off by the application of the wrong size spanner or by the ravages of corrosion. A self-grip wrench can sometimes solve the problem. Obviously the nut is already ruined and so further damage is totally irrelevant. A pipe wrench (or Stillson wrench) will give even more grip since once it is properly adjusted it actually gets tighter and tighter as pressure is applied to it.

And don't forget that when a nut and bolt are scrap, you could always grind off the entire nut using a mini-grinder with grinding disc attached.

One gadget which should not be overlooked is that painful sounding old faithful, the nut splitter. This consists of a chisel point which is driven into the nut by tightening the bolt on the splitter. It is a very clean and effective way of removing a nut but it does have the disadvantage that it is not always possible to get the tool into a constricted space and in many cases, small nuts just won't reach far enough into the body of the splitter to enable it to do its job properly. Having said that, the nut splitter does such a good job when the circumstances are right for it that it is a tool well worth investing in.

What if all the above ideas have been to no avail and all that has happened is that the nut has gone 'free' as it has been turned. "It's coming off at last!" you think, before the stud or bolt shears and drops on the floor. All too often the remains of a vital stud is left in place which has just **got** to come out. It is here that a good stud extractor will prove its worth. The extractor takes the form of a tapered rod with spiral fluting with a left hand 'thread'. To use a stud extractor a hole has first to be drilled in the end of the stud before the extractor is inserted and turned in an anti-clockwise direction. When inserted into the pre-drilled hole and rotated until it can go no further it should — you hope — turn the stud itself. So much for the more obvious type of fixing. But what about trim such as door trim or chrome beading which snaps onto concealed fixings? Removal of this can all too often damage paintwork, bend the chrome plated strip or damage the door panel. Several tool makers make a tool especially for the job of removing such concealed fixings, which consists of a double pronged fork, rather like the claw on a claw hammer, which is extended into a handle.

Even when armed with the best gadgets that money can buy, there can be no universal way of freeing stubborn fixings. The best ammunition is the sort of advice that has been presented here coupled with the most important ingredients of all — the ingenuity and common sense of the person working on the car. In a vicious combination, Murphy's Law (If a Thing Can Go Wrong – It Will Go Wrong) and Sodt's Codicil (– And In The Most Difficult Circumstances Possible) will always place ingenuity at a premium. And who knows, your ingenuity could lead to the invention of the gadget that everyone has been waiting for and a fortune for the inventor. After all, even Mr. Snap-On had to start somewhere.

Light Crash Repair – front end damage ∎

Phil's daughter passed her driving test first time and so pleased was he that he let her drive his little Talbot Samba. You could guess what happened the first time she took it out – and you'd be right. The only consolation was that the crash damage was light, no-one was hurt and Phil's girl learned another driving lesson the hard way. Here's how the damage was put right; it's a job that any keen amateur could tackle at home, even if the final spraying was left until last and the finish coat put on in a professional body shop.

CD1. The car was bumped as it went into a ditch and came up against a stump. Of course, the headlamp was broken and this was removed first. It was not thrown away at this stage because more than one make of unit was used on the Samba (as with most cars) and it made an unarguable reference when ordering parts over the counter of the local main dealer.

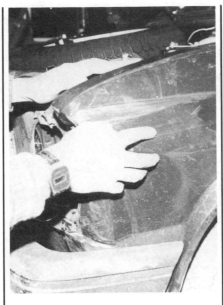

CD2. When the structural bodywork was examined it became clear that the wing was badly damaged and would need repair but fortunately the shock of the crash had not transmitted itself into any of the supporting panels. More modern cars are designed to be easier to repair than their predecessors and the Samba's bolt-on front wings are no exception.

CD3. The front bumper-cum-spoiler is designed to be flexible but it had all been a bit too much for this one which had shattered beyond repair.

CD4. The front bumper was taken off by undoing the four bolts (two of them arrowed) which lie behind the front panel and are accessed from beneath the front of the car.

CD5. The deep front panel (left) had torn away from the bottom of the wing but it was normally held in place by a couple of nuts and bolts passing vertically through both panel and wing. That is how the two new parts would have to be re-assembled of course.

CD6. The trim strip on the side of the wing would live to fight another day. It was removed by carefully prising it away from the panel with a flat-point screwdriver.

CD7. This is how it was held in place. The rear of the trim strip contained a pair of spring clips which pushed into the two corresponding holes in the wing panel. Most trim panels spring or pop off in this way, but some have bolts set into the trim panel and nuts – often plastic nuts – holding the trim panel in place. Carry out some investigation before trying to force a trim strip off and in any case take great care not to buckle or otherwise damage thin or delicate trim.

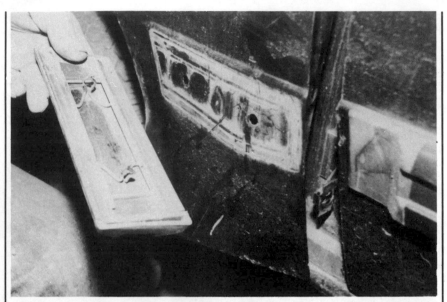

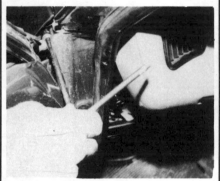

CD8. A couple of screws held the front wing in place where it fitted to the door pillar and were reached with the door open. A long cross-point screwdriver was used here along with a tommy bar for extra purchase.

CD10. The easiest bolts, in a line along the wing drain channel, were left until last, because these top bolts will support the wing from above while the lower ones are removed.

CD11. Finally, the damaged wing was lifted away and consigned to the scrap heap.

CD9. Underneath the arches, more screws (this time with hexagonal heads) were found holding the wing to the bulkhead. On anything but a new car, this area has to be thoroughly cleaned before the bolts can be seen and it is usually necessary to apply releasing fluid and heat (after stripping out the adjacent interior trim) before a screw at this point will begin to move from its corrosion 'cement'.

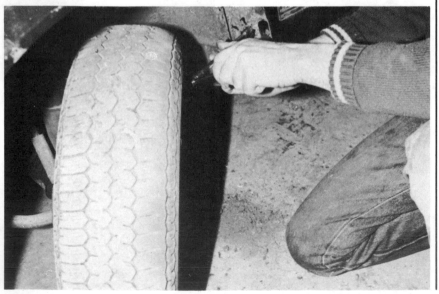

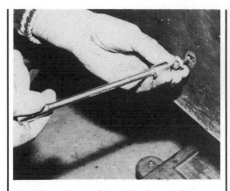

CD12.   Apart from the four bolts linking the front panel to the front wings, the only other fastenings were easily visible with the bumper/spoiler removed. The front panel also joined the old wing on the scrap heap. The home body-repairer might have considered spending the time and effort necessary to salvage this part by strengthening it out, but on a commercial exercise such as this, it's just not worth while because the cost of the time spent would have exceeded the cost of the new panel.

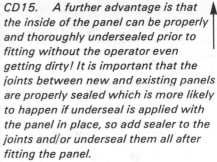

CD15.   A further advantage is that the inside of the panel can be properly and thoroughly undersealed prior to fitting without the operator even getting dirty! It is important that the joints between new and existing panels are properly sealed which is more likely to happen if underseal is applied with the panel in place, so add sealer to the joints and/or underseal them all after fitting the panel.

CD13.   The new front panel and wing were prepared whilst off the car. This is a real advantage of bolt-on parts compared with weld-on panels. Weld-on panels can't be painted until they have been fitted because the welding would simply burn the paint off again.

CD14.   Bolt-on panels can not only be prepared in a convenient position, but all their 'hidden' surfaces can be properly painted and protected as well, helping to prevent corrosion from getting a hold along the metal-to-metal joints where it particularly flourishes.

CD16.   Next, the new front panel was fitted into place (reversing the removal sequence) ...

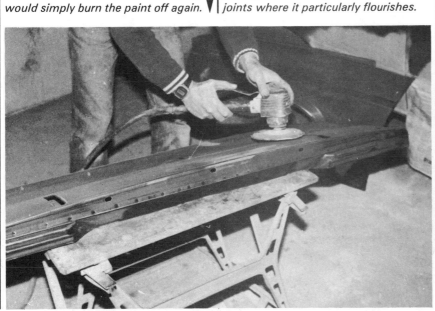

CD17.   ... and the new wing fitted up to it. All the screws and bolts were fitted into place but at this stage none were tightened fully to allow for adjustment. Also, if you tighten the first bolts to go in, later ones can prove difficult to fit into place.

CD18.   Unfortunately Talbot, in their infinite wisdom, did not see fit to include the holes for fixing the trim in the panel they supplied. (Perhaps it also suited a more down-market version of the car with no trim strip). The positions of the holes on the old panel were measured ...

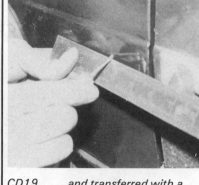

CD19.   ... and transferred with a scriber to the exactly identical position on the new panel.

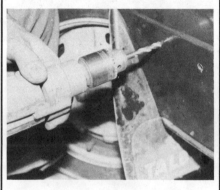

CD20.   The new holes were drilled and then painted for protection from rust. If you have any doubts about the drill slipping when carrying out this job, try sticking some masking tape over the place being drilled and rotate the chuck and drill bit a few times by hand to make a tiny 'start' to the drill cut.

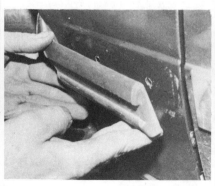

CD21.   The trim was replaced simply by holding the trim in place and banging the trim clips into their holes with the flat of the hand.

CD22.   The front bumper was fitted up and then the business of closing door and bonnet and checking all round for a good, even fit carried out. Sometimes it is not possible to attain an absolutely perfect fit without drastic panel surgery, but a compromise fit where a not-quite perfect alignment is shared out between the various adjacent panels is usually quite acceptable. For instance, if the wing-to-bonnet fit is perfect against the established right-hand wing but too wide against the new left-hand wing (in this case, they were both right straight away), try slackening the bonnet fixing screws off a little and sharing the available gap equally between both sides. Sometimes it is even necessary to lever the whole bonnet hinges over a little if no more adjustment is available.

CD23.   The new sidelamp was held in place by a retaining bracket which was held in place by a self-tapping screw which passed through the front panel from behind it.

CD24. *Fitting the new unit itself and the lense was easy and the wires were reconnected to the colour coded connections behind the lamp unit.* →

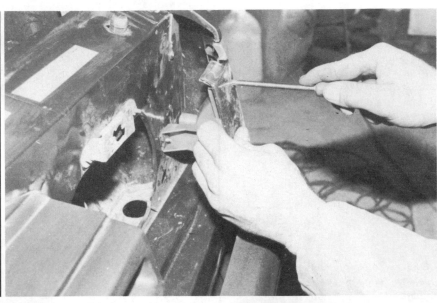

CD25. *Phil also wanted another small bump put right at the same time as the rest of the repairs were carried out. One dent was behind one of the trim strips already described. There was no access to the rear of the panel and so a puller was improvised, held by a self-grip wrench ...*

CD28. *A little more damage was filled flat in the normal way. It wasn't necessary to remove the trim strip here but note how it is protected with a strip of masking tape.*

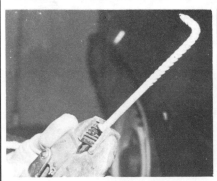

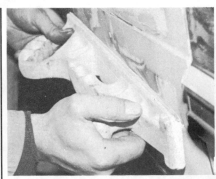

CD26. *... and made from nothing more glorious than a large bent nail. The holes used, of course, were the trim strip fixing holes.*

CD27. *Final imperfections were filled and flatted, as described elsewhere in this book.*

CD29. *The whole area was sprayed with primer/filler ...*

CD30.   ... and after careful flatting, the edges of the primer and the surrounding panel were compounded with T-cut to remove any haze from the surrounding panel and ensure a good colour match and also to achieve a very fine, invisible feather-edge to the extremities of the primer.

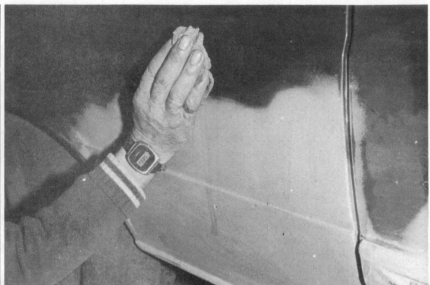

CD31.   You should always try to 'lose' the edge of a panel being repainted against a body feature of some kind. Here there was no handily placed trim strip only a body fluting which was too soft to hide the hard edge of new paint. A rather clever trick was used to soften the edge of the paint: a piece of masking tape was placed along the body flute in the normal way, and then another one was stuck along it but only held in by its top edge, most of the tape sticking out like a wavy paper ledge. When the panel was sprayed, this ledge had the effect of bouncing air and paint particles back down the panel and away from the edge of the masking tape and so softening the line. (Of course, the spray was not directed hard at it). When the tape was removed and the panel compounded with T-cut, the edge of the repair was absolutely invisible.

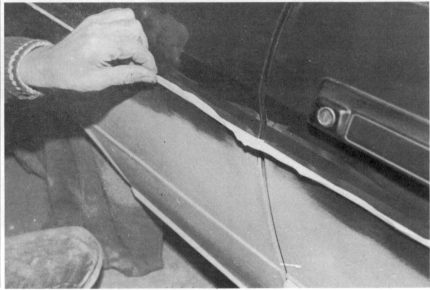

CD32.   The finished job, and you wouldn't know that the car had ever had a bump in its life. Which was, of course, the aim of the exercise!

Light Crash Repair – side damage ■

It really doesn't take much of an impact to knock the bodywork on your car quite badly. A good scrape down the side panel hurts the pride and the ego far more than the basic structure of the car, but it still costs a lot to have it repaired for all that. Changing a door skin, knocking out a few dents and

changing a sill are all within the scope
of the careful amateur who has bought
or can hire simple welding equipment.
Anything from a Welding Centre
portable welding kit or an SIP arc
welder with brazing attachment
through to a full MIG welder would be
suitable for this sort of job. The work
here was carried out by CARS Ltd of
Stourport, England.

*LSD1.   Front and rear wings were
both badly scraped and a little dented
in this crash and the door panel
knocked about. Although the sill can
hardly be seen in this shot, it was
damaged too, and the impact had
shown up some underlying corrosion.*

Damage to body panels can be
classified as either direct damage or
indirect damage. Direct damage is the
damage caused by direct impact while
indirect damage is the result of the
damaging force being transmitted
through the surrounding areas. The
metal is bent beyond its elastic limit
and the result is a series of valleys or
buckles. In nearly every case a repair
should be carried out as the reverse of
the original damage. In other words,
indirect damage should be repaired
first and the correcting force should
lead inwards to the source of the most
immediate direct damage, or the place
where the impact first took place. If
corrective work is to be carried out
properly, the rear of the panel should
be cleaned of any sound deadeners,
underseal or road dirt, so that tools can
be used on clean metal.

*LSD2.   Here the impact to the front
wing can be seen to have created a vee
corrugation which extends to the door
panel. Note how this distortion has
created further distortion in the wing
fit, as the panel has been pulled past its
elasticity limit.*

*LSD3.   At the rear, most of the
damage has been confined to the door
panel which has been both scraped
and rippled but the line of the rear wing
where it lies adjacent to the sill has
also distorted.*

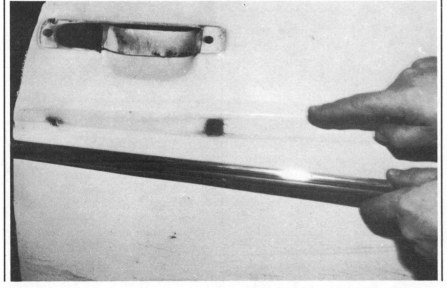

*LSD4.   Before commencing any
remedial work, fittings which get in the
way such as bumpers and trim should
be removed. In this case, the car had
shed its side strip in the collision, but
the way to remove it is to prise it from
its square fixing strip with a flat-blade
screwdriver, taking care not to damage
the trim strip.*

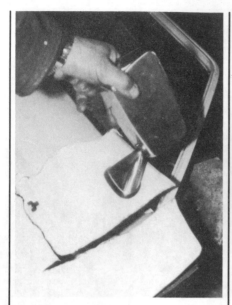

LSD5.   New door skins are usually cheap and relatively quick to replace so an early decision was taken not to attempt to repair the door panel but to replace it. The door mirror was to be re-used so it was cut away with its surrounding metal before work commenced on the door but after removing it from the car.

LSD7.   The door skin was removed by grinding the outer edge of the door skin away ar 45° and by using a hacksaw where the skin was welded into place at the top.

LSD9.   The old skin now lifted off as a simple, flat sheet of steel. Note that the top of the skin was only lightly welded in place and that the flange was hooked over the adjacent part of the frame.

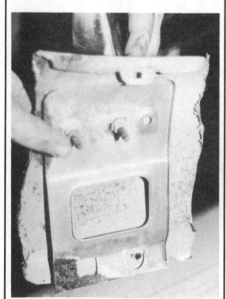

LSD6.   This clever move gave perfect access to what would otherwise have been half hidden nuts. In addition, it became a simple matter to apply releasing fluid and a little heat to ensure that the threaded studs did not shear off.

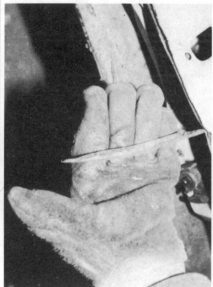

LSD8.   After grinding the edge away, the old flange, folded around the door frame, simply peeled away. Wear a pair of heavy industrial gloves for this job because the metal is razor sharp.

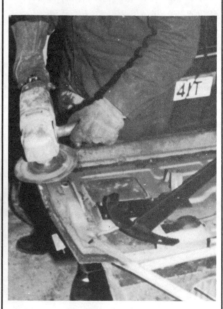

LSD10.   The steel inside the fold of the doorskin was covered in surface rust, which shows that where different pieces of metal are trapped close together and moisture is allowed to get in, rapid corrosion can take place. Wearing goggles, gloves and particle mask, the CARS body-man linished the edge of the door frame back to bright metal.

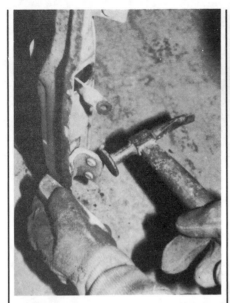

LSD11. The door frame was also distorted in the accident and this was dressed true with the hammer and dolly.

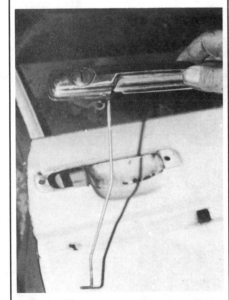

LSD12. Removal of the door handle and lock was also left until the door skin was removed, taking care to disconnect the linkage carefully as the skin was lifted away. Next, the door handle was transferred to the new door skin prior to fitting.

LSD13. The new door skin was placed face downwards on a protected raised surface and the door frame lowered onto it.

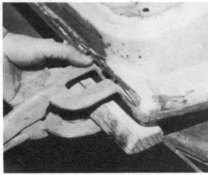

LSD14. The frame and skin were carefully clamped together, a piece of wood being used to protect the surface of the door skin from the marking effects of the clamp.

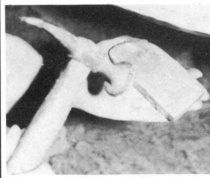

LSD15. A panel beater's hammer and flat dolly were then selected for turning over the raised flange of the new door skin.

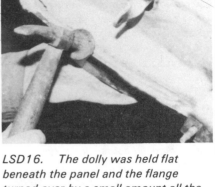

LSD16. The dolly was held flat beneath the panel and the flange turned over by a small amount all the way round. Then another 'circuit' of the flange was made, this time folding it almost flat.

LSD17. Finally the flange was hammered tight down with the cross-pein end of the hammer. Great care must be taken here not to hammer too heavily or with the hammer tilted and so mark the panel.

LSD18. An alternative way of turning a door skin flange over is to use a purpose built tool sold by Sykes-Pickavant. The flange is gripped between the jaws of the tool ...

LSD19.   ... and folded as far as it will go. Then the tool is reversed and the jaws used to crimp the flange tight. Many pros are very resistant to accepting something new (which is understandable if they are getting good results from tried and tested methods) but the Sykes-Pickavant tool could be especially useful to the amateur. It has a nylon pad on one of its jaws, but care still has to be taken in order to ensure that the outer face of the door skin is not marked. Of course, if the tyro should mark the panel through inexperience, it would easily be made flat again with plastic filler.

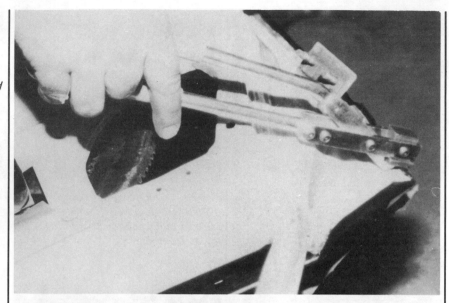

LSD20.   The next job is to re-fit the door so that its shape acts as a reference point for the surrounding areas. In any case, any tack welds that are to be applied to the door should not be made until the door has been re-fitted. Sometimes a re-skinned door can twist (or go 'out of wind' as woodworkers put it) and it can be easily twisted back again using brute force and ignorance before it is welded up.

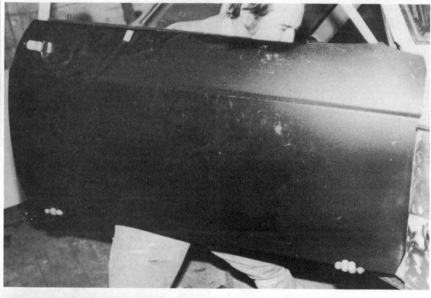

LSD21.   Before the front wing is repaired, it must be cleaned up with a power linishing tool (or lots of elbow grease!)

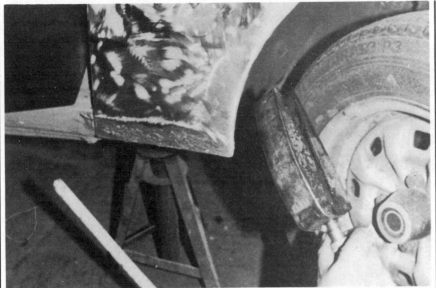

LSD22.   This crab's claw is in fact a hydraulic 'wedge' or 'spreader'. Pumped in the same way as a hydraulic jack, its purpose is to open up and spread panels apart; in this case the wing against the bulkhead footwell panel. The DIY repairer can use a combination of a squarely used hammer and a strategically placed lever, such as a tyre lever, used against a wooden pad to prevent it from causing more damage than it repairs. Remember always to work from the outside of a damaged area, inwards to the centre of the damage.

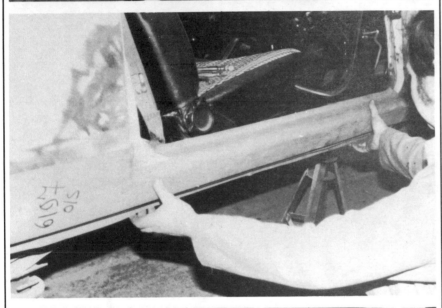

LSD23.   Next the replacement sill was held in place over the old one and used as a template to show where the old wing had to be cut off. Note that the car is held on axle stands in such a way that it won't distort when the sill — one of its major structural supports — is cut away. In any case, the door must be closed at regular intervals to check that no distortion is taking place.

LSD24.   The old sill was cut away with a chisel. The inner sill was found to be corroded, which just goes to show how salt-laden winter roads had affected the insides of a car that was then only a few years old. This area had to be plated and painted before fitting the new sill.

LSD25.   The new sill was clamped into place along its top flange with the inner sill. In a repair of this sort, the old sill flange is normally left in place, the new sill forming another slice to the sandwich. This seam can be seam welded along the top edge or the 'sandwich' can be spot welded together, provided that the surfaces are cleaned up first to make a good electrical contact.

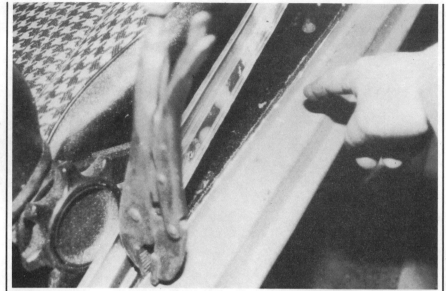

LSD26.   The glare of the SIP MIG welder obscures all sight of the nozzle as the sill is tack welded into a place at the rear wing. It is important that the sill be no more than tack welded before the door is closed and the fit examined closely. One huge advantage of MIG here is that little heat is generated relative to gas welding so that very little trim has to be stripped out and panel buckling is minimised. It is also a very great deal quicker.

LSD27.   The dents in the rear wing were mostly taken care of by the new sill and the slight marks that remained were flushed over with filler. When the finishing and spraying process was completed by CARS Ltd, the Escort was a car that its owner could once again be proud of.

Fitting a Replacement Bolt-on Wing ■

BW1.   Bolt-on wings are undoubtedly the easiest of body panels to change and many manufacturers have introduced them in recent years in recognition of that fact. Their reasoning is quite simple: lower repair costs. For the home repairer, bolt-on wings come easily within the realms of the possible but with one proviso. If the wings have corroded badly enough to require replacement, it is highly likely that the surfaces beneath the wing will have corroded in such a way that welding is necessary. Still, if you live close to a body repairer or you can find someone who will do the work on your premises, even if you can't do it yourself, replacing a bolt-on wing will still be straightforward in most cases.

BW3.   First step in removing a rotten bolt-on wing when the bolts are underneath it, is to chisel the wing away. Your instinct is to grovel beneath the wing, trying to find the securing bolts, but if it's to be scrapped anyway, why bother? Incidentally, bolts in this position are usually corroded solidly into place. See the Section on 'Removing Stubborn Fixings' for tips of their removal.

BW5.   Door pillars are always prone to corrosion because of their exposed position. Typically, the Morris Minor pillar rots out at its base. This one would have to be replaced before the new wing was fitted: see Section on 'Removing Stubborn Fixings' for details of replacing captive nuts.

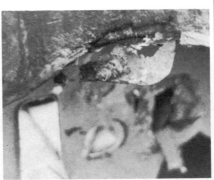

BW2.   When a wing has deteriorated to the point where the headlamp is held on with adhesive tape, something needs to be done! Be prepared to buy new headlamp bowls too. Feel behind the wing, crumble the built-up mud out of the way with your fingers and see if the headlamp backs are sound or holed.

BW4.   Most of the inner wing on this car was perfectly sound but the suspension bump stop was in need of welding: this is a typical fatigue spot on an older car with weak suspension.

BW6.   Behind this old wing, a very badly corroded headlamp bowl shows just how bad things can get! Replacement bowls come in plastic and steel varieties and are usually supplied without their fixtures and fittings so either be prepared to save all your old clips and screws or to pay a little more when buying.

BW7.   Having had to pay the cost of wing corrosion once, it would be the height of folly not to attempt to do something about making the new wings last a little longer. Here, the wing flange is being sprayed with aerosol, the back of the wing (at the bottom here) having been sprayed already.

BW8.   As a general rule, the areas most prone to rusting should be given the most thorough treatment. Look out for: welded seams, which trap moisture, and mud traps such as this one behind the headlamp bowls. Here, and in areas subject to 'machine-gunning' by road grit and water from the tyres, a heavier undersealant has been used. Don't expect underseal or rust inhibitor of any sort to last forever. Be prepared to clean the underside of the car and re-treat at least annually if you want to stand a chance of keeping rust at bay.

BS9.   As well as new front wings, new rear wings were also fitted to this car and they too are of the bolt-on variety. Here, a bead of seam sealer is being applied. Another has to go on the wing flange itself and the wing beading will be sandwiched between the two, like bread between two fillings. Incidentally, **do** remember to insert and line-up the beading before fitting the bolts; it can be very frustrating to have to take the wing off again because you have forgotten it.

BW10.   Before attempting the actual fitting, offer the wing up and see how it looks. Motor factor's wings (i.e. non-original equipment) can sometimes be a poor fit and may need some modification to make them fit. Even OE wings are not always perfect and may need bolt holes enlarging or moving a little. This is especially true of cars with long production runs where shapes may alter subtly as the factory replaces its tooling.

*BW11.   Don't fit any ancillaries until the wing is in place: the freer the access to those hidden nuts the better! Always clean out and lubricate captive nut threads before fitting the wing – the bolts go in so much more easily that way. **Don't** whatever you do tighten up any of the bolts until all are in place, so that there remains room for manoeuvring of the panel right up until the end.*

BW12.   This area is actually held by bolts that pass through the chrome trim on the Minor. For the purposes of alignment and location a couple of standard bolts are preferable.

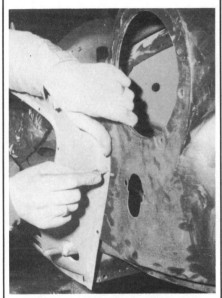

BW13.   Fitting the wing so that the wing-door gap is consistent is essential but it is equally important that the door opens and closes without fouling and with sufficient clearance that the build-up of paint on the panels will not cause paint rubbing or chipping later on.

BW14.   Where there is some degree of door hinge adjustment, the doors themselves can be brought into the game ...

BW15.   ... while the bonnet itself completes the external triangle of adjustments and compromises between the fit of the various panels and their gaps. At this stage, slightly uneven gaps always look far worse than when the panels have all been painted the same colour. Once the best compromise possible has been achieved, all the bolts can be finally 'nipped' up tight and the ancillaries fitted into place.

Removing and Fitting a Welded-on Wing ∎

This 1960 Mk. 1 Austin-Healey Sprite (known colloquially as the 'Frogeye' or 'Bugeye') was suffering from a severe state of corrosion in one of its rear wings. In many ways, the removal and principles involved are similar to those involved in fitting a replacement wing to a more modern car but there are significant differences worth pointing out here. The first problem is that classic cars very rarely have manufacturers' original panels available. (The exceptions to this rule are cars like the VW Beetle, the Mini and the MGB which had long production runs so that while the earlier examples are often fairly established as 'Classics', later panels can often be of use.) It is occasionally possible to pick up new panels for earlier cars from garages disposing of 'new-old' stock or from autojumbles, but you can't really bank on it. In the case of very rare and valuable cars, the only option open is to have wings specially built. This is a process beyond the scope of this book and is very skilled, labour-intensive and costly. Happily, however, more and more specialist suppliers are arranging to have panels produced in limited production runs while other manufacturers have gone into the business of making reproduction panels for a vast range of cars mainly to satisfy the demands of 'the trade'.

Wings produced by the former source are generally no-frills panels which may require some final detail work such as the cutting·out and positioning of light apertures, while the latter group, the repair panels, are often crude in a different way. They are usually made to fit over existing panels (in the case of sills and chassis members) or over the remnants of wings, for instance, but not back to the manufacturer's joint line. Built to provide a cheap method of cobbling cars together where the cost of OE (Original Equipment) panels would be too high, they can be an acceptable medium-term solution to accident or corrosion problems, but they frequently do nothing to overcome inherent corrosion.

However, the main point about fitting non-OE panels of any type is that they will inevitably require some tailoring to make them fit – read on for more details!

WW1.   All steel wings are held on around the wheelarch by the in-turned flange which matches that on the inner wing. The drill for removal is to grind away the corner of the flange so that inner and outer panels become separated. The flange of the outer wing can be removed later as a separate strip of metal.

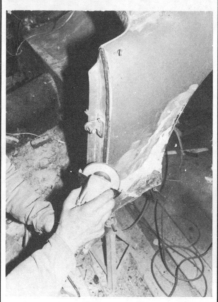

WW2.   Similarly, the edge of the door pillar has a flange which has to be ground away in the same way. If a rear wing is to be fitted to a saloon, a cut may well have to be made to separate the wing from the rear pillar. Carefully measure the replacement wing to determine where the cut is to be made and leave an overlap – it's easier to trim back later rather than to have to add on.

WW3.   There are a variety of ways of cutting sheet steel in these circumstances. Using a hare v. tortoise analogy, the Monodex cutter shown here is most definitely the tortoise; and it always gets there in the end! It's finger-achingly slow but it causes virtually no distortion whilst it carves a thin slot with its beak.

WW4.   Here a thin bladed bolster chisel is being used to cut 1 cm or so away from the joint of the old wing. Make sure that the chisel is sharpened regularly: sharp tools are safe tools and, also, a chisel that requires less thumping with the hammer can be positioned more accurately and causes less percussion damage to the surrounding areas.

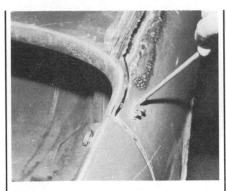

WW5.   It's too easy to overlook any fixtures and fittings, throw them away with the old wing and then find that they are irreplaceable. Take them off and store them safely in labelled plastic bags for easy reference, or leave them on the old wing which is retained until the job is finished.

WW7.   The 'gas' cutting torch is used by holding it in place like an ordinary welding torch then, when the steel melts, the torch is turned at a steep angle as shown, the oxygen trigger pressed and a stream of almost pure oxygen directed through the metal. This cuts the metal rather than burning it and is capable of doing so quite neatly.

WW9.   The remains of the inner wing were an ugly sight. This is one of the biggest and most typical problems encountered when working on a classic. Because of the car's special interest status it will probably have had its outer panels cobbled together many times just to keep it looking good, but because of its age, the inner panels are likely to have deteriorated most severely. Before the inner panels were repaired, the rest of the old outer wing was still in place and needed to be taken off.

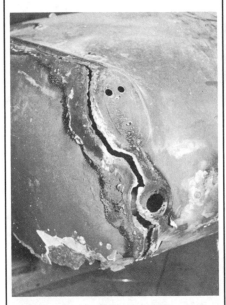

WW6.   At the rear of the wing things were looking a bit delicate and so, to prevent unnecessary damage, the oxy-acetylene cutting torch was used. Note that the base of the wing had corroded right out and so no cutting was needed there.

WW8.   As the old wing was lifted away the worst could be seen. Note that the edges of the old panel were razor sharp, especially where that had been ground away. It is always best to wear leather gloves when handling panels at this stage. Ray, one of The Classic Restoration Centre's panel beaters, whose hand is in the picture hates wearing gloves. But then they're **his** fingers.

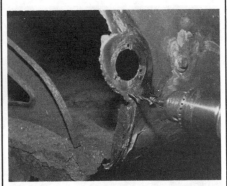

WW10.   The flange of the old wing, where it joined the two lamp mounting plates, had been spot-welded in place on the production line. The positions of the spot welds were found by linishing the surface of the steel, when they became apparent as small craters in the surface of the steel. The centre of each spot-weld was drilled out with a small drill. Sometimes the old flange comes straight off in this way but it usually needs to be helped off with a hammer and thin-bladed bolster chisel. If it seems to need a lot of bashing, you've probably missed some of the spot welds!

WW11.   We made a saw cut to separate the flange from the top of the top rear lamp plate. The point here is that every job is different and no prescribed pattern can be laid down for every job; you need commonsense and sometimes a little ingenuity as part of your tool box. But then, that's what makes restoration so interesting!

WW13.   A further flange was wrapped around the outer edge of the door pillar and this too was removed after simply drilling out the spots.

WW15.   The tapered box member, level with the boot floor at its top face, had totally disintegrated. It was a fairly complex shape and had to be tailored to fit the curve of the outer wing when it was fitted. The top and other surfaces were first made in card then transferred to steel. The base of the box was fitted up from the inside **after** the outer wing was fitted.

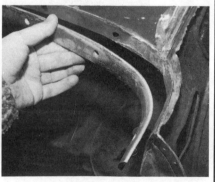

WW12.   The top of the wing was joined to the inner panel by a concealed, downward turning flange which is virtually impossible to get at with a drill with the wing in place. Between the two flanges was a strip of beading and this, being part of an arc-weld sandwich, had also to be drilled through.

WW14.   This trim strip was held on with a series of small nuts and bolts, most of which were easy to get at but one was virtually inaccessible with the wing in place. It was, of course, easy to remove with the wing taken off. It can often be easier to strip trim, mirrors and other fittings with the old wing taken off.

WW16.   To digress at this juncture: a less severely corroded wing could have been repaired with a repair panel such as this one. Many classic cars (and non-classic) no longer have full panels available for them, but smaller repair sections are often to be had. Enquire at your local factor if the car is modern; at your specialist supplier or car club if the car is a classic.

WW17. *Whether a repair panel or full panel is being used, the inner wing has to be repaired just the same. The easiest way to do so when no repair panel is available is to cut a piece of plywood around 1 cm thick into the same curve as the wheel arch. Then use the plywood as a former around which a strip of steel can be folded — grip the steel to the ply with a series of self-grip wrenches. Make the sections in a number of short length pieces; it's easier to fold, easier to fit and more economical with the steel sheet that way.*

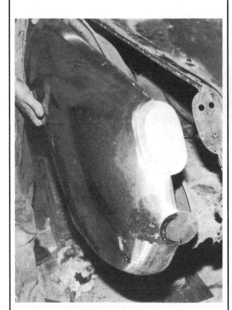

WW18. *With all the preparatory work out of the way, it's time to start fitting the wing. Offer it up and, unless it is a panel made by the original manufacturer, expect to have to carry out some tailoring.*

WW19. *Blank plates were fitted to this wing at the positions of the rear lamps. The original plates were perfectly OK and so the spot welds holding the new plates in place were drilled out and the plates removed. The original plates were already drilled for the correct fitting of the lamps of course; the new ones would have had to have been correctly drilled and filed out.*

WW20. *Holding the replacement wing in place can often require some ingenuity. Here a rack clamp and a pair of welding grips have been pressed into service. Self-tapping screws can be very useful for this purpose, especially if the wing is to go 'out' for its final welding into place.*

WW21. *Underneath, the reverse flange was gripped with standard self-grip wrenches. (The lamp is simply an owner's accessory.) This flange has to be welded up later, even though it is awkward to get at.*

WW22. *In the final stages of fitting, the wing was tacked a few times with braze, to hold it solidly into place prior to welding. The advantage of braze tacking is that the braze can later be softened with the welding torch and the panel moved around a little if that should become necessary.*

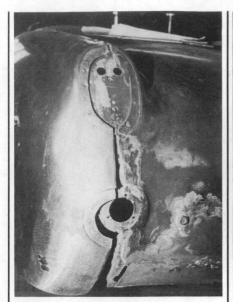

WW23.   Here is a typical problem with 'reproduction' panels: the bottom lamp aperture is set too low. The problem could only be overcome with a series of compromises. The braze at the top, rear was softened and the wing pushed up slightly. Then, with the wing held solidly at the top, it was carefully raised further with the jack, so increasing the curve at the wing top. Any deficiencies that remained were made up by lead loading the area around the lamp mounting. (See Section on 'Lead Loading' for details.)

WW24.   Another problem was encountered where the wing adjoined the sill. The front of the wing fitted perfectly but where it should have contacted the rearmost part of the sill it was simply too long.

WW25.   The solution was to cut a narrow 'vee' out of the wing, to close it up until it fitted perfectly and then to MIG weld the joint back up again before finishing the weld flat.

Renewing a Door Skin ■

Replacing a door skin is a job which can be tackled by the sort of person who is serious about getting to grips with the simpler principles of panel beating but who may have done very little in the past. It involves the use of few special tools but the transformation in the appearance and structural condition of the door can be dramatic.

Professional body shops will often fit a new door skin in preference to carrying out quite minor rust or accident damage repairs to a door. The reasoning is simply that because doors consist of large, flat panels, they are difficult to make 'true' and flat again, and door skins are basically so straightforward to fit.

Basically, a door's structure is made up in two parts. The inner part (the door frame) consists of a large, pressed steel dish with a lip around three sides. The outer part (the door skin) is a more or less flat section which is placed onto the frame and the outer edges folded round.

DS1.   Doors on older cars, such as this MGB, are often held to their hinges by three or four machine screws. They are often very tight and are best released with the aid of an impact screwdriver. Modern cars often have their hinges welded to the door and hinge post. In this case, the hinge pins holding the two halves of the hinge together must be drifted out. It is possible to make up a drift to knock the pin part of the way out then grip it with a self-grip wrench to complete the job. Hinge pin removal kits are available from good DIY motor factors.

DS2.   When you are ready to pull the door away, be prepared for its weight! This sports car door with all of its internals removed was not too bad, but a complete door from a medium sized 2-door car can be really quite heavy. It is not always necessary to strip out a door before reskinning it, but be sure to obtain new door weather seals and their clips because they attach to the skin itself.

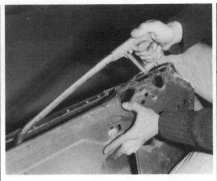

DS3.   Turn the door upside down and start to remove the skin. Rather than attempt to unfold the outer edge, simply grind through it, rather like slitting open the flap on an envelope. A coarse grit sanding disc mounted on a rubber pad will do the job perfectly. Remember to wear goggles!

DS5.   On the MGB, the only place where the door skin is welded is across the quarterlight area. Cut through the middle with a hacksaw or, alternatively, drill out the spot welds. Most doors have some sort of fixing point that is unique to that car. You'll just have to think it out!

DS7.   ... then cut out the corroded metal.

DS4.   Continue up each side of the door. The now redundant folded strip will peel itself away. Wear heavy gloves when handling it; it will be razor sharp! You may have to ease it away in places with the aid of a thin bladed chisel.

DS6.   Door bases are usually sound on newer cars. The surface is likely to be rust pitted however, so clean back to bare metal. If the base is corroded mark out the sound metal with chalk ..

*DS8.   Many cars have specialist-made door bottom repair kits already available. If not, you may have to fabricate such a repair yourself. Beware that cutting the frame about can cause the door to distort badly. Check the shape **very** carefully before welding the repair panel into place and only tack on a new door bottom after the skin has been lightly fitted and the whole door has been refitted to the car. Then, when you are sure that the door frame shape is still okay, weld in the repair.*

DS9.   This is the door skin and frame base repair panel for the MGB. This base panel includes both bottom corners which could be rather tricky to make up. If the door frame on your car is badly corroded and there are no repair panels available, it could be time to buy another door — even a repairable second-hand one.

DS10.   The repair panel is firmly clamped into place (or held with steel pop-rivets or self-tapping screws) and tacked, checked for fit, then welded onto the existing door frame.

DS11.   Whether you have repaired the door frame, or whether you have started with a sound one, now is the time to dress it to the right shape with accurately formed flanges.

DS12.   Now paint the inside of the door frame and the inside of the door skin, too. If you wish to use them, stick sound-deadening panels to the insides of the skin while it is so easily accessible.

DS13.   Place the door skin upon the floor, flanges uppermost. (NB Door skins are always supplied with the fold at 90°, ready to be completed by the fitter.) You may have to hook a lip on the top of the door skin over a corresponding shape on the door frame.

DS14.   The door frame is located on top and the whole assembly placed upon a wooden board. The upright flange should be tapped inwards a few degrees all the way round, ensuring that the door frame is snugly located down into the skin at the point where folding is taking place.

DS15.   The fold should be made a little at a time, going around the whole length of the flange several times until it is complete.

DS16.   The expert panel beater will use a hammer and dolly to make the fold really close. One way for the amateur to achieve a good fit without the risk of marking the panel is to finish off with a piece of wood as shown. Note how the door has been tipped so that the part being hammered is always in contact with the board beneath it.

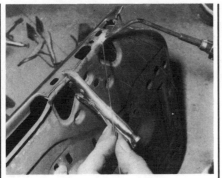

DS17. Most door skins are simply tack welded in two or three places. **Before** welding, fit the door onto the hinges and check it for fit. If it has twisted, pull it in the opposite direction until it lies true.

DS18. The repaired door can now be refitted to the car. If you have stripped the 'innards' out of the door, put them back in before you attempt to line the door up on its hinges. The weight of the door gear could easily make a difference to the fit of the door.

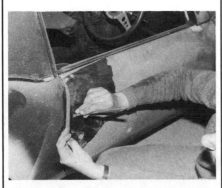

DS19. Many door skins are supplied without holes for door handles and locks. Here the author has cut the corner of the old door skin away in the place where the handle was fitted and he is using it as a template to mark out the exact location of the handle in the new skin.

Whenever possible, buy an original equipment door skin from the manufacturer rather than one from one of the many repair panel suppliers. The latter's panels are often poorly made and bear little more than a passing resemblance to the original! Skilled panel beaters can often make use of them (at the cost of considerable time) but the beginner should steer clear of them unless they are demonstrably of a good quality or unless there is no alternative.

Repairs Using a DIY Patch Panel ■

Rear valance/boot floor

Many modern cars can be repaired using one of the repair panels available from main agents or the specialist manufacturers of repair panels. Quite a lot of older cars only have a very limited range of 'patch panels' available while many have none at all. And even the panels that can be bought are sometimes frighteningly expensive especially for the more exotic breeds of motor car.

The following sequence shows how the rear valence and the rear of the boot floor were repaired, using a couple of Austin-Healey Mk. 1 'Frogeye' Sprites as subject cars. Obviously, this technique is suitable only where fairly simple curves are encountered but on older cars especially, that is often the case anyway.

DPP1. The rear corner of this 'Frogeye' Sprite had corroded really badly; so much so that the bottom couple of inches of the rear valence were missing. This area can often look this bad, although it is often concealed with body filler. The area beneath the number plate was a little tricky, having dished curves, and this was repaired first using a number of small hand-made repair sections.

DPP2. You really need plenty of access for this sort of work. The 'Frogeye' was supported on a pair of stable axle stands with a baulk of timber between axle stands and car to give firmer support and to spread the load. Note that the fuel tank has been removed. This is a **vital** step to take when welding in this area to prevent the very real risk of explosion.

DPP3. As always, the first task is to clean back to sound metal by linishing the panel and sanding out any filler that may be present. Wear goggles and a particle mask. Note that the disc is held so that the angle of rotation (clockwise, viewed from the spindle end) takes the disc downward across the edge of the panel. If linishing is carried out with the disc rotating upwards, it will tend to dig in and rip within a few seconds.

DPP4. The corroded areas were marked out with a straight edge and marking pen ...

DPP6. The inevitable rear end dings that were discovered beneath the filler were repaired with a hammer and with the dolly held against the rear of the panel. This area is normally inaccessible so it paid to take advantage of the access to be had with most of the valence out of the way.

DPP8. The rear of the boot floor had been cut away similarly on this car and, where repairs were needed, they were carried out at this stage.

DPP5. ... and the corrosion cut out with a pair of snips. It is always much easier, as well as much more successful, to repair back to a line that is straight and to where metal is free of corrosion.

DPP7. The tricky little repair sections around the number plate indentation were gas welded into place in order to achieve the flattest possible weld.

DPP9. The rear valence area on this car was corroded in a far more straightforward fashion. All the cutting away was completed and a flat piece of steel cut to shape and offered up behind the panel. Note how felt pen marks have been made upon the repair panel and upon the adjacent body area. This is so that the repair can be trimmed and held in exactly the same place each time it is offered up, to give a consistent frame of reference.

DPP10. The repair panel is shown here being held in place with a line of self-tapping screws. This is a useful technique for the DIY repairer who does not possess welding equipment or who does not trust his own welding. The job can be fully prepared and a professional welder brought in just to tie the job together.

DPP11.   Notice how the repair panel being fitted in the last shot has been pulled to the contour of the main panel. Another strip of steel is held in place here and the arch of the valence drawn onto it.

DPP13.   Then the end-to-end folding process is shown being continued, but this time the flange is being sharpened by hammering it over.

DPP15.   In an attempt to sharpen the fold still further, a wide bolster chisel was placed right into the corner and used as a light dolly. In addition, the chisel was given a few light taps into the corner of the fold.

DPP12.   The home repairer can produce excellent results given the simplest equipment, some ingenuity and a great deal of care. Here the curved flange on the boot repair panel is being started a piece at a time by being held in the vice while the steel is pushed over a little at a time by hand.

DPP14.   Smooth continuity of the flange was assured by holding the dolly against the inside edge. Beware! Too much hammering here, especially on the full face of the dolly, will stretch the metal.

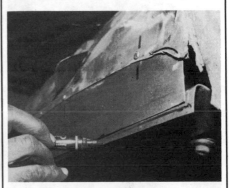

DPP16.   It would have been impossible to judge the depth of the flange exactly and so it was marked off from the depth of the new rear valence (which has not yet been welded into place). The best panel beaters are invariably pessimists and only weld things into place when they are **certain** that everything is going to go together properly.)

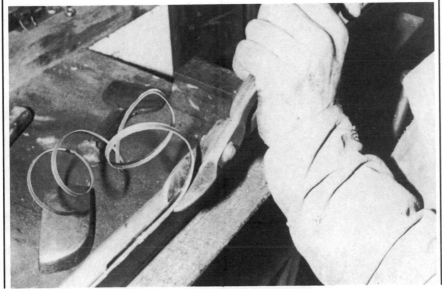

DPP17.   The easiest and safest way of trimming steel from a piece of metal such as this is to clamp it down securely. This piece was held between two pieces of angle iron held in the vice. The nearest end (out of shot) was held closed with a G-cramp.

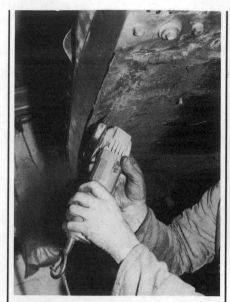

DPP18.   This shot shows one of the reasons just why easy access is so important. The surface of the boot floor was linished thoroughly back to bright, shiny metal.

DPP19.   A series of welding clamps was used to align the flanges properly (ordinary mole grips or even more self-tapping screws would have been fine).

DPP20.   The boot floor repair panel was clamped into place and tack welded to the boot floor using gas welding. The SIP MIG would have coped here but gas was chosen because it gives a flatter weld with less linishing back necessary on steel with some corrosion on its surface.

DPP21.   Ever cautious, the valence was first spot welded into place using the SIP MIG. Note that the boot repair flange now sits a little lower than was originally envisaged. It often happens that, as final fitting-up takes place, this kind of final adjustment must be carried out. It may not be 'text-book' in the strictest sense – but it **is** reality! The excess would later be trimmed off or, alternatively, a seam weld could be run down the edge of the outer panel and final trimming carried out later. The outer edges of the valence repair panel were later completed with smaller repair panels shaped to take account of the slightly different shape at this point and welded to the major panel.

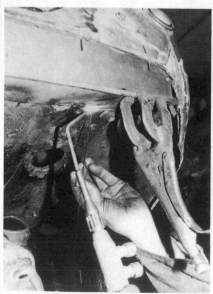

Front wing

The bottoms of wings are prime rot-spots and can quickly get to the point where filler is not a long-term disguise for the problem. Anyone who owns or can hire a welder can get over the problem by creating their own unsophisticated patch panel repair which is effective on straight panels as well as on simple curves.

DPP22.   The base of this wing had rotted badly and was easy to poke away with the inquisitive screwdriver. Filler could have been used here but the repair would have been strictly temporary and only a fraction as strong.

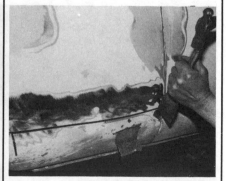

DPP23.   The bottom of the old wing was cut away with a thin bladed bolster chisel. The little flap cut out beforehand was a way of discovering what sort of condition the panel behind was in. It was sound.

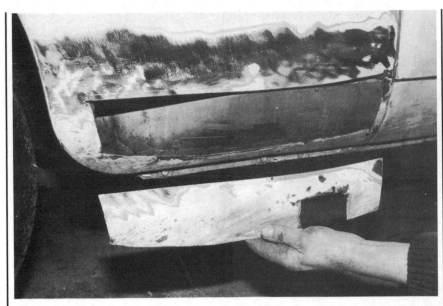

DPP24. The panel was cut out beyond the area of the rusty metal (there's no point leaving rotten metal in place to start off the rotten-apple-in-the-barrel process all over again) and all of the dirt and mud found behind the repair was cleaned out. If any rot had been found in the inner wing, that would have been repaired next.

DPP28. Then the panel was bent upwards so that it took on the curve of the base of the wing. The earlier shots will have shown that sufficient of the old wing was sound and in place to form the shape of the panel. Note that the paint had already been linished off the wing at the line where the patch panel was to be welded into place.

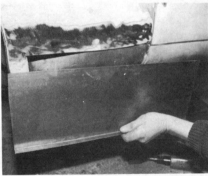

DPP26. A rectangular piece of steel was cut out ready to fit to the repair, complete with a flange made to fit the flange at the base of the wing.

DPP29. The SIP MIG welder was used to create a line of tack welds along the top of the patch, which were welded over later with a series of seam welds when the wing fit was found to be satisfactory. The excess metal at the front of the wing was carefully trimmed back to the wing line and welded up. All that remained was to flush over the joints with filler after first linishing the welds flat.

DPP25. It makes sense to hold back any future rusting as far as possible. All the enclosed surfaces were brushed over with Waxoyl corrosion inhibitor. If you were to use gas welding, it would be best to inject the fluid after completing the job, otherwise the highly flammable Waxoyl could cause a fire inside the box-section that could be very difficult to put out.

DPP27. Slots were cut in the flange, so that they fitted around the screws at the base of the wing, and the bottom flange clamped into place.

The conclusion was a wing repair that could be carried out easily by the home repairer and which would give far more long-lasting results than could be achieved by filler or fibreglass. The methods used may not have been as 'pure' as those practised by the best bodyshops, but there is no doubt that the outcome looked fine and would last easily as long as a professional beater's repair.

Bonnet/Front Damage Repair ■

MGB1.   The front of any car's bonnet is vulnerable to accident damage. In a big crash, there's usually nothing to do but replace the bonnet, but in the flyweight class of High Street butting, damage is usually slight. In the case of the MGB shown here, damage to the front bumper over-riders was rectified by slackening the over-rider bolts and repositioning them, and the grille was very easily pulled back to shape and a new badge was purchased.

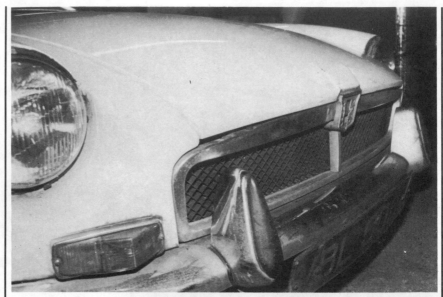

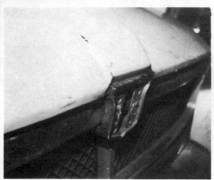

MGB2.   The bonnet had taken a punch right on the end of its hooter and looked just a little bit crumpled.

MGB3.   With the bonnet lifted and grille removed, the front panel could be seen to be just a little bit put back. Its leading edge was crinkled slightly, so this was straightened out using a flat dolly below and a hammer with a cross-pein above.

MGB4.   Sorting out a supporting structure first is always the best way of working. Once the front panel was finished, the bonnet itself could be sorted. It is important to establish that you are working with sound metal and so the paint around the damaged area was linished off back to bare metal. In this case, there was no filler clogging up the works.

MGB5.   The shape of the bonnet at this point was slightly curved and so a dolly with slightly less curve was held beneath the panel. Again the cross-pein hammer was used and the 'edge' of the hammer used in a series of sharp, accurate blows along the crest of the upwards kink. This had the dual effect of pushing the kink back down and also pushing the leading edge of the bonnet back where it belonged. It was important not to heat the kinked area because, although it would have made it easier to get rid of the ridge, the soft metal would have compressed into itself without pushing the front edge of the bonnet further forwards.

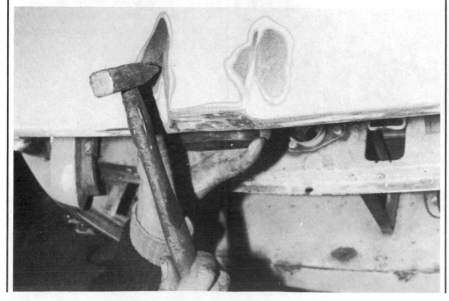

MGB6.   Any very slight ripples remaining can be lightly filed or flushed over with body filler. It then only remains to flat and finish, as detailed elsewhere in this book.

Front Wing Damage Repair ■

Cars like this Triumph TR7 with exotically shaped bodywork can be quite tricky to repair. In fact, when anything more than light damage is encountered, it makes sense to fit a whole new panel. The other complication with this particular car — and it applies to many vehicles nowadays — is that it was painted with a clear gloss coat of paint over a matt colour coat. Check by very lightly flatting with a fine grade wet-and-dry. If the colour you remove is the colour of the car, the finish is **not** clear-over-base; if it's a virtually colourless, perhaps milky colour, you know that you are flatting a clear coat.

FWR1.   You can pick out the high spots of dents and distortion best by lightly running the flat of your hand over it, like this. Use long strokes of the hand, keep it flat on the job and sense the hollows and high spots through the palm rather than the tips of the fingers.

FWR2.   It is virtually essential to have rear access in a case like this. Here, panelbeater Ken Wright finds a way in to the mainly enclosed area behind the wing.

FWR3.   He chooses a panel beating hammer with a general purpose head and a heavy spoon that will act as a dolly in this instance. (See 'Panel Beating' section for more information.)

FWR4.   Starting furthest away from the point of impact, Ken lightly taps the raised area while holding the spoon behind it. In one or two places where the panel is hollowed, he holds the hammer on the job and slaps inside with the spoon.

FWR5.   Then he works steadily forwards, towards the point of impact. It is vitally important not to hammer too much or the metal will stretch and you could be worse off than when you started. If the metal is stretched a little, it is better to leave it slightly low and bring the surface up with a thin skin of filler than to leave it too high.

FWR6.   In order to dress the flange, Ken chose one of the Sykes-Pickavant dollies with a shape to fit inside the wheel arch.

FWR7.   Then, with the dolly in place, he carefully beat the flange true ...

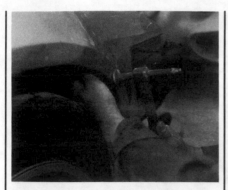

FWR8.   ... once again, working from the 'shock' damage which went through the panel, towards the point of impact.

FWR11.   With the general shape looking good, Ken could now go back and get rid of one or two areas of very light damage. He uses a cross-pein hammer here to tap out the raised 'vee' ...

FWR14.   He also masks off the surrounding trim areas.

FWR9.   In reality, you can often be wholly unconventional and yet achieve a better job. A slight kink in the flange is bent out with nothing more sophisticated than a pair of pincers.

FWR12.   ... and then, feeling that much more hammering could stretch the metal, which could take a lot more time to remedy (and perhaps more skill than most DIY-ers could muster), he looks for the couple of slightly raised areas that remain and dings them down.

FWR15.   He uses the angle grinder with 40 grit sanding disc to linish the paint off, defining the full area of the repair first. Sparks from this tool can embed themselves immovably in the glass, which is why it must be covered. It makes sense to keep the whole engine bay clean, too.

FWR10.   This can cause its own minor distortion and a couple of light taps are being used here to put matters to rights.

FWR13.   Next, he covers up the surrounding area, paying special attention to every scrap of exposed glass.

FWR16.   The whole repair area is linished back to bare metal ...

FWR17.   ... when (and this is the reality, not the textbook theory!) it is possible to discover any remaining high spots that you may not be happy with.

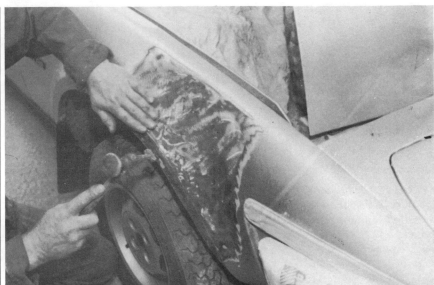

FWR18.   Now body filler has a bad name because of its use over rusty panels, but in this case, to bring the surface back smooth without hours and hours of work, it is perfectly acceptable. Indeed, for the amateur who can cause more problems than are solved by trying to take panel beating too far, the use of filler as a surfacing agent is highly desirable!

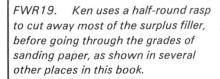

FWR19.   Ken uses a half-round rasp to cut away most of the surplus filler, before going through the grades of sanding paper, as shown in several other places in this book.

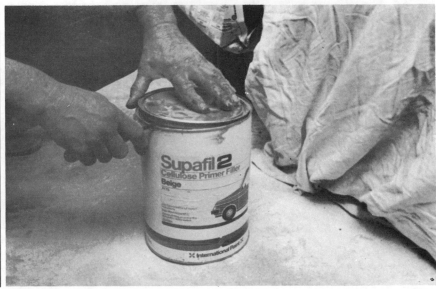

FWR20.   When he has the surface as level and smooth as he wants it, down to about 120 grit dry (400 grit wet-and-dry), he chooses a high-build primer-filler. Good quality primer-fillers are very worthwhile; cheaper ones don't give the depth to get rid of small imperfections. Don't use a poor quality thinner because it will show through in the final paint.

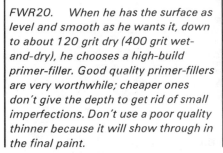

FWR21.   The primer-filler is sprayed on more heavily than finish paint, although sags and runs do take a long time to dry. The repaired area and a couple of inches of the old paint (pre-flatted) are 'blown' over.

FWR22.   When dry, a very light mist of finish paint is 'blown' over the primer and flatted, the contrast in colours showing up any minor imperfections.

FWR23.   The next job is to paint the panel with the base colour, starting with the inside of the wheelarch flange ...

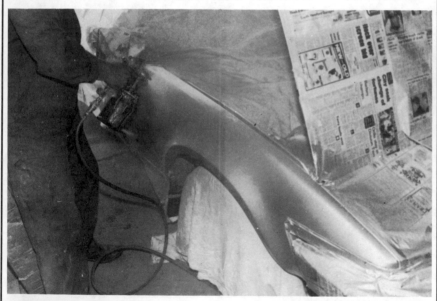

FWR24.   ... and going on to paint the whole panel in the normal way. Beware of any imperfections because they will show up right through the final coat.

FWR25.   The final coat is of clear paint and this brings the matt finish up to an incredible shine and also offers some protection. Be sure to use a cellulose base paint for both coats — there is a great deal of 2-pack clear-over-base available, but it is unsafe to spray it without using the correct protective breathing apparatus.

FWR26.   The finished result shows the car looking 'as new' again and indeed it is, with even the rust-proofing on the insides of the panel undamaged.
     (For details of how the '2-litre' badge was removed and replaced, see 'Body Fittings' section.)

Old-Timer Body Repairs ■

OT1. This early-1930s Austin with Swallow bodywork, belonging to Paul Skilleter, Managing Editor of Practical Classics *magazine, was beautifully built but ravaged by time. The rear wing, for instance, had rotted badly at its leading edge, near where it met the running board.*

OT2. Here, a repair patch has been made up, faithfully following the lines of the old wing, and the old rot has been cut away. Thicker steel can be used than on modern cars, to match the original, and that makes the job of welding so much easier.

OT3. Complex shapes such as these have to be produced on a piece of specialist equipment known as a wheeling machine. This work is really beyond the scope of the amateur ...

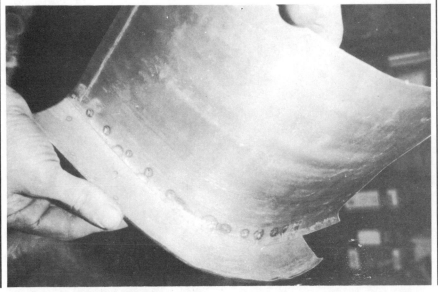

OT4. ... but there's no reason why you should not be able to find a specialist capable of making the sections, leaving you to jigsaw-piece them back together. This repair section was made in two pieces, then spot-welded together: a case of modern equipment making an old-fashioned job so much easier!

OT5.   One of the front wings had
gone right through where the tyre had
rubbed against the wing on full lock. A
piece was cut out with oxy-acetylene
and a new one made up and welded
straight in with butt-joints.

Adjustments – tips in fitting panels and doors ●

Bonnet

A1.   Correct adjustments start right
back here, when you're carrying out
major repairs to the car. When dealing
with a unitary or monocoque
construction, it is possible to weld
major structural components, such as
this MGB sill, in such a way that
distortion is locked into the body,
making it at best impossible to fit parts
correctly and at worst, making the car
unsafe.

A2.   The way to avoid this problem is
to build replacement body structures
around known datum points like doors,
and to support the body structure in
such a way that it cannot sag whilst old
structural members are being replaced.

A3. One of the most crucial gaps is that between the bonnet and wings. The catch at the front almost always has both up-and-down and (some) sideways adjustment, although the bonnet must be adjusted for side-to-side movement at the hinges.

A4. Adjusting a bonnet is best carried out by two people. Slacken the hinge nuts on both sides until the bonnet can **only just** be moved on its hinge adjustment. Bring the bonnet down and pull the panel one side or the other until the gap between it and the wings is the same on both sides and at the rear. Take care that the bonnet doesn't foul the firewall/bulkhead panel as it is lifted up.

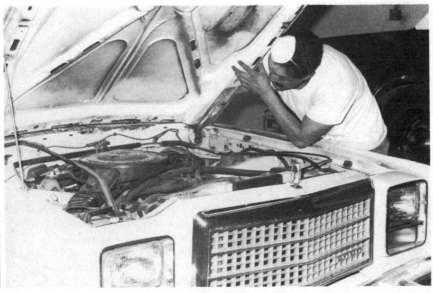

A5. If the bonnet is low at the rear, lift both sides up on the adjustment so that when it is closed both rear corners are too high. Then gently press each side down until the correct level is attained, reopen the bonnet and retighten. If any of the bump rubbers are missing from the inside of the wing rain channel, they should be replaced because they also help determine the correct position of the bonnet.

Wing

Many American cars have wings with adjustment brackets, which enables them to be moved around to give the best obtainable fit. However, many American and European cars' wings are welded on and there is, of course, nothing that can be done once they are in place, which makes it essential that they are fitted up around other panels, such as doors and bonnet in the first place. Bolt-on wings without special adjustments can be adjusted by filing out the holes through which the fixing bolts fit. It means that a great deal of time has to be spent putting on and taking off the panel until the fit is acceptable.

Doors

Doors generally have some adjustment built into the points where the hinges join the hinge pillar and the door itself. It is not possible, of course, to adjust welded-on door hinges. The position of the door striker plate is critical to the fit of a door, both in the up-down plane and as far as door protrusion is concerned. Never try to fit a door accurately without the sealing rubbers in place as they can make a large difference to the fit. The same procedure applies to the boot lid, too.

    If you come across a door which is twisted, so that when it is flush at, say, the top – rear, it is proud or low at the bottom – rear, you can usually twist it back quite easily, although the method sounds quite brutal! Place a block of wood between the door and the surface against which it closes, behind the rear corner where it is low. Shut the door against the wood and spring the high corner of the door inwards, taking the twist out of the door.

    If a welded-on door or one without front-end in-and-out adjustment is fitted and the leading edge is below the level of the wing, you can level it up in a similar way. Place the block of wood between the front edge of the door and the door pillar and push the door as if to close it. (Don't push too hard!). The leverage on the door will spring the front of the door outwards but because you can easily overdo it, do it a little at a time.

Trim

A6.   *Bumpers, grilles and the like should always be polished before refitting because it is easier to be thorough that way. Be prepared to open out fixing holes in grilles or to adjust bumper brackets so that the trim looks even and square-on.*

Second-hand Parts ●

Salvaging a Panel

It's not often that you might want to cut a good panel out of a scrap car, but there are occasions when they can be useful. One such occasion is when a panel is no longer available from a manufacturer, or perhaps it is only available as a complete, complex and expensive sub-assembly when all you want is a small part.

Owners of rare or classic cars may, in fact, not be strangers to the need to salvage what they can from spare parts. For this sequence the author can be seen using the small, handy but powerful welding set supplied by The Welding Centre.

SP1.   *This is the remains of a scrap Austin-Healey 'Frogeye' Mk1 Sprite bodyshell. The only panel worth having from it was the rear centre panel, the place where the boot goes on most cars. This type of panel has no value if you don't need it, but for the person who wanted this particular one, it was invaluable; how else could you obtain one for such an old car other than from a scrapped car? Before removing a scrap panel, note carefully how it is fitted to its surround parts. Obviously it is better to cut too much metal away rather than risk ruining a hard-to-find part.*

←

SP2.   *Here the Welding Centre's kit really comes into its own. It's so light and easy to carry that it can be taken to the most inaccessible car. Make certain that there is no fuel tank nor any other combustibles around before starting work. Here the author is cutting using a welding torch; it is possible if it's all you've got but it is slow. Start by melting a hole in the metal then turn the oxygen up a long way, when you will be able to cut after a fashion.*

SP3. The Welding Centre supply a cutter which fits onto the torch in place of the welding nozzle. See the appropriate section for more information on how to use a cutter.

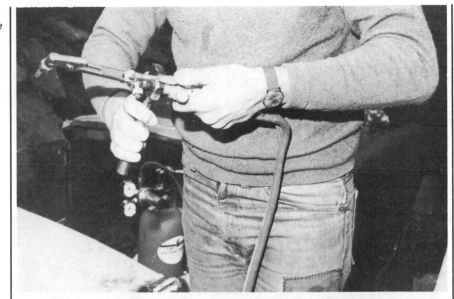

SP4. The only additional point to make regarding cutting technique is to tilt the flame in the direction you are travelling when cutting thin steel. This cut is being made about 1 inch (2cm) outside the flange holding the rear panel in place; in fact the wing is being cut through. The rear light housings were cut out complete; you can decide how much to trim off later.

Fitting a salvaged panel

Cars can corrode in some of the most ridiculous and unpredictable places! This Citroen Dyane was a very sound car in every area except its windscreen lower surround. There, corrosion had eaten right through the steel allowing torrents of water to come cascading into the car. One solution would have been to purchase a complete front panel from Citroen, but to let the whole panel in would have been an unnecessary extravagance and, in any case, the panel may not have included the dash top panel which was badly corroded. The answer chosen here was to visit a breaker's yard and find a Dyane with no corrosion in this area.

SP5. The whole rear panel is lifted away in one complete section. Although the rest of the car was a rotten hulk, this panel was sound at the base where they usually rot. Moral: just because your car has rotted in a certain place, don't assume that all the cars in the breaker's yard will have corroded in the same place. There can be remarkable differences between different cars, even those of the same model year.

The task proved simple as Dyanes rarely rot out in this area – and that's the whole point of this section. Cutting out a repair patch from a scrap car can save you a lot of money and you can also make sure that you get all the bits *you* need rather than the bits the manufacturer may have needed when the car was being produced.

*SP6.   The windscreen lower panel had rotted through to an alarming degree. The corrosion had not seemed to be anything like this bad until the windscreen had been taken out. It was well past patching with home made repair panels, or at least if it **had** been patched, the work involved would have been disproportionate to the value of the car.* ➜

SP8.   The repair patch was seated well down onto the panel it was to replace, and the outer edges scribed around carefully. The panel did not go down quite far enough but that didn't matter at this stage because the panel that was in its way was going to have to be cut out anyway.

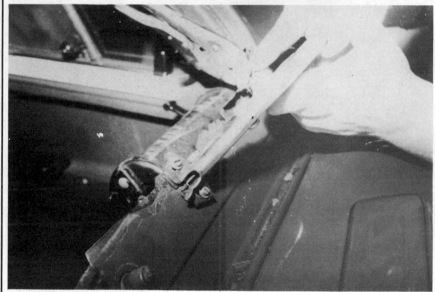

⬅

SP9.   The Monodex cutter was used to cut the unwanted metal away. Although slow in operation the Monodex was chosen because it distorted the thin steel hardly at all. Vertical cuts were simply made with a hacksaw. The metal was cut away about $\frac{1}{2}$ inch (1 cm) above the marked line to allow an overlap.

➜ *SP7.   This is the salvage panel removed from the scrap car. It had been cut out quite a lot bigger than it was required to be (see section on cutting out a salvage panel) and was then accurately cut back to a trim line (to disguise the welding) and to a width which suited the area of corrosion involved.*

SP10.   The panel was fitted first of all with a line of about 15 pop rivets and also by the windscreen wiper mechanism. This was to ensure that no movement and as little distortion as possible takes place. The panel was held in place by a series of short braze tacks; amply sufficient for this type of work where few structural loads are involved.

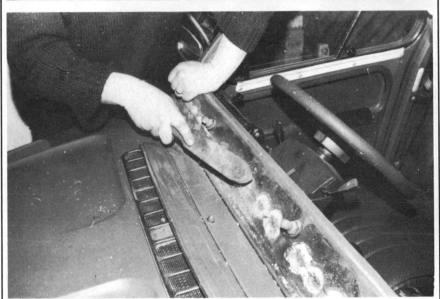

SP11.   Naturally, the paint in the surrounding area had burned off and this was thoroughly cleaned up with a wire brush. Special care had been taken not to ignite any of the wiring behind the dash; it had all been tucked away safely.

SP12.   In order to seal the gap off thoroughly and also to help prevent any filler from cracking, the joint was reinforced with fibreglass. First, a coat of resin was painted on ...

SP13.   ... then two layers of very fine glass fibre tissue was stippled into place. Ordinary glass fibre mat would have been too coarse and could have been difficult to restore to an even surface. Finally, the area was filled, finished and sprayed, as detailed elsewhere in this book.

Types of salvage panels

The cost of new body panels can be frightening, especially if you own an imported car. Even small items like bezels, badges and clips can knock a hefty hole in your pocket, but fortunately there is often a way out. Vehicle dismantlers do a roaring trade in good second-hand body panels and it's well worth visiting your local yard, or ringing round a few that are further afield to see what they have in stock. The shots in this section were taken at Rollie's Auto Wrecking Yard, Sun Valley, California, but the principles involved are the same wherever you live, with the few exceptions pointed out in the captions.

SP15.   Screens are shown stacked here with the model identification clearly chalked onto the glass.

SP16.   Complete front-ends in a unit are a US speciality. Check that the one you buy includes any hard-to-get trim and other details.

SP14.   Rollie's don't seem to throw anything away! Most yards seem to sell off the old engines, and other useless bits for scrap but when you find a yard that hangs onto its stuff, you can locate some real nuggets among the dross. Note the selection of grille panels hanging like trophies around the perimeter fence.

SP17.   Bumpers as far as the eye can see! They're often scuffed or slightly bent, so check carefully. Outside the sun belt, where corrosion isn't a problem, also check for corrosion at the rear and pitting through the chrome. Scrap-yard dirt can obscure such blemishes!

SP18.   Wings and doors are commonly damaged in a light accident and can cost an arm and a leg to replace new. In addition, brand new doors come as bare as a new born babe and can take a good deal of fitting up while second-hand doors usually have their gear intact! In rust-smitten climates, check carefully for rust in used panels.

SP19.   Sometimes a panel will have escaped rust for no apparent reason, sometimes a car will have been fitted with a new panel just a couple of years previously, while there are some cases where a small amount of welding will make a panel which is a great deal better than the one you have got – but be prepared to haggle with the dealer.

SP20.   The type of scrapyard where donor bodies are left lying around until everything useful has been transplanted from them can be useful for older-car owners where even some of the simpler bits and pieces can be hard to get hold of. It's especially useful when the yard owner groups cars of each type together such as at this yard, Stourport Car Dismantlers, Worcestershire, England.

Beautiful Wing Beading ∎

Several BMC/BL sports cars used a method of finishing off the joint at the tops of wings that looked attractive enough when new but which has proved to be prone to corrosion and to be the devil of a job to repair if done by the most obvious method. Here is a quicker and less traumatic method of beautifying wing beading, developed by the author. ⟶

The number of 'Frogeye' Sprites with front and rear wing tops flushed level with filler is testimony to the dilemma facing owners suffering from the problem of corroded wing beading. The problem lies in the nature of the stuff and the way it is held in place. Wing beading is made in a T-section, the top of the 'T' being the thin, rolled, fluted strip which you can see on the tops of MGB/GT and Spridget rear wings (as well as all round the 'Frogeye') whilst the upright is slotted down between the outer wing flange and that of the inner panel, as shown in Fig. BB1. The whole sandwich is spot welded together which means that the 'proper' method of replacing the beading – drilling out the spots, pulling out the beading, re-welding – is not on, because there is no room to get the drill into place. At the same time, the thrice-rolled beading is a perfect moisture trap, especially in its top hollow section and it does rust out.

BB1. *If the whole wing is being replaced as part of a restoration, beading replacement can be carried out at the same time. (Indeed, the beading comes attached to the wing on manufacturers' original panels). However, since it is usually just the beading top that corrodes it is possible to do something about replacing it without having to disturb the wing at all.* ⟶

BB2. *The old beading can easily be chiselled away with a sharp thin-bladed chisel leaving the upright part of the 'T' still sandwiched in place.*

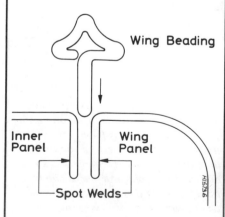

Wing Beading

Inner Panel

Wing Panel

Spot Welds

Figure BB1. This section through the wing beading and surrounding panels shows how they fit together!

BB3.   If the wing has been levelled over with filler it will, of course, be necessary to linish every scrap of filler away. The surfaces each side of the wing joint have to be thoroughly linished in any case, to give a strip of bright, clean metal, completely free of any paint or rust to a width of about 1 inch (2½cm) each side of the joint.

BB4.   If the joint itself looks a bit murky, you can clean it out by using a purpose-made cutting disc in the angle grinder. Be most careful not to jam or twist the disc or it could break up with very dangerous consequences.

BB5.   Another way of cleaning out the wing joint is to fit a small drill bit into the electric drill and use it like a milling cutter. You can expect to break a couple of drills in this way but at least it will churn out quite a lot of corrosion. If the gap between wing and inner panel has been spread open because of the pressures of rust, try to clear out all the corrosion and carefully pull the pieces back together from beneath with a welder's clamp before going on. Of course, if you manage to separate completely the wing and inner panel in this way, you could insert the new beading and braze it into place from beneath. Usually, though, it's not practicable.

BB6.   Where much of the inner strip is missing, it is a good idea to build the wing gap up with braze. This restores the strength to the joint and also gives a more level finish, ready for the subsequent stages.

BB7.   At the bottom is a strip of beading as it comes from specialist supplies, such as Spridgebits; at the top is the thin top section only which is needed for this job.

BB8.   With the tongue of the beading held in the vice, the top section is cut away with a hacksaw, the blade being turned 90° from its more usual position. (This is easy to achieve: slacken the wing nut, remove the blade, turn the blade holders, refit and retighten).

BB9.   The beading is going to be held in place with body solder which, although it combines reasonably well with a steel surface, does not have the close affinity to steel that it has with, say, copper. Thus, the surface of the joint is painted with solder paint, a mixture of liquid flux and solder grains held in suspension. Remember to stir really well first.

BB10.   The back of the beading strip has to be carefully de-greased and also coated with solder paint. Cleanliness is vitally important at this stage because solder **chemically combines** with the surface of the steel; it does not simply stick like glue. So, anything that acts as a barrier prevents the molecular connection from taking place.

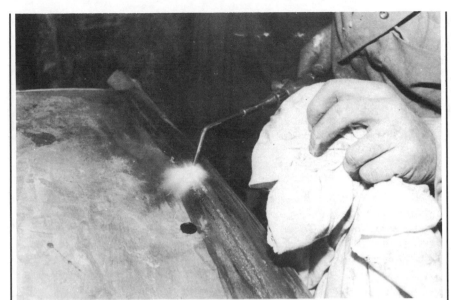

BB11. Using a soft (carbonising) flame on the welding torch, or even a simple butane gas torch (e.g. Ronson Variflame) the solder paint is heated until it 'flushes' into the characteristic silvery-white globules in a wash of brown flux. If using the welding torch, brush the flame lightly over the surface; don't concentrate on one spot as in welding.

BB12. After flushing the solder paint on the beading, start to solder the beading down. Either build up a goodish layer of body solder on and in the joint, place the beading on top and heat until the solder softens and they settle together or, starting at one end, heat the panel and feed in some solder rod in the conventional way. Several points must be noted here: 1) it is easy to apply too much heat, burn through solder and flux, and oxidise (blacken) the surface of the metal, preventing solder from 'taking'; 2) solder requires far less heat than braze (it softens at 180°C (360°F) and runs at 260°C (500°F) and so the flame should be used sparingly; 3) the panels will retain enough heat to keep the solder molten once they are warmed up, so feed solder into the heat of the panel, not the heat of the flame and have an assistant hold down the beading with a couple of pieces of wood until the solder 'freezes'.

BB13. There will invariably be a few gaps down the edge of the beading. If you're very brave, you will use more body solder (and risk detaching the beading). If you're like the author, you will use body filler, fingered into place.

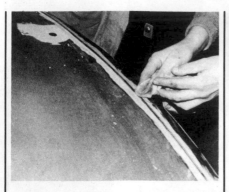

BB14. Having the beading fluting clear is a kind of hallmark of originality. Clean out any surplus filler with thinners on a rag before it sets.

BB15. A sharp edge can be restored by hard sanding using the edge of a piece of abrasive paper. Don't machine-sand at this stage; powered lead dust can be most harmful.

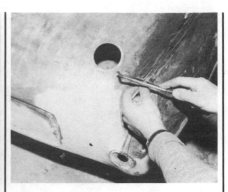

BB16. It only remains to cut the beading to the correct length using a junior hacksaw. Note the angle at which it is being used.

BB17. Then the 'flap' created by cutting at that angle can be hammered flat in the hope of keeping out a little corrosion-inducing moisture.

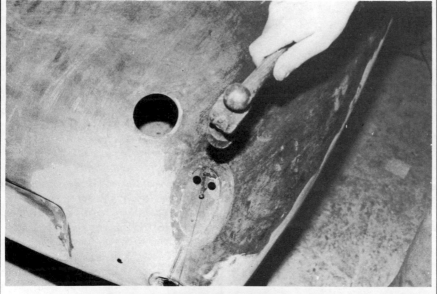

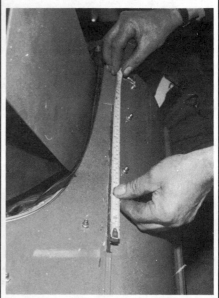

BB18. Sometimes, wing beading will deteriorate in one specific area such as beneath the hood seating on this MGB. Measure out the area to be removed and cut a piece of beading to match.

BB19. Cut the ends of the beading to be removed with a junior hacksaw to define their positions sharply. Then linish and clean off in the usual way.

BB20.   Simply let in the new piece using the technique shown. It is crucially important that the new beading is correctly aligned with the old. Remember that solder goes 'soft' at 180°C and doesn't melt until 260°C. Use that to advantage by softening the solder without melting it, then pushing the beading around until it lines up perfectly.

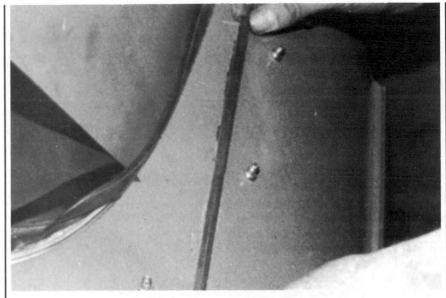

Blast Cleaning ●

Anyone who has spent hours of back-breaking rust-scraping would be delighted to find a way of getting back to shiny metal without any effort at all. There *is* a way and it's the most efficient method there is because it gets right down into rust pits and other crevices: blast cleaning is the answer. Blast cleaning is the use of compressed air to blast an abrasive at a chassis or bodywork to scour all the old rust and paint away. It's so efficient that you would swear the operator was blowing clean shiny metal **on**, rather than blasting the rubbish off!

There are five main types of blast cleaning, not all of which are suitable for motor car use.

Shot Blasting

Blasting with round steel balls is

suitable only for heavy industrial applications and is not suitable for any motor car work, being far too abrasive.

Dry Grit Blasting (pressurised supply)

With this method a large container of grit is usually used which is pressurised from a heavy-duty compressor. All 'mobile' blast cleaners use this method. The material used is grit rather than steel balls and there are various grades available. This method is ideal for chassis but is often too robust for thinner panels. The pressure can create ripples in the panel even when it does not blast straight through, unless a fine grade of grit is used at low pressure. A

lot depends on the user's expertise.

Clean off *all* underseal and grease because they absorb the force of the grit. They take ages to blast off – which costs you money – and before they are blasted away, the surrounding area could have been blasted through. Remove all brake and mechanical components and wiring and have the work carried out well away from the house or workshop – the grit seems to go everywhere, and it's the very last thing you want near anything mechanical. If anything is to be left in place which must not be blasted, cover it with many layers of PVC insulation tape and point it out to the operator.

Dry Grit Blasting (suction supply)

This is the sort of system which can be used by the DIY-er, but note all the earlier comments about dust and damage to certain components. Glass is easily etched by a blast cleaner.

BC1.   A small gun costs about the average price of a tyre but takes a large compressor to run it continuously. If you are prepared to wait for pressure to build up every few minutes, you should be able to use one with a 9 cu ft FAD compressor, (around 14 cu ft displacement.)

Dry Bead Blasting

This uses glass beads which remove paint and contamination without affecting the critical tolerances of parts being blasted. It is much slower than dry-grit and so more costly and a dry bead blasted surface can be rather 'spikey' and difficult to clean.

Vapour Bead Blasting

Although more expensive than dry-bead blasting, this is a superior system which gives the original 'polished' surface to aluminium items such as cylinder heads and gearbox casings. The glass beads are blasted on with pressurised water, which helps to close the grain of the surface of the aluminium and gives an even smoother finish.

Blast cleaning of any type will make it so much easier to work with elderly panels or components but, best of all, it chases corrosion out from every place it exists. But do entrust your work to a reputable firm. Once a part is blasted into extinction, it's gone for good!
(See the following Sections for photographs of a dry grit blaster in operation).

Chassis and Sub-frame Repair ■

Separate chassis and sub-frames

This is a brief story of an MGA chassis repair. Many older cars were built on a separate chassis to which the car's mechanics and body were hung. To repair them properly they have to be stripped down to the bare bones, which is, of course, a massive task. Detachable sub-frames, such as those on the BL Mini or 1100/1300 series, can be treated in a similar way to a full chassis, although the strip-out will require very much less work.

CRP1.   Having gone as far as to strip the thing down, there's only one way to get rid of all the rust, and that is to sandblast it. A 'mobile' sand blaster was called in, carrying the blaster unit and sand on the back of a truck and towing a very heavy-duty compressor.

CRP2.   Martin Griffiths, the fella doing the sandblasting could almost have passed for Neil Armstrong when dressed like this, which is some indication of the power of the blaster and the volumes of all-pervasive dust it gives off. Do it **well** away from a house or a workshop or any sort of machinery.

CRP3.   The blaster hosed rust off a treat, but didn't want to know about old undershield. To save a great deal of expensive sand-blasting time, always clean off all traces of undershield or other soft materials beforehand.

CRP4.   Back in the workshop, a system of sturdy axle stands and chains stretched down to hooks in the floor was used to hold the chassis rigidly. It was trued up in all directions with a spirit level.

CRP5.   Where a complete sidewall had rotted out, it was cut out and replaced whole, the jack pushing up lightly just to hold the member true.

CRP6.   A smaller area of rot was cut out with an oxy-acetylene cutting torch.

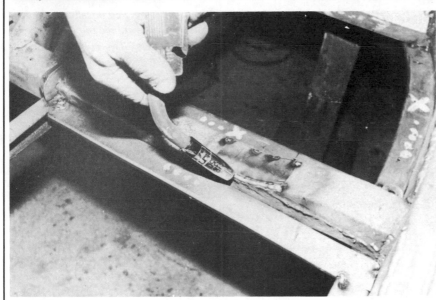

CRP7.   Then a plate was tacked down at one end, tapped down flat with a hammer ...

CRP8.   ... then after tack-welding all the way round, seam welded with the MIG.

CRP9.   The floor bearers had corroded into insignificance along with one or two other small brackets. They were fabricated, generally from a thinner steel than that required for the chassis itself, and welded into place. Dimensional accuracy of every part is vital here because the chassis is literally the skeleton of the entire car. If you can't check measurements of one part from another symmetrically-positioned part, (you should really measure any frail components before you have the sandblasting carried out), try to get hold of some original drawings from your specialist one-make club, or perhaps just measure another enthusiast's car. Remember that accuracy and soundness are the keynotes to your chassis-based car's safety and appearance. In fact, you would be wise to have a specialist check your chassis on a jig before starting work and then again after the work is complete to ensure that the welding process has not caused any distortion to occur.

Unitary Chassis

Manipulating the 'chassis' on a semi-monocoque framed car (i.e. one where the body itself provides a good deal of strength but where there are also 'chassis' rails welded in as an integral part) is a more skilled task. The following section shows how the job can be done but, if the damage is severe, there's no way that an amateur can do it or should attempt it. The following information holds true only for slight damage.

CRP12.   Assuming that the damage is purely localised, it is sometimes possible to use a bottle jack to push out light damage. (Spread the load at both ends with timbers). Incidentally, some bottle jack valves won't work in this position.

CRP13.   It may be possible to hire a professional hydraulic ram, which is capable of exerting great power. Go little by little and, again, spread the load.

CRP10.   First, mount the car or body shell on stands, on a perfectly true surface. Check for level with a large spirit level used in several different directions.

CRP11.   Make sure that the shell is level by measuring from known datum points: don't just accept a couple of measurements but take several. You should then use a builders plumb-bob, which is a piece of cord with a pointed weight on the end. You hold the cord against two symmetrically-placed datum points at the rear, for example a particular pair of spring mounting bolts, and two at the front, such as points on the front suspension. Where the pointer on the bottom of the plumb-bob touches the ground, an accurate pencil or chalk mark should be made. Measurements between the diagonally opposite points will give you an idea of whether the car's frame is twisted or not and the height measurements will give further clues. If the overall shape seems twisted, play safe and go to a specialist with a body jig. ➡

⬅ CRP14.   You can sometimes help prevent all the pushing loads being taken in one area (particularly one you **don't** want to move!) by supporting it from behind with baulks of timber which go back to other structural members.

CRP15.   Once again, accurate measurement is the key to success, the distance between parallel members being an easy one to check.

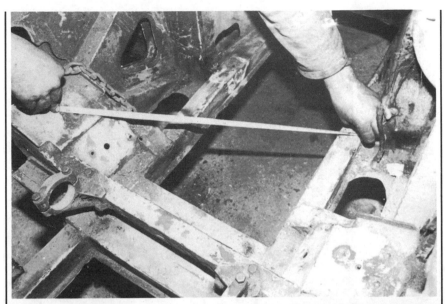

CRP16.   Overall shape is best checked by measuring diagonals. Here a suspension strut to engine mounting is measured ...

CRP17.   ... while here the distance between the opposite pair is compared. Always measure from the edge of a hole or nut – otherwise you will be guessing the centre – and measure from the first digit on the tape rather than from the end, because it's more accurate.

Safety Note:

It cannot be over emphasised that *any* chassis repairs should be checked over by a specialist with highly accurate equipment after they have been carried out, and if the repairs are more than of a very minor nature, they should be carried out by a specialist. A faulty door skin can ruin your car's looks but a faulty chassis can ruin a car's safe handling and cost lives.

⑥ Repairs on a Shoestring

Cutting out Rust – short-term panel and paintwork repairs ■

Jennifer Shaw had run her 105E Ford Anglia for years and, as well as needing the car as a means of getting to and from work, she felt quite attached to it. Frankly, it looked a mess and she ought to have considered replacing it but she liked the car and in any case, couldn't afford another one. Her husband, Geoff, went over the car with her and weighed up the pros and cons. Mechanically, the car was in fine fettle; it was using little oil and never failed to start first time. Underneath, it was remarkably sound and it had just passed an MOT test. They decided that they would try and patch up the holes that were appearing everywhere,

of being able to afford a replacement runabout.
but especially in the front wings, and save hard for another year in the hope

SSR1.   The car's front wings were its worst point. The rear of the wings, around the door hinge pillars were particularly badly corroded and, further forwards, there were rust scabs beneath the trim and beneath where a section of the trim had once been. The wheel arches were not rotted through at any point although most cars at this stage of deterioration are particularly bad in that area. The 'explosion' visible in the middle of the door is evidence of

bad corrosion coming though from inside the door: the window winder gear presses against the inner panel via a felt pad. This had collected water which had run through the faulty window weather strip. Since the rest of the door was very sound (and when checking, always look hard at the bottom of the door, especially from underneath) it was decided to repair the corrosion.

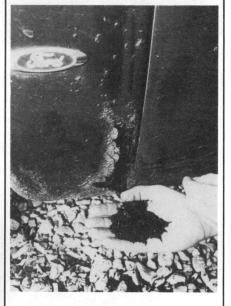

SSR2.   When the bottom of the wing was lightly attacked with a screwdriver, it disintegrated and handfuls of fine silt fell to the floor. This demonstrates the importance of ensuring that inner wing, sill end plates and other under-wheel arch areas are sound and closed-off from the ingress of water-borne dirt. Where it collects, it traps salt-laden water with the same effect on panel-work as the felt 'sponge' fixed to the inside of the door.

SSR3.   Geoff felt that, even in the case of a temporary repair, it would be best to cut out the corroded metal. Here he's using a Monodex cutter, which is excellent for cutting out steel without distorting the surrounding panel. It consists of two plates and a 'finger' which is pushed inside the panel. As the handles of the Monodex are squeezed together, the finger lifts upwards between the plates and curls a thin strip of steel out between the plates. Its major drawback is that it's hand-achingly slow.

SSR6.   With the first stage of the operation complete. Geoff checked visually that the all-important door hinge pillar was sound. He double-checked by attempting to lift and lower the door while watching out for signs of movement. All seemed fine in that department so Geoff felt that it was OK to carry on with a purely cosmetic repair. If the hinge pillar had shown any signs of movement, that would have indicated an unacceptable degree of corrosion requiring major surgery; in other words, the car may well have been scrap.

SSR7.   Neither filler nor fibreglass will stick to thin air, so before a hole can be filled some sort of supporting material has to be let-in. At the quickest end of the scale, even a piece of cardboard could be used to support fibreglass until it goes off, and perforated aluminium (which has no inherent strength to speak of) is also often used. Geoff decided to use a piece of aluminium and to pop-rivet it into place. Here, the aluminium has been cut to shape and is already held with a couple of pop-rivets. Geoff used the ball of the hammer to create a shallow dent ...

SSR4.   Before using the Monodex, you have to drill a hole large enough to enable the cutter to fit into place. If you try to start off where the steel is corroded, the thin, brittle, rusty steel simply jams the cutter. In any case, you need to cut well back to sound metal.

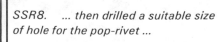

SSR8.   ... then drilled a suitable size of hole for the pop-rivet ...

SSR5.   Another handy tool in this situation is an old or cheap woodworker's chisel. Purpose built bolster chisels are often too heavy for this job but a thin-bladed wood chisel can be very useful.

SSR9. ... before snapping it into place. Always make certain that both pieces of metal are tight up against one another before pulling the gun handles together, otherwise the rivet will make a poor, loose fit.

SSR10. Next, the surface of the aluminium and the surrounding steel were roughened with a coarse sanding disc held in the electric drill. This has the dual effect of forming a key for the filler to bond to and it also removes any surface rust that might remain.

SSR11. No rust 'killer' works 100%, as far as the author has ever been able to discover. One of the more effective rust treatments is 'Trustan' which Geoff is seen painting on here. The idea is that any rust which has formed tiny craters, and so couldn't be reached by the sander, will be held back by the rust killer.

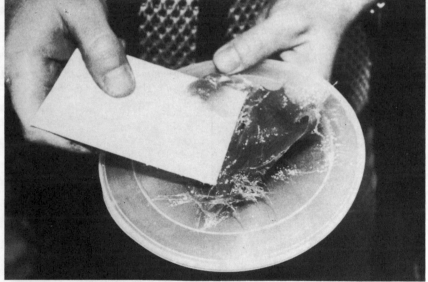

SSR12. Geoff mixed up some filler with short strands of fibreglass included in it. This is much stronger than ordinary polyester filler which is rather brittle when set. Chopped-strand impregnated filler is not as easy to mix with its hardener but must be mixed just as thoroughly. It is recommended that gloves are worn when handling it.

SSR13. When set, the filler can be ground down to a suitable contour. Power tools create an unacceptable health hazard here: not only is filler dust flung into the air by the sanding disc, but tiny particles of glass (from the glass fibre) also enter the air which the operator is breathing. It is best to use a single-cut file or, if power is used, to wear an efficient particle mask and, of course, goggles. It is obviously common sense to be careful when collecting up, and disposing of sanded particles as well as when knocking the dust out of clothes and overalls.

SSR14.   Towards the front of the wing, the rust scabs can be seen clearly. They started forming behind the chrome trim strips and are the result of there being holes in the steel which have not been properly sealed and also probably because of electrolytic reaction between the different metals involved.

SSR15.   They must be thoroughly sanded back to bare metal and once again treated with rust preventative to discourage pitted rust from starting its destructive work again.

SSR16.   This picture shows a range of the most basic materials required for carrying out this work. On the left is the filler (actually, two tins will be required – one of plain filler and one with chopped-strands of fibreglass included); then the bottle of rust inhibitor is shown. At the back are three sheets of wet-or-dry paper showing a coarse, an intermediate and a fine grade and at the front are two grades of coarser abrasive paper, used for shaping filler. Machine papers such as these are often useful because they resist clogging well; ordinary glasspaper is almost useless in this respect.

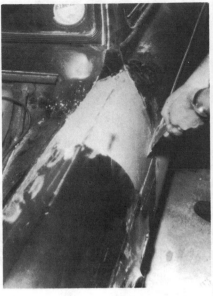

SSR17.   A thin wipe of ordinary filler is spread over the repair by Geoff, taking care to hold the spreader at a narrow angle. Try to obtain something like the correct shape but with just a little more height to it. You can, of course, slap on a mountain of filler and sand it away later but that just adds to the health risk, takes far too long and makes it more difficult to achieve the correct shape.

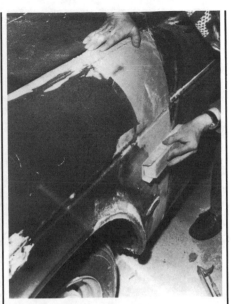

SSR18.   When rubbing down to achieve the final shape, it is important not to leave ripples in the surface as they will be super-apparent beneath the glossy coat of paint, even if your eye can't detect them in the filler. Always wrap the paper around a flat block when sanding flat or convex surfaces.

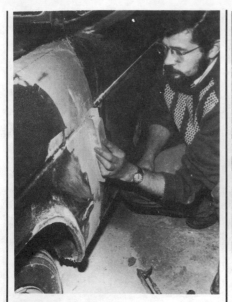

SSR19. Geoff sanded in both directions to make extra sure that no rippling occurred. He sanded first with the coarsest grade of paper and then used the finer grade, ensuring that all of the coarser scratches were sanded out.

SSR21. With the benefit of hindsight, Geoff conceded that the engine bay would have remained cleaner if he had masked it off first. Here he used the flats of his fingers as a 'rubbing block' for the small, concave area at the wing top. If it is necessary to sand a longer area with the fingers, your fingers should be held at a right angle to the direction of sanding (i.e. you sand sideways) to avoid the formation of grooves.

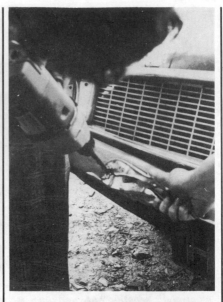

SSR23. At this stage, Geoff realised that it was no good trying to leave the trim in place! Still, better late than never. Only one of the bumper bolts could be undone from behind; all the others turned in the bumper. Geoff hit upon the idea of gripping the head of the bumper bolt with a self-grip wrench, and drilling the bolt head off, after first breaking through the chrome plated surface with a heftily made centre-punch mark.

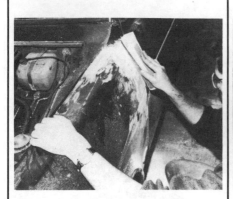

SSR20. The convex curve of the wing should only be sanded in an up-and-down direction, or better still, diagonally, moving the block across as it goes up. If Geoff had sanded lengthways, he would have been certain to have created flats and ripples here.

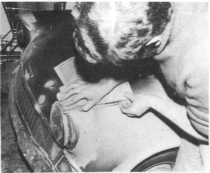

SSR22. Geoff tried a slightly different system here. He used a sanding belt with a piece of wood slotted into it. This gives a double-sided sander with extremely long lasting, clog-resistant properties. Industrial belt sanders use these sanding belts and they can usually be purchased from tool hire shops.

SSR24. The aluminium grille came off after taking out the self-tapping screws holding it in place. In this case, the lamps looked a little rusty behind the wing so, in view of the envisaged short life-span of the car, they were left in place and masked off. The business of taking them out and replacing them can be too time consuming for this sort of job and, worse still, they can disintegrate if corroded badly.

SSR25.   Jennifer Shaw came to help out with the masking off. Large areas such as the windscreen are best masked off by running a length of tape down one side of a piece of newspaper and then placing the tape very carefully along the edge of the area being masked.

SSR26.   At the back of the car, Geoff used some wider masking tape on a broader strip of trim which was left on the car. Wide tape can be very useful for neatly masking off lamps without having to use newspaper.

SSR27.   With the car out of doors, the spray gun hose was used to blow out every trace of dust from trim, slots and other traps, otherwise such dust will be thrown out when the car is sprayed with depressing results; the dust will settle on the paint and ruin the finish.

SSR28.   Geoff wanted someone else to do the actual spraying for him, so the author stepped into his oldest clothes, pulled on his DIY face mask and made a start on the roof. Spraying out of doors is distinctly healthier than spraying inside but the weather, the time of day and the time of year all have to be taken into account: rain, gnats and small flies can all wreak havoc, especially with the finish coat.

SSR29.   Er, actually, leaning on the roof is not such a good idea if you get grease from your fingers onto the panel, but then spraying a roof as high as this is not easy either. Note the size and diameter of the Apollo sprayer air line. The air is high volume/low pressure and gives an excellent finish with less wastage than most spray systems.

SSR30.   Note how small areas had been spot primed after rubbing down and stopping with body filler. This gives a depth of paint which can be flatted down to get rid of small scratches. Note also that wheels have to be masked off, too.

SSR31.   The trouble with a smaller sprayer is that the width of the spray pattern is relatively narrow; be prepared for an aching arm as the gun is held for long periods. It is important that the air line is held away from the surfaces already sprayed.

SSR32.   It is possible to spray the finish coat out of doors, again painting the roof first, then spraying the rest of the body, starting at one corner and going all the way round.

SSR33. We flatted the first finish coat, then transferred to the garage for a second. Inside the garage, Geoff watered the concrete floor to lay the dust which would normally be stirred up when walking around the car.

SSR34.   This is the exciting part, and Jennifer couldn't wait to get the masking tape and paper off the car. Don't risk removing it before the paint is dry and hard, however! Incidentally, when leaving the car to dry, it is important that no draughts (especially damp draughts) are allowed to play on the paintwork through door gaps, etc; otherwise paint will bloom (become cloudy).

SSR35.   Before refitting chrome and trim, Geoff carefully cleaned every piece: it is so much easier to clean the brightwork whilst it is off the car and attractive chromework adds a very great deal to the car's final appearance — as any car salesman will tell you!

SSR36.   Jennifer Shaw was delighted with the finished appearance of her car. The finish was excellent from the Apollo spray gun but if you end up with a dull finish, don't worry; it can be polished up with T-cut or similar abrasive paint polish. This Anglia certainly **looked** ready for its expected 12 months service.

One final job that Geoffrey had to carry out was to brush plenty of underseal on the undersides of the repaired surfaces. As every schoolchild knows, rust requires both oxygen (from the air) and water to carry out its deadly work. The more you can seal out, the longer the repairs will last, although don't be deluded; you can never seal out corrosion permanently, just delay its progress.

Bodywork Repair and Improvement from a can ■

Does your car look a disgrace to the neighbourhood? Or do you fancy buying a banger for a song and making it look presentable? Either way, this section shows a host of techniques and tricks for putting a shine on a car for which the spotlight has long gone out. Make no mistake the following tips won't make the car last a lot longer; they won't make it go faster or stop better; most important of all, they won't make it any safer. It is only worthwhile carrying out any of the cosmetic repairs that follow if the car's structure and running gear are safe. That is something that you must determine for yourself, if necessary with the aid of a professional tester. But it is surprising how even a basically sound car can be so badly knocked about and neglected that it looks far worse than it really is. So, if you are tired of punk rockers wanting to take your car home as a souvenir, or of patrol men pulling you up to count the rust bubbles, this chapter could be just what you have been waiting for. Read oN! The author – with a little help from his father and friends – shows how it's done.

BC1.   Well, this is it! I picked this one up with no MOT roadworthiness certificate, no Road Fund Licence, and a clutch that had rust-welded itself onto the flywheel. The owner was just about to chop off the rear axle and turn it into a trailer when I spotted the chariot's startling potential (!) and for around the cost of a dozen pints of Best Bitter, the deal was struck, leaving the ex-owner alcoholically ecstatic and the new owner stone cold sober at the realisation of what was to come.

The car's underframe was sound, everything shone, tooted and flashed as it should and, by dramatic and distinctly unorthodox means, the clutch was freed in a trice.

Sizing up

BC2.   There were several places where rust was disturbing the surface of the paint and I knew that many of these would reveal gaping holes when they were prodded.

BC3.   At the rear of the same wing, the bubbling was even worse, and pushing a screwdriver into the corroded metal was as easy as breaking thin ice. Quite a big patch was going to be needed here.

BC4.   This body scratch is typical of the sort of calling card that some morons leave behind to greet you on your return to the car park. It was worse than it looks in this picture and you could feel and see a shallow dent right along the line of the scratch.

BC5.   The frame is worthy of the picture! Wheels look terrible without their trim but that was easily fixed. The rust on the wheel would have to be rubbed down and the wheel arch was of the back-to-nature variety; it was rapidly returning to its original metallurgical state!

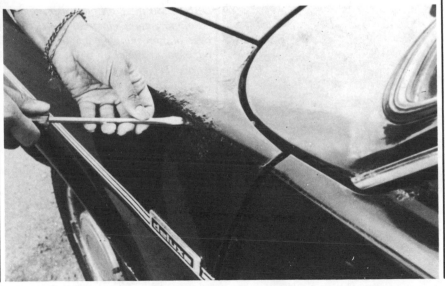

DR1.   This sequence of photographs deals with the repair of the dent and paintwork damage shown in this photo. The procedure will be similar for the repair of a hole. It should be noted that the procedures given here are simplified — more explicit instructions will be found in the text.

DR2.   In the case of a dent the first job — after removing surrounding trim — is to hammer out the dent where access is possible. This will minimise filling. Here, the large dent having been hammered out, the damaged area is being made slightly concave.

DR3.   Now all paint must be removed from the damaged area, by rubbing with coarse abrasive paper. Alternatively, a wire brush or abrasive pad can be used in a power drill. Where the repair area meets good paintwork, the edge of the paintwork should be 'feathered', using a finer grade of abrasive paper.

DR4.   In the case of a hole caused by rusting, all damaged sheet-metal should be cut away before proceeding to this stage. Here, the damaged area is being treated with rust remover and inhibitor before being filled.

DR5.   Mix the body filler according to its manufacturer's instructions. In the case of corrosion damage, it will be necessary to block off any large holes before filling — this can be done with zinc gauze or an aluminium patch. Make sure the area is absolutely clean before ...

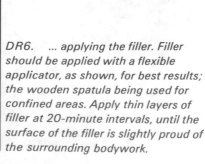

DR6.   ... applying the filler. Filler should be applied with a flexible applicator, as shown, for best results; the wooden spatula being used for confined areas. Apply thin layers of filler at 20-minute intervals, until the surface of the filler is slightly proud of the surrounding bodywork.

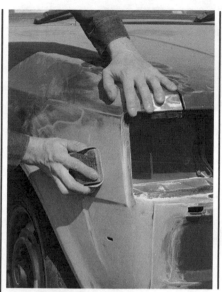

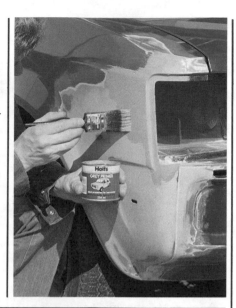

DR7.   Initial shaping can be done with a Surform plane or Dreadnought file. Then, using progressively finer grades of wet-or-dry paper, wrapped around a sanding block, and copious amounts of clean water, rub down the filler until really smooth and flat. Again, feather the edges of adjoining paintwork.

DR8.   The whole repair area can now be sprayed or brush-painted with primer. If spraying, ensure adjoining areas are protected from over-spray. Note that at least one inch of the surrounding sound paintwork should be coated with primer. Primer has a 'thick' consistency, so will fill small imperfections.

DR9.   Again, using plenty of water, run down the primer with a fine grade of wet-or-dry paper until it is really smooth and well blended into the surrounding paintwork. Any remaining imperfections can now be filled by carefully applied knifing stopper paste.

DR10.   When the stopper has hardened, rub down the repair area again before applying the final coat of primer. Before rubbing down this last coat of primer, ensure the repair area is blemish-free – use more stopper if necessary. To ensure that the surface of the primer is really smooth use some finishing compound.

DR11.   The top coat can now be applied. When working out of doors, pick a dry, warm and wind-free day. Ensure surrounding areas are protected from over-spray. Agitate the aerosol thoroughly, then spray the centre of the repair area, working outwards with a circular motion. Apply the paint as several thin coats.

DR12.   After a period of about two weeks, which the paint needs to harden fully, the surface of the repaired area can be 'cut' with a mild cutting compound prior to wax polishing. When carrying out bodywork repairs, remember that the quality of the finished job is proportional to the time and effort expended.

BC6.   Even with a hubcap fitted, the wheel arch looked terrible when Michelle, a friend and neighbour , called around and said "Oh, look how this comes apart when you touch it!" Who needs enemies ... But seriously, it just shows how weak rust is, and how filler applied some time ago will pop straight off again under the force of expanding rust beneath it.

BC7.   Michelle tried the same trick with the front wing but this time the paint just flaked off revealing sound metal beneath. You never can tell just by looking.

BC9.   ... Ouch! Just to make things equal, my wife clobbered the other side of the car the very next day. Now, believe it or not, denting cars is not something we make a habit of. It's just that there's a real psychological difference to the way you treat a car when it looks respectable.

BC10.   Michelle seems to be saying, "How on earth d'you think you are going to repair this?" I didn't even try but simply visited the local breaker's yard and bought a more presentable seat along with the hub cap that replaced the one missing from the rear right-hand wheel.

BC11.   The makers of Holts products supplied virtually all of the 'canned car' used throughout this set of pictures. Their products are ideal for car care and repair and include everything from rust eater, through filler, primer and paint to underseal and a range of polishes for finishing the job off. This is the selection I started with.

BC8.   This was NOT staged! It just goes to show how you can disregard an already battered looking car. I normally pride myself on being able to judge a car's dimensions but this time ...

Paint breakdown — sound metal

BC12. I started off by nibbling away at a bubbling area with an old woodworking chisel. The paint scraped and flaked away quite easily and revealed metal that was pitted but which hadn't yet gone right through. The paint was scraped back **beyond** the obvious area of rust, out to shiny metal. That way, you make sure that you don't miss any rust that might have started to creep under the paint without anything showing on the surface.

BC13. Next the Rust Eater was applied according to the instructions and with the brush supplied. I've always had reservations about how well any of these rust killers actually work, but they **might** help to hold it back a little and they surely can't do any harm.

BC14. I've missed out all the filling and masking pictures (see the other sections for details) but note that once the filler was flatted it was sprayed with primer then with a light coat of finish paint straight away. Filler is absorbent and I didn't want it soaking up any moisture whilst the rest of the car was attended to. Incidentally, after using the Rust Eater but before applying the filler, the metal was sprayed with several coats of Holts Zinc Spray. Now, I **know** that zinc helps to hold back rust.

Rusty rear wing

BC15. This wing hadn't been bumped (how did we miss it?) so the corroded metal and flaking filler were cut away and the profile built back up with body filler. Although there's only one shot here of this being done, in truth the filling/sanding routine had to be carried out several times before the correct shape was sculptured. Unless you're **very** lucky don't expect to be able to get there with only one or two shots of filler.

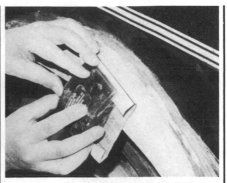

BC16. Here I'm using a rubbing block with some medium grade production paper (dry sanding) wrapped around the flat part of the block. The outer flat lip of the rear wing is being sanded first.

BC17. The back of the block gives a convex surface and this is handy for when you want to sand into concave surfaces.

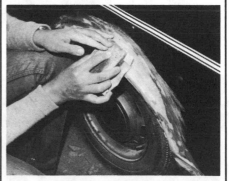

BC18. The fairly strong curve of the rear wing is shown being sanded with left-to-right movements of paper and block. This is the sort of area that is impossible to machine sand both because of its shape and also because hand work allows finer judgement than a machine sander, which can rapidly remove more material than you intend.

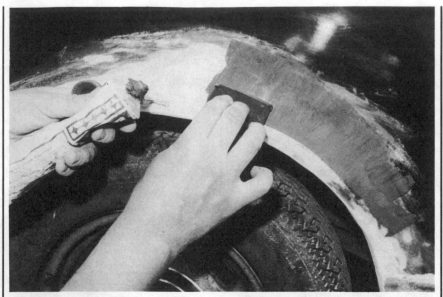

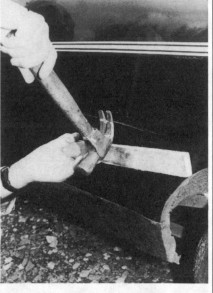

BC19.   After achieving the correct shape it was found that there were lots of scratches and other small blemishes in the surface of the filler. I used a cellulose stopper which is air drying and can only be used for this purpose in a thin coat. It doesn't have the strength of filler and if used too liberally will shrink back as it dries, leaving you with an indifferent surface again. Ordinary filler can be pressed into service for this purpose provided that it is spread as thinly as this, but it doesn't possess the easy-flat properties of stopper.

Pulling out a dent I

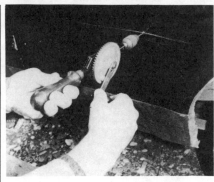

BC21.   If you recall, the deep scratch down the left-hand side panel was accompanied by a valley in the panel itself. There was no ready access to the rear of the panel without time consuming stripping-out of the trim panels. First, a hole was drilled in the centre of the dent, using a $\frac{1}{8}$″ drill.

BC23.   The art of improvisation! A woodworker's claw hammer was used to grip the screw head while a strip of wood was used both as a fulcrum point and as a cushion to prevent the hammer marking the panel. The dent will come out really easily; the trick lies in not overdoing it.

BC24.   When the dent had been pulled out all the way along its length (and actually, it was left just a little low, which is greatly preferable to creating a raised ridge) the paint was prepared for the application of filler by roughening the surface with medium grade production paper. If filler is applied over shiny paint, its adhesion is poor, it becomes prone to cracking out and it won't feather edge properly so its edges always show.

BC20.   So little of the stopper has to be removed that a piece of fine grade production paper, hand held, will do the job perfectly well and should leave the surface ready for spraying primer.

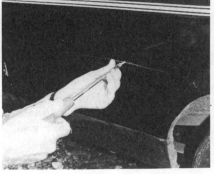

BC22.   Then a self-tapping screw with a flat head was screwed into the panel, making sure that it didn't go so far in that it damaged anything behind the panel but taking it in far enough to get a strong grip.

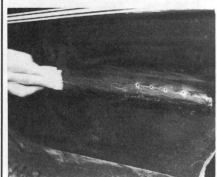

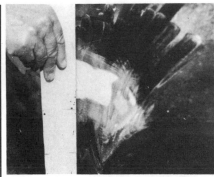

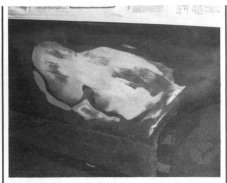

BC25. You can buy filler in pots right up to this size, which is made for commercial use but would be a more economical way of buying the stuff if you were going to use a lot. Try not to use the same surface twice for mixing your filler otherwise you will pick up hard pieces of filler from the previous mixing which will then drag across the surface as you attempt to spread the filler, leaving furrows which are infuriatingly difficult to get rid of.

BC28. An excellent way of checking the 'trueness' of the surface is to hold a straightedge against it. This is a strip of Perspex (Plexiglass) which cost a song from a local supplier, bought as an offcut. Its machined edge is very straight; use it by looking for gaps between straight edge and panel. Use the straight edge at several different angles when checking for rippling. It is also very useful when held against convex panels as it can be held in a curve against the shape of the car's bodywork. Good tools need not always be expensive.

BC29. Leaping ahead now to the time when the filling is almost finished a tin of spray paint was used to spray a very thin coat of paint called a 'guide coat' over the surface of the filler. The can was held further away than normal so that the paint landed as an almost dry, dusting coat.

BC30. When flatted off with a rubbing block and a fine grade production paper, the paint was removed from the high spots leaving the low areas standing out in stark relief. Depending on how deep these areas are, they can be brought out with filler or stopper, as already described. When using a guide coat, choose a colour that contrasts with the surrounding colours.

BC26. Here a 'professional' sanding block is being used. It accepts ready made strips of self-adhesive backed production paper strips (any paint factor will stock them) and helps to create a true, flat surface. Attaining a flat surface is easier if you sand in more than one direction. Coarse production paper can be used at this stage.

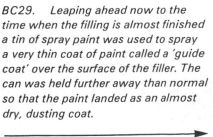

BC27. My father lends a hand here, using his power sander which really shifts the dust! That's why he is wearing a particle mask, and a hat to keep the dust out of his hair. While the power sander's quicker, it's not so easy to produce a flat surface over a large flat area.

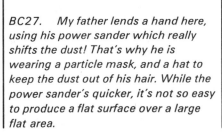

Pulling out a dent II

BC33.   A small kink was left inside the wheel arch and this was easily knocked back into line using the panel beater's hammer.

BC35.   The repaired area was flatted with medium grade production paper, as were the scratches to the rear of the wing and the front of the door.

BC31.   The dent on the front wing was in a very awkward place, just where the wing formed a fairly complex wheel arch extension. The DIY tools used here were an ordinary woodworker's G-cramp and the ubiquitous piece of wood again!

BC36.   The surfaces were filled, as shown and described earlier ...

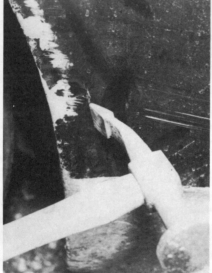

BC32.   The G-cramp was used right behind the worst part of the dent and then again each side of the first 'pull', to force the dented metal back to the line of the wood which was the same as the rest of the wheel arch. If the head of the G-cramp had not fitted so snugly inside the wheel arch, I would have used another, smaller piece of wood, shaped if necessary, to pull the metal to car correct shape.

BC34.   Well, all right, the G-cramp did leave a small mark. Unfortunately it had pushed a little of the concave curve out of line, but it was easily restored to the correct position with the cross-pein end of the panel beater's hammer.

BC37.   ... and the concave curve was flatted, this time using a slightly different technique. The production paper was rolled into a tube, the shape of which followed that of the concave part of the wing.

BC38.   The flatter areas were sanded as before, but this time the paper was wrapped round a flat piece of wood. Once again, the sanding was carried out in several different directions to ensure a flat surface.

BC39.   And finally, the filler was sprayed with primer to protect it from the elements.

Cutting out corrosion

BC40.   Rust frequently takes its strongest hold in the places where mud becomes lodged, and this area at the top of the wing is one of those places. When the surface was lightly tapped with the old wood chisel, the metal just fell into holes.

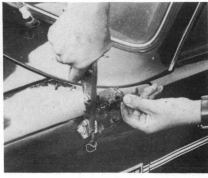

BC41.   I started off by cutting all the rusty steel away using the Monodex cutter, leaving only sound metal in place. A couple of fiddly bits wouldn't come out using the Monodex and they were finished off with a hammer and the trusty old wood chisel.

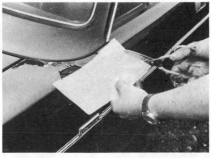

BC42.   Included in the Holts body repair kit was a sheet of aluminium mesh. This can be bent and folded easier than card and can even be cut with scissors. It isn't intended to impart any strength to the job but just acts as a bridge for fibreglass and filler while it goes off. You can't fill a gaping hole without putting in a support first and aluminium is ideal because it doesn't encourage the steel to start rusting again.

BC43.   The aluminium mesh was cut so that it covered the area of the holes and then a dollop of filler was placed on each corner of the mesh.

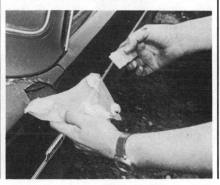

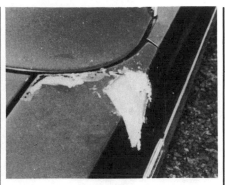

BC44.   You can't fully see what is going on here without having your X-ray specs on, but the mesh is being pushed into position from beneath the wing while the filler acts as a glue to hold it in position. Aluminium mesh is so soft that it can easily be pushed into the contours of the wing with light hand pressure

BC45.   The kit provides resin (a thick liquid), hardener, and a spatula for stirring as well as a sheet of fibreglass mat. The hardener was mixed with resin to the prescribed proportions and then resin was spread over the mesh and the edges of the steel. (The Rust Eater brush proved ideal). Then pieces of fibreglass mat were cut to size, placed over the mesh and stippled down with resin until the mat became almost transparent. See the section on 'Getting to Grips with GRP' for more information.

BC46.   The resin was left to go hard, then a scrape of filler was taken from the tin and mixed with the appropriate amount of hardener.

BC49.   As an alternative to using a professional sanding block, I used a sheet of P80 grade self-adhesive backed production paper and mounted it onto ... that piece of wood again!

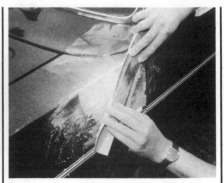

BC51.   ... and then the other, turning and turning about every six to ten strokes, to avoid the very real risk of rippling the surface.

BC47.   Filler was then spread over the depressed surface of the repair in the knowledge that there was a fairly sound foundation beneath. Note that the edges of surplus fibreglass are treated as irrelevant at this stage.

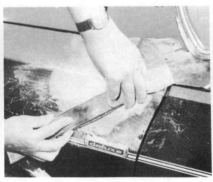

BC50. Remember to sand first in one direction ...

BC52.   Here, ordinary filler was used, finely spread, as a stopper. It works quite well but it really sets too hard for easy flatting and it also fails to spread as finely as cellulose stopper.

BC48.   The whole lot was sanded flat using a medium grit disc fitted to a mini grinder. A rubber pad and disc fitted to an electric drill would have done the job just as well. It is extra important that you wear an efficient particle mask when carrying out this job because as well as particles of solidified polyester filler, there are also particles of glass fibre floating around, and this can be extremely dangerous to health if inhaled.

Painting the patches

BC53. There's no way with a job of this sort that you're going to want to remove the badges and sidestripes, so simply mask them. Take care in doing so because poor masking and overspray can look almost as bad as the rust you have spent so much time cutting out.

BC54. Fortunately there is not so much power in an aerosol can that overspray is a real problem, so masking off to within a couple of feet of where you are spraying should be adequate. On the other hand, if you are working out of doors the ultra-light spray can carry on the wind. If it's windy, either transfer indoors, find a really sheltered spot or wait for a calmer day. Here, a coat of primer is being sprayed, working a strip at a time across the repair.

BC55. After priming the panel and allowing the paint to harden off thoroughly, rub the edges of the primer and the surrounding area with an abrasive paint polishing compound. This serves two purposes: it gives a very fine feather edge to the edge of the primer, so blending its thickness into that of its surrounds; and it polishes the oxides and traffic film off the surrounding colour which brings it back to its original colour and increases the chances of a good colour match with the paint you are spraying.

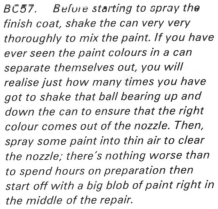

BC57. Before starting to spray the finish coat, shake the can very very thoroughly to mix the paint. If you have ever seen the paint colours in a can separate themselves out, you will realise just how many times you have got to shake that ball bearing up and down the can to ensure that the right colour comes out of the nozzle. Then, spray some paint into thin air to clear the nozzle; there's nothing worse than to spend hours on preparation then start off with a big blob of paint right in the middle of the repair.

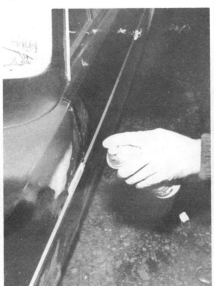

BC56. As implied in the previous caption, the purpose of abrasive cutting compound is to remove some of the paint; you should polish until paint comes off and colours the cloth you are using like this.

The Car Bodywork Repair Manual

BC58. Spray on a light first coat; don't even try to cover completely the colours beneath but spray on a coat which is light enough to let them show through. The paint should dry within a couple of minutes after which the second and later a third coat can be applied.

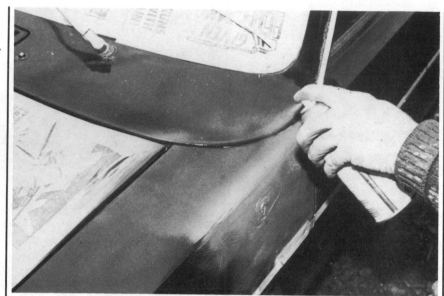

BC59. Each coat should be sprayed as a series of horizontal or vertical strips, each coat half covering the one that went before. (If you get runs, you're passing too slowly or you're too close.) If you get a dull, dry finish, you're passing too quickly or you're holding the can too far away. Only trial and error can determine what will be exactly right for you and the conditions you are working in. Remember that a gust of wind will 'bend' the spray and spoil your aim and that damp air will cause blooming, i.e. the surface of the paint will go a milky colour. (Blooming can sometimes be polished out if it hasn't gone too deep.)

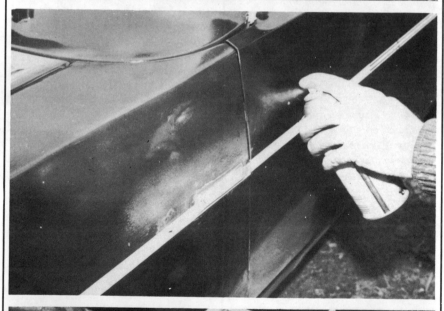

BC60. Finally, here's a tip to remember when putting masking paper in place. Put a line of tape down the edge you want to protect taking care to place it accurately, then put a strip of tape half over the edge of a piece of newspaper before sticking that down to the first piece of masking tape. If you try to position the tape plus paper you will find it too cumbersome to handle easily.

Finishing touches

BC61.   This car had already had its sills and door bottoms covered in undershield, probably to disguise work carried out on these areas in the past. It also prevents stone chipping in these vulnerable areas. When used in this sort of area, spray-on undershield gives a far better looking finish than brush-on undershield.

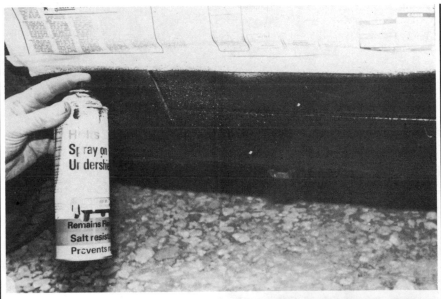

BC62.   Removing the masking tape can be quite exciting as it unwraps a 'new' car. Be sure not to fetch the masking off before the paint is dry and properly hard – it would be a shame to spoil it!

BC64.   There were several small scratches and chips on this car and, while they certainly weren't bad enough to warrant spraying, they could only get worse if nothing was done. Here, some of the Holts finish paint is being sprayed into the cap from where it could be brushed on with a fine-bristle kiddies paint brush. Paint for spraying is too thin for brushing; leave the cap to stand for a while to let the surplus solvent evaporate off before using it for painting.

BC65.   Don't forget to polish all the chromework – it can make an incredible difference to the appearance – and also clean all the windows to help to give the car a spring-cleaned, fresh appearance.

BC63.   Brush-on undershield should now be used beneath all of the repaired areas to keep out the damp and dirt from the especially vulnerable repair patches. If you don't underseal them, the patches will break through in no time at all.

BC66. After spraying random patches and panels the rest of the paintwork will look horribly dull by comparison. This car was polished with a light abrasive polish, a small area at a time, until it shone like the new paint. Then the whole car, chrome and all, was treated to a wax polishing to help to keep the shine in for a little longer.

BC67. Tricks of the trade! You will never see a car in a showroom with anything but uniformly black tyres. The old Morris Marina was just about purring to itself as the tyrewall black was painted on.

BC68. Next, the engine bay was cleaned up for what seemed like the first time ever. Aerosol degreaser was sprayed all over, allowed to soak in, worked in with a brush and then hosed off. Don't expect to use the car straight away if you try this, especially if you get water into the electrics.

BC69. I knew that this car had leaked in from around the top corner of the windscreen. The only long-term cure for this problem is to remove and refit the windscreen but with a car of this sort, a good medium-term answer is to inject a good bead of windscreen sealer behind the rubber using the nozzle supplied with the tube. Cover a distance well to each side of the apparent source of the leak; water can creep disconcertingly before coming through.

BC70. The old Morris Marina now had a real sparkle to it that it hadn't had for years. It seemed to sit an inch higher on its springs and certainly didn't look a candidate for being driven into the nearest gatepost. As I said right at the start, the car was only cosmetically improved but, in the sense that we all like a car to project a bit of our own image, who wants to drive a car that shouts out, 'I'm a scruff!' And, since you can revamp your car from a can, who needs to?

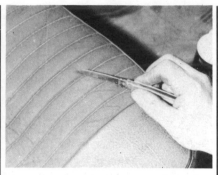

BC71. If your car has untidy and stained velour pile seats, improve them by first scratching off any hard deposits with a blunt knife ...

BC72. ... then squirt some velour upholstery foam cleaner onto the cloth or onto a rag and wipe the cloth clean, without actually soaking it.

BC73. Black bumpers loose their crisp blackness really quickly and they can be perked up with a cleaner made just for the job – and so can black sunroof fabric, vinyl roof coverings and sportscar vinyl rag-tops, each of which seems to have a product made especially for the job.

BC74.   Just scrubbing deeply sculptured or wire wheels with soapy water and a stiff brush can make a real improvement to the general appearance. And don't forget to clean the window glass really thoroughly all the way around — your car contains a large area of glass and smears will detract from the brightest paintwork.

Smartening up an older car is one of the cheapest jobs you can carry out but with dramatic effect. Allow plenty of time and be prepared for some fairly hard work — more power to your elbow!

7 Glass-fibre Bodywork

Repairing GRP Body Damage ●

'Fibreglass', Glass-Fibre and Glass Reinforced Plastic are all names for a material that was once going to shake steel from its rust-ridden throne as king of the car panels. Although high-performance car manufacturers like Corvette in the USA, Lotus, TVR and many others in the UK and Renault-Alpine in France took to it, GRP has only ever been used on a small number of cars. Although GRP can split when put under stress, it has the great advantages that it *never* rots and it is one of the most suitable substances for DIY applications used in car bodywork. Thanks are due to the GRP experts, Smith & Deakin of Worcester, England and especially to Tom, who went to a great deal of trouble to help in the preparation of this section.

GFR1. The basic equipment you will need to carry out work with GRP, apart from the most basic workshop tools, includes a 1½inch paintbrush, a pair of rubber or plastic gloves (ensuring that the plastic is not the type dissolved by resin), a container in which to mix the resin (again, some plastics are unsuitable), a mixing stick and plenty of newspaper on which to work. Very useful, but not essential is a roller which ensures absorption of the resin by the mat.

Materials: 1oz (25g) mat — meaning its weight per square foot — the heavier, the thicker. Pre-activated lay-up resin, sold by weight and nearly always sold complete with sufficient hardener. Barrier cream — strongly advisable. Resin stripper, for removing the resin from brushes on which it has gone hard, is useful for beginners. Ordinary washing powder is excellent and cheap for cleaning brushes provided it is used as a thick paste made with hot water and worked in really well before the resin goes hard. Acetone, though, is the recognised brush cleaner but brings its own hazards — check with your supplier.

Safety — The following points are strongly recommended:

a) the wearing of goggles and, b) the use of barrier cream and gloves when working with liquid resin, c) the use of gloves when working with 'raw' mat, i.e. handling or cutting it, and d) it is essential to wear an efficient respirator when sanding or cutting cured laminate, unless it is cut with a knife whilst in its soft, 'green', semi-cured state. In addition I would add that GRP should be cut or sanded away from children and pets and preferably, out of doors — breathing in the tiny air-borne particles is literally to inhale powdered glass. Not nice!

GRP — The how and why

Firstly 'Fibreglass' is, correctly speaking, the trade name of the American company which markets the strands of silicone (or 'glass') which, when loosely bonded together make the familiar white coloured 'mat' with which we shall be dealing. The correct term for the substance is Glass Reinforced Plastic — quite literally a plastic of the thermo-setting type (i.e. it can't be re-softened by heating, unlike 'plastic' plastics) which, when reinforced by the glass, forms a material which weight for weight, is stronger than steel.

Within the glass-fibre mat itself, each strand is microscopically thin, thousands of these hair-like strands

being drawn together to form the thicker fibres which make up the visible strands of mat. Although the mat appears white, this is only the colour of the bonding agent which holds the strands together enabling the mat to be handled in sheet form. The behaviour of this bonding agent is important when it comes to impregnating the mat with resin as will be shown later.

The resin, technically known as Polyester Resin, is a long chain monomer. This is really a clever way of saying that all the molecules are linked together in long lines rather like the chain on a boat's anchor. While the resin is liquid, the chains are free to slip over one another, but the addition of hardener sets off a chemical reaction (confirmed by the fact that resin gets warm as it goes off) which bonds the lines of molecules in an extremely complex criss-crossed interlocking mesh.

If more than the maker's recommended quantity of hardener is added, the resin will go off more quickly and produce more heat. The reverse is also true. The greater the heat added, the more quickly will the resin go off. In hot weather less hardener should be added if you want to avoid the frustration of seeing your expensive resin turn in rapid succession from liquid to jelly to a solid lump, ruining your brush and temper in the process. Conversely, cold weather should be countered by the addition of extra hardener, or heat, which should only be applied generally to the work area and not directly to the job. Too much heat or too much hardener result in a weakened laminate. Confused? You won't be ...

By itself, the resin is very hard and brittle; combining it with the glass-fibre mat, however, transforms it almost miraculously into a substance that is far stronger than the sum of the two separate substances. This phenomenon is not restricted to GRP of course, reinforced concrete being another commonly used material which takes on additional strength in a somewhat similar way.

To be precise, hardener alone will not cause resin to go off in the way described. A further substance, Cobalt Naphthenate (an unfriendly sounding substance if ever there was one), has to be mixed with the resin. This component of the mixture is known as 'accelerator'. Most resin manufacturers supply their product with the accelerator ready mixed in, though it is possible to buy it separately. As its name implies, the more the accelerator added, the quicker the resin goes off. For various reasons it is far better to leave non pre-accelerated resin well alone. The most obvious reason is that when you buy ready-mixed resin you can be fairly sure that the manufacturers have added the optimum amount of accelerator for thorough and strong curing of the resin. Just be sure when you buy your resin (either from a specialist supplier to the public or from a boatyard or other specialist user) that the resin *is* pre-accelerated. If not, obtain accelerator too. **NB. Never mix neat accelerator with neat hardener. They react explosively!!**

Basically, as far as resin for repairing GRP is concerned, that's it. There are in fact different types of resin, both chemically and practically speaking, such as gel-coat, flame retardant and casting resins and so on, as well as a range of 'accessory' materials to enable all sorts of jobs to be carried out. But really, it would take a book ...

Getting down to it

A golden rule for repairing local damage is, 'don't try to do too much at once'. Glass fibre is awfully messy at the best of times and soggy feather edged patches of the stuff splodged all over your car will do your morale no good at all. Instead, be sensible and tackle a small part of a panel at a time, the smaller the better, until you have built up some experience of the materials you are using.

You should, however, strip off all the paint from the panel you are working on. With the paint off you will be able to see all of the stress damage developing in the painting process which might take months to show through. Even if you achieve a perfect feather edge between your repair, the existing panel and the old paint, the thinners in the new paint will cause the existing paint to lift slightly, showing up some months later as a hollow around the repair.

Any paint stripper will remove the paint but unfortunately most types soften the gel coat of the existing bodywork. It will harden off again later but it is all too easy to cause extra work for yourself as your scraper digs in. Nitromors produce a stripper specially for GRP which takes a lot longer to work but gets there surely and rather more safely.

Once the old paint is off, the repair procedure to be followed will fall into a certain category depending upon the extent and type of damage found. The first item described is a general technique used in all GRP repair where more than surface blemishes are to be dealt with.

Laying up

1) Cut a piece of mat to fit the work to be carried out either by tearing against a straight edge or with scissors.
2) Pour the required amount of resin into a container (but **not** glass) and thoroughly stir in a measured amount of hardener.

The manufacturer's literature will say how much, but remember to use more in cold weather, less in hot weather.
3) Paint resin liberally onto the surface on which the GRP is to be layed up.
4) Place the mat over the repair and stipple more resin briskly with a stiff, downward dabbing movement until the mat looses its whiteness and becomes translucent. Do not try to wet thoroughly the 'mat' a bit at a time. Get some resin over the whole surface then come back and start stippling from the place where you started, having given the resin a chance to soak in.
5) Consolidate the resin well into the mat by rolling it thoroughly in all directions. If resin hardens onto the roller, it can be burned off, but outdoors only, because it gives off dense, dangerous, choking fumes. Your hands and brush don't benefit from being coated in resin and should be cleaned off straight away with Swarfega (or other hand cleaner) and washing powder respectively.

Star Cracks

Star cracks and other surface crazing are the most common GRP faults. Often they seem to 'just happen' although flying stones or having the surface pushed in can also produce the same effects. The surface all around the cracks must be ground away, preferably by using a grinding disc on an electric drill, until the cracks themselves are no longer visible (wear a mask and goggles). Then a coat of lay-up resin should be applied to the whole surface followed, when set, by body filler applied in the normal way.

Really severe cracks, ones which can be accentuated by flexing the panel, should be treated as described but in addition the surface should be ground quite a lot more deeply and one layer, or two if possible, of 1oz (25g) mat should be layed-up over the repair before the filler is added. In severe cases of damage it would also be strongly advisable to add a couple of layers of mat to the back of the panel as well.

Bits missing

Apart from light star cracks, every other type of GRP damage must be repaired from the back so that sufficient strength can be restored to the panel without the repair being in any way evident. Cars which are constructed of double-skinned GRP *must* have a section cut out of their inner skin to enable the damaged outer skin to be repaired properly. The section can be fixed back in place later using a small modification of the basic repair technique shown for larger repairs.

Dealing with small repairs first of all, it is possible to place masking tape over the outside of the hole, clean up the inside of the damaged area for about 6 inches (150mm) around it using a sanding disc on an electric drill or angle grinder, and then lay up five or six layers of resin-impregnated mat across the hole and for an additional 6 inches (150mm) or so on each side.

When the resin has thoroughly gone-off turn your attention to the 'good' side and sand down any excess resin, which will have oozed under the edges of the masking tape, and also a margin of two to three inches around the patch to give the filler something to grip on to.

Then apply a good layer of Plastic Padding or other 'fine' type of plastic filler over the patch and the sanded margin around it. If, when the desired level has been achieved imperfections are found, don't be tempted to try to sand them out. Nothing looks worse than a repair which is perfect except that it can be seen as a dip in the panel. Remember that inaccurate levelling is quite hard to spot on a matt section of filler but once it is painted, the gloss finish will always show up any mistakes. Pin holes, which are tiny craters left from cutting into air bubbles incorporatd into the filler at the mixing stage can be simply dealt with by ignoring them. Until, that is, you have flatted the area and applied primer, when they can be filled by applying the thinnest smear of cellulose stopper before flatting down again in readiness for painting.

Larger Repairs

Large repairs are no more difficult to deal with – just bigger. In much the same way as with steel panels, it is sometimes necessary to 'patch-in' a repair section, the main difference being that the patch does not have to be fitted quite as accurately as would be necessary with steel. Owners of Reliant Scimitars, TVRs and the like are in the fortunate position of being able to purchase replacement panels from which they can cut a suitable patch, keeping the edges as neat as possible. This can then be placed over the damaged area, drawn around and the damaged piece cut out.

Under impact, glass fibre bodywork tends to break up in much the same way as a broken eggshell and the pieces retain their original shape and dimensions so it is possible to pick up the wreckage and piece it together in best Humpty Dumpty fashion, bonding in one piece at a time. If a panel does suffer a mishap it makes repairs much more simple if the owner has the presence of mind or the opportunity to collect the bits from the scene of the misfortune.

Owners of rarer cars such as Rochdale or Berkeley may have to make their own mould either by using another complete vehicle or by doing a 'bodge' repair on their own panel with filler which is finished as accurately as possible so that a mould can be taken from the repaired panel. A repair section can then be taken from the mould before cutting out the 'bodge' and repairing the panel properly.

Repair patches should be held in place using bridging pieces of aluminium screwed across the gaps in several places on the outer or the 'good' side. Hold them in place by drilling clearance holes in the pieces of aluminium (drill all holes before the aluminium is cut up into strips; it's easier and safer to grip that way) and drill pilot holes in the GRP before attaching the clips with self-tapping screws on the 'good' side of the panel.

If pop-rivets are used with the idea of later drilling them out, be sure not to use those with steel shafts since the bits left inside the repair will eventually corrode causing a rare sight in GRP bodywork – rust bubbles!

Then masking tape must be stuck length-ways along the joint between the patch and the panel to prevent excess resin oozing through the crack and down onto good bodywork causing more cleaning-up work than is necessary.

Strips of mat, about 6 inches (150 mm) wide and five or six layers thick should be layed-up over the length of the joint, after first cleaning up the inside of the panel in the way described for smaller repairs. The GRP should be given time to go off really thoroughly before the clips are removed – about a day should suffice; longer in really cold weather – and then the wisdom of placing your clips on the outside will manifest itself. If you had put them on the inside they would of course now be lost underneath six rock hard layers of GRP. It is possible to use filler to restore the surface. However, there will be more structural strength in the repair if the seams on the outer surface are now 'Vee'd, so that the edges of the panel and the replaced section gradually taper to meet each other. In effect the outer surface is tapered so that at the joint itself the panel is almost through to the supporting mat on the reverse side. The surface level should then be restored by applying layers of resin impregnated mat until the surface is slightly proud. When the mat has cured the repair is rubbed down level and any imperfections made good with conventional filler.

For safety's sake you must wear gloves when handling glass-fibre, even though the professional shown here chose not to. See also the 'Safety' Section on P194.

Large-scale body repair

GFR2.   This Reliant 3-wheeler had received a bit of a punch on the cheek. As usual, the GRP had disintegrated under the shock of the crash.

GFR3.   No, this isn't an instant repair! It's a replacement panel from a scrap car placed over the top, although new panels can be bought in the normal way. Second-hand panels, provided they are not damaged, are as good as new ones, of course, in GRP.

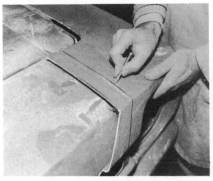

GFR4.   The 'new' panel was marked out, leaving in place most of the sound fibreglass of the car being repaired, and the excess cut off from the repair panel. The damaged shell was marked out to suit.

GFR5.   Here, the old panel is cut out with a special GRP cutter blade fixed to a mini-grinder ...

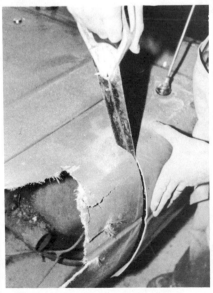

GFR6.   ... but it is almost as easy and far less dusty to use a panel saw, although GRP will quickly blunt a sharp saw (You MUST wear adequate breathing protection because GRP dust can, quite literally, be lethal).

GFR7.   More of the old panel was cut away ...

GFR8.   ... until all of the old, damaged portion was removed.

GFR9.   At this stage, it is essential to ensure that the repair section is correctly located. GRP is so easy to use that it's easy to get carried away and fit the panel without lining it up properly. Use a rule and check measurements from all directions using the undamaged side of the car as a reference point.

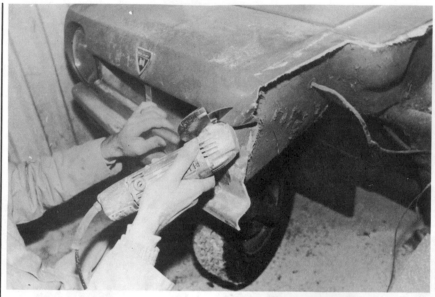

GFR13.   Look inside the repair panel for any loose joints, strengtheners, or old repairs, and make sure that all joints are properly bonded. If they're not, roughen the surfaces and bond them together with extra layers of GRP.

GFR10. Now, in the manner of manuals the world over, you were just told to cut the damage away and trim the repair panel to suit. Actually, in the real world, it's a bit slower than that! You should cut off the damage, then a little more and a little more until you reach a) sound GRP and b) a good position to join up the new panel.

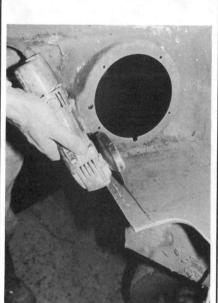

GFR12.   Here, part of the grille trim is being offered up as a double-check that the correct position of the new panel is being maintained.

GG11.   Similarly, trim off enough of the repair panel to stop it being unwieldy but cut back to exact shape later, in conjunction with trimming the old panel.

GFR14.   Roughen all the surfaces to be joined, using a mini-grinder and ...

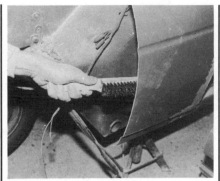

GFR15. ... clean off the inner surfaces of both existing and repair patches and wipe down with a spirit wipe – grease is a major enemy of successful GRP bonding.

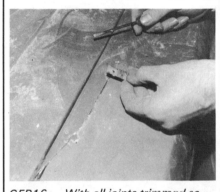

GFR16. With all joints trimmed so that there is only a small gap between existing and repair panels, cut out some strips of thin steel or aluminium ...

GFR17. ... drill pilot holes ...

GFR18. ... and screw the strips across the joints to hold the two panels accurately together.

GFR19. Next, place a strip of masking tape firmly over the joint, pressing it down carefully around the joint strips.

GFR20. Mix up some ordinary lay-up resin with hardener, according to the supplier's instructions.

GFR21. Place a piece of card on the floor and 'lay-up' three strips of mat. (Cut them out **before** you start, or the sticky resin will make it an almost impossible task.)

GFR22. Use suitable gloves or at the very least an effective barrier cream for this part of the work. Bear the section of mat on brush and hand, offering it up to the repair joint.

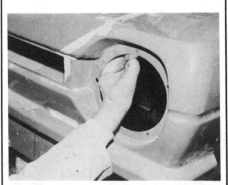

GFR23. Press it firmly into place, trying not to pull it off again as you take your hand away.

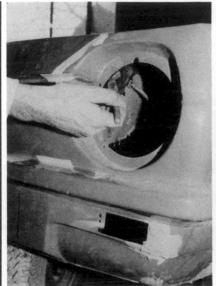

GFR24. Then stipple the mat with the resin brush as thoroughly as you can to 'wet-out' the mat. Do the same with the next section of the repair, overlapping the second patch with the first to make a good bond.

GFR27. ... and proceed to sand and flat the repair as you would any other.

Repairing a small hole

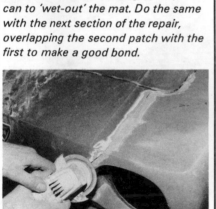

GFR25. Next, feather the edges of the repair inwards a little using the mini-grinder and a coarse sanding disc.

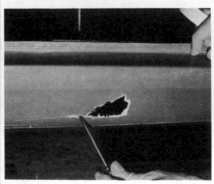

GFR28. In the same crash, a small hole had been punched into the car's lower bodywork. The full extent of any cracks was investigated so that they too, could be repaired.

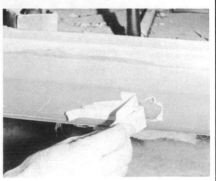

GFR30. ... and wetted-out mat applied as in the previous section.

GFR26. Spread filler into the shallow valley you have created ...

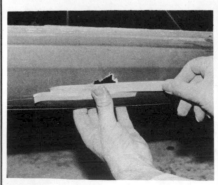

GFR29. Masking tape was used to build up a temporary cover over the hole ...

GFR31. After the GRP has 'gone off' the tape can be removed ...

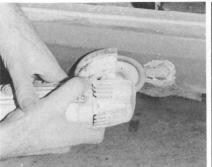

GFR32.   ... the proud surface of the GRP ground back ...

Repairing a tear

GFR35.   Edge damage in GRP frequently takes the form of a tear, like this. (You can prevent it by beefing up the edge of the panel with a flange or even just with extra layers.)

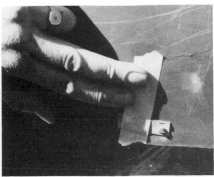

GFR37.   ... masking off the joint and then laying-up GRP on the inside before grinding and filling the outside of the tear in the normal way. If, as sometimes happens, the split is accompanied by delamination, the affected area should be ground away from the outside after the internal reinforcement is in place and then replaced by new layers of mat and resin.

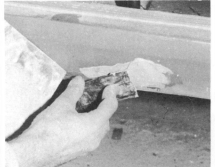

GFR33.   ... and the surface filled and finished in the usual way.

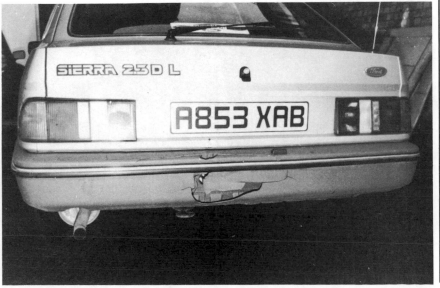

GFR36.   Repair the tear by screwing a clip or clips in place as in the earlier section ...

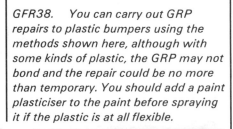

GFR38.   You can carry out GRP repairs to plastic bumpers using the methods shown here, although with some kinds of plastic, the GRP may not bond and the repair could be no more than temporary. You should add a paint plasticiser to the paint before spraying it if the plastic is at all flexible.

GFR34.   A useful tool for removing a larger area of filler without causing ripples is a large single-cut file (i.e. with one row of teeth, so it doesn't clog so easily). Work it half-a-dozen strokes in one direction, then the same number in another to help avoid rippling, which looks awful when the gloss paint goes on.

Painting

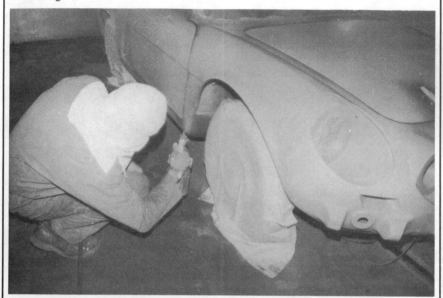

GFR39. GRP can be sprayed with perfect success, but don't attempt to get rid of crazing in GRP just by filling over the top (see 'Star Cracks' earlier in this section) otherwise the cracks will, with absolute certainty, reappear through the paint in weeks or even days.

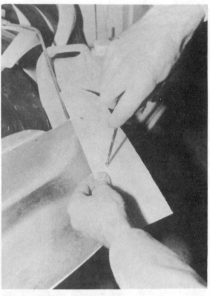

CP2. This spoiler has a small internal flange. Obviously, if you laid fibreglass over the outside of the panel and wrapped it round the flange, you wouldn't get the original panel out of the mould! A strip was screwed onto the flange ...

Copying a GRP panel ■

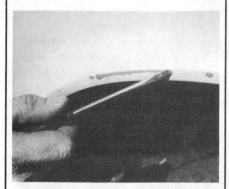

GFR40. The surface of GRP must be well flatted, it must be wiped over with a degreasing spirit wipe and sprayed first in self-etch primer, which eats a key into the surface, otherwise paint will flake off like this.

CP1. In the UK Mustang front spoilers are fairly easy to get hold of, but are outrageously expensive, and the same is true of most panels imported into one country from another. Because it is non-loadbearing, this is an ideal panel to copy, provided that the owner can get hold of one to copy from. First, a negative copy of the panel has to be made.

CP3 ... which stuck out beyond the edge of the panel. This is essential, but it is easier to explain what it does by showing it in the pictures to come.

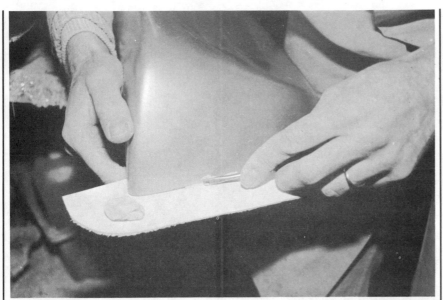

CP4. The joint between spoiler and extension strip was sealed with modelling clay so that no resin could get in there.

CP5. A release agent was wiped onto the surface of the panel, otherwise the GRP would bond itself to it, ruining the original panel. **Remember**: 1) Make sure you cover every inch with release agent. 2) Use only a wax polish **without** silicone additive. Most of them have it but your GRP supplier will be able to supply suitable wax if all else fails. 3) It may be best to operate a 'belts-and-braces' approach: apply wax release agent plus a paint-on PVA release agent. Ruining a good panel or mould can be expensive in terms of both time and money.

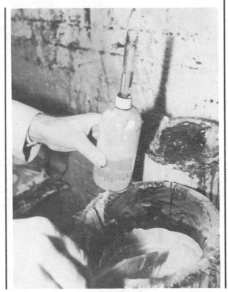

CP6. Mix up some gel-coat resin to the supplier's recommended resin/hardener ratio ...

CP7. ... and paint the gel-coat on to the master shape; in this case, the spoiler. Aim to get a good, heavy, even coat, right up to the edges. Don't leave gaps or the mat will show through, and don't use ordinary resin for this job: gel-coat resin remains tacky even after hardening, which is ideal for bonding on the following layers.

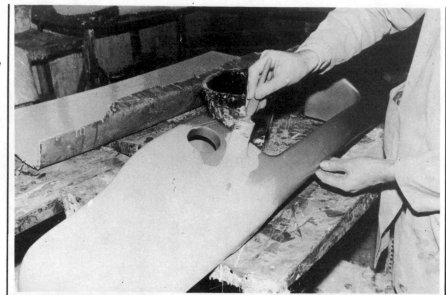

CP8. Place a layer of mat all over the master shaft after the gel-coat has 'gone-off'. Use gloves and, preferably, a heavy coat of barrier cream, even though this Smith & Deakin's worker doesn't go much on gloves.

CP9. Then stipple on lay-up resin to which you have added hardener. 'Wet-out' the mat thoroughly until it loses most of its whiteness, goes thoroughly floppy and takes on a yellowed appearance.

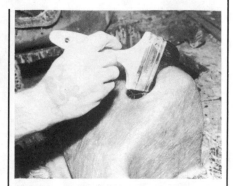

CP10. Make absolutely sure that the mat is down tight in all the corners because any gaps or air bubbles will severely weaken it.

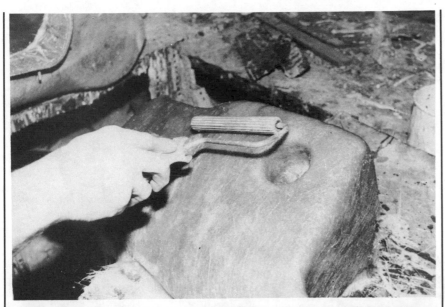

CP11.   You can make quite sure that all the air is out by using a special metal roller, sold by most GRP suppliers.

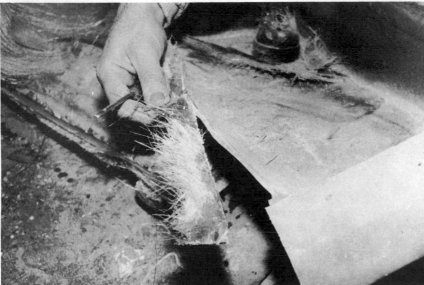

CP12.   You should have 'laid-up' right over the edge to be sure of getting a good thickness at the edge. If you can catch the resin just as it is 'green' you can cut it with a sharp knife. Otherwise, use a saw taking care not to damage the master, or mould.

CP13.   Remember the strip stuck over the flange? It has to be trimmed round and the screws undone then taken off. The surface made up of the original flange **plus** the extension now made up of fresh fibreglass is treated thoroughly with release agent.

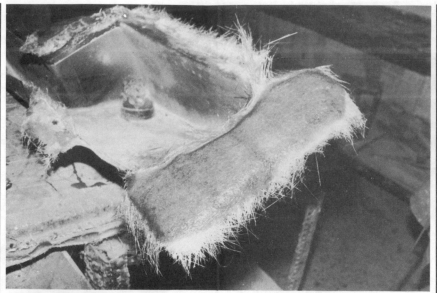

CP14.   Then, with the master spoiler still inside the mould, a pad of GRP is laid up across the whole flat surface, flange and all, but remember: there's release agent between this pad and the surface beneath.

CP15.   After the resin has gone off, but before removing the pad, it and the mould were drilled through in two places, so that later, when bolts and nuts are placed through these holes, the pad can be put back onto the mould in exactly the same place.

CP16.   The pad can now be removed from the mould and trimmed.

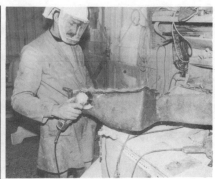

CP17.   The whole mould is trimmed back to the master. Here, Tom is wearing a fully protective air-fed breathing set. See your local factor for something almost as good for mouth and nose only and take note of the safety advice regarding the potentially lethal glass dust mentioned earlier in this section.

CP18.   The surplus has also to be cut off the air vent ...

CP19.   Even with release agent, the two won't just fall apart. Hitting all the edges fairly hard with a rubber mallet helps them to start.

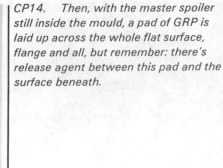

CP20.   *Protrusions like this are particularly bad sticking points. Just give it a few sharp cracks with the mallet and keep working at it.*

CP23.   *On the left is the negative or 'female' mould, while on the right is the original. To make a perfect copy, all you do is bolt the 'pads' of GRP back on to both ends, and lay up **inside** the mould; including inside the corners made by the two pads — they give the two flanges. To remove, take off the two pads, and hey presto! And not only will the copy be absolutely identical to the original, it could also be stronger!*

CP21.   *You can also try driving a smooth thin tapering piece of wood into the joint ...*

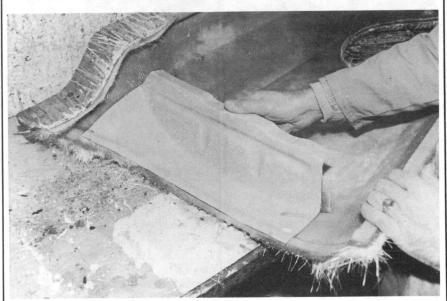

CP24.   *Some pieces can't be cast-in even without removable pieces, as shown. This is the support on the inside of an MGB wing. Make it separately and, after putting at least two coats of mat into the mould, put it in place and lay up more mat over all the edges to hold it in place.*

CP22.   *... hammering it all the way round.*

Incidentally, if you expect a mould to last a long time and provide many copies, make it with at least four layers of mat — but don't lay up more than four layers, *maximum* at one go, because the heat generated can cause problems. Also remember to leave the job on the master or in the mould for a couple of days; those nasty, rippled GRP panels you may have seen were probably caused by taking out the panel too soon.

With GRP work you are only restricted by your own imagination, and your ability to make a master of the shape you want, although you can use all sorts of materials to do it. But do remember that GRP copies everything — right down to blemishes and scratches, so spend time making sure that your master is as perfect as possible.

Fitting GRP repair panels in place of steel ■

FP1.   In the previous Chapter, Jennifer Shaw's beloved 1964 Ford Anglia was patched together for what seemed like the last time. Two years after the work was carried out, the car was still going strong and, if you recall, the original intention was to keep it going for only another 12 months. However, the car was beginning to look a little shoddy again and Jennifer was wondering what to do with it. One day a car pulled out in front of her while she was driving down the High Street and poked her little Anglia in the eye. In purely economic terms, that should have been that. The insurance company took the same view and wrote the car off. Jennifer, however, decided to keep the car so she bought it back off the insurance company, picked up a pair of fibreglass wings and decided to have them fitted.

Fibreglass wings cannot be fitted to a car where they form part of its structure without a great deal of structural re-strengthening being carried out on the car's bodywork. The strength left in this Anglia's original wings was negligible and in any case, it appeared that the wings did not form a significant part of the car's structural strength. However, regulations on this issue can change over a period of time and also from country to country, so always check that, a) the fitting of fibreglass wings is legal in your area, and b) that your car is going to be structurally OK after you have fitted them.

The other drawback with fibreglass wings is that they very rarely fit properly, needing quite a lot of manipulation and often ingenuity before they will go on: this is truer of cars which normally have weld-on wings than those which have bolt-on wings, naturally. The advantages however, are that they never corrode (although they do crack and craze), they are often a great deal cheaper than steel wings and, especially in the case of less highly regarded cars, they may be the only type of wing available at all.

FP2.   The bump was not a severe one by any means. Although the lens glass on the headlamp was not even cracked the wing was by now so weak that the headlamp had been pushed right back. The other accident related problems were that the grille was damaged (being made of thin aluminium, it was going to be tricky to straighten); the bumper was slightly bent, as was the front valance, and the sidelamp lens was broken. The whole sidelamp was in need of replacement so it was decided to replace it with a scrapyard lamp.

FP3.   Critical points to examine on this type of car before deciding whether it is actually worth fitting any sort of wings at all rather than scrapping the car, are the tops of the inner wings and especially the load-bearing tops of the struts.

FP4.   Here, corrosion had spread as a result of the accumulation of mud under the wing tops. It was going to be necessary to carry out some repair work here. The door hinge pillars are quite close to this area; the corrosion here didn't bode too well!

FP6.   Before dismantling anything, the battery was disconnected and lifted out of the way to give easier access to the inner panels. If you try messing around with electrics with the battery still connected up, especially with older, probably deteriorated, wiring, you're asking for a fire.

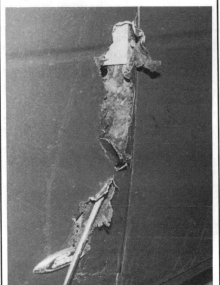

FP5.   It was quite instructive to poke out some of the old filler which had been slapped into place two years previously. Here, where filler had gone over 'rust-proofed' steel, the filler had been pushed out unmercifully by the steady advance of corrosion. Above, where the corner of a piece of aluminium can just be seen, and where all of the old, corroded steel had been cut away, there was remarkably little corrosion; certainly far less than had been originally expected.

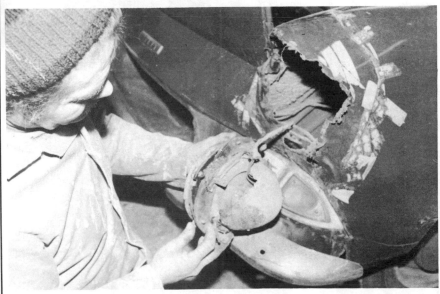

FP7.   The left-hand headlamp came out after the gentlest of tugs. The headlamp bowl was found to be severely corroded and in need of replacement. The sealing rubber was saved for further use and the wiring carefully disconnected.

*FP8.   The grille was cunningly held in place by a number of self-tapping screws fitting into the bodywork. In most cases like this, it is necessary to do a little detective work to find out how things go together. After all, it's quite reasonable for manufacturers **not** to want to have ugly nuts and bolts standing out like sore thumbs.*

FP9.   Restoring the grille to shape would have been extremely difficult because the aluminium had stretched. It could have been made to look acceptable if not original, but a local garage was found with an Anglia grille in new-old stock which they agreed to sell for a song. It's often well worth ringing round all the local main dealers to see if they have got any left-overs still in stock. An even better source is often an ex-main dealer who has gone over to another make. He would probably be only too pleased to let you have what he has got at nominal cost.

FP10.   On the right-hand side of the car, the headlamp was removed by more conventional means. First, the three extra-long self-tapping screws (again, partly concealed) were located and removed.

FP11.   Then the headlamp body was removed from the wing. Note that it was not necessary to strip the headlamp down at all; the glass-retaining ring was left in place.

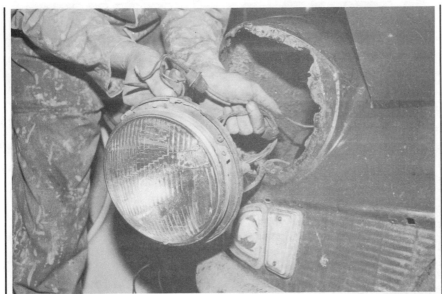

FP12. *The wiring grommet was carefully removed from the inner wing so that it could be used again, some of the surplus wire was pulled through from the engine bay to make the wiring clips more get-at-able, and the bullet connectors were disconnected. In this case, it was clear where they had to be reconnected, but if there is any doubt at all, it is best to tag the leads with masking tape and so save a great deal of time later. Be prepared to have to solder new bullet connectors on to the ends of the wires; old wiring often pulls straight out, leaving the connector stuck fast in the sleeve.*

FP13. *The indicator lenses were removed, too.*

FP14. *Behind the lens was a sealing grommet. Such things are often found to be irreplaceable and without them, the inside of the lamp would corrode and malfunction very quickly indeed. Try very hard to preserve them.*

FP15.   Inside this lamp was a
*supplementary lens. Again, take very
great care to preserve such things as
their replacement could be extremely
difficult on anything but the newest of
cars.*

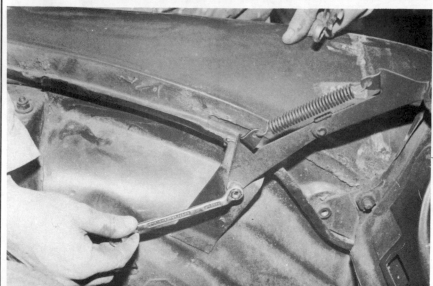

FP16.   *Next step was to remove the
bonnet. The bonnet stay was held in
place with a pair of nuts locked onto
one another.*

FP17.   *The stay itself was simply
pushed off the captive bolt and the
spring assembly left complete. It
makes sense to dismantle as little as
possible and in this case the stay
assembly was left attached to the
bonnet.*

212

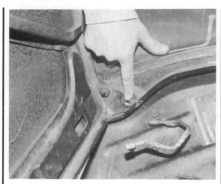

FP18.   The bonnet itself was held in place via a swivel bracket, bolted to the front inner wings.

FP20.   It was fairly simple for one person to lift the bonnet out of the way. Remember always to put some protective coverings on the floor to protect whichever end of the bonnet it is to be rested on. It is also important to cover the surface of the bonnet; it's all too easy to damage it whilst it's in storage.

FP19.   The bolts themselves would have been quite a struggle to reach with everything in place but with the headlamp taken out, access was easy. Where you have got to remove a scrap panel, it can often be useful to hack away the unwanted part and so make it easier to get at fixings that are normally tucked out of the way.

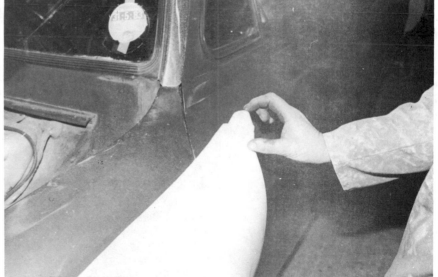

FP21.   Before hacking the old wings off, offer up the new ones and assess how much of the old wing needs to be removed and how much has to be left in place. The upper corners of our new wings were very badly misshapen so we decided to cut off that part of the fibreglass.

FP22.   The old wing was measured up to fit and a hacksaw cut made right across the position of the new joint.

FP23.   A sharp bolster chisel was used to remove the old wing ...

FP25.   Lifting the wing away revealed that there was perhaps less corrosion in the top of the inner wing than anticipated — a rare occurrence! It had to be plated of course. Note that the jagged edges of chiselled steel have been cleaned up. Fot this, a mini-angle grinder would be ideal, or a small pair of body repairer's tin snips.

FP24.   ... and the wing was lifted away and dumped.

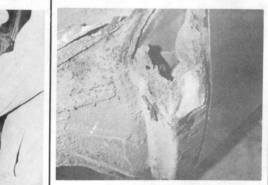

FP26.   This view of the door pillar presents another story! Although it was quite sound at its base, the pillar had corroded very badly indeed where mud has been trapped around the top of the wing. The door hadn't come loose, but it must have been a close thing. This demonstrates the fallacy of the belief that you don't need to have welding carried out if you're going to fit fibreglass wings. If the wings are bad enough to require replacement, some of the inner panels are bound to be as bad.

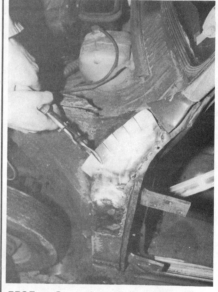

FP27.   Once the rust has been cleaned away from the door pillar, the curved section at the top was welded-up in a non-sophisticated but effective way. A plate was first welded onto the side of the pillar, then 'tags' were snipped along the edge of the over-sized plate. A pencil line had already been drawn, showing where to cut to.

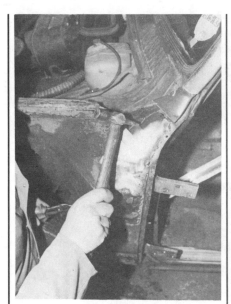

FP28.   Then, one at a time, the tags were folded over using a hammer. To have created a proper flanged, curved panel would have been far too time consuming for a car that by any account had a short life, but the quick method adopted is sound enough if not pretty.

FP29.   For the top face, again, an oversized panel was cut to shape.

FP30.   Then, too, the edge facing the inner wing was tagged to make a curved flange.

FP31.   This time the flange was created by turning up the tags using a pair of pliers.

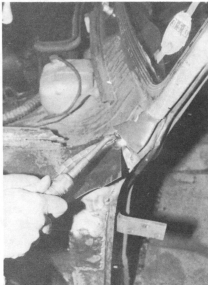

FP32.   The top of the plate was tack welded into place at its far end ...

FP33.   ... then the plate was pushed down to follow the curve of the hinge pillar using a large screwdriver (you lean on it with your shoulder leaving both hands free), and the plate tack welded down.

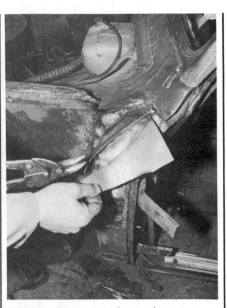

FP34.   Excess steel was then trimmed off and everything welded solidly into place. The flanging system described here is certainly not suitable for the purist or for the owner of a 'classic' car, but a welded flange is far stronger than a straightforward edge weld.

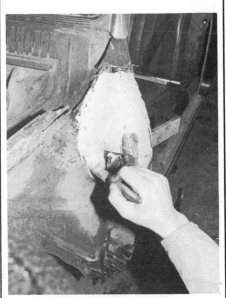

FP35.   Even though the repair was considered temporary, slapping a coat of paint over it cost next to nothing.

FP36. You should always remove trim from any area in which you are welding but even then, it is easy to set fire to a coating of oil, old fibreglass repairs or underseal. Having a proper fire extinguisher available when welding is vital, but for putting out those small, highly localised fires, a washing-up bottle full of water is quick, easily directed — and free! Never be tempted to make this a stand-in for a purpose built fire extinguisher; lives could depend upon it. See the section on 'Safety' for further information.

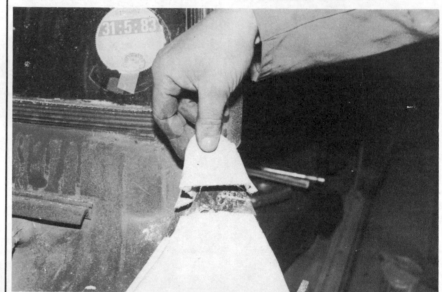

FP37. With the top part of the fibreglass wing trimmed to fit the steel panel, the new wing was offered up and placed in position.

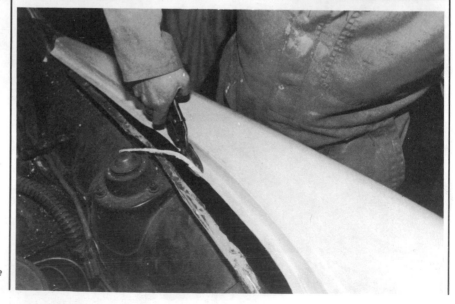

FP38. The rain channel flange was far too wide so it was cut down using the snips. Be careful not to crack the fibreglass if you choose this method but remember that it is far healthier than using any sort of power or abrading tool that can cause particles of fibreglass to fly around and enter the lungs.

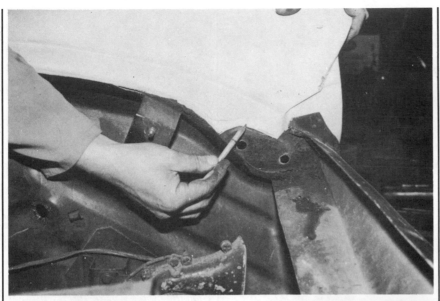

FP39.   At the inside-front of the wing, it was necessary to make a cut-out to allow for the refitting of the bonnet swivel plate. This illustrates one of the ways in which these wings are never made to fit precisely.

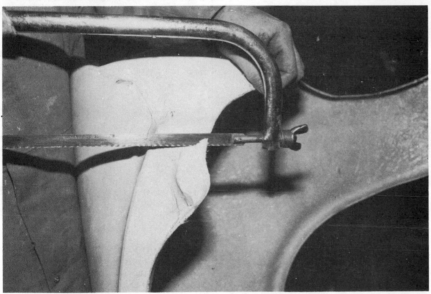

FP40.   This time a hacksaw was used because the risk of splitting this larger, flatter panel with the snips was too great.

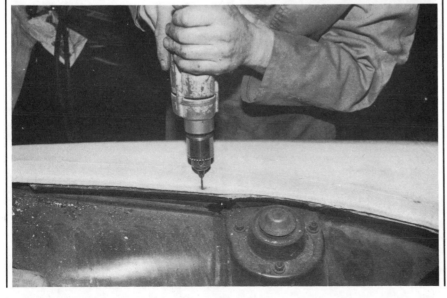

FP41.   Once the wing was deemed to fit properly it was held in place while a small hole was drilled through the wing flange and the steel rain channel at the top of the old inner wing.

FP42.   The wing was then located using a self-tapping screw and a large washer underneath the head of the screw to spread the load. Be prepared to remove and refit more than once if necessary, to ensure a good fit. Follow this up by fitting a line of fixing screws.

FP44.   It is then a simple matter to go around all the fixing points, drilling more pilot holes ...

FP46.   The front valance was easily pulled back into shape and here, where it seemed impossible to find any means of joining the fibreglass to the steel, fibreglass mat and resin were used to bond the two surfaces together, after first scuffing them both to give a key. Then the profile was restored with body filler.

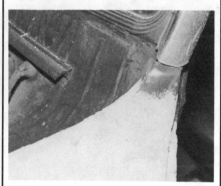

FP47.   At the other end of the wing, the joint was made using chopped-strand impregnated filler paste. When scuffing fibreglass to give a 'key', always remember to wear a mask to avoid inhaling particles of fibreglass dust which can be very harmful to health.

FP43.   The wing was then joined down the door pillar and at the bottom, onto the sill, in the same way. Be sure to put the minimum number of screws in at this stage, just in case you have to go back and make any readjustments.

FP45.   ... and putting in more self-tapping screws on the principle of 'the more the merrier'. Fibreglass takes localised stresses very poorly because its surface cracks badly. Thus, it follows that the greater the number of stress points, the less the load placed upon each one.

FP48.   On the other side of the car now, the fitted wing looked a good deal less scruffy than the old one.

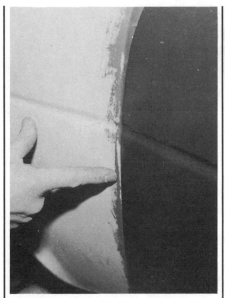

FP49.   Fibreglass is thicker than
steel, and one of the most common
problems is to find the front of the door
catching on the rear corner of the wing.

FP51.   One of the wings had a bald
patch! The gel-coat (outer surface) had
broken away at one point and so the
patch and the surrounding area were
ground back to the fibreglass. **Use
goggles and a face mask!**

FP50.   One solution, where there is
insufficient hinge adjustment available,
is to bend the door hinges out just
enough to clear the obstruction. (It
looks like a 'bodge' but is in fact
standard bodyshop practice.) Place a
block of wood in the gap between half
opened door and hinge pillar and push
the door towards the closed position.
The leverage of the door acting upon
the fulcrum of the wooden blocks,
forces the front of the door slightly
outwards.

FP52.   Fine fibreglass was dabbed
into the patch with resin to restore
strength in that area ...

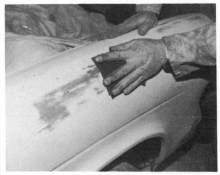

FP53.   ... then rubbed down, filled
and rubbed down again, back to the
profile of the original wing.

FP54.   The next problem was that of fitting the headlamps back into place. The headlamp bezel was held in place and used to establish the exact centre of where the headlamp was to be fitted.

FP55.   Then, the rubber headlamp gasket was measured to find the size of the headlamp bowl.

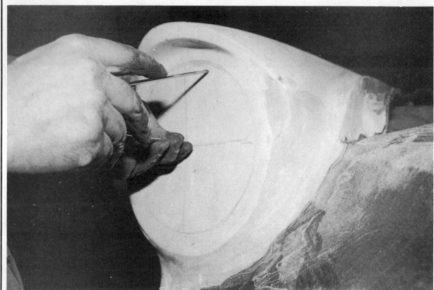

FP57.   Scribing a line with the makeshift dividers was easy ...

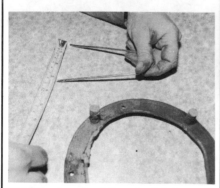

FP56.   A makeshift pair of dividers can easily be made up using a piece of thick welding rod sharpened at both ends. Half the diameter of the rubber gasket was transferred to the 'dividers'.

FP58.   ... but it was necessary to emphasise the line with a pencil otherwise it would have been too faint.

FP59.   A series of small holes were drilled then made into one hole big enough to ...

FP60.   ... insert the blade of the power jig saw. The amount of dust created is amply illustrated in this picture.

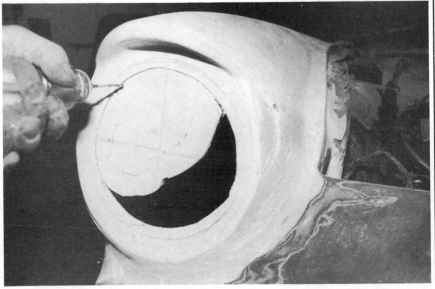

FP61.   Because of the 'eyebrow' at the top of the wing, it was not possible to get the jigsaw all the way round so an alternative method of cutting out was used: a series of holes were drilled around the perimeter of the marking out, then linked together using the drill as a sort of milling cutter, i.e. moving sideways through the thin bridges between the holes.

FP62. The size of the hole was right first time. It really pays to measure up and mark out properly right from the start.

FP63. The headlamp was held in place by drilling small holes and holding it to the fibreglass with self-tapping screws. An alternative would have been small nuts and bolts with washers to the rear but they would have been the very devil to get out again once rust took a hold on their threads.

FP64. The wires were reconnected and the earth wire clamped back to the body in the position it came from. Many cars don't have an earth wire running from each unit but earth the lamps through the wing itself. In that case it is necessary to run an earth wire from the body of each lamp to the car bodywork before the lights will work.

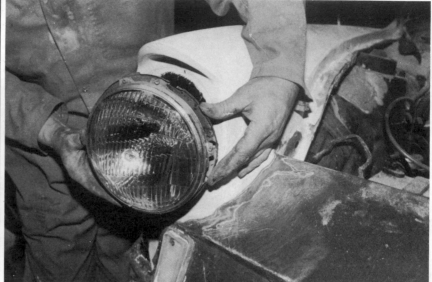

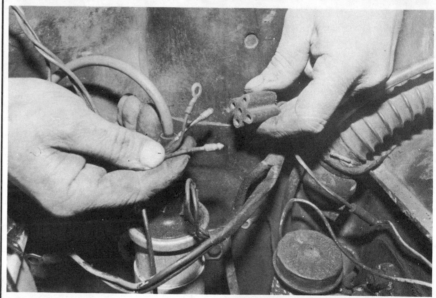

FP65. With all the fitting procedure complete, the wings were masked off and sprayed. Fibreglass wings are notorious for having a poor finish with lots of scratches in the surface. Use several coats of primer-filler or even one of the high-build spraying fillers for which you need more spraying pressure than this little Apollo gun is capable of delivering.

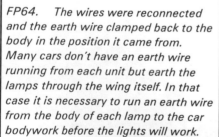

←

→

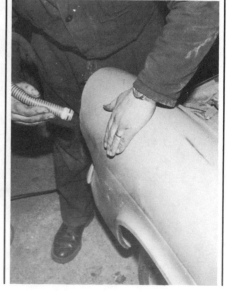

FP66. The surface was thoroughly flatted then all dust carefully blown from all crevices.

FP67. *Both wings and most of the front panel were sprayed in cellulose paint for which the little Apollo is ideally suited. The finish is excellent and drying time reduced because of the slightly warmed air which the gun emits.*

FP68. *After spraying the wings and refitting the bonnet, the bonnet paint seemed really dull. After all, it was two years old and wasn't often cleaned! The original shine was quickly restored using one of the mildly abrasive shine restorers.*

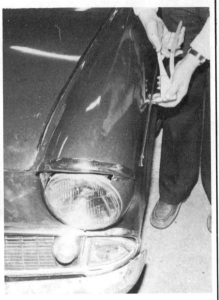

FP69. *It only remained to fit the trim, but with fibreglass, that can be a major headache. The original-type clips were pop-riveted into place but, because they were designed for steel, would not reach through the fibreglass and constantly pulled right out again. In desperation, the chrome strips were drilled and pop-riveted direct to the panel using extra-long aluminium pop rivets. Note that a different type of sidelamp had to be fitted to the left-hand side until a suitable replacement could be found in a breaker's yard.*

Fibreglass wings can be useful to get the owner of a car of little worth out of a spot and they are certainly cheaper than steel wings in most cases, and cover a wider range of cars. It should never be imagined however, that fibreglass wings are a soft option and easier to fit. As the foregoing pages should have pointed out, they aren't!

Glossary

GRP (Fibreglass, 'glass, glassfibre) – a composite material consisting of matting woven from filaments of glass embedded in a chemically-hardened plastic bonding material.

Mat – fibres of glass bonded or woven together to form different types of weights of loose mat.

Resin – plastic liquid which is impregnated into mat and which goes hard after the addition of hardener. Actually starts life as a solid which has been dissolved in a Styrene solvent.

Gel-coat – the outer layer of GRP. A layer of plastic not impregnated into mat because it would show through its surface.

Gel-coat resin – A thixotropic (run-free) resin painted onto the mould first. Retains 'sticky' layer when exposed to air, thus facilitating adhesion of following layers.

Lay-up resin – doesn't leave a sticky outer layer. Stippled through mat.

Laying-up – the process of forming layers of resin impregnated mat.

Wet-out – to thoroughly impregnate mat with resin.

Green – newly gone off: firm but slightly rubbery and not completely hard.

⑧ Doors, Windows & Soft-tops

Stripping Out Door Gear ●

Sometimes you have to take out door gear because the mechanism goes wrong and sometimes you have to remove it to repair a door. There are several different types of door gear and the main ones are shown here. There has been no attempt to cover every different make, however — that would clearly be impossible — but most types of door trim and window gear are shown here so there should be enough information contained in this chapter to apply to whatever car you are working upon. Before removing any type of window mechanism, remember to prop the glass up or have an assistant hold it there or it can crash down and cause a nasty injury.

When replacing glass channels and winder mechanisms, remember to replace everything without tightening up. Then make sure that everything operates smoothly before finally tightening nuts and bolts.

Stripping early doors and later Van and Pick-up doors

BDS2. *Unscrew the two crosshead screws holding the door pull in place (lift the fold-down handle on earlier models).*

BDS3. *Door catch bezels "break" in the middle — they clip apart then slide out.*

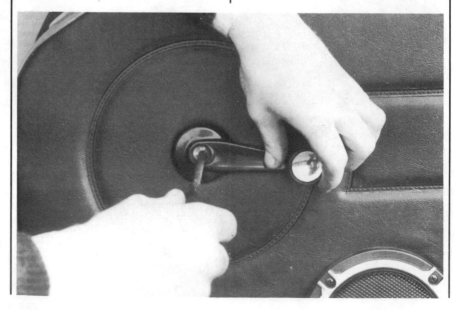

BDS1. *Start by removing the trim rail at the top of the door (2 crosshead screws at each end), then remove the single screw which holds the window winder in place.*

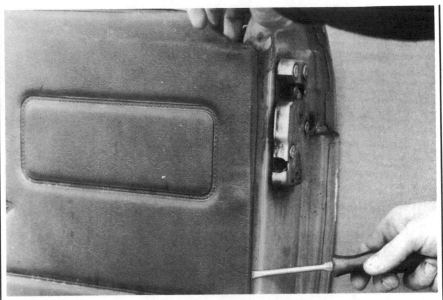

BDS4. *Remove door speakers if fitted.*

BDS5. *The door trim clips forwards and off. Take care, if the trim is an old one, to lever near to the spring clips.*

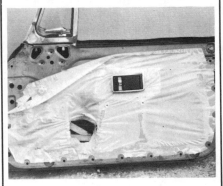

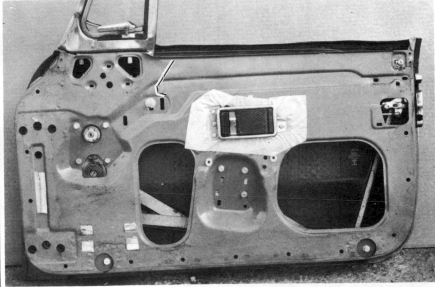

BDS6. *The protective plastic sheet should be carefully removed and reused later if not damaged.*

BDS7. *Open wide. This won't hurt! This now gives access to the door's internals.*

BDS8. *Carefully screwdriver off the spring clip which holds the latch release rod in place ...*

BDS9. *... and the one which holds the locking lever.*

BDS10.   Pull them forwards and out of location with the latch.

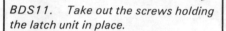

BDS11.   Take out the screws holding the latch unit in place.

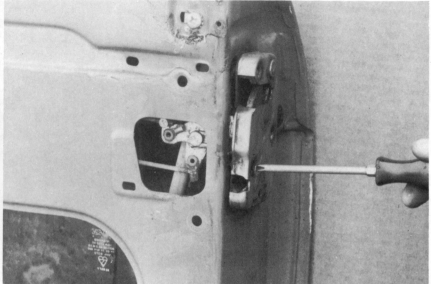

BDS12.   Remove the latch unit.

BDS13.   Remove the four screws holding the latch pull in place ...

BDS14.   ... and remove it.

BDS15.   Take out the window runner top screw.

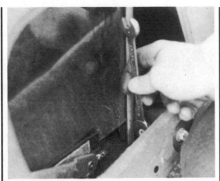

BDS16.   Unbolt the bottom of the runner, either inside the door ...

BDS17.   ... or from outside, removing the bracket as well. Leave the runner loose, inside the door.

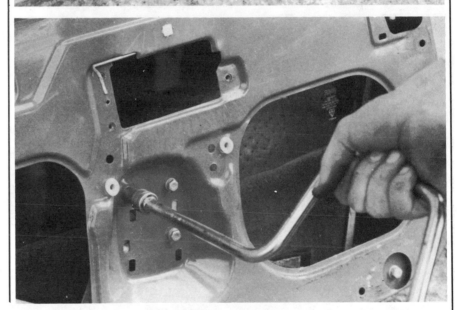

BDS18.   Remove the window regulator extension screws.

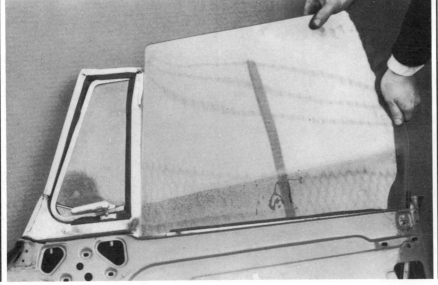

BDS19.   Remove the regulator securing screws. Slide the rollers out of the bottom of the channel fixed to the bottom of the window glass.

BDS20.   Lift the glass up and out of the door.

BDS21.   Lift the rear glass channel out of the door.

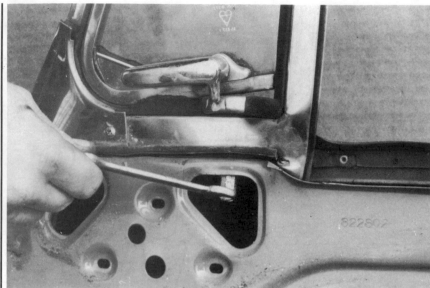

BDS24.   Remove the two nuts which hold the quarterlight from beneath and the one which holds it from the front of the door.

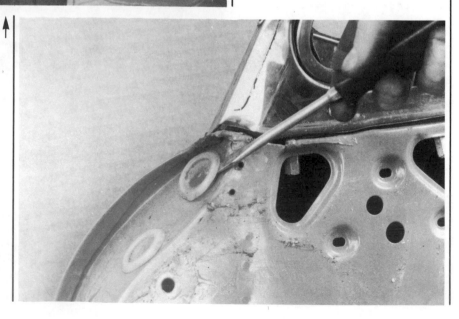

BDS22.   "Persuade" the regulator assembly out of the holes in the door.

BDS23.   Lever the front grommets out of their holes in the front of the door.

BDS26.   *Lift the quarterlight assembly out of the door.*

BDS25.   *Undo the two nuts which hold the front window channel (an extension of the quarterlight).*

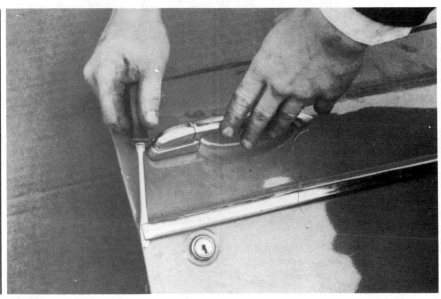

BDS27.   *The chrome trim clips forwards and off (be very careful not to distort it), the door push is held by two nuts — two screw threads protrude from the handle, backwards through the door skin — and the lock is held by a spring clip which slides into a groove in the lock, tight against the inside of the door skin.*

BDS28.   *Voila! The now denuded door skin is ready for whatever work is to be carried out.*

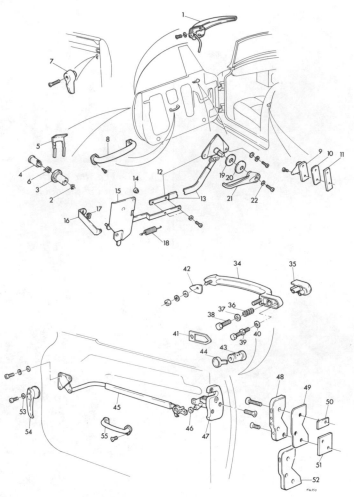

Figure DS1.   MGB door mechanism

The door mechanism shown here is typical of those fitted to many cars

Items 1 to 22 apply to earlier sports-tourer only, with pull-out exterior door handles.

1   Outer door handle
2   Spring clip
3   Lock housing
4   Lock barrel
5   Lock retaining clip
6   Self-centring spring
7   Inner locking knob
8   Door pull
9   Striker
10 Packing
11 Tapping Plate
12 Remote control lock
13 Anti-rattle sleeve
14 Outside door handle buffer
15 Lock
16 Operating link
17 Spring clip
18 Tension spring
19 Fibre washer
20 Finisher
21 Inner door handle
22 Spring washer
34 Outer door handle

35 Pushbutton
36 Spring
37 Shakeproof washer
38 Set screw
39 Set screw with locknut
40 Shakeproof washer
41 Fibre washer
42 Fibre washer
43 Lock barrel
44 Retaining clip
45 Remote control link
46 Anti-rattle washer
47 Lock
48 Striker
49 Shim – 0.003 in or 0.006 in
    (0.08 mm or 0.16 mm)
50 Tapping plate (upper)
51 Tapping plate (lower)
52 Striker lock
53 Spring washer
54 Inner door handle
55 Door pull

Stripping Mini door trim

Early type

MDS1.   Start by taking out the trim finishers which simply push into each end of the door pocket.

MDS2.   Take out the screws that hold the trim into the base of the door pocket.

MDS3.   Take out the card trim, taking care not to rip it.

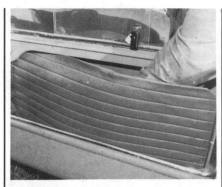

MDS4.   Next ease your arm behind the main door trim and push it forwards in the centre so that it bows forwards and comes clear of the door frame at one end.

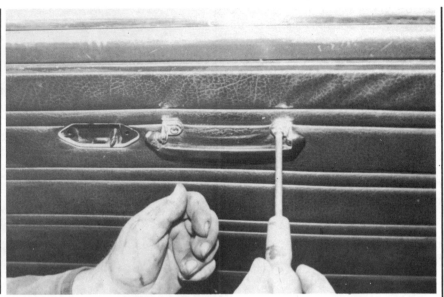

MDS7.   Next the door pull handle is removed by taking out the two screws which hold it in place.

MDS5.   Lift that end upwards and lift out the main trim board as shown.

Later type ──────────────▶

MDS6.   Take out the cross-headed screws that hold the window winder knob and the door catch handle (top right). Each handle then pulls off its square shaft.

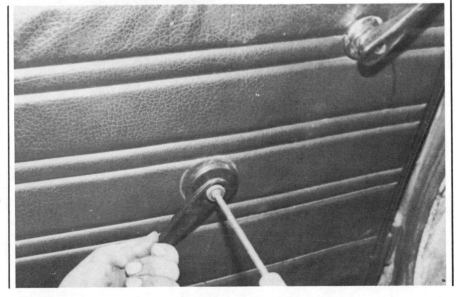

MDS8.   The trim board is held to the door by a ring of clips which snap into holes in the door frame. Carefully ease a screwdriver behind the trim board and snap the clips out one at a time. Avoid snatching at the clips or they may pull out of the trim board, especially if it has started to age and lose its strength.

Figure MDS1.   Exploded view of Mini Van, Pick-up and early Saloon models' door lock and handle assembly.

MDS9.   When the two sides and bottom of the trim panel have been snapped away, the top of the panel is eased downwards out of its retaining flap at the top of the door. There should be a waterproof covering behind the trim panel and if this has to be removed, re-glue it into place before refitting the trim panel.

Stripping early doors and later Van and Pick-up doors See Figure MDS1.

MDS10.   Start by taking off the screw which holds the lock handle spindle in place. (Fig 2, 1) Use a straight point screwdriver.

1   Lock handle spindle fixings
2   Lock body retaining screws
3   Interior handle
4   Seal
5   Exterior handle

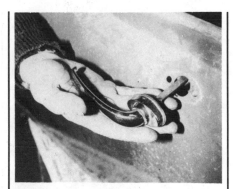

MDS11.   *The exterior handle can now be removed, but not before ...*

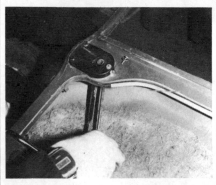

MDS12... *the interior handle (Fig 2, 3) has been eased off the spindle with a screwdriver. Some are held in place with a pinch screw and this is being undone in the photograph.*

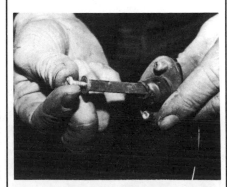

MDS13.   *Keep the oddly sized, oddly threaded retaining screw and its washer safely by putting them straight back into the end of the spindle.*

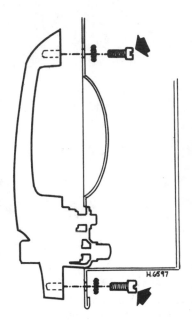

Figure MDS2.   Later type Mini door handle assembly.

See figure MDS2. With door trim out of the way, later-type door handles are removed by unscrewing the two screws arrowed here. The screws holding the internal handle and lock in place are also clearly visible with the trim out of the way, while the latch assembly is screwed to the rear closing face of the door.

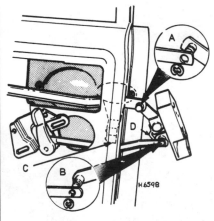

Figure MDS3.   Front door lock removal

A   Remote control handle operating rod
B   Interior lock operating rod
C   Exterior handle lock link
D   Latch lock rod

See Figure MDS3. Front door lock removal: note that clips at A and B have to be removed *after* all three mechanisms have been disconnected from the door. With the handle taken off, the lock barrel and push button can be dismantled as follows: 1) Prise off the retaining clip which holds the lock barrel to the handle. 2) Insert the key into the lock and use it to pull out the lock barrel. 3) Undo the screw that fixes the retaining plate to the exterior handle. 4) You can now take out the push button after lifting off the retaining plate, operating link, washer and spring.

See figure MDS4. On earlier models the plunger cap (B) can be adjusted by screwing in or screwing out to give around 1mm to 1.5mm of free movement before the door lock release lever begins to move.

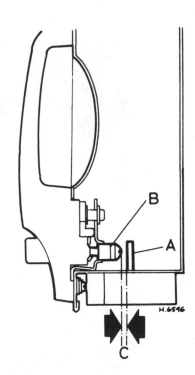

Figure MDS4. Door handle push button plunger adjustment

A   Lock release lever
B   Plunger cap
C   = 0.031 to 0.062 in
      (1.0 to 1.5mm)

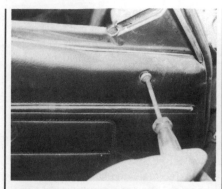

Volvo door strip

VDS1. The top of the door trim is held in place with self-tapping screws. Be sure to retain the cup washers.

VDS2. Door handles push onto a splined shaft and are held in place with a spring 'hairgrip' clip.

VDS3. This is best removed by 'fishing' for the loop end of it with a wire hook, whilst the door trim panel is pushed back far enough to give access.

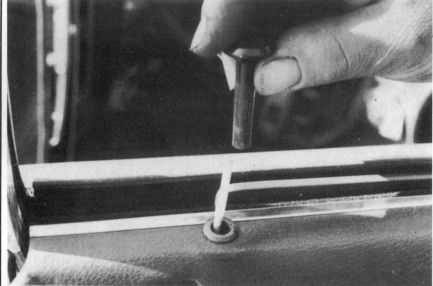

VDS4. The door lock button simply unscrews, leaving a threaded pin protruding.

VDS5. Around the interior latch handle, the plastic bezel springs on — and off.

VDS6. Now, like most door trims, the concealed clips around sides and base are eased away ...

VDS7. ...leaving the trim panel free to be lifted up over the door lock pin and away.

VDS8. Next, the four bolts holding the mechanism to the door casing can be removed, but ensure that the glass is supported.

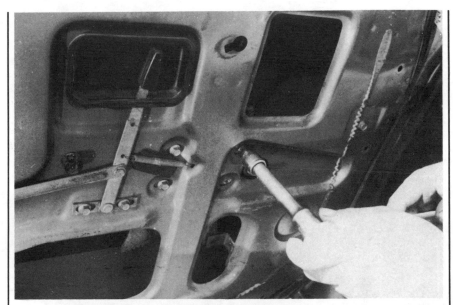

VDS9. Now, this is cheating! This clip is found on the assembly at the bottom of the glass, inside the door casing, facing away from you (i.e. facing the outside of the car), so there's no other way to photograph it!

VDS10. By feeling up inside the door casing, the spring clip has to be raised over the pin and pushed off ...

VDS11. ... followed by a spring and washers. All the while, the glass must be supported, preferably by an assistant.

VDS12. Next the quarter light and door glass channel rubbers are eased out (use liquid soap to help ease them back in, using a blunt screwdriver for 'persuasion').

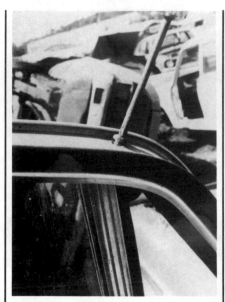

VDS13.   Take out the top screw
holding the glass guide in place ...

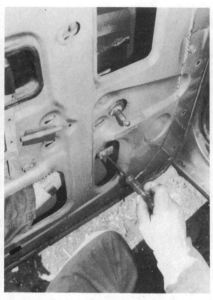

VDS15.   Then remove the bottom
attachment screw ...

VDS16.   ... leaving the channel to be
lifted upwards and clear.

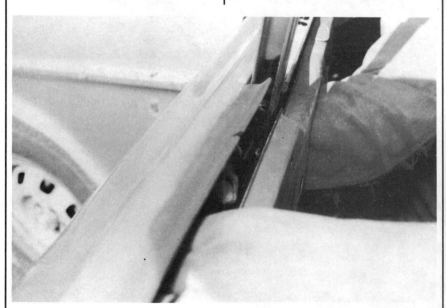

VDS14.   ... and the screws holding it
just below the top of the door frame.
This tightly-squeezed view is through
the gap from whence the glass appears
when wound upwards.

VDS17.   Now the glass is free to be
lifted up and away through the top of
the door and the mechanism can be
taken out through one of the bottom
apertures.

Chevrolet (Full-Size Models) 1969 through 1981 door strip

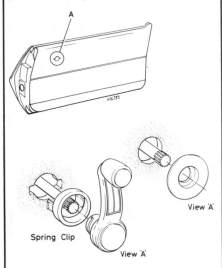

Figure DS2.   Chevrolet window handle installation

On some models, the door handles are fitted as shown (see 'Volvo' section for removal details) while others are held on with screws. Door trim is screwed or clipped into place and the door pull handle and armrest are screwed on. After removing the trim panel, note the installation of the water seal beneath and ensure that it is refitted correctly later. When reinstalling the clip-type winder handles, first fit the clip to the handle, then hold the handle in place and strike it home with a sharp blow from the palm of the hand.

To remove the front door glass:
1) Remove the door trim as shown.
2) Take out the weatherstrip clips, the travel stops and the stabiliser guide assembly.
3) Half-lower the window and remove the lower sash channel nuts. Now raise the window glass completely and remove the other nuts.
4) Mark the position of the bolts and remove them, disengaging the guide from the roller, and rest the guide in the bottom of the door.
5) Tilt the top of the glass until the rear roller is clear of the inner panel and then lift the glass from the door.
6) You can remove the regulator by itself after propping the window in its fully open position. Mark the positions of the cam attaching bolts before removal. Disconnect the wiring harness from power-operated windows when fitted.

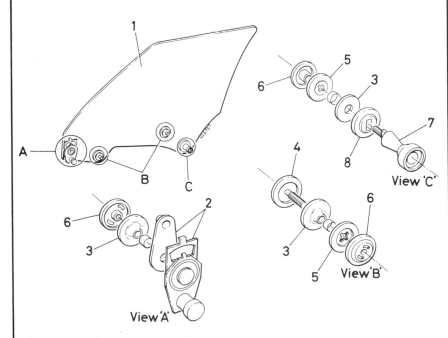

Fig. DS3.   Front door window components

1	Window assembly	5	Washer (plastic)
2	Window assembly (bell crank)	6	Nut
3	Spacer	7	Window roller
4	Bolt, inner panel cam	8	Washer (metal)

Buick Regal and Century door strip

(Refer to Figure DS4 under 'Chevrolet Camaro' for door hardware and components).

1) Door trim and panels are removed in the normal way. Winder handles use the Chevrolet/Volvo-type attachment method. (See earlier Sections).
2) Remove the decorative cover plate from around the inside door handle by prising away carefully with a screwdriver. Remove the screws which hold the handle in place, take off the remote control rod from the back of the handle and remove the handle.
3) Unscrew the locking knob from its shaft.
4) Remove the control escutcheon and control cable from the remote mirror control, where fitted.
5) Remove the armrest or armrest-cum-doorpull by unscrewing the retaining screws which are sometimes hidden beneath decorative plugs.
6) The trim panel unscrews and/or unclips in the conventional way.
7) If power windows are fitted, removal is not a DIY job and should be left to your dealer.
8) If manual windows are fitted, remove the inner water shield, then the up-travel stops at the front and rear of the door.
9) Loosen the front and rear belt trim support retainers located at the top of the door in the window channel.
10) With the glass three-quarters of the way down, remove the lower sash channel to glass attaching nuts through the special access holes in the inner door skin.
11) Lift the window straight up and out of the channel, aligning the rollers with the notches provided in the inner door skin.
12) If the regulator is to be removed, remove the window first, as described.
13) Disconnect the regulator from the inner door by undoing the nuts and bolts or if rivets have been used (later models) carefully drill them out with a $\frac{1}{4}$ inch drill bit. Remove the regulator through the large access hole.
14) If rivets were drilled out, replace the regulator using 20 x $\frac{1}{2}$ inch screws and U-nuts on the regulator body.

Chevrolet Camaro door strip

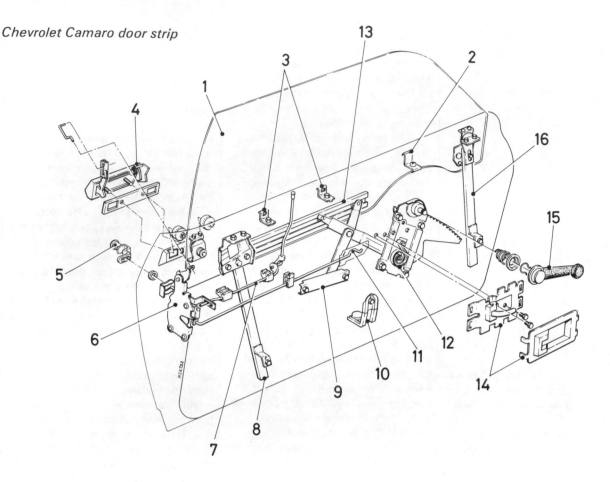

Figure DS4. *Camaro door mechanism components*

1	Window assembly	7	Inside locking rod	12	Window regulator (manual)
2	Trim pad hanger plates	8	Rear guide	13	Lower sash channel cam
3	Trim pad hanger plate and stabilizer strip	9	Inner panel cam	14	Remote control handle assembly and escutcheon
4	Door outside handle	10	Window down travel bumper support	15	Window regulator handle
5	Lock cylinder	11	Remote control to lock rod	16	Front guide
6	Lock assembly				

Remove the door trim panel and also the door window glass and manually operated regulator following the instructions for Buick Regal and Century.

Power Windows: Note that if the following description of how to remove this type of power system is not followed, severe personal injury could be the result.

1. This system incorporates an electric motor and an independent control switch for each of the door windows. The driver's door has a master control switch permitting operation of all the windows.

2. The electric motor which powers the window regulator is a reversible-direction motor and operates with 12 volts. It features an internal circuit breaker for protection. The motor is secured to the regulator with bolts.

3. The electrical motor can be removed from the regulator with the remainder of the window system intact only if the door glass is intact and attached to the regulator. If the door glass is broken or removed from the door, the motor must be separated after the regulator is removed from inside the door.

Glass intact and attached

4. Raise the window and remove the door trim panel and water shield as described in the previous sections.

5. Reach inside the door access cavity and disconnect the wiring harness at the motor.

6. It is imperative at this point that the window glass is taped or blocked in the up position. This will prevent the glass from falling into the door and possibly causing injury or damage.

7. Since the bolts used to secure the motor to the regulator are inaccessible, it is necessary to drill three large

access holes in the metal door inner panel. The position of these holes is critical. Use the full-size template shown in Figure DS5. This template should be positioned on the door with tape after properly aligning it with the regulator attaching rivets (late models) or bolts (early models).

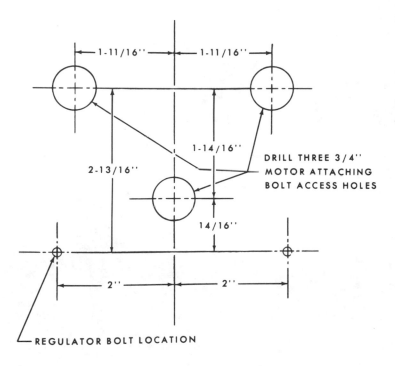

ALIGN TEMPLATE WITH APPROPRIATE REGULATOR
LOWER ATTACHING BOLTS ON DOOR

1-11/16''
1-11/16''
1-14/16''
2-13/16''
DRILL THREE 3/4''
MOTOR ATTACHING
BOLT ACCESS HOLES
14/16''
2''
2''
REGULATOR BOLT LOCATION

Figure DS5. Template used for gaining access to the power window motor bolts.

8. Use a center punch to dimple the panel at the center of the template access holes and then drill the $\frac{3}{4}$-inch holes with a hole saw.

9. Reach through the access hole and support the motor as the attaching bolts are removed. Remove the motor through the access holes, being careful that the window glass is firmly supported in the up position.

10. Before installation, the motor drive gear and regulator sector teeth should be lubricated.

11. Upon positioning the motor, make sure that the drive gear engages properly with the regulator sector teeth. Install remaining components by reversing the removal order. Waterproof tape can be used to seal the three access holes drilled in the metal inner panel.

Glass Broken or Not Attached

12. Remove the window regulator as described. Make sure that the wiring harness to the motor is disconnected first.

13. It is imperative that the regulator sector gear be locked into position before removing the motor from the regulator. The control arms are under pressure and can cause serious injury if the motor is removed without performing the following operation.

14. Drill a hole through the regulator sector gear and backplate, install a bolt and nut to lock the gear in position. Do not drill closer than $\frac{1}{2}$ inch to the edge of the sector gear or backplate.

15. Remove the three motor attaching bolts and remove the motor assembly from the regulator.

16. Prior to installation, the motor drive gear and regulator sector teeth should be lubricated. The lubricant should be cold weather approved to at least -20°F. Lubriplate Spray Lube 'A' is recommended by GM.

17. When installing the motor to the regulator make sure that the sector gear teeth and drive gear teeth properly mesh.

18. Once the motor attaching bolts are tightened, the locking nut and bolt can be removed. Install the regulator and don't forget to connect the motor wiring.

Fiat door strip

This is a cable type of winder system and is, if anything, easier to dismantle than any other because there are no bulky and mischevious mechanisms to handle.

FDS1. *The chrome bezel around the base of the door handle is carefully levered off.*

FDS2. *Once again, the handle is of the splined shaft/concealed spring clip variety.*

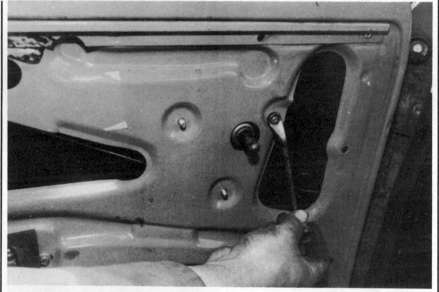

FDS6.   *The channel can be removed through the bottom of the door.*

FDS3.   *Door pull/armrest comes away after unscrewing the two retaining screws.*

FDS4.   *The window channel is held at the top of the door frame by a screw ...*

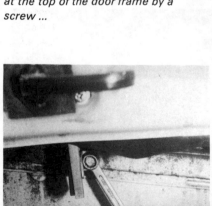

FDS7.   *The winder regulator is held to the door frame by three nuts ...*

FDS5.   *... and at the bottom, inside the door casing, by a bolt.*

FDS8.   *... but when removing, be careful not to get the cable itself into a tangle.*

FDS12.	Carefully lower the glass to the bottom of the door ...

FDS9.	The cable can be removed from the bottom pulley ...

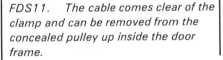

FDS10.	... and the window eased down far enough at least to expose the cable clamp. One of the screws must be taken out completely but the other need only be slackened.

FDS11.	The cable comes clear of the clamp and can be removed from the concealed pulley up inside the door frame.

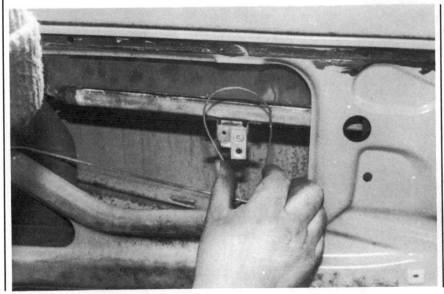

FDS13.	... and lift it over the bottom edge of the frame and out.

Ford door strip

FODS1. This particular Ford system is neither unconventional nor difficult to remove and it is common. Remove the three screws holding the regulator arm support from the door, after propping the glass in the ¾-down position.

FODS2. Take out the screws holding the regulator winder mechanism to the door.

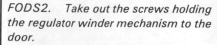

FODS3. With the mechanism free inside the door casing, slide the rollers out of the channels on the bottom of the window glass.

FODS4. Ease the mechanism out of the bottom of the door ...

FODS5. ... and the glass out of the top as shown.

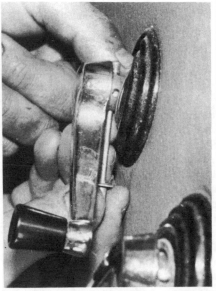

General

GDS1. Remember that old doors will undoubtedly have had a good few gallons of water pass through them! Soak all fixing nuts, bolts and screws with a spray-on releasing fluid well before starting work.

GDS3. Some internal door handles are held on in a way that's a bit difficult to understand at first. Push the trim inwards and behind the bezel you may find that the shank of the handle and the squared shaft it pushes onto have a pin passing through them. It may or may not be a tapered pin, but if it is tapered, push from the narrow end, of course. Push the pin out with a thin punch or nail as shown – you may need to give it a tap with a hammer.

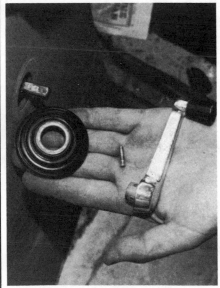

GDS2. On some older cars, quarter-light or vent assemblies were often attached to the glass runner so look out for screws holding the whole thing in place and not just the runner.

GDS4. Then the handle and bezel just pull off. The trim may have a spring behind it placed around the squared shaft, to keep the assembly up tight.

Windscreen Replacement ●

Most windscreens are fitted in place using one of two methods. The more traditional method uses a rubber seal in which the glass is set, and replacing it requires a little know-how but not necessarily a great deal of skill. If you do intend replacing your own windscreen glass take a close look at the condition of the rubbers holding it in place. Old rubber becomes hard, loses its flexibility and tends to crack as it is being fitted so, if in doubt, get hold of a new one before you start.

More modern fixing methods involve the use of an adhesive to hold the screen in place. Sometimes these are cold setting adhesives, applied and used like ordinary mastic (except that they are designed to set) and sometimes they are set by passing an electric current through a hot wire which passes through the adhesive. The heat softens the adhesive which sticks the glass in place then re-sets as it cools down.

Some cars have a great deal of trim around their windscreen rubbers which may or may not be simple to remove; much depends on the degree of competence and confidence of the individual. The first of the following sequences shows how to remove a simple rubber windscreen fitting system, and while others using this system may *look* more complicated, the principle will be the same.

Windscreens held by rubbers

WR1.   This windscreen had shattered, just as they normally do, with no advanced warning at all, presumably because of a stone thrown up by another vehicle. Other reasons for replacing a screen can be because a screen is chipped, because a sandstorm (which can occur in certain parts of the world) has pitted it, because the wipers have indelibly marked or scratched the screen or simply because the owner wants to fit a 'Sundym' tinted screen or a heated rear screen.

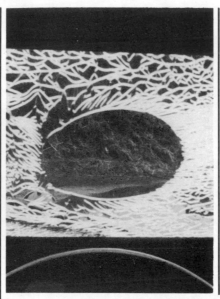

WR2.   This screen had the clever and useful facility of a clear patch remaining in the driver's eye-line after it had cracked. If you're refitting this type of screen, make sure that the clear patch goes in front of the driver. (Most screens, being curved, are not actually reversible of course.)

WR3.   Windscreen Services of Worcester came out to show how a screen swap was carried out. First they put masking tape over all the windscreen demister vents. Many cars are fitted with trim or other mouldings around the inside of the screen that also has to be removed.

WR4.   As it comes out, a broken windscreen separates into a thousand different pieces and goes in a thousand different directions. Covering the seats, the floor and the dash is an essential step to take if you don't want to spend hours picking sharp splinters of glass out of every conceivable nook and cranny.

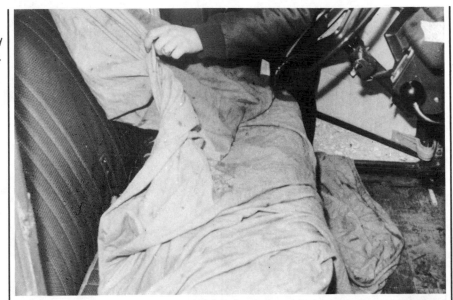

WR5.   The old screen was unceremoniously but rather carefully knocked back into the car and onto the cloth draped over the interior. People who are doing this sort of thing all the time become blasé about the risks but it would obviously be wisest to wear a pair of thick gloves from this stage on and a pair of goggles too, to protect the eyes.

WR6.   Next, all the glass that is still sitting in the rubber channel must be removed. The larger pieces can be pulled out with a pair of pliers but most of the glass will simply push out with a straight-point screwdriver.

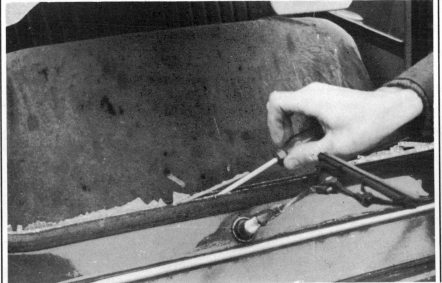

WR7.   There will be lots of pieces of glass sitting on the bonnet and on top of the dash and all the bits can be swept right into the car and onto the cloth inside.

245

WR8.   The screen rubbber was lifted straight out by the Windscreen Services fitter, whereupon even more pieces of glass fell out as if from nowhere. That stuff really gets into every crack imaginable!

WR9.   The cloth inside the car was then folded in from the outside, so that every scrap of glass was collected up. Be very careful when handling smashed glass and take great care to dispose of it safely.

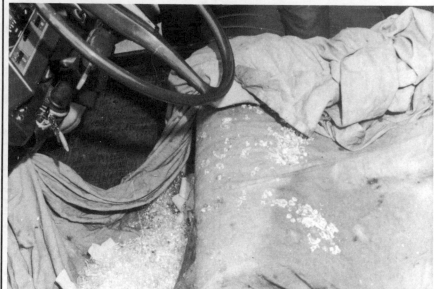

WR10.   A rag dipped in paraffin (kerosene) was used to wipe the flange around which the rubber fitted so that all the old sealant was removed. If allowed to remain, old sealant might prevent the screen from sealing properly when refitted and so cause one of those irritating leaks where the water always seems to land on the driver's right foot.

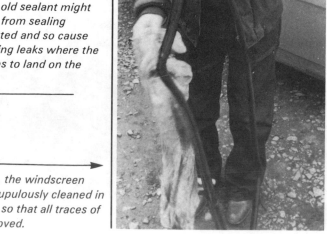

WR11.   Similarly, the windscreen rubber must be scrupulously cleaned in all its sealing areas so that all traces of old mastic are removed.

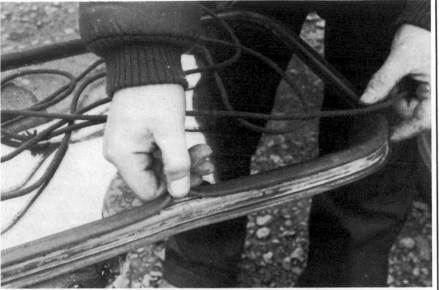

WR12.   The new screen was placed on a soft surface at the right working height (a kitchen stool such as the one shown here is ideal) and the rubber slipped around the outside edge of the glass. Ensure that the outer flange of the sealing rubber is situated on the outside of the windscreen glass.

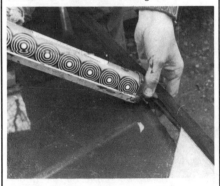

WR13.   Windscreen sealing mastic can be purchased from a paint factor or from any windscreen specialist. Squeeze sealing mastic into the rubber-to-glass joint on both sides. Mastic was not squeezed into the rubber before fitting it because that would have made it difficult to get the rubber far enough onto the screen and the whole assembly into the windscreen aperture.

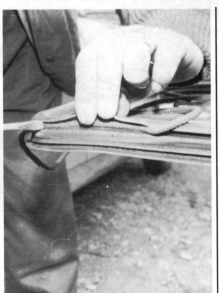

WR15.   On the outside of the rubber there were a pair of lips, one to seal against the outside of the windscreen panel and one which had to be pulled over the windscreen panel flange. The way to pull it over is to slip a piece of cord into the seal all the way round the screen.

WR16.   Here the cord is shown being inserted into the seal, starting near the bottom corner ...

WR17.   ... and continuing all the way round the rubber. Where the two ends of the cord meet, make them actually cross over with both ends of the cord inside the rubber seal for a distance of 3 or 4 inches (75mm to 100mm). ↓

WR14.   The windscreen rubber can be seen to have two lips on its inner face, the lower of which is the one for the glass.

WR18.	Then put a run of sealer behind the edge of the front lip, the one that fits up against the outer windscreen panel, **not** the seal into which the cord has been inserted.

WR19.	The fitters offered the screen and rubber up to the car and made sure that all the surplus cord fell inside the car so that none of it lodged in between the rubber and the windscreen panel .

WR20.	After sitting the rubber and screen onto the bottom ledge of the windscreen panel, screen and rubber were pushed lightly into the aperture. Of course, it wouldn't go all the way in because the innermost lip was up against the windscreen flange.

WR21.	You can see here what is meant by crossing the cord over inside the rubber. While one of the fitters pushed hard on the screen rubber from the outside, the other carefully held one piece of cord taut while pulling harder on the other. This made the sealing lip begin to flip over the windscreen panel flange.

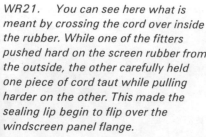

WR22. The end of the cord that was first started continued to be pulled while the screen and rubber continued to be pressed inwards from outside the car.

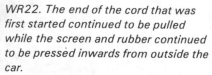

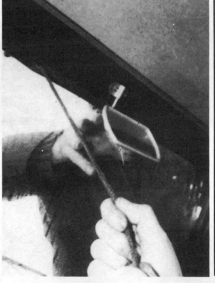

WR23.	As the cord is steadily pulled out all the way around the screen, it is important to ensure that the rubber lip comes clearly over the flange, otherwise the cord could just pull right out, leaving the rubber on the wrong side of the flange! If any small hiccoughs are encountered the rubber can be encouraged to come over the flange using a blunt ended screwdriver.

WR24.	After pulling the cords right out, the inside of the screen was wiped clean ...

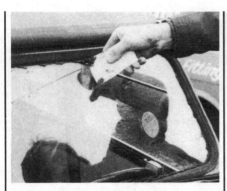

WR25. ... and the excess mastic sealer that had oozed out from under the rubber was scraped away using a plastic scraper used for spreading body filler.

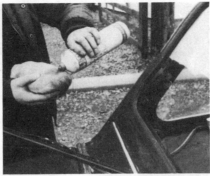

WR26. Smears of mastic were left on the screen and on various other parts of the body, but these all came off with the greatest of ease with a rag dampened with paraffin (kerosene) or white spirit (turps substitute).

WR27. Last but by no means least, the windscreen wiper blades were minutely examined for trapped particles of glass and wiped off thoroughly with the paraffin dampened rag. There must be little that is more demoralising than to fit a brand new windscreen and then ruin it the first time the wipers switch on and score indelible scratches across the glass!

WR28. Some screens of this type have the additional feature of a rubber spreader strip which is let into yet another slit in the front of the windscreen rubber. This has the effect of pushing the rubber into closer contact with both screen and glass. It can be fitted using the special tool shown, or a more long-winded alternative is to use a pair of screwdrivers: one broad bladed to open up the rubber and one to push the filler strip down and into place. Wiping washing-up liquid over the filler strip makes it considerably easier to get into position.

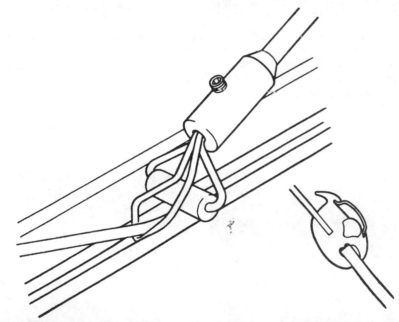

WR29. Quite often a windscreen will leak just because the rubber and the mastic inside it have dried out, allowing water through. Here the 'boss' from Clearview Windscreens of Worcester shows how you can pipe in a bead of windscreen mastic, following both sides of the rubber and preventing any further leaks.

Safety

If you replace a broken windscreen and the screen has smashed into small pieces before you can seal off all the vents as shown in this sequence, be sure to remove all heater and demister ducting to remove any fragments of glass which could so easily be blown into the face of an occupant of the car when the blower unit is next switched on.

Sports car windscreen

Many earlier sports cars have separate windscreen surrounds which are usually constructed of cast or extruded aluminium and which must first be removed from the car complete with windscreen glass before the glass can be changed. The method of holding the surround to the body varies from car to car but it is generally held in a pretty straightforward manner. This is especially so on older cars where the purists ideal was to whip off the screen and fit a pair of tiny aeroscreens. But we won't go into *that* particular form of masochism ...

The following sequence is based on the biggest-selling open top sports car of all time, the MGB, but the principles involved are applicable to many other cars.

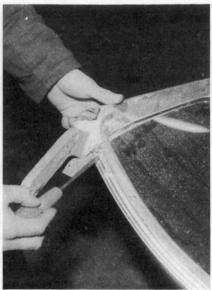

WR31. Take out the two outer crosshead screws from each end of the top rail of the frame. Note the two rivets by the fitter's left hand — on later cars these are screws, too, which should be left in place.

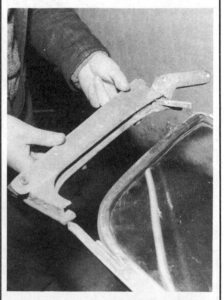

WR33. Bottom screws (2 each side) are found beneath the rubber sealing strip which must first be pulled out of its seating and removed.

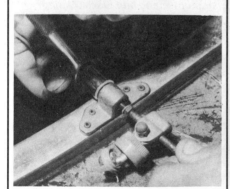

WR30. The bottom bracket of the centre steady will have been disconnected when the screen was removed. Take off the domed nut which holds the top of the steady to the frame bracket.

WR32. It is not unusual to find an immovable screw. When this happens, the only recourse is to drill off the screw head, drill out the remainder of the screw after the frame has been disassembled and clean up the thread with a tap.

WR34. The side frame slots into the top and bottom rails and can be pulled off with all the screws removed. Top and bottom screws are of different lengths — make a note of where they come from!

WR35.   Frame joints are often tight and have to be tapped apart with a wooden mallet.

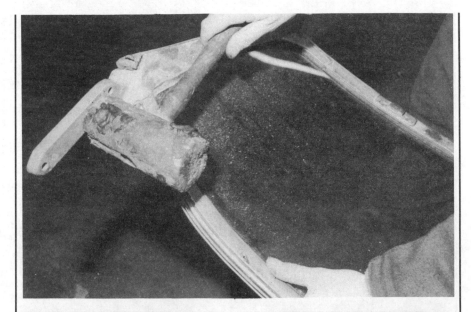

WR36.   With both side frames removed, pull off the top rail, starting at one end and pulling the sealing rubber out of the frame as it is removed.

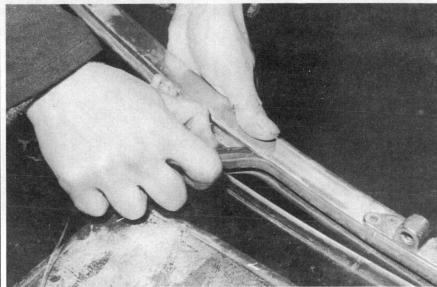

WR37.   Remove the bottom rail in the same way. Note how a padded stool makes an ideal "work surface".

WR38.   Take off the sealing rubber taking care not to be cut by any pieces of broken glass ...

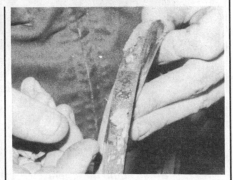

WR39.   ... and clean all the old, hardened sealer from the rubber.

WR40.   Take this opportunity to clean the frame and to grease threads before reassembly. Remember that care must be taken not to twist the screen and so cause it to crack.

WR41.   Use a proprietary brand of screen sealer (available from motor factors) and inject a bead of sealer into each side of the rubber strip which has now been placed around the new screen.

WR43.   ... and also inside the top and bottom rail channels.

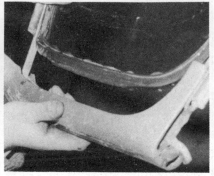

WR45.   Slot the side rails into place.

WR42.   Brush liquid detergent (washing-up liquid) around the outer edge of the rubber sealer ...

WR44.   Push top and bottom rails onto the rubbers (ease them on slowly). They will push out the excess sealer as they go.

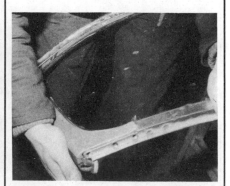

WR46.   Ensure that the screw holes line up properly. Bang the side rails into place with the open hand if necessary.

WR47.   If it is found difficult to pull the top and bottom rails sufficiently together, use a woodworker's sash cramp, but tighten SLOWLY — give the excess sealer time to ooze out.

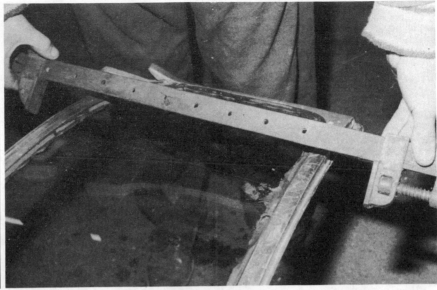

WR48.   Replace top and bottom screws. Make absolutely certain that the correct screw lengths are used in the corresponding holes.

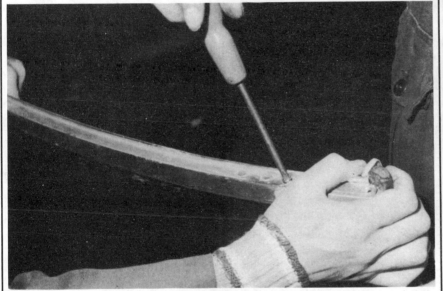

WR49.   Scrape off the excess sealer from around the screen. Paraffin (kerosene) used on a rag will remove what remains.

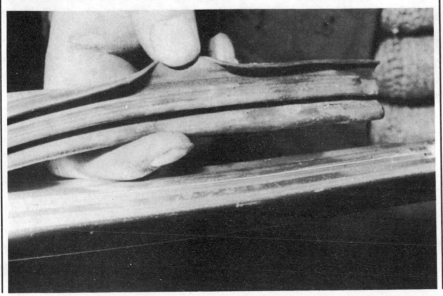

WR50.   The bottom rail to car body sealing rubber has to be fitted properly with the contours of the rubber fitting the contours of the bottom of the frame and the lip shown held open here, wrapped around the edge of the frame.

WR51. Only apply liquid detergent to the frame if the rubber will not go in dry. If it goes in too easily, it will come out easily as well.

WR52. Slide the leading edge of the rubber into the slot on the bottom of the frame and push it to the end.

WR53. Work the rest of the rubber into place with a blunt screwdriver. You can see why Windscreen Services only employ fitters with four hands!

WR54. Apply a good, heavy bead of screen sealer towards the front of the rubber ...

WR55. ... place the rubber corner seals in place and apply more sealer to the bottom of the corner rubber before refitting to the car.

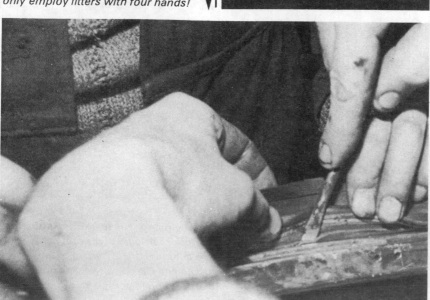

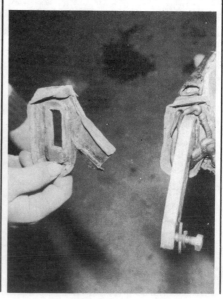

Fitting a Soft Top ■

Fitting a new soft-top (or hood, in Britain) to a sportscar can make all the difference in winter between continuing to enjoy the car and half freezing to death! In addition, elderly soft top rear windows tend to go cloudy and difficult to see through which is certainly inconvenient and unsafe, and quite possibly illegal too. The author visited the MGB Centre to see a hood or soft-top being fitted there.

Watching "Smiling" Steve Langdell is a revelation! He makes fitting a hood to an MGB look like child's play – and it's not! But you CAN fit one yourself and avoid a nightmare of sags, draughts and flapping vinyl by working carefully and methodically, as shown in the following step-by-step instructions.

The first job and probably the most important one, is to buy the best hood that you can afford. If you can get an original factory hood the advantages are that it is very likely to fit much better than those made by outside concerns, it may be better made and it will be constructed of the correct material. The disadvantage of a factory fresh hood is that it is likely to cost a great deal. If you have to buy one from one of the hood specialists try, if you can, to avoid buying without seeing first (there are some horribly mis-shapen offerings) and get yourself a hood with the clips and stud fastenings already fitted if possible. The small extra cost saves a lot of work – not to mention the risk of getting it wrong!

ST1.   Work methodically and – provided that the hood is a good one – there shouldn't be any problem. Choose a warm day so that the vinyl (if that type of hood is being fitted) is supple but avoid the heat of high summer for then the hood will be too soft and easily over-stretched. Laid out in the foreground here are all the materials necessary, plus the two earlier types of hood sticks used prior to the Michelotti design fitted to the subject car.

Do ensure that the hood is (a) the right one for your car, and (b) that it fits, before removing the old one or attempting to alter the new one. The fit can be checked by the simple expedient of draping and smoothing it over the old, erected hood and checking for shape and size. There will be some useful sized overlaps where the manufacturer has allowed for adjustment during fitting.

ST2.   First step is to open the doors, fold the hood back, remove the rubber cant-rail sealing strip and drill off the pop-rivet heads found beneath.

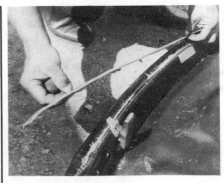

ST3.   Lift away the aluminium channel being careful not to distort it.

ST4.   Unscrew the hood where it is folded and held down to the ends of the cant rail. Only a coat of adhesive stands between cant rail and removal of the front of the hood – peel them apart. Rub the cant rail down and re-paint it to give a smooth finish under the new hood.

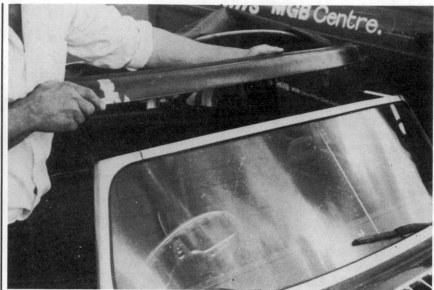

ST5. Slip the steel bar (which clips onto the two chrome "claws" on the rear bodywork) out from the old hood and, right away slide it into the new hood – before you forget which way round it goes!

ST6. Refit the bare cant rail to the top of the screen frame.

ST7. Clip the rear of the hood in place, after fitting the hood frame (if not Michelotti, in which case it will be attached to the cant rail) ...

ST8. ... and after folding the front-most part of the hood back on itself, measure with a tape and mark the centre of the hood with chalk.

ST9.   Apply glue, with a brush, to the central third of the cant rail ...

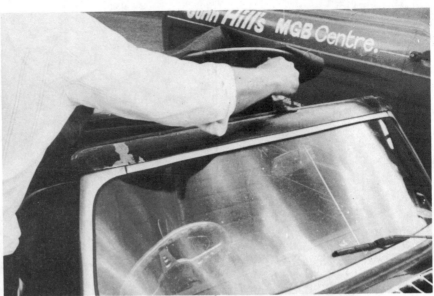

ST10.   ... and to the corresponding part of the inside of the hood.

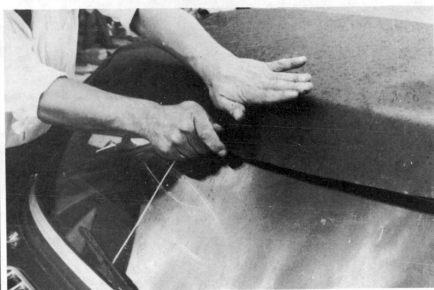

ST11.   Pull the hood forward, aligning the chalk mark with the windscreen steady bar and ensuring that the hood is taut.

ST12.   Make absolutely certain that the sides of the hood line up with the closed door glasses.

ST13. Fold back each front corner, apply glue to it and the cant rail.

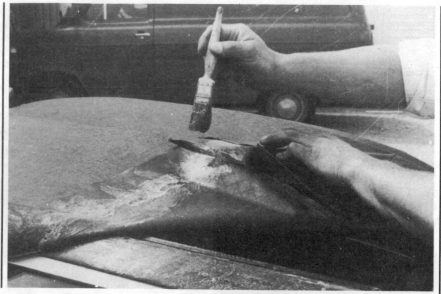

ST14. Stretch each corner forwards just enough to get rid of any sags or wrinkles – but not so much that you will need a team of three to close the hood on a cold day when the material has contracted!

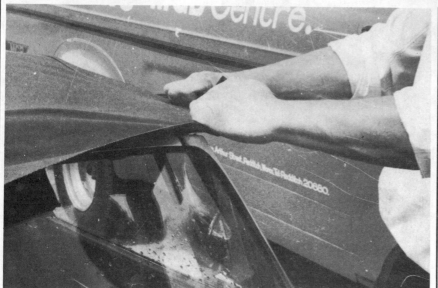

ST15. Fold the draught excluder corners down onto the cant rail, pierce them with an awl and fit them into place with the crosshead screw and cup washer removed earlier.

ST16. Glue the flap at the front onto the face of the cant rail which sits on the top of the screen frame.

ST17. Glue down the draught strip channel in order to prevent leaks behind the strip itself remembering to line up the holes with an awl before the glue dries.

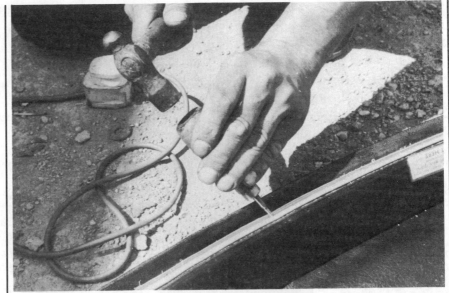

ST18.   Pop-rivet it back down then refit the draught excluder rubber ...

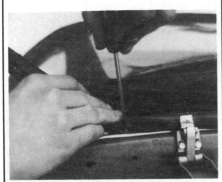

ST19.   ... carefully easing it into the channel with the aid of a screwdriver.

ST20.   Snip the surplus hood material around the front frame clips ...

ST21.   ... then cut off the surplus with a craft knife.

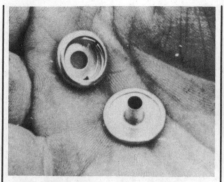

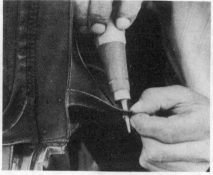

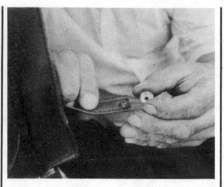

ST22.   Press-stud clips known in the trade as "cocks and hens" ...

ST23.   ... have to be fitted to the tags provided one on each side, at the bottom of the window aperture. First, pierce with an awl ...

ST24.   ... push in the "cock" from beneath, place the "hen" on top and spread the hollow tube on the cock with a centre punch and hammer, using another hammer as an anvil beneath. Although fitting the press-studs with the hood in place is awkward, it is the only way of ensuring that they align with the buttons on the car.

ST25.   If at all possible, buy a hood with the rear clips already fitted. If this is not possible, pierce the cloth as shown on this sample and push the claw part of the clip into place through the material.

ST26.   Place the material on the bench with the claws sticking upwards through the material and locate the retaining plate over the claws before bending them inwards with a light hammer.

Four seater soft-tops

The principles behind fitting a soft-top to a four-seater are just about the same as those for a two-seater except that sometimes, especially on older cars such as the Minor and 'Beetle' convertibles, the soft-top is pinned to a wooden body rail mounted at the rear and a wooden cant rail at the front. It is still normal practice to fit the rear of the hood first followed by careful stretching of the hood forwards before fixing the front of the hood to the cant rail. But it must be borne in mind that most four-seaters hoods are rather more complex and certainly more cumbersome affairs and so require rather more time spent to ensure a good fit. For that reason a closer examination of the old hood as it comes off and, notes jotted down on any of its idiosyncracies will pay dividends when it comes to fitting the new hood properly.

Watch the Weather

Professional trimmers advise anyone fitting a hood to choose a mild, dry day or failing that, a reasonably warm garage. Vinyl is affected by temperature and in cold weather you just won't be able to tension the hood correctly – if you fit your hood on a very warm day the vinyl will stretch too easily and the result will be that the hood is dragged and may even be so tight that on a cold, wet day the seams will part, or you won't be able to raise the hood or fasten it down.

Fabrics such as 'double duck' or mohair should be fitted dry and will self-tension themselves to some degree once they get wet, but do tension them reasonably well in the first place. Because of the shrinkage factor the makers often leave these hoods a little wide. Don't try to compensate for this by applying uneven tension at the cant rail.

Energy-Absorbing Bumpers

There are a number of different types of energy absorbing bumpers, some of which include an energy-absorbing strut of the kind shown here on this 1980 model Chrysler K-car. Upon impact, the bumper and forward portion of the strut collapse inwards, compressing the energy absorber and, one hopes, preventing damage to the body.

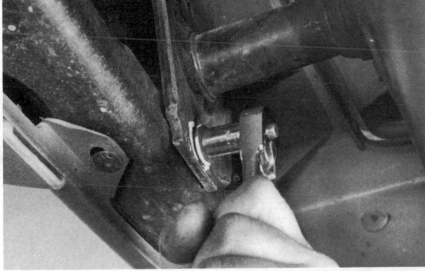
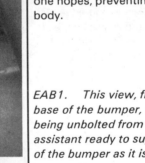
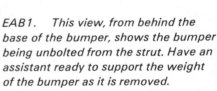

EAB1.   This view, from behind the base of the bumper, shows the bumper being unbolted from the strut. Have an assistant ready to support the weight of the bumper as it is removed.

EAB2.   This is the strut itself coming off the car, having been simply unbolted from the body. The bumper itself was bolted to the plate held in the mechanic's right hand.

⑨ Accessories & Improvements

Fitting Simple Accessories
●

Mirrors

First of all check that the mirrors are going to be in the right place by sitting in the driver's seat while someone else holds each mirror in turn and moves it to the best place. Too far away, and your rear vision will be restricted and the mirror will be difficult to see clearly in a hurry; too near or too low and your view of the mirror could be obstructed. Work out the correct position first, or your mirror will be no more than a showpiece.

SA1.   Place several strips of masking tape on the panel in the area where you intend to fit the mirror. The tape is easy to mark as you measure out the exact position of the mirror and it protects the panel if you slip a little with drill or file.

SA2.   The Black & Decker cordless drill is ideal for outdoor uses like this. A small pilot hole was drilled first, then a larger one. Before the first hole was cut, the drill and chuck were turned by hand until the drill cut through paper and paint and started itself in the steel beneath. (You could use a centre punch, tapped lightly with a hammer). If you don't do either of these things, the drill will almost certainly skid across the panel, gouging the paint.

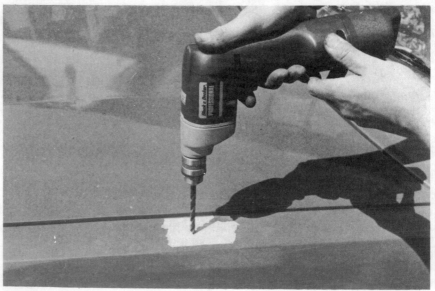

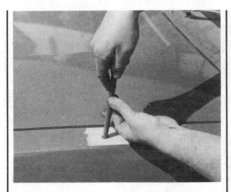

SA3.   Then the hole has to be opened out, if necessary using a round file.

SA4.   A good wing mirror should have a sealing rubber above and below the hole, a flat washer beneath the bottom rubber and a lock washer directly above the nut.

SA5.   It is difficult to get paint onto the edges of the new hole in the panel, but if you don't do something, it will certainly corrode. Waxoyl rust preventer or even grease could be spread around the hole and the mirror fixing.

SA6.   There's rarely a lot of room to get at the fixing nut. A ring spanner gives you smaller turns than an open-ender, but you may have to get hold of a long box-spanner. Remember to adjust the mirror accurately before final tightening-up.

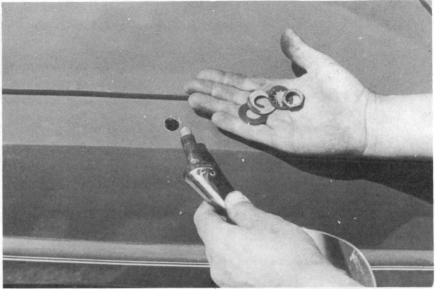

Wing-mounted aerial

Position the aerial and cut out the hole as shown in the previous section. Make certain that there is room beneath the panel for the aerial body to fit and try to choose a place that won't be splashed with water and mud, particularly if you are fitting an electric aerial. Generally, place the aerial away from the car's electrical system to cut down on interference and make sure that its fixing clamp can earth (ground) onto bare metal.

SA7.   Work out the order in which the tilt/fixing clamps go together. The clamp held in the right hand here goes beneath the panel while all the others go above it.

SA8.   Fit the aerial into place, then extend it and adjust it to the angle you want.

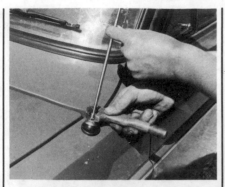

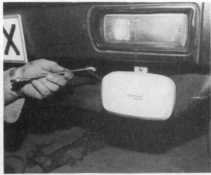

SA9.   Finally, tighten up the fixing nut. In the case of electric aerials, it will be necessary to fit a supporting strap (supplied with the aerial) to locate the weighty base of the aerial. Screw, bolt or pop-rivet it into place against the car's inner bodywork.

SA13.   With this lamp, the mounting bolt also tightened the lamp swivel. You can only set the lamp position really satisfactorily on the road.

SA14.   Fitted to this TR7, these driving lamps look the part and are useful in dull conditions for making the car's presence known to other road users and for lighting up the road for that time just before headlamps are really necessary.

Front auxiliary lamps

SA10.   One way of being certain of buying good quality parts is to buy those sold for your make of car. These Unipart lamps were chosen for that reason. The electrical side of things is detailed in the instructions and all the wire and wiring clips are supplied too.

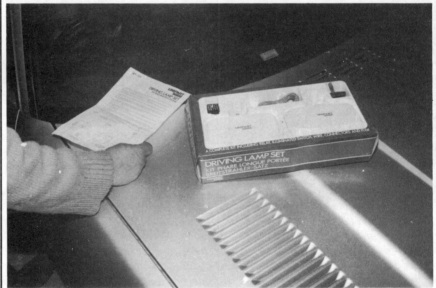

SA11.   Start by choosing carefully where you want your lamps to go. Try to make them compliment the existing features and lines of the car, but don't fit them as low as this if you want them to illuminate the road a long way ahead.

SA12.   Mark the position of the lamp and drill a mounting hole. Use a rust preventer or grease around the hole to protect the bared metal from rust.

264

New number/license plates

Mud flaps

SA15.   New plates make a car look terrific, especially after it has just been resprayed. Remove the old one and clean any loose rust or dirt from the supporting plate, using a wire brush or scraper.

SA18.   Then, just bolt your new plate in place. Special plastic nuts and bolt are also available to match the background colour of the plates.

SA19.   Mud flaps made specifically for one particular model of car will fit so much better than the 'universal' types freely available.

SA16.   Paint it, or brush on a liberal coating of rust preventer so preventing dirt and moisture trapped there from causing any more problems.

SA17.   Place the old plate over the new one and drill the mounting holes, using the old plate as a template.

The Car Bodywork Repair Manual

SA20. The best way of finding where to drill is to clamp the mud flap in place. Here a Sykes-Pickavant body clamp is used. It's specially shaped, wide spread jaws make it ideal for clamping panels and parts together.

SA21. The mud flaps are held in place with nylon bushes which push into the holes you drill and then act as anchors for the self-tapping screws screwed into them

SA22. Before inserting the nylon bushes, they were dipped in rust-preventer to protect the steel panel around them and the self-tapping screws from corrosion.

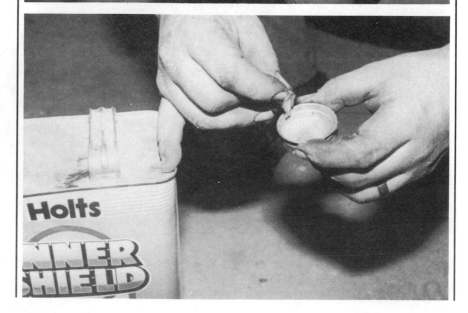

266

SA23.   Screwing the mud-flap into place is the easiest part of all!

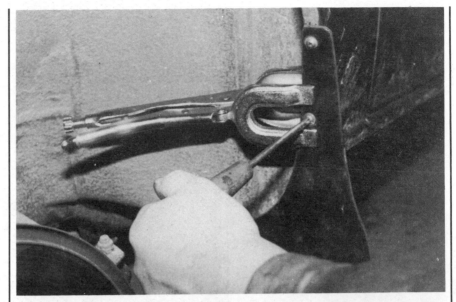

SA24.   'Universal' type mud flaps are usually clamped in place with pinch clamps supplied as part of the kit.

SA25.   Here the mud flap has been supported on blocks of wood whilst clamped into place. The same blocks were then used at the other side of the car to ensure that both mud flaps were at the same height.

Soundproofing

You make a car less noisy by carrying out lots of small sound-deadening jobs rather than any big ones. One of the most fruitful areas to tackle is in the bulkhead/firewall and in the floor of the car, especially around the gear-change, where lots of small holes can let in a lot of noise. Use new grommets or mastic to block off any holes you may find.

SA26.   Flat panels exaggerate sound by resonating. You can damp that out by sticking on a self-adhesive sheet which reduces the vibrations in the panel. This is the Supra Dedsheet, having its protective layer pulled away from it.

SA27. It's then a simple matter to stick the Dedsheet onto any large, flat panels where resonance can cause a noise problem.

SA28. Another Supra product are these thick soundproofing mats which come in easy-handle large squares. They can be trimmed to fit the shape of the floor and inner bulkhead and glued into place beneath the carpet.

Sports car roll-over bar

SA29. A roll-over bar is a sensible safety accessory which also lends a 'macho' appeal to a sports car, if that is what you want! They almost always come complete with a fixing kit, so that they simply bolt through the sports car's bodywork. Make certain that the one you buy will fit beneath the soft-top when it's erected, because some versions made for use on the track don't.

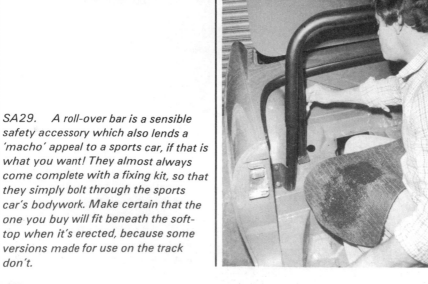

Fitting a tow bar

Of course, every car is an individual when it comes to fitting a tow bar but there are a few general points that can be made. It's best to buy a ready-made tow bar, rather than make one up yourself, because the manufacturer will have worked out how best to spread into the body of the car the considerable loads involved and how to make it as unobtrusive as possible.

SA30. In almost every case, the rear bumper of the car will have to come off, so squirt plenty of releasing fluid onto all the bumper retaining bolts well in advance. Support the rear of the car well off the ground on ramps or axle stands.

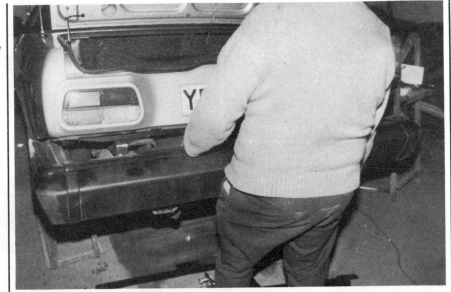

SA31. Get out all the parts supplied and lay them out on the floor, beneath the car. Read through the fitting instructions and check that they make sense (their interpretation sometimes needs a little nimble thinking!) and that all the parts are there. You will probably find that you have to carry out some filling-out of holes to get everything to fit properly.

SA32. You usually start by fitting the main member; the one that carries the actual tow hitch.

SA33. Get someone to hold it firmly in place while you drill any mounting holes.

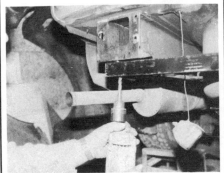

SA34. Then, lightly assemble the parts that reach forwards under the car and again drill out the mounting holes, using the bar itself as a guide. Be careful not to drill into any wires, fuel pipes or the spare wheel or anything else the other side of the panel you are drilling through. Don't tighten anything up until **all** the bolts are in place.

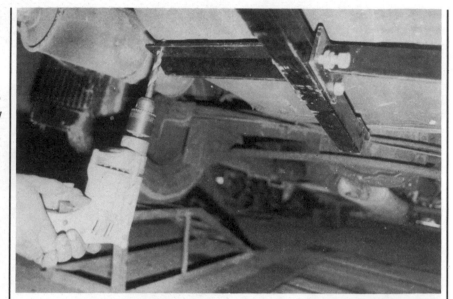

SA35. With the bar in place, you can fit your hitch and wire up your electrics, or take the car along to your local auto-electrician if wiring puzzles you.

Fitting and Maintaining a Sunroof ■

Sunroofs are becoming more and more popular as accessories fitted to cars of all ages, shapes and sizes. As well as making the car so much more pleasant to own they add extra light, fresh air and a breath of sunshine in the summer — and they also increase the car's value. Tudor Webasto, one of the leading suppliers and fitters of sunroofs, kindly showed how they fit one of the least expensive and popular sunroofs to an Austin Metro. This was quite a straightforward job but Tudor Webasto strongly recommend that DIY fitting be avoided. They say that some roof structures are quite complex and require expert attention, that headlinings can degenerate into a flapping nightmare if handled wrongly and that, if a mistake is made cutting out the roof ... it could all end in tears!

SR1. First job for the Tudor Webasto fitter was to cut the headlining; just a small cut-out for access at this stage.

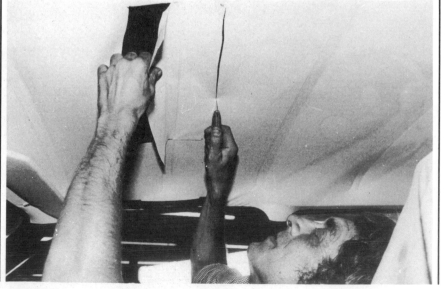

SR2.   Then he placed masking tape around the area where the sunroof was to be fitted, accurately marked out the area to be removed and (gulp!) drilled a hole into the roof panel.

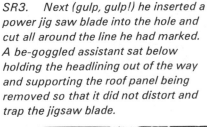

SR4.   The roof panel was lowered and fitted into the accurately cut aperture.

SR3.   Next (gulp, gulp!) he inserted a power jig saw blade into the hole and cut all around the line he had marked. A be-goggled assistant sat below holding the headlining out of the way and supporting the roof panel being removed so that it did not distort and trap the jigsaw blade.

SR5.   This was clamped from beneath by a frame which has screws passing upwards and into the frame above. The two compress together to form a seal. The unwanted headlining was cut back and the headlining edges and screw heads hidden from view with trim strips.

SR6.   The smoked glass panel slotted into place via a pair of clips-cum-hinges. In use, the sunroof can be raised at the rear or, in hot weather, it can quickly be lifted right out — a reversal of the fitting process seen here and a work of moments.

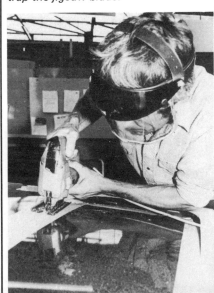

SR7. Last job for Tudor Webasto and just about the only piece of maintenance for the owner is to keep the glass clean. This type of sunroof should never leak (although a downpour after a long, hot, dry spell can temporarily catch the sealing rubbers out) but it must be said that cheap sunroofs are notorious for leaking with depressing regularity.

SR8. From one end of the scale to the other. Tudor Webasto can fit a range of sunroofs from the simple opening glass light, through their luxurious 'off-the-peg' sliding roofs (**definitely** not for the amateur) ...

SR9. ... through to bespoke tailored sunroofs made in a workshop pleasantly scented with beechwood shavings, and with wooden templates on the walls. This piece of wood is actually part of the sideframe of what Tudor Webasto claim to be the biggest sunroof in the world. It was made as a 'one-off' for a six-wheeled Range Rover for a certain Eastern gentleman who used it for shooting-parties. The roof, it was specified, had to be strong enough for the whole shooting-party to sit around it, sunroof open, with legs dangling inside!

SR10. It's always pleasant to see a company taking care of their own products from years ago. This Volvo P1800 was in the process of receiving new fabric for its sliding roof, a step guaranteed to improve the appearance of any older car with a sliding sunroof.

SR11. Sliding sunroofs don't need a great deal of maintenance but the sliding mechanism should be kept lubricated and clean. Periodically, wipe the slots out with a cloth and spray in some aerosol silicone lubricant; it's far more effective than anything else for this purpose and cleaner than oil.

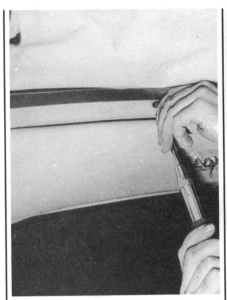

SR12.   Removing a sliding sunroof, either because the car is being resprayed or in order to replace the fabric section, is quite an easy job. Three or four screws will be found holding the rear of the roof in place from inside the car. Occasionally, on an older car, one will shear because of corrosion weakness. All you can do is to drill out the stud remains with the fabric off the car and re-tap the hole.

SR14.   Concertina all of the fabric together and turn the sunroof fabric so that it sits diagonally across the sunroof opening. One by one the rails can be eased out of their runners, leaving the fabric and rails free.

SR15.   Refitting is the reverse of this procedure. In this shot you can see the guides at the end of the front rail which have to be manoeuvred out as described.

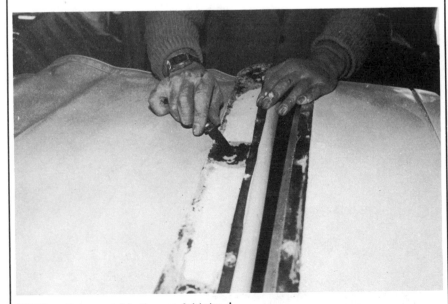

SR13.   From outside the car, fold the rear of the sunroof back and you will see a heavy encrustation of sealer which can be scraped off with a knife.

SR16.   Before screwing down the back rail, but after all the runners have been fitted into place, fold the back rail over so that the base is uppermost and 'ice' it with mastic. Place a swirl of mastic around each of the screw holes and a double line across the edge where mastic had originally been placed by the manufacturer. All that remains is to re-insert the screws from inside the car.

Fitting Side Windows to a Van ■

Fitting side windows to a van can make it a more versatile vehicle for a number of purposes. There are a number of different types of side window kit and a number of different kinds of van structure. A specialist can advise on which type to use and, as in the case of the company featured here, can supply DIY kits or can fit side windows for you.

VSW3. *After cutting a 'starting hole' in the panel ...*

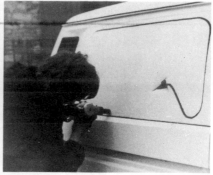

VSW4 *... the panel can be cut out and removed. This is an industrial-type 'nibbler' attachment. You could hire one, use a cheaper, drill mounted version or even use an electric jig-saw with metal-cutting blade.*

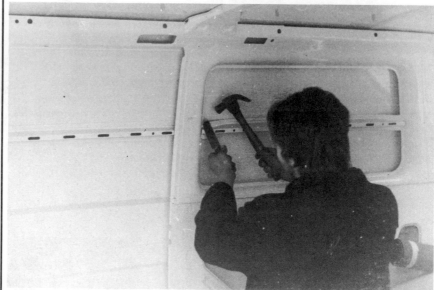

VSW1. *From inside the van, carefully chisel the horizontal panel strengthener away from each end. You can neaten it up afterwards with a mini-grinder – but **before** the glass goes in. (Vehicle Windows are using a hacking knife here).*

VSW2. *After marking the height and horizontal position where the glass is to be situated hold the glass or sliding window frame against the outer panel. (A couple of balls of 'Blu-tack' will stop the glass from slipping). Mark around each window or frame*

VSW5. Then the self-sealing type of glazing rubber is pushed over the edge of the aperture all round ...

VSW7. The filler strip — rubber or 'plastic chrome' - is fitted using a filler tool. Either make one of these up yourself, beg, borrow or hire one, or get a windscreen fitting firm to come along and fit it for you. It should not cost a great deal.

VSW8. Fitting a sliding window is the same as fitting glass, the frame having a lip which seats into the rubber in the same way as the glass.

VSW6. ... and the glass eased into the rubber surround, with the aid of a screwdriver blade which lifts the edge of the rubber out of the way allowing the window to fully enter the glazing rubber.

VSW9. The finished vehicle looks smart and gives greatly improved visibility and ventilation.

(Photographs and information supplied by Vehicle Window Centre, Pudsey, West Yorkshire).

Polishing Faded Paint ●

In time, paintwork of any sort is likely to lose the deep lustrous shine it had when sitting in the showroom, even though there is no corrosion in the panels beneath the paint and though the paint itself may be perfectly sound. Ordinary polishing may not bring it back to life, so this is the time to try something a little more vigorous. The results can be remarkable, transforming what previously looked like an old banger into a very respectable looking car – as any used car dealer can tell you!

Simply, paint fades when the top surface of the paint is affected by sunlight (which 'weakens' its colour – reds, oranges and yellows being particularly prone to sun bleaching) and it goes a dull, matt finish as it oxidizes.

Many ordinary polishes contain a tiny amount of abrasive so that when you polish your car regularly, you will also be taking off a microscopically thin layer of paint – that's why the polishing cloth ends up the colour of the paintwork. There are, however, special compounds available which enable you to cope with the job of taking off a larger (though still microscopic) layer of paint when fading or bleaching is notably bad.

Rubbing compounds, as they are called, are like flatting papers; the coarser grades cut faster but produce deeper scratches and, like flatting paper, if you start with the coarser grade of compound, you must work through the grades and finish with a fine grade in order to produce a high quality shine. Beware if you are attempting to polish a thin coat of paint! The compound can break through and, with some colours, the result will be an apparent dark ring around the area that has broken through. Polishing compounds are generally only available through a trade paint factor (they almost all sell to whoever comes up to the counter). The DIY cutting compounds, such as T-cut, are too fine to remove anything but a very light amount of dull paint, unless you are prepared for a marathon, arm-aching rubbing session.

A third source of discoloration is so-called 'industrial fall-out' when chemical or particle discharge from industrial plant is carried by the wind, lands on a car's surface and causes discoloration. Such contamination is by no means restricted to immediately around industrial areas (indeed, some Scandanavian countries claim to be affected by 'acid rain' discharged from British factories). The results of such contamination must be polished out while the effects are still slight otherwise the damage can go deeply into the paint. if you suspect that heavy contamination has taken place, try to remove it by washing the panels affected in a solution of 10% oxalic acid. Remember to take the usual stringent precautions regarding skin and eye protection and safe storage of acids.

PFP1.   Most people won't have access to a power tool and will therefore entrust the work to the power of their own arm. Bad cases of hazing or fading (and not forgetting that orange peeled paint can be flatted using the same process) are best approached using a cutting compound. It is probably best to avoid the coarser grades of cutting compound – you can actually hear them roughing away at the paint surface – and go for a smooher grade. It might mean using a little more elbow grease, but that is preferable to overdoing it and rubbing straight through the paint. Rubbing through is most likely to happen on edges and raised body lines, so take it easy in those places.

*Use a clean cloth to rub the compound off and to polish the surface of the paint. Turn the cloth regularly to avoid too heavy a build-up of compound on any one part of the cloth. Try to keep the area being compounded at any one time relatively small. Hand polishing is quite hard work and fairly time consuming so approach it a section at a time. Polish **ONLY** in straight lines, following the line of the bodywork; rotary polishing will leave rotary marks.*

PFP2.   'T-cut' or any other similar proprietary polishing compound is used last of all (remember the analogy with flatting papers?) to get rid of the minute scratches left by the cutting compound and to bring up a deep shine on the surface of the paint. Wet the soft cloth you use for polishing then wring it out very thoroughly to leave it damp; this stops the cloth soaking up the compound.

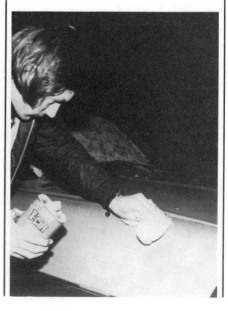

PFP3.   Here a 'pro' polishing mop is being used with cutting compound and of course this speeds the job up perhaps by as much as a factor of ten. Note that the use of a polishing mop requires a certain degree of skill to avoid cutting through the paint or burning the surface of the paint. Such polishing machines can be bought fairly cheaply to run from a compressed air source but their air consumption is massive, (at least in terms of workshop equipment output) and the great majority of DIY compressors come nowhere near having enough capacity to cope.

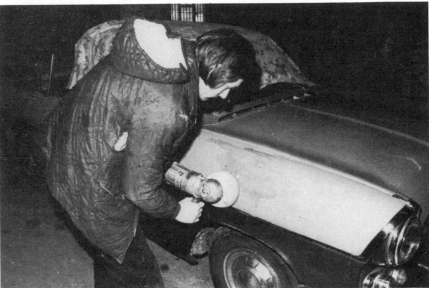

PFP4.   Electric machines are around 50% more expensive, though they can usually be hired from tool hire stores. Alternatively an ordinary electric drill can be fitted with a soft backing pad and lambswool mop (you need a different mop for every grade of compound you use) but most professionals would consider that an electric drill spins too quickly for this purpose, even set at its slowest speed, so if you use this method avoid burning the paint by keeping the mop moving over the surface of the paint and apply only very light pressure; you'll also be doing a big favour to the bearings in your drill, which are not really intended for side pressure.

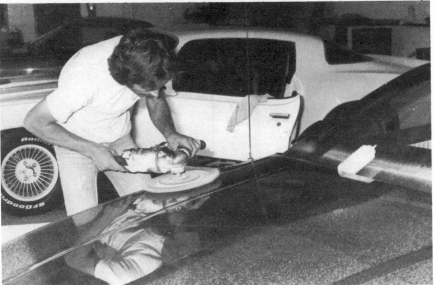

Polishing hints

● When using compound either thin it with water or dampen the cloth or mop (take care where electrical components are involved) and apply even less pressure as the polish dries out.

● Take special care when machine polishing sharp curves and edges, perhaps leaving such areas for hand polishing along with the areas around door handles and accessories where the polishing mop can't reach.

● Always keep polishing mops clean. Excessive paint and polish residues in the mop increase friction at the point of contact and increase the tendency to burn the paint.

● Avoid all substitutes! Polishing compounds are specially formulated from materials which will not harm the paint. The same cannot be said of metal polish and other abrasive polishes designed for other uses.

● Take special care when compounding metallic finishes; only ever lightly compound them. If too much paint is removed, the metallic content will 'shear' and the finish will be ruined in a way that can only be cured by re-painting.

● Finish off with a good quality wax polish to deepen the shine and protect the surface. **NEVER** wax polish paint that is less than four or five weeks old otherwise the paint can go dull (it absorbs the wax) or can develop a tendency to watermark.

● Cover the car windscreen and wear old clothes when machine compounding. The stuff tends to fly around a bit!

Thanks are due to Autotech Ltd of Belbroughton, Worcestershire, England and Village Detail, Thousand Oaks, California for their help with the photographs used here.)

Pinstriping and decals ●

Decal graphics are used on nearly all US cars nowadays and on a large number of European cars, too. Sometimes they are used where a chrome plated badge would have been fitted formerly, but often they are used to give stylish bodywork effects. Many owners may be interested in fitting pinstripes or decals to improve the appearance of a plain looking vehicle, but even when fitted from new the material gets damaged or discolours after a period of time and replacing it really improves the appearance of a car. The material is available from accessory shops when being applied as an additional feature, or from a dealer when it is being replaced; just order it like you would an engine part or door knob.

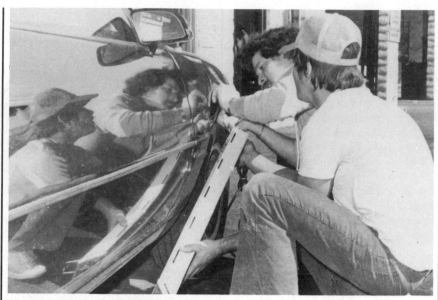

P&D2.   The idea is to soften the gum holding the pinstripe or decal in place. It helps if someone else can hold the heat source in place while you pick and peel the old tape away.

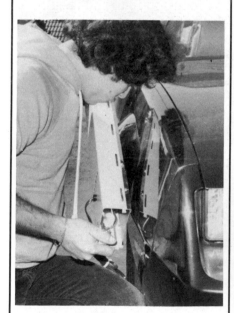

P&D1.   When replacing an old pinstripe or decal, the first job is getting the old one off without damaging the paintwork beneath. Start by heating the tape with a radiant heater (as shown here), or a professional air gun. Even a hand-held hairdryer at its hottest setting is better than nothing.

P&D3.   Here Ron Samuel is using a spirit solvent to wipe away the residual gum. Don't, obviously, use a solvent such as cellulose thinners which could react with and damage the paintwork.

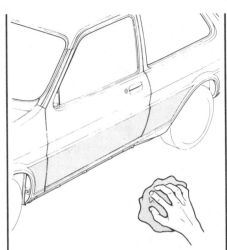

P&D7. Carefully position the stripe as you go ...

P&D8. ... Easing it round any curves. If the stripe is to go straight down the side of a car, position 6 inches (300mm) or so, of one end, then peel back the tape for several feet before positioning the next part of the tape, say, where you come to the edge of a door. Pull it fairly tight before making the second point of contact so that the tape is bound to be straight. Do the same with the third and subsequent points of contact but get down on a level with the tape and sight along it to ensure its straightness. Then go along and smooth the whole tape down.

P&D4. Before fitting a new decal or stripe, or after removing an old one, make sure that all traces of grease are removed using a spirit wipe. Methylated spirit would do the job equally well as a proprietary brand of wipe, and has the added advantage that it reacts with virtually no type of paint.

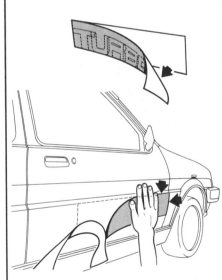

P&D5. The new decal or stripe will have a protective sheet of paper on its reverse. Peel part of it back, locate the start of the decal or stripe **accurately** (it's not easy to remove again) and smooth out the decal or stripe, pulling the protective paper off as you go.

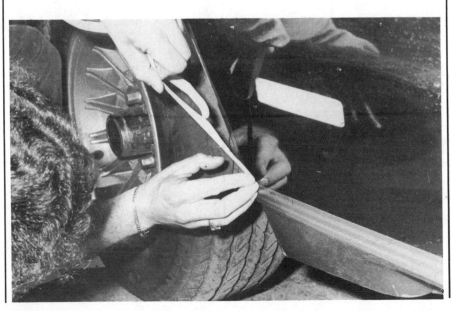

P&D6. Treat a stripe in exactly the same way, but leave some overlap beyond where you want the stripe to fit.

P&D9.   As shown here, you must smooth all air out of the tape using a rubber, a clean cloth or just your hand. You can accurately pencil the correct position for cuts ...

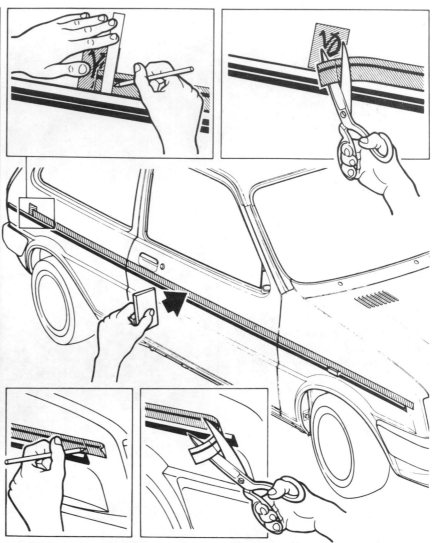

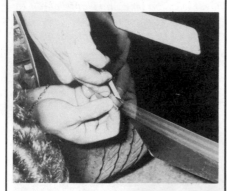

P&D10.   ... or do as Ron Samuel does and trim accurately in place with a sharp razor blade or craft knife.

P&D11.   When fitting a decal, it's even more important to push out all the air, working from the centre outwards. Then, finally, peel back the top coating (which is sometimes clear plastic) starting from one corner.

P&D12.   Sometimes a thin stripe will tend to lift up again with the top coating. If this happens, lift the first couple of inches, separate the two, push the stripe very carefully back down and continue to remove the top coating. If your strip bridges two or more panels, don't bother cutting to the length of each panel but take the stripe right over the panel gap. Trim it to fit afterwards.

P&D13.   Similarly, where a decal fits behind a side marker/flasher, take the unit off, cut the decal to suit the hole after it has been fitted, then refit the lamp.

Fitting self-adhesive trim

P&D14. Before attempting to replace stuck-on trim, make certain that there are no traces of grease or other contamination present on the surface of the panel. Here the author is using International Paints proprietary Spirit Wipe but methylated spirit would do the job just as well. Obviously, you can't use thinner on many paint types – unless you want to fetch the paint off as well!

P&D15. Carefully measure and mark out the position of the trim or badge taking a look at the other side of the car or at another similar car if necessary. Use a water-based felt-tipped pen if you're worried about getting rid of any superfluous marks afterwards.

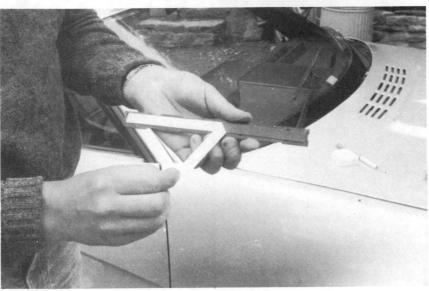

P&D16. This type of trim is stuck down with double-sided tape. Factors sell it by the roll but it is obviously more economical if you can buy or cadge a short length from your friendly local body shop. Peel off one side of the protective covering, stick the tape down to the badge then expose the sticky surface on the other side of the tape as shown here.

P&D17.   Position the badge or trim with very great care – you can't just lift it off and replace it or it wouldn't hold down well enough to do the job – and press it down well all over.

SWA1.   If you are painting wheels that consist of more than one colour, be prepared for an awful lot of fiddling around with masking tape. **Don't,** however, waste time in trying to follow every tricky little curve with masking tape. Instead, stick tape over the colour joint, rub it down really well so that the bit you want to stay in place actually does so during the next phase, and carefully cut along the joint line with a sharp craft knife. Then peel away the unwanted tape. Of course, to save having to do this twice, you can spray your first colour without having any masking in place, then just mask-up for the second colour.

SWA3.   The basic rules of preparation, flatting and priming, apply to wheels quite as much as to ordinary bodywork. Make sure that you sand off every trace of rust and also treat the afflicted areas with a rust killer to be certain, if you don't want it to break out again in double quick time.

(All graphics in the preceding section are courtesy of Austin-Rover Ltd, and the picture sequence was carried out at Ron Samuel's body shop, Village Detail, Thousand Oaks, California.)

Steel Wheel Appeal ●

Steel disc wheels can be one of the least obtrusive areas of the car but if they look good they will lift the whole appearance of the car while if they look shoddy and down at heel, so too, will the rest of the car.

Wheels are very vulnerable to damage from stone chips and are constantly subject to every destructive influence that the road can throw at them – and all from only a few inches away! For that reason, it is best to use paints that have been specially produced for use on wheels; although ordinary paint can be used, it simply won't last as long before it needs more attention.

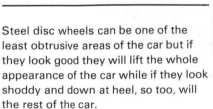

SWA2.   The areas between the cut-out masking tape are, naturally, much easier to mask-up in the normal way. Choose your colour carefully. Silver often looks too bright and garish but a steel colour (sold as such) usually suits steel disc wheels very much better.

SWA4.   An easy way to smarten up the wheels quickly when still on the car is to clean them up as recommended, then make an instant spraying mask with a piece of cardboard. To do this hold the card firmly against the wheel rim and press through the card to the edge of the wheel rim with your thumb to leave an indentation and a mark on the card. (If you've got a dirty 'workshop thumb', the mark will be all the clearer!)

SWA5.   Then accurately cut around the curve you have marked on the card with a pair of scissors.

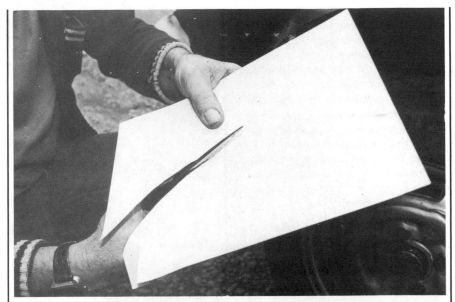

SWA6.   You can hold the card mask against the wheel rim while spraying the wheel and so prevent getting unsightly overspray onto the tyre sidewall, moving the mask around the wheel as you spray around the rim of the wheel. Of course, if you do slip up and get paint onto the tyre, nil desperandum! It's not recommended in top bodyshop circles, but you can simply paint over the overspray with tyrewall black. Then, as the black gets worn and rubbed away, so does the overspray!

Aluminium wheels can be protected by spraying a clear sealer onto their surface but if they are suffering from the all too common surface corrosion, they are best resuscitated by being taken to a specialist wheel polisher and then treated with sealer, which should be re-applied at regular intervals.

Interior Trim – renovation and repair ●

Although interior trim is not strictly a part of bodywork, it is likely that the owner who wants to improve his car on the outside will welcome the chance to make the inside look a lot tidier, too, so here are a number of ways of improving seats, carpets and door trim. Incidentally, several different types of door handles and door trim are shown being removed in the 'Stripping Door Gear' Section in Chapter 9.

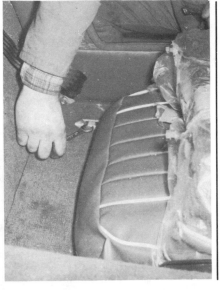

IT1.   Virtually all car seats are bolted down to the floor of the car. Some, such as sports car seats, can be a little hard to get at and you may have to slide the seat forwards to undo the rear bolts and back for the front ones. An even more common difficulty is that of seized nuts and bolts. Try soaking them in releasing fluid well before starting work, try applying heat, (but carefully, taking note of the promixity of fuel lines beneath the floor and flammable trim above it) but if all else fails, it may be necessary to drill out the bolts and replace them with new ones; preferably of the rust-resistant bright zinc-plated variety.

*IT2.   Quite often the seat covering will go saggy without anything actually being wrong with the structure of the seat at all. Alternatively, the cover may have split and it may be possible to get hold of a new cover from a specialist supplier or a good second-hand one from a breakers yard. (Slip-on, tie-on accessory covers are not shown here because they are just **too** easy to fit.) In this shot, the old cover has been removed and a layer of thin foam is being glued over the shoulders, back and base of the seat.*

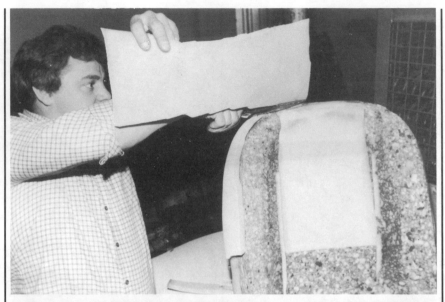

IT3.   Then, so that the new cover will slip on without binding on the surface of the foam, a plastic bag is split open and glued over the shoulders of the backrest

IT4.   The cover is then pulled down on to the backrest and stretched down carefully, easing out any wrinkles or bunching as it is pulled on. The clips and method of fixing used by the manufacturer are reused to hold the cover down, if possible.

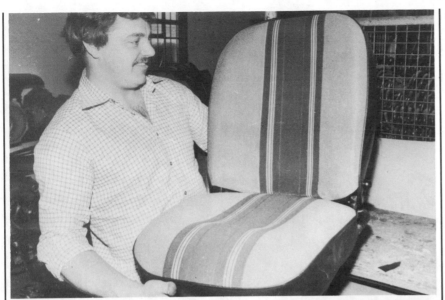

IT5.   The recovered seat will have all the smoothness and tautness of a new seat, especially if you took the opportunity to renew any worn springs or a rubber diaphragm while the seat was stripped down.

IT6.   A few cars have leather seats, these being aesthetically beautiful to see and smell and touch but painful to the pocket when they need repairing. You can invariably strip off the leather cover in the same way as for cloth covers and you can then restitch any broken stitching using the existing stitching holes in the leather. You could even let-in a repair patch yourself from a second-hand seat. Be sure to use strong, upholsterer's thread.

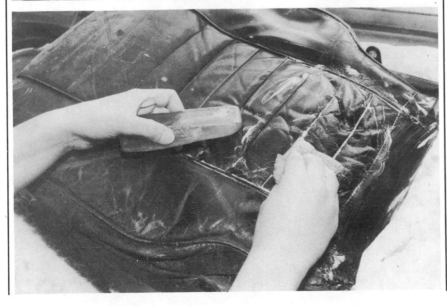

IT7.   Old leather can be cleaned up using saddle soap and then treated with hide food to stop it from splitting by making it supple again. Specialists such as Woolies and Connolly Brothers (see 'Classic' motoring press for addresses) can even supply recolouring kits which can bring leather seats back to almost-like-new.

IT8.   The far more common vinyl type of seat covering is also prone to splitting as the material age-hardens. Splits can be repaired using vinyl adhesive, available from motoring and DIY shops, after first roughening the edges of the split with fine sand paper.

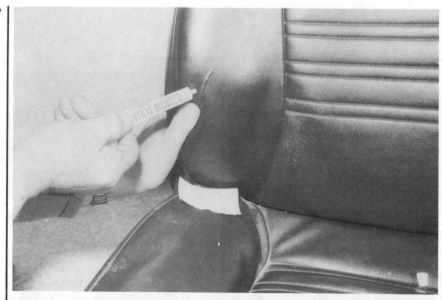

IT9.   Really bad splits need support from behind, especially if they are unsupported by padding. The base of this seat was held on with claws which were bent open with a screwdriver, allowing the cover to be pulled loose.

IT10.   Then a piece of card was slid up behind the tear. This was used as a slipway for a piece of vinyl which was also slid up behind the tear – it would otherwise have dragged on the padding inside the seat.

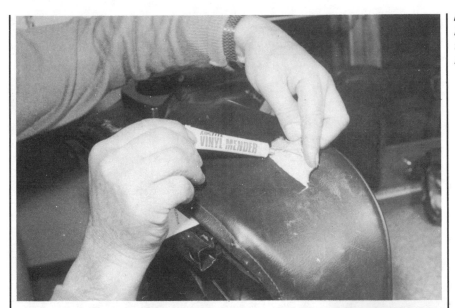

IT11. After roughening the edges as before the flaps of vinyl were lifted and the vinyl glued down to the vinyl backing piece behind ...

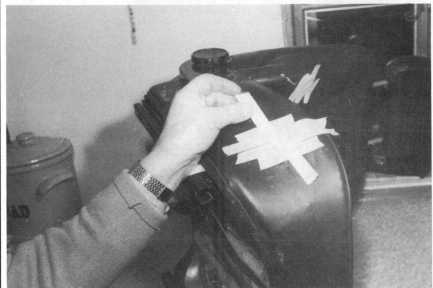

IT12 ... and the edges were pulled close together with masking tape and the tape left in place until the mender was completely dry.

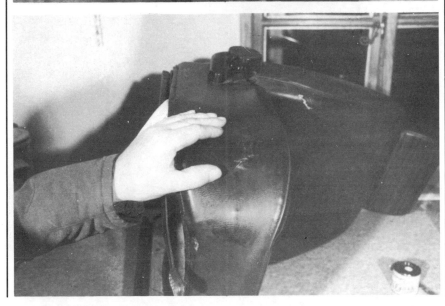

IT13. While the finished repair was far from invisible, it was vastly preferable to a gaping tear.

IT14.   Vinyl seating can become dull wthout your really noticing it, but a good clean-up can make a dramatic difference. Here Turtle Wax 'Vinyl Plus' has been rubbed onto the right-hand half of the seat. The extra shine it gave did not disappear even when the polish was completely dry – as indeed it was in this picture – and the vinyl actually felt more supple.

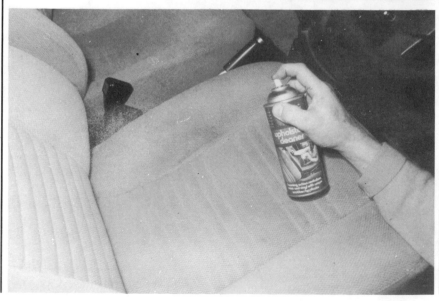

IT15.   Cloth upholstery can be a little more difficult to clean if only because it absorbs more dirt! Start by scraping off any clods of chocolate or dirt that might have embedded itself into the fabric, using a blunt table knife, then spray on an aerosol upholstery cleaner, taking care not to soak the fabric which could cause shrinking to take place.

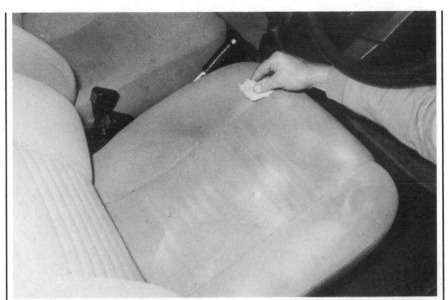

IT16.   Then rub off the cleaner with a clean cloth. You can fetch off a surprising amount of dirt in this way, but be prepared to have several goes at a really dirty seat, allowing the cloth to dry out between each cleaning.

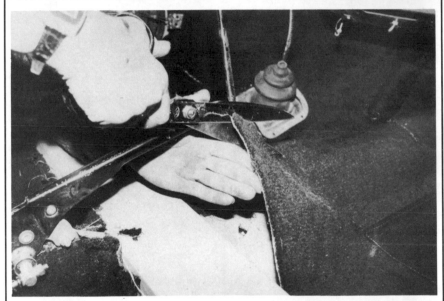

IT17.   It seems that with replacement carpets almost more than anything else, you get what you pay for — and no more! Top-quality carpets sold by a main agent or a specialist in your car should fit straight into place, but even only slightly down-market carpets may need a considerable amount of trimming to get them to fit properly.

IT18.   Unless carpets are clipped down they will slip about, look untidy, and make a thorough nuisance of themselves. When you receive your new carpets and, if necessary, after you have trimmed them to shape, start by placing them in the car, feeling for the position of the stud and marking it with chalk. Press the clawed ring down onto the top of the carpet ...

IT19. ... so that the claws protrude through the carpet.

IT20. Place the clip over the claws and fold the claws inwards with a screwdriver.

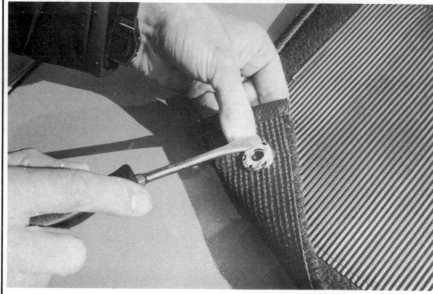

IT21. It may be that the floor clips are missing for some reason in which case it is a simple matter to fix new ones in place using self-tapping screws or pop-rivets. If you fit sound-deadening materials beneath the carpets it will be necessary to raise the position of the studs using pieces of plywood placed beneath the stud, and longer screws.

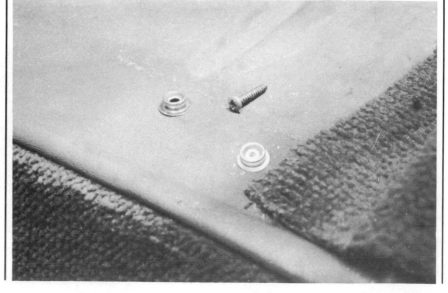

IT22.   It is then simplicity itself to clip the carpets into place with the added bonus of being able to unclip them in a moment for cleaning out the car.

IT23.   Plasticised seat covers and door trim materials can be given a new lease of life by painting them with upholstery paint. Fumes from the paint could be dangerous if used in a confined area, by the way, so ventilate the work area thoroughly. The wrinkling you can see in the painted door panel at the rear disappeared after a day or two, presumably as all the solvent dried out. Strangely, this type of paint always seems to have covered properly when it is still wet only to look patchy when dry, so buy enough for two coats. Paint only in straight lines so that brush marks don't show.

Manufacturers of Equipment & Materials

Apollo Sprayers Ltd
47/57 Bishop St, Birmingham B5 6LT.

Austin-Rover Ltd
Longbridge, Birmingham.

Black & Decker
Maidenhead, Berkshire SL6 3PD.

BOC Ltd
Great West House, Great West Road,
Brentford, Middlesex TW8 9DQ.

C.A.R.S. Wilden Trading Estate,
Stourport, Worcestershire.

Celette-Churchill Ltd
PO Box 10, London Road, Daventry,
Northants NN11 4PZ.

Clearview Windscreens
Lowesmoor Trading Estate, St Martins
Gate, Worcester.

De Vilbiss Company Ltd
Ringwood Road, Bournemouth.

Holts Products Ltd
Wilmslow, Cheshire SK9 1QT

International Paints Ltd
(via Leedex Ltd)
1-17 The Parade, Birmingham
B1 3QD.

John Hill's MGB Centre
Arthur Street, Redditch,
Worcestershire B98 8JY

Murex Welding Products
PO Box 32, Oxford Street, Bilston,
West Midlands WV14 7EQ

Sifbronze
Gipping Works, Stowmarket, Suffolk
IP14 1EY.

SIP (Industrial Products) Ltd
Gelders Hall Road, Shepshed,
Loughborough, Leicestershire
LE12 9NH

Smith & Deakin Fibreglass Products
Tolladine Road, Worcester.

Supra Chemicals & Paints Ltd
Hainge Road, Tividale, Warley
B69 2NF

Sykes-Pickavant Ltd
Warwick House, Kilnhouse Lane,
Lytham St. Annes, Lancashire
FY8 3DU.

The Welding Centre
165 Nether Auldhouse Road, Glasgow
G43 2YP.

Transpeed Mail Order
213 Portland Street, Hove, Sussex.
*Suppliers of a huge range of workshop
and DIY tools.*

Tudor Webasto
(via Media Men Ltd)
7 Albert Terrace, Union Street, Bedford
MK40 2SF.

Unipart
Unipart House, Cowley, Oxford
OX4 2PG

Vehicle Window Centre
Cranshaw Close, Pudsey, W. Yorks
LS28 7UF.

Waxoyl (Finnigans)
Eltringham Works, Prudhoe,
Northumberland.

The following lists the names of
leading manufacturers in the US of
various equipment and materials.
Addresses of local suppliers should be
found under the relevant headings in
Yellow Pages.
For welding oxygen and fuel-gas:

Amerigas, Union Carbide

For welding equipment:
Victor, Lincoln, Miller, and Hobart

For body repair tools:
Proto, Snap-on, Streamline, and
Dynatron

For automotive paint:
Dupont, Sherwin-Williams, Ditzler, and
Nason

For paint spraying equipment:
Binks, DeVilbiss, and Sharp